SCENIC DRIVING
NEW ENGLAND

Help Us Keep This Guide Up to Date

Every effort has been made by the author and editors to make this guide as accurate and useful as possible. However, many things can change after a guide is published—establishments close, phone numbers change, hiking trails are rerouted, facilities come under new management, etc.

We would love to hear from you concerning your experiences with this guide and how you feel it could be improved and kept up to date. While we may not be able to respond to all comments and suggestions, we'll take them to heart and we'll also make certain to share them with the author. Please send your comments and suggestions to the following address:

The Globe Pequot Press
Reader Response/Editorial Department
P.O. Box 480
Guilford, CT 06437

Or you may e-mail us at:

editorial@GlobePequot.com

Thanks for your input, and happy travels!

INSIDERS' GUIDE®

SECOND EDITION

SCENIC DRIVING

NEW ENGLAND

STEWART M. GREEN

INSIDERS' GUIDE®

GUILFORD, CONNECTICUT
AN IMPRINT OF THE GLOBE PEQUOT PRESS

INSIDERS' GUIDE®

Copyright © 1997, 2006 Morris Book Publishing, LLC
Previously published by Falcon Publishing, Inc.

Interior photographs by Stewart M. Green
Maps by Völker Schniepp & IFB © Morris Book Publishing, LLC

Library of Congress Cataloging-in-Publication Data
Green, Stewart M.
  Scenic driving New England / Stewart M. Green. — 2nd ed.
     p. cm. — (A Falcon guide) (Scenic driving guides)
  Includes index.
  ISBN-13: 978-0-7627-4060-4
  ISBN-10: 0-7627-4060-4
     1. New England—Tours. 2. Automobile travel—New England—Guidebooks. 3. Scenic byways—New England—Guidebooks. I. Title. II. Series. III. Series: Scenic driving guides

  F2.3.G74 2006
  917.404'44—dc22

                                                                2006043544

Manufactured in the United States of America
Second Edition/First Printing

CONTENTS

The Scenic Drives

Connecticut

Rhode Island

Massachusetts

Vermont

New Hampshire

Maine

ACKNOWLEDGMENTS

New England is one of those special landscapes that you can return to again and again. Its old terrain and long history give visitors a sense of America's origins. Researching this book gave me the opportunity to return to that place where I spent formative college years in the early 1970s. Back then I was interested in climbing the New Hampshire cliffs, kicking around Boston and enjoying its cultural events, and discovering the ragged seacoast, which was a new diversion for a native Westerner.

My thanks go to Falcon Press for originally publishing this book, and to my editor, Randall Green, and the staff that copyedited and designed it. Kudos also go to the park rangers and interpretative staffs who reviewed portions of the book. I add special thanks to Nancy Spencer-Green for traveling many of the drives with me, taking notes, helping to keep track of information, proofreading, and providing moral support. Another debt of gratitude is owed Martha Morris for creating all the maps, proofreading the chapters, making comments and changes to the manuscripts, and lending inspiration and ideas gleaned from her fifteen years in northern New Hampshire. Thanks also to editor Heather Carreiro and The Globe Pequot Press staff for creating this stunning second edition.

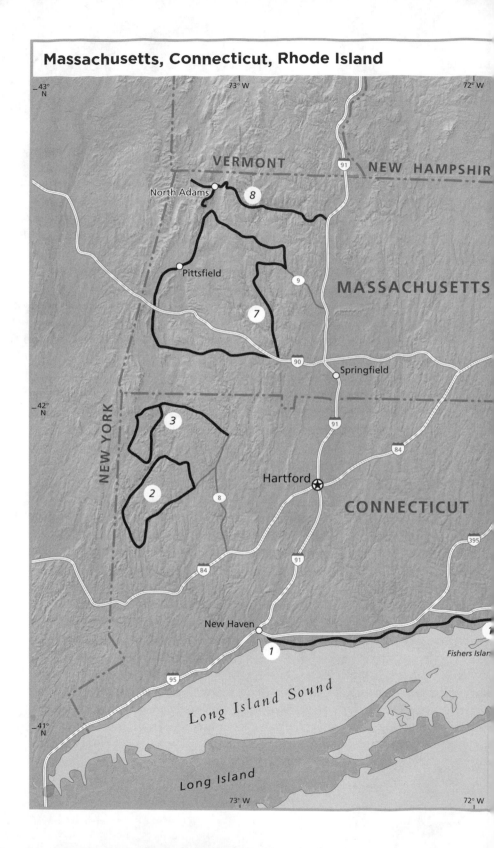

Massachusetts, Connecticut, Rhode Island

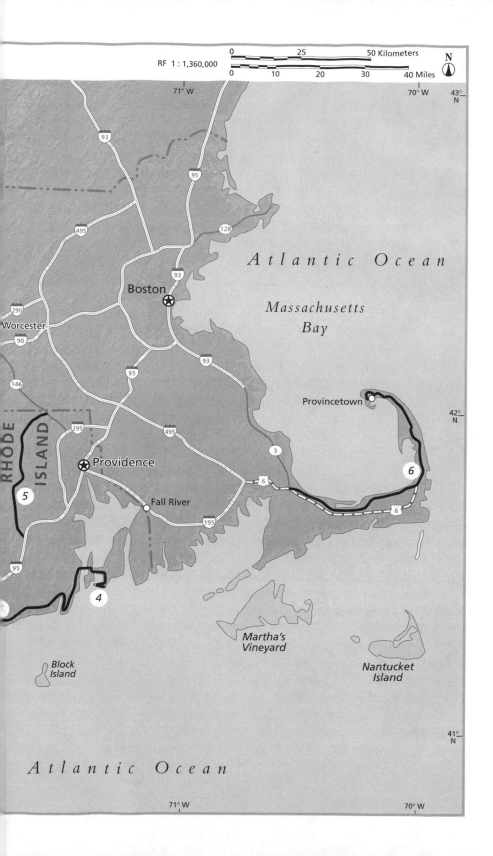

0   25   50 Kilometers   **N**

0   10   20   30   40 Miles

71° W   70° W   43°
N

Atlantic Ocean

93

95

495

128

93

Boston

290

Worcester

90

146

95

Massachusetts Bay

295

93

495

RHODE

ISLAND

Providence

3

Provincetown

42°
N

6

5

6

Fall River

195

6

4

95

Martha's Vineyard

Block Island

Nantucket Island

41°
N

Atlantic Ocean

71° W   70° W

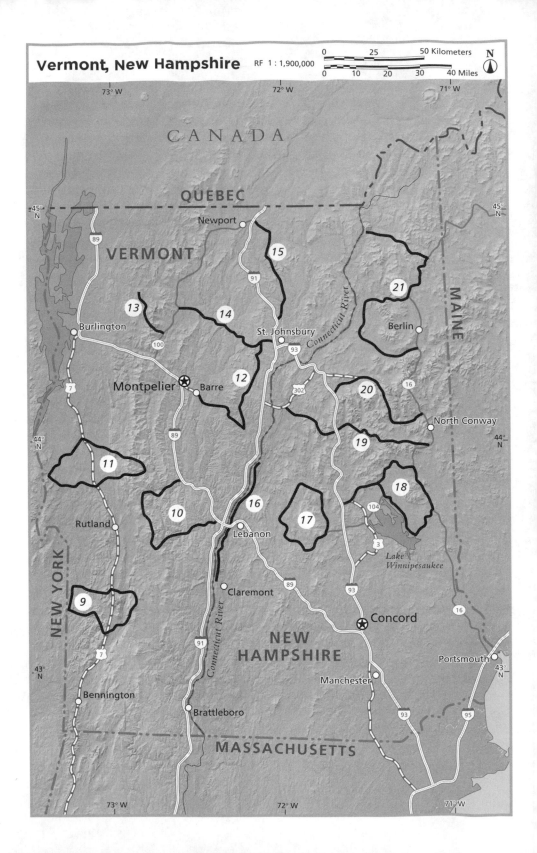

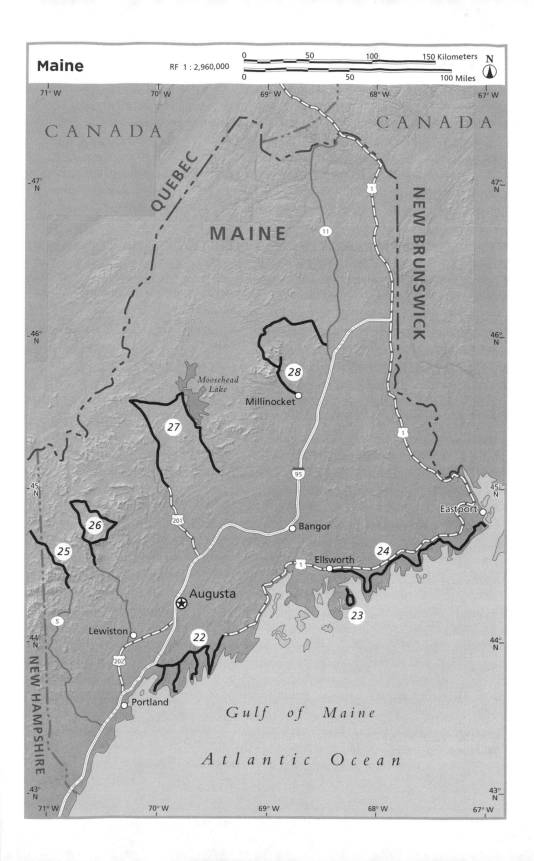

Map Legend

Transportation

Limited Access Freeway	
U.S. Highway Featured U.S. Highway	
State Highway Featured State Highway	
Local Road Featured Local Road	
Trail	----------
Railroad	
Interstate Highway	(91)
U.S. Highway	(5)
State Highway	(16)

Boundaries

International Line	
State Line	
National / State Park / Forest Wildlife Refuge Management Area	
National Seashore	

Population

Capital	⊛
City	◉
Town	○

Grids

Latitude / Longitude Number and Ticks	46° −12′ N

Hydrology

Reservoir or Lake	
Stream / River	
River / Creek	
Waterfall	

Physiography

Cliff / Scarp	

Terrain (Shaded Relief)

Mountain, Peak or Butte ——————— ▲ Peak

Valley _____

Symbols

Visitor Center	?
Ranger Station	
Point of Interest	■
Campground	▲
State Park	♠
Wildlife Refuge	
Ski Area	
Picnic Area	⊼
Trailhead	
Gate	•—•
Pass / Notch	‿
Bridge	
Covered Bridge	
Historic Site	
Museum	🏛
Tunnel	⊢⊣

INTRODUCTION

New England nestles along the northeastern edge of the United States, a forested wedge of mountains and valleys set against the watery Atlantic Ocean rim. The region, encompassing Rhode Island, Connecticut, Massachusetts, Vermont, New Hampshire, and Maine, forms its own little, insular kingdom. The region's 66,608 square miles, about half as many as belong to most western states, offer a diversity of geography, natural history, character, and history that is unmatched by the rest of the nation. New England offers explorers an old landscape filled with contrast and wonder—ragged mountains and broad valleys, sprawling cities and pastoral hills, rocky coastlines and sandy beaches, pounding surf and pristine ponds, swift rivers and trickling seeps, towering white pines and tiny jewel orchids, and salt marshes that echo with the cries of winter waterfowl.

New England is a place of startling variety. Wild, primeval lands lie within comfortable reach of its great cities, cultural institutions, ethnic neighborhoods, and famed universities. It is also a place of history, a place that defines what it means to be an American. Here grew the men and women who founded this country. Here were fought the famous battles of the American Revolution. Here began the Industrial Revolution that transformed the face of the nation. Here is where the North's anti-slavery movement began. This rich and varied past is peopled with Native Americans who called New England home for thousands of years; Pilgrims who first alit on Cape Cod in 1620; simple farmers who cleared the land of stones and trees; patriots who sounded the cry of independence from Britain, taxes, and tyranny; communities of Shakers living a utopian dream; and sailors, whalers, and lobstermen eking a hard-won living from the ocean.

Rural New England is also a landscape that lives in the American imagination. Its images—weathered red barns as sentinels over autumn cornfields, church steeples soaring above white saltbox houses, and covered bridges spanning rocky rivers—evoke a yearning for the simple lifestyles of yesteryear.

Geographic Provinces

New England is roughly divided into several geographic provinces—the Atlantic Seaboard, a long rock-and-sand coastline; the New England Upland, a sloping plain; the Appalachian Mountains, a complex spine of hills and mountains; and the Connecticut River Valley, following New England's longest river. Each distinct area is defined by its underlying geological structure, which, coupled with the vagaries of climate, temperature, and precipitation, determines New England's diverse ecology, that web of relationships between the plants and animals inhabiting the land.

The coastline, twisting 6,130 miles from northern Maine to southwestern Connecticut and surrounding countless islands, fronts the cold North Atlantic Ocean. About half the region's shore is the foggy, rockbound Maine coast, a landscape of inlets, bays, coves, cliffs, and the only fjord on the eastern seaboard. The southern coast offers long, sweeping sand beaches interrupted by broken rock outcrops and Cape Cod, a fishhook-shaped peninsula that juts far out into the ocean. Most of New England's population lives along the coastline in large cities such as Boston, Providence, and Portland, as well as numerous small towns and villages that were settled as early as the 1600s.

The New England Upland, also called the Piedmont, is a sloping, plateau-like region in southern and central New England that gently rises away from the seaboard. The low-relief upland was dissected and flattened by rivers and streams and is broken by occasional individual mountains that tower above the lowlands, including the famed Mount Monadnock in southern New Hampshire. Many cities and towns arose on the upland along the fall line of large rivers that provided water power to fuel the Industrial Revolution in the nineteenth century.

The mountain skyline, New England's most definitive feature, stretches along the western and northern edges of the region. These old, rounded ranges are the Taconic Mountains along the Massachusetts, Vermont, and New York border; Vermont's Green Mountains and its southern extension, the Berkshire and Litchfield Hills in western Massachusetts and northwestern Connecticut; the White Mountains in northern New Hampshire and northwestern Maine; and the lofty Mount Katahdin massif in central Maine. New England's high point is 6,288-foot Mount Washington in New Hampshire's Presidential Range, a division of the White Mountains.

The Connecticut River Valley is a lowland carved by New England's longest river, which neatly cleaves the region in half. The valley's broad lowland, covered with towns and farms, reaches south from the New Hampshire border to the Connecticut coast. Above that stretches a long, sharply incised river valley that forms the boundary between Vermont and New Hampshire. The border agreement between the states, however, left the river itself in New Hampshire.

East Topsham, Vermont, is a classic New England village nestled among hills.

During long periods of glaciation, at least four in the last three million years, ice sheets descended from the north and spread across New England. These massive sheets, the last retreating a scant ten thousand years ago, scoured, excavated, sculpted, and shaped New England. The ice, reaching thicknesses of 2 miles in places, compressed and crushed the land, rounded mountain ridges and summits, chiseled immense cirques and valleys, and left huge moraines and eskers, or gravel piles and ridges, in their wake. Today, the glacial legacy includes thousands of lakes and ponds, characteristic U-shaped river valleys, the drowned seacoast of Maine, and Cape Cod, the world's largest glacial moraine.

New England's six states present not only a geography of seascapes and mountains, but a diverse variety of flora and fauna. The fragile alpine zone, dotted with tiny flowers like those found in northern Canada, perches atop the highest peaks with islands of tundra left after the ice ages. The great forests that once blanketed primeval, pre-European New England are now long gone, the clear-cut victims of farms, firewood, the Royal Navy, industrial interests, and paper factories. Today, enough forest has returned to cover three-quarters of the area. During the nineteenth century as much as 80 percent of southern New England was cleared of trees. Without the cities, highways, and agriculture, forests would cloak all of the region save the salt marshes and the treeless mountaintops.

The woodlands growing across New England fascinate visitors with their dramatic differences due to climate and latitude over the 500 miles from southern Connecticut to northern Maine. The spruce-fir evergreen forest forms a relatively small part of the New England woodland, covering the coolest and wettest mountains in the northern states and along Maine's cool northern coast. The northern hardwood forest, mantling most of northern New England, is dominated by maple, birch, and beech along with the conifers spruce, white pine, and hemlock. This lovely woodland, with an open canopy, offers the region's brilliant fall colors. Maples weave a tapestry of red and orange while birch and beech offer bright yellow and gold highlights. An oak-hickory forest blankets southern New England, except for southeastern Massachusetts where the dominant forest species are oak and pitch pine.

Scenic Driving New England

New England offers travelers a spectacular assortment of natural and scenic wonders, historic sites, and varied recreational opportunities. The region's national parklands include popular Acadia National Park and Cape Cod National Seashore along with many historic districts. Numerous state parks, forests, beaches, and recreation areas preserve slices of superlative landscapes, including Maine's Baxter State Park, New England's largest state parkland. White Mountain and Green Mountain National Forests spread across their respective ranges in Vermont and New Hampshire, managed by the USDA Forest Service for multiple uses. Thousands of lakes and ponds and numerous rivers and brooks offer boating, swimming, canoeing, and angling choices for outdoor enthusiasts. The Appalachian Trail winds across New England's mountains and valleys to its northern terminus atop Mount Katahdin in northern Maine, while the Long Trail threads along the crest of Vermont's Green Mountains. The cities, towns, and villages, from the urban centers of Boston, Providence, and Hartford to myriad tiny villages dotting the green hills of Vermont and New Hampshire, are filled with culture and steeped in history.

Scenic Driving New England, an indispensable mile-by-mile highway companion, explores and discovers the wonders of this compact region. Its twenty-eight scenic drives follow almost 2,000 miles of highways and back roads, sampling the region's colorful history, beauty spots, hidden wonders, and scenic jewels. Along the drives, highway recreationists find the stunning diversity and variety that is New England. Drivers traverse lofty wooded gaps including Smugglers and Crawford Notches, wind along ragged sea cliffs and headlands pounded by the restless ocean along the Maine coast, loop around Mount Katahdin's pristine wilderness, marvel at classic villages set among the green Vermont hills, pass rural birthplaces and burial sites of the notable and the notorious, wander among shifting sand dunes on Cape Cod's outer beaches, and climb atop Mount Greylock, the highest

The gates are seldom closed on the back roads along the Lake Winnipesaukee Scenic Drive.

point in Massachusetts. Most of the drives leave the urban sprawl and interstate highways behind, setting off into the beautiful heart of the region.

New England is laced with highways and roads, some dating back to the earliest paths that once connected colonial settlements. This book's twenty-eight drives sample some of the region's best scenic venues. Area natives will undoubtedly wonder why some roads are included and others omitted. I chose these routes for their beauty, unique natural history, and historical implications. I left out some worthy roads for one reason or another, but mostly due to the burgeoning development along those asphalt corridors in an amazing labyrinth of highway possibilities. It was simply impossible to chart all of New England's scenic routes in a single book since, in a sense, almost every New England highway could be considered a scenic or historic drive.

Use these described drives to win a new appreciation and understanding of this marvelous land. Take them as a starting point to embark on new adventures by seeking out other back road gems in Vermont's Green Mountains, in the Massachusetts Berkshire Hills, among the low hills and vales of northeastern Connecticut, in the historic towns and old hills of southern New Hampshire, and in the remote and little traveled north Maine woods.

Being Prepared

Be prepared for changing weather when traveling New England's scenic highways, especially in winter when snow and ice encase the roadways. Most of the drives, except for bits and pieces, are paved two-lane highways that are regularly maintained. Services are available on almost all the drives, and every little village offers at least some basics during daylight hours. Use caution when driving. Many of the roads twist and wind through valleys and over mountains, with blind corners. Follow the posted speed limits and stay in your lane. Use occasional pullouts to allow faster traffic to safely pass. Watch for heavy traffic on some roads, particularly during summer vacation season and on fall-foliage weekends. Be extremely alert for animals crossing the asphalt, especially on the rural highways in northern New Hampshire and Maine. The moose hazard is serious, and drivers are killed every year in moose-auto collisions. Take care at dusk, just after darkness falls, and in the early morning.

The region's fickle weather creates changeable and dangerous driving conditions. Make sure your windshield wipers are in good shape. Heavy rain can impair highway vision and cause your vehicle to hydroplane. Snow and ice slicken mountain highways. Slow down, carry chains and a shovel, and have spare clothes and a sleeping bag when traveling in winter. Watch for fog and poor visibility, particularly along the Maine coast. Know your vehicle and its limits when traveling and, above all, use common sense.

Travelers are, unfortunately, potential crime victims. Use caution when driving in urban areas or popular tourist destinations. Keep all valuables, including wallets, purses, cameras, and video cameras, out of sight in a parked car. Better yet, take them with you when leaving the vehicle.

These scenic drives cross a complex mosaic of private and public land. Respect private property rights by not trespassing or crossing fences.

Remember also that all archaeological and historic sites are protected by federal law. Campers should try to use established campgrounds or campsites whenever possible to avoid adverse environmental impacts. Remember to douse your campfires and to pack all your trash out with you to the nearest refuse container.

New England is a magical place. Its magnificent landscape of historical and natural riches awaits. Drive its scenic highways and you will soon discover its secrets. Out there are glimpses of things and places that are not soon forgotten— wave-swept beaches, snowcapped mountain peaks, weathered buildings, majestic rivers, and quiet villages. The highways featured in this book celebrate the spirit of New England, its regional and ethnic character, and its hard-won history.

Every road we travel offers its own promise and special rewards. Remember Walt Whitman's poetic proclamation as you drive New England's scenic highways: "Afoot, light-hearted, I take to the open road. Healthy, free, the world before me."

Connecticut Coast Scenic Drive

General description: A 71-mile scenic route along southeastern Connecticut's historic coastline.

Special attractions: Mystic Seaport: The Museum of America and the Sea, Mystic Aquarium, Bluff Point State Park, Fort Griswold Battlefield State Park, U.S. Navy Submarine Force Museum, Rocky Neck State Park, Old Lyme, Lyme Academy of Fine Arts, Old Saybrook, Florence Griswold Museum, Hammonasset Beach State Park, Guilford, Whitfield House, historic houses and sites, picnicking, camping, fishing, swimming, beaches.

Location: Southeastern Connecticut.

Drive route numbers: U.S. Highway 1, Interstate 95, Connecticut Highways 156 and 146.

Travel season: Year-round.

Camping: Rocky Neck State Park has a 160-site campground that is open from mid-April through the end of September. Hammonasset Beach State Park has the William F. Miller Campground with 558 sites and beach access. Call (203) 245–1817 for park campground information and reservations.

Services: All services in Pawcatuck, Mystic, Groton, New London, Niantic, Old Lyme, Old Saybrook, Clinton, Madison, and Guilford.

Nearby attractions: Watch Hill (RI), Misquamicut State Beach (RI), Nehantic State Forest, Becket Hill State Park, Connecticut River, Selden Neck State Park, Gillette Castle State Park, East Haddam, Brainard Homestead State Park, Haddam Meadows State Park, Cockaponset State Forest, Chatfield Hollow State Park, New Haven attractions.

The Drive

This scenic route traverses 71 miles of southeastern Connecticut's coastline, passing numerous historic areas and towns, and crossing the unspoiled mouth of New England's longest river while offering tranquil vistas of sandy beaches, salt marshes, and dense woodlands. Worlds away from the Nutmeg State's busy urban centers, this lovely drive parallels coves, inlets, and beaches along Long Island Sound between Rhode Island and the outskirts of New Haven. This section of coast boasts a long and colorful seafaring history, with many of its towns, including some of the state's oldest villages, drawing sustenance from the ocean.

The nineteenth-century Industrial Revolution, which transformed and urbanized much of southern New England, mostly bypassed the fishing and whaling villages along the southeastern Connecticut coast. Instead, industry developed inland at the fall line of the region's rivers, with rapids and waterfalls generating power for mills and factories. Today this shoreline, lying just off Interstate 95 and the hectic Boston-to-New York corridor, is generally overlooked by passing drivers. Those who do venture off the interstate are treated to quiet country roads and a look at Connecticut's rich maritime heritage.

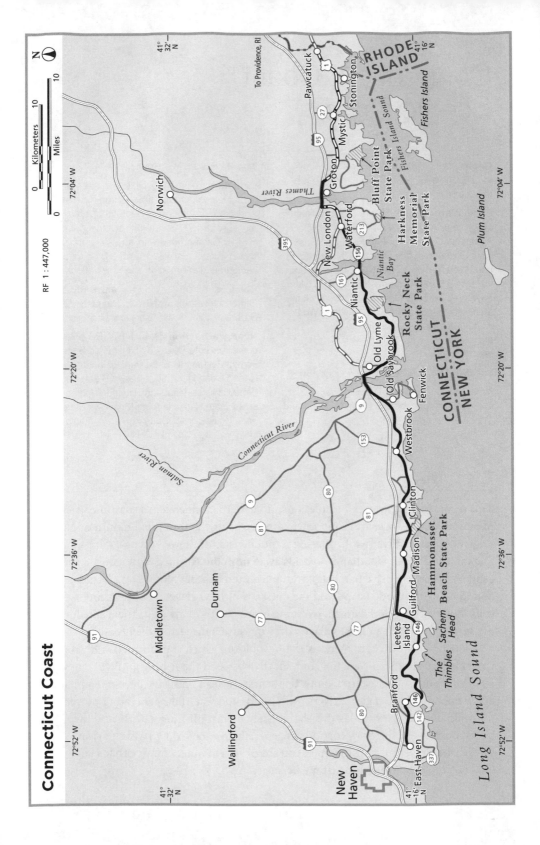

Connecticut Coast

RF 1 : 447,000

Heading west from Rhode Island to New Haven, the drive begins in Pawcatuck on the west side of the Pawcatuck River, across from Westerly in Rhode Island. Pawcatuck is easily reached from I–95. Take exit 2 and drive south a few miles on Connecticut Highway 2 to its junction with U.S. Highway 1, the East Coast's celebrated main thoroughfare. US 1 roughly follows the old Boston Post Road, the colonial road between Boston and New York. Head west through Pawcatuck on US 1 past many large homes and leave town after a mile. A few miles later is U.S. Highway 1A; jog left here to Stonington.

Stonington

One of Connecticut's loveliest coastal villages, **Stonington** sits on a narrow peninsula jutting south into Fishers Island Sound. The town, dubbed the "Nursery for Seamen," offers a superb, protected harbor that nourished its profitable whaling, sealing, fishing, trading, and shipbuilding industries through the nineteenth century. This once-busy town, settled in the 1640s, figured prominently in early Connecticut history when the local militia repelled British naval attacks during both the Revolution and the War of 1812.

The latter battle is commemorated by a historical tablet on Water Street that reads: "The brave men of Stonington defeated a landing force from the British ship *Ramillies* bent on burning the town and its shipping. August 10, 1814." Cannon Square holds a pair of eighteen-pound cannons that the patriots used to repulse four British warships, which were commanded by Captain Thomas M. Hardy and armed with 140 guns. The invaders sent a note ashore warning the villagers to abandon the town within one hour or face their wrath. Stonington replied, "We shall defend the place to the last extremity; should it be destroyed, we shall perish in its ruins." Captain Jeremiah Holmes tacked an American flag over the town's earthen breastworks, averring "That flag shall never come down while I'm alive." The subsequent two-day British barrage injured only one person, while the local cannons killed twenty-one British sailors, wounded fifty more, and almost sank the *Dispatch* before the ships withdrew.

This seaport town, at one time the third largest in the state, was a bustling commercial hub at its zenith. Stonington's two main avenues were jammed with seamen, whalers, and sailors and lined with buildings, warehouses, and the opulent houses of wealthy merchants and sea captains. Ships based here fanned out around the globe, including the *Betsy*, the first American ship to circumnavigate the world. Captain Nathaniel Parker sailed from here on a sealing expedition in 1820 and discovered Antarctica. The town, with as many as seventeen separate tracks, was also an early railroad center with passengers arriving by rail from Boston and departing for New York on ferries.

Stonington still retains its colonial charm with cobblestone streets and many Federal and Greek Revival–style homes. A walking tour brochure details important sites, including homes once occupied by poet Stephen Vincent Benet and painter James Whistler. With its narrow streets hemmed in by restored buildings and houses and numerous shops, Stonington is a great place for walkers, rather than drivers, to roam and explore.

Be sure to stop at the **Old Lighthouse Museum** at the end of Water Street, overlooking the Atlantic. The sturdy granite lighthouse, built in 1823, was the first erected by the federal government. Inside is an eclectic collection of local artifacts and memorabilia, including distinctive Stonington salt-glaze pottery, ship models, whaling gear, cannonballs from the Battle of Stonington, and treasures brought back from the Orient. Circular stone stairs lead to a small chamber atop the lighthouse and marvelous views of the surrounding harbor, Block Island to the southeast, and even the tip of Montauk Point on Long Island to the south.

Return to US 1 by taking Water Street north and following signs for US 1 and I–95. Back on US 1, head west past the upper end of placid Stonington Harbor, past a turnoff to Lords Point, and run through a forest dotted with homes. After almost 5 miles the road bends northwest and enters Mystic, the best known of New England's living history museum-villages.

Mystic

Mystic, named from the Indian word *mistick* or "tidal river," was, along with its neighbor Stonington, one of Connecticut's most prosperous and important seaports. The fabled town, straddling the banks of the Mystic River where it empties into Mystic Harbor, flourished not only as a port but as one of the nation's premier shipbuilding centers in the nineteenth century. Reaching 6 miles inland from the ocean, the wide, calm river channel with its gently sloped banks was ideal for constructing the variety of ships needed by the country's growing clipper trade. The nearby forests of cedar, white pine, ash, spruce, and white oak offered plentiful raw materials. Hundreds of clippers, packets, sloops, and whalers, as well as fifty-six steamers for the federal navy, were launched from Mystic's shipyards. Mystic's ships often made the hazardous 110-day journey around Tierra del Fuego to San Francisco during the Gold Rush days, and competing shipbuilders vied to build the fastest vessel. The *Andrew Jackson*, built in Mystic in 1860, still holds the record—eighty-nine days and four hours. The town also flourished as a whaling port from 1832 to 1860 when petroleum began replacing whale oil for illumination and lubrication.

This colorful maritime history is commemorated at **Mystic Seaport: The Museum of America and the Sea** on the waterfront just north of the scenic drive on Connecticut Highway 27. The seventeen-acre museum recreates a typical nineteenth-century New England seaport with more than sixty historic buildings and homes relocated here. On the site of two old shipyards, it is a living history site displaying restored sailing ships that nudge against piers and interpreters who practice traditional maritime crafts. The replica village gives a uniquely vivid glimpse back to the 1860s during the heyday of the tall ships. Visitors ramble through the streets past the town tavern, shops, schoolhouse, church, bank, and print shop, and along the wharves where the ships are anchored. Dozens of exhibits include whaling tools and a video; a collection of figureheads; the Preservation Shipyard where visitors watch a ship restoration; and the N. G. Fish Ship Chandlery, which outfitted sailors and ships for voyages that lasted as long as five years.

The *Charles W. Morgan*, a 113-foot-long whale ship built in 1841, is the centerpiece of the Mystic fleet. The ship, a National Historic Landmark, made thirty-seven voyages in eighty years under the command of twenty-one different captains—and made almost $1.5 million for its New Bedford owners. Other tall ships parked here are the two-masted *L.A. Dunton* fishing schooner, the SS *Sabina* steamboat, and the *Joseph Conrad*, a square-rigged Danish training ship. Mystic Seaport is open year-round. Allow a full day to visit the museum and discover New England's rich maritime heritage.

Before leaving Mystic, park and walk around the town. Its sidewalks, often crowded with museum visitors, are lined with shops, cafes, and historic colonial homes. A few points of interest include the 1764 **Whitehall Mansion,** the 1717 **Denison Homestead** (furnished by eleven generations of Denisons), and the **John Mason Monument** remembering a 1637 battle between the Pequot Indians and early settlers. In retribution for an earlier Indian raid that killed thirty colonists, Mason and his men attacked a Pequot fort and massacred between 400 and 700 Indians, including women and children.

The **Mystic Aquarium,** on the north side of town, displays more than 6,000 sea creatures, as well as seals and sea lions. The scenic drive threads through Mystic on US 1 as it crosses the river on a drawbridge, passes through downtown Mystic and West Mystic, and twists west through wooded hills. A few miles later is the turnoff to **Bluff Point State Park.** This 806-acre parkland, encompassing a forested neck that reaches down to Long Island Sound, is the largest remaining stretch of wild, undeveloped coast along Connecticut's 253-mile-long shoreline. Overlying metamorphic gneiss and schist rocks, the park is a wintering area for waterfowl, including brant and scaup. Nearby is Bluff Point Beach and a narrow sandspit or tombolo that ends at Bushy Point, a small island at high tide.

Groton

Past the park turnoff, the highway enters Groton, one of the larger cities along this stretch of coast. Groton, spread along the east bank of the Thames River, was originally part of the Pequot Plantation founded in 1646 by John Winthrop Jr. In 1705 it was incorporated and given the name Groton to honor Winthrop's English estate.

During the American Revolution Groton was the site of the only major battle in Connecticut, fought at Fort Griswold. This dark episode, one of the most savage and brutal fights of the war, occurred on September 8, 1781. The turncoat traitor Benedict Arnold led a British assault on Groton and New London. When Groton was attacked by two regiments, Lieutenant Colonel William Ledyard mustered 165 militiamen to defend Fort Griswold, a 12-foot-high stone fort overlooking the Thames River. The fort was surrounded, but Griswold's defenders refused to surrender. The British force of 800 began a determined attack but was repulsed several times before breaking into the fort. The British suffered high causalities, fifty killed and more than 150 wounded, while only three patriots were killed. Ledyard surrendered his garrison, handing his sword to the opposing commander in subjugation. The Tory officer, irate after the brutal battle, promptly ran Ledyard through with the sword. A slaughter ensued, with the British soldiers massacring eighty-eight of the surrendered Americans after their weapons were laid down.

The story of this infamous encounter is now preserved at **Fort Griswold Battlefield State Park** on Fort Street in Groton, and the memory of the murdered defenders is kept alive with a 134-foot granite obelisk. The names of the slain men are engraved on the monument and a spiral staircase winds to a panoramic viewpoint atop the tower. The star-shaped fort remains in remarkably good shape. An on-site museum offers a diorama of the battle and exhibits of Groton history.

Today Groton is famous as the "submarine capital of the world." The town, with the nation's largest submarine base, is also the birthplace of the nuclear-powered submarine. After building seventy-four subs during World War II, General Dynamics also built the first nuclear sub, the USS *Nautilus,* in 1954. The *Nautilus,* now decommissioned after twenty-five years of service and almost 500,000 miles, is open for free tours year-round. Visitors can explore this fascinating National Historic Landmark, viewing bunks for the 111 crew members, officers' quarters, the torpedo room, and the attack center. Nearby is the **U.S. Navy Submarine Force Museum,** exhibiting the history of underwater warfare, multimedia shows, and numerous midget subs.

New London

In Groton, follow signs to I–95 South. Get on the interstate, cross the Thames River, and take exit 84 to US 1. The drive and US 1 head south and west through a dense business district where **New London,** one of Connecticut's venerable coastal cities, spreads along the west bank of the Thames River opposite Groton. The town was originally settled in 1646 by a group of forty Puritan families from Massachusetts led by John Winthrop Jr. It was named for London, England, of course, and in keeping with that theme, the newcomers appropriately renamed the Monhegan River, the Thames River. New London boasted one of the finest deepwater ports on the southern New England seaboard and quickly prospered with West Indies trade in sugar, molasses, and rum.

During the Revolutionary War New London was the base for some of the war's most notorious privateers—pirates who worked for the government by seizing and capturing enemy ships. The New London privateers raised British ire by their constant harassment. In 1781 Benedict Arnold led a British armada of thirty-two ships and a military force of 1,700 soldiers against New London and Groton, leading not only to the Fort Griswold massacre but also to the burning and destruction of much of New London. After the war many New London residents migrated west to Ohio and land given by the federal government to compensate for their wartime losses.

The town, along with New Bedford, became a leading whaling port between 1784 and 1909. The whale wealth built Whale Oil Row, a line of four Greek Revival mansions built in 1830. Other historic sites in New London include the **Downtown New London Historic District** and the granite block **U.S. Customs House,** built in 1833, one of the nation's oldest operating custom houses. The city offers a host of historic buildings and homes, many open for tours, including the 1678 and 1759 Hempsted Houses and the 1756 Shaw Mansion. One of the most interesting is **Monte Cristo Cottage,** the childhood home of famed American playwright Eugene O'Neill. O'Neill, who won a Nobel Prize and four Pulitzer Prizes, based some of his works on childhood experiences at the house. The O'Neill Theater Center runs a museum at the house and mounts productions of his plays every summer.

New London is also home to the **U.S. Coast Guard Academy** on a 125-acre site along the Thames River, the elegant **Lyman Allyn Art Museum** with a fine collection of Connecticut painters, and the informative **Science Center of Eastern Connecticut** with natural history displays on the Thames River basin.

Waterford to Old Lyme

Wind west through New London, following US 1 through a residential district before leaving town. The next 15-mile drive stretch runs from here to I–95 exit 70 at Old Lyme. In just a few miles more, the highway enters **Waterford,** a quiet town that was part of New London from its 1645 settlement until its incorporation as a separate entity in 1801. A collection of historic buildings gather about the Jordan Village Historic District, including the Beebe Phillips Farmhouse with exhibits on farm living in the 1800s; the quaint 1749 Jordan School House, Waterford's oldest public edifice; and the Stacy Barn with farm implements and wagons. South of town on Great Neck Road is 230-acre **Harkness Memorial State Park,** which includes a forty-two-room Italianate villa with formal gardens overlooking Long Island Sound.

Bear southwest (left) in Waterford on Connecticut Highway 156 West to the historic district, the turn to the state park, and to continue the drive. CT 156 leaves the city behind and heads through wooded hills studded with homes. The road skirts Niantic Bay before crossing the Niantic Bay Bridge, a drawbridge above a marina and harbor with a stunning view of the bay. The route then runs through **Niantic** itself. This peaceful coastal village offers several historic homes, pleasant seaside views, and nearby beaches. The Thomas Lee House, open for summer tours, was built in 1660 and is the oldest remaining wood frame house left in Connecticut. It was originally a one-room cabin that may have been built as early as 1641 before later expansion. The house is furnished with rare seventeenth-century English furnishings, as well as an original casement window.

After a mile the highway exits Niantic. Look down the road for a couple of miles until you see the left turn to **Rocky Neck State Park.** This popular 708-acre state park offers a dazzling mile-long, white-sand beach, one of a few state-run beaches in Connecticut. The gently sloped beach, warm seawater, and easy interstate access make this a busy summer destination. Off-season it is less crowded.

Four Mile River, a tidal river, borders the park on the west. The river's east side is a large salt marsh that offers great birding opportunities, with common sightings of heron, teal, mallard, and osprey. The park also offers a 160-site campground, 4.5 miles of hiking trails, saltwater fishing, picnic tables, and other recreational facilities.

The drive continues through a thick mixed hardwood forest and after a few miles bends inland along the east bank of the broad Connecticut River to Old Lyme with its marshes and dense thickets. The Connecticut River, emptying here into Long Island Sound, is one of the only major East Coast rivers with an undeveloped mouth. The longest river in New England, it flows 407 miles from its source at the Canadian border to the sound, dropping 1,618 feet and draining more than 11,000 square miles. The river's name (and the state's) derives from the Algonquin Indian word *Quinatucquet,* meaning "on the long tidal river." In the 1600s, the river formed the dividing line between the Dutch colonies along the Hudson River and the English settlements in Massachusetts and Rhode Island.

Old Lyme

Set on the east bank of the Connecticut River, **Old Lyme** is a classic New England village. Its First Congregational Church, built in 1817 and rebuilt and fire-proofed after a 1907 fire, is a beautiful building fronted by Ionic columns and topped with a tall, graceful steeple. The town, which split from Saybrook in 1665, was an old shipbuilding center and home port to many sea captains. It was named for the English port of Lyme Regis.

At the end of the nineteenth century, however, Old Lyme became a flourishing artists' colony and center of American Impressionism. The gorgeous scenery and bucolic woodlands along the river valley and seacoast attracted many talented painters, including Childe Hassam, Henry Ward Ranger, and William Metcalf, who found the surrounding countryside, light, and color palette similar to that around Paris. One of the Impressionists' favorite subjects was the village church. The **Lyme Academy of Fine Arts,** with exhibits by today's local artists, is nearby. Florence Griswold, spinster daughter of Captain Robert Griswold, opened her inherited Georgian mansion to the landscape painters and became a patron of the arts. The artists adorned her dining room with romantic landscape murals. Today the rest of the 1817 house is an art museum with a collection of works by more than 130 American artists, including many lovely Impressionistic pieces.

Old Saybrook to Guilford

Continue the drive by heading up CT 156 to I–95. Take the interstate across the half-mile-wide Connecticut River before leaving it again at exit 68 to US 1 and Old Saybrook. The next 20-mile drive section runs from here to Guilford. **Old Saybrook** has the honor of being the first colonial settlement on New England's southern shore. The village, located at a place the Indians called *Pashbeshauke* or "place at the river's mouth," was founded in 1635 as Saybrook Colony by Puritan settlers. Old Saybrook was the initial home of Yale University, founded here in 1701 as the Collegiate School before moving to New Haven fifteen years later. It was also the home to inventor David Bushnell, who, after putting himself through Yale at the age of thirty-one, built a sea craft he called a "sub-marine" for use in the Revolution. His submersible, dubbed the *American Turtle*, was meant to maneuver underwater to the hull of enemy ships, upon which would be attached an exploding, timed mine of his invention.

Old Saybrook spreads along Main Street southeast of US 1 to Saybrook Point, a peninsula jutting into the Connecticut River's mouth. A walking tour on Main Street gives a taste of the village's colorful history. The Humphrey Pratt Tavern, on the National Register of Historic Places, was an old stage stop as well as Saybrook's first post office. The 1840 Greek Revival–style Congregational Church is the congregation's fourth building since 1646. The **General William Hart House,** a handsome house-museum open for tours, is a superb example of a pre-Revolution colonial home. The restored house, built in 1767, is surrounded by colonial gardens with fruit trees, roses, and herbs. At Saybrook Point are numerous lovely old homes overlooking the river mouth, along with Cypress Cemetery and the earthen 1636 Saybrook Fort, the state's first fortification.

A stony beach at Hammonasset Beach State Park edges Long Island Sound.

The drive continues west along US 1, passing through Westbrook, a village settled in 1648. The town's picturesque Congregational Church overlooks the Westbrook Cemetery, with many old gravestones from the 1700s. Nearby is the restored 1756 house of settler Jedediah Chapman. The highway meanders above curving Westbrook Harbor before bending inland to Clinton. This quiet community with tree-lined streets dates from 1663. The 1850 **Captain Elisha White House,** a brick house open on summer weekends, was lovingly restored after a fire gutted it at the turn of the twentieth century.

The highway leaves Clinton and crosses the Hammonasset River. The turnoff to **Hammonasset Beach State Park** is just west of the bridge. This 919-acre parkland makes a great stop, offering a 2-mile strand of sandy beach and the state's largest park campground. Like Rocky Neck, it is easily accessible to I–95 and much of Connecticut's population, so it is crowded in summer. The park spreads across a wide neck that reaches into Long Island Sound. A good hike lies along the cobbled shoreline at Meigs Point, with spectacular views south across the sound to the forest-fringed outline of Long Island. A nearby nature center interprets the area's natural history with nature programs and walks. The extensive marshlands along the river attract shorebirds, waterfowl, and birders off-season.

Madison is the next coastal town on US 1. The town was originally part of Guilford but separated in 1826 and was named for President James Madison. Its stately village green is surrounded by many homes that date from the 1700s along with the ubiquitous Congregational Church topped with a small gold-domed steeple. The house to visit here is the **Allis-Bushnell House and museum.** The two-family house, originally built in 1785, was once home to Cornelius Scranton Bushnell, an organizer of the Union Pacific Railroad, shipbuilding magnate, and financier of the *Monitor*, a famed ironclad ship from the Civil War.

Guilford

Next the highway leaves Madison, passes an old cemetery, and rolls through wooded countryside interrupted by occasional stone walls around pastures with grazing sheep and cattle. Five miles later the scenic drive enters the historic settlement of **Guilford,** the seventh-oldest town in Connecticut. This beautiful village, dating from 1639, surrounds a tree-shaded green lined with old houses, four churches, and the town hall. The green, like all New England village greens, was used as a pioneer burial ground and a place to pasture cattle and horses, flog common criminals, and drill the local militia.

Reverend Henry Whitfield and forty Puritan men and their families bought land from the Menuncatuck Indians and settled here as farmers. In the eighteenth century, Guilford prospered through its shipyard, fishing, and trading. During the Revolution it avoided destruction by the British and kept intact its heritage of several seventeenth-century houses, as well as more than 400 eighteenth- and nineteenth-century homes.

The **Henry Whitfield State Museum,** lying south of the green on Old Whitfield Street, is the town's most famous structure. The house, with parts of it built in 1639 by the town's founder, is reputed to be New England's oldest stone dwelling. The house was meant to be not only home to the Whitfields, but also a fortress to protect the first settlers from Indian attacks. Over the last three centuries, the house has changed dramatically, and Whitfield would scarcely recognize his old home. The house does, however, illustrate daily life in early Connecticut with its 33-foot-long Great Hall, leaded glass windows, whitewashed walls, and rare seventeenth- and eighteenth-century artifacts and furnishings. Other local houses in Guilford are typical New England saltboxes including the 1660 **Hyland House** and the 1774 **Thomas Griswold House.** Both are restored and operated as museums. On the south side of town fronting the ocean is Chaffinch Island Park with a picnic area, Jacobs Beach, and the town landing and marina.

Guilford to New Haven

The last drive segment begins in Guilford and runs 18 miles through Branford to East Haven and I–95. Find this road section by keeping left on CT 146 or Boston Street at its junction with US 1 on the east side of Guilford. After leaving Guilford, the highway is a designated Connecticut scenic highway for the next 12 miles. The narrow asphalt road dips and rolls among low rocky hills blanketed with dense forest and skirts salt marshes, inlets, and coves. Occasional ocean views unfold beyond the trees.

Sachem's Head, a stubby peninsula jutting into the water south of the highway, possesses a rich history. It was named after a Mohegan chief, Uncas, killed a captured Pequot enemy sachem, or chief, here and wedged his severed head in the fork of a tree during the Pequot War in the late 1630s. Uncas allied his tribe with the new colonists to eradicate the rival Pequot Indians. The Pequots, their name meaning "destroyers of men," were the most fierce of the sixteen Connecticut tribes. The Pequots and Mohegans had been allied until Uncas was spurned as the leader of the two tribes. In retaliation he lined up an uneasy alliance with the colonists against the Pequots, who had raided and killed many settlers.

Past Island Bay, the road reaches Leetes Island, the site of a 1777 skirmish where the Guilford militia doused a British raiding attempt. The highway continues west within sight of the coastline and offers views of the Thimble Islands archipelago. This offshore group of 365 islands, named for the abundant thimbleberries found on the wooded isles, forms one of the most scenic portions of the Connecticut coast. Unfortunately, they are all privately held and trespassers are not highly regarded. The notorious pirate Captain Kidd supposedly buried a still unfound treasure on one of the Thimble isles in 1699. Several vessels offer daily sightseeing excursions among the islands from Stony Creek Dock at the end of Thimble Island Road.

The highway rolls westward through Pine Orchard and Indian Neck before turning north to **Branford.** This village was, like most other coastal towns, an early settlement. It was purchased from Indians in 1638 and settled the following year. Historic houses, three churches including a lovely Congregational Church topped with a steeple and clock tower, and the town hall surround the old Town Green.

To end the drive, continue west on US 1 from Branford a few miles to its intersection with I–95 and exit 51. An alternate and longer ending follows Connecticut Highways 142 and 337 down along the coast and up the east edge of New Haven Harbor. This winding road passes through numerous residential suburbs amid low granite hills. CT 337 ends at exit 50 on I–95. The New Haven metropolis awaits the traveler immediately west.

The 1639 Whitfield House in Guilford is reputed to be the oldest stone house in New England.

2

South Litchfield Hills Scenic Drive

General description: This 58-mile loop drive travels across scenic hills and valleys, through historic Litchfield, then follows the Housatonic River Valley south to New Milford.

Special attractions: Litchfield, Kent, Kent Falls State Park, Housatonic River, Bull's Bridge, Macedonia Brook State Park, Kent, Sloane-Stanley Museum, Mount Tom State Park, White Memorial Conservation Center, Lake Waramaug State Park, Mohawk State Forest, Appalachian Trail, hiking, camping, fishing, canoeing, rock climbing, nature study.

Location: Northwestern Connecticut. The drive lies north of Danbury and New Milford in the southern Litchfield Hills.

Drive route numbers: U.S. Highways 202 and 7, Connecticut Highways 45, 63, and 4.

Travel season: Year-round. A good time to visit is May through October. Spring brings new greenery to the hillsides and flowering shrubs. Summers are pleasant, but can be hot. Autumn brings warm weather and spectacular fall colors. Winters are cold and snowy.

Camping: Macedonia Brook State Park, west of Kent, offers fifty-one sites April through September. Lake Waramaug State Park near New Preston has seventy-seven sites April through September. Housatonic Meadows State Park at Cornwall Bridge (just north of the drive on U.S. Highway 7) offers ninety-five sites April through September. All are fee areas. Call the state parks at (860) 424–3200 or (866) 287–2757 for information and reservations. White Memorial Foundation has two campgrounds: Point Folly with forty-seven sites and Windmill Hill with eighteen sites. Several private campgrounds are found along or just off the drive.

Services: All services in New Milford, Litchfield, and Goshen; limited services in other towns along the route.

Nearby attractions: Housatonic Meadows State Park, West Cornwall covered bridge, Housatonic State Forest, Bartholomew's Cobble, Berkshire Hills, Hartford attractions.

The Drive

Sprawling across northwestern Connecticut, the Litchfield Hills form one of New England's most charming landscapes. The rounded, rolling hills are broken by sharp wooded vales and transected through their pastoral heart by the broad Housatonic River. Classic white saltbox farmhouses and red barns scatter across the hills, and old stone fences, some wildly overgrown, mark the edges of cleared fields and pastures. Amid this bucolic splendor sit some of New England's best preserved eighteenth- and nineteenth-century villages, including Litchfield, Cornwall, and Kent. The South Litchfield Hills drive, a 58-mile loop that begins in New Milford, travels across rustic countryside, explores picturesque towns, and discovers natural wonders and hidden beauty.

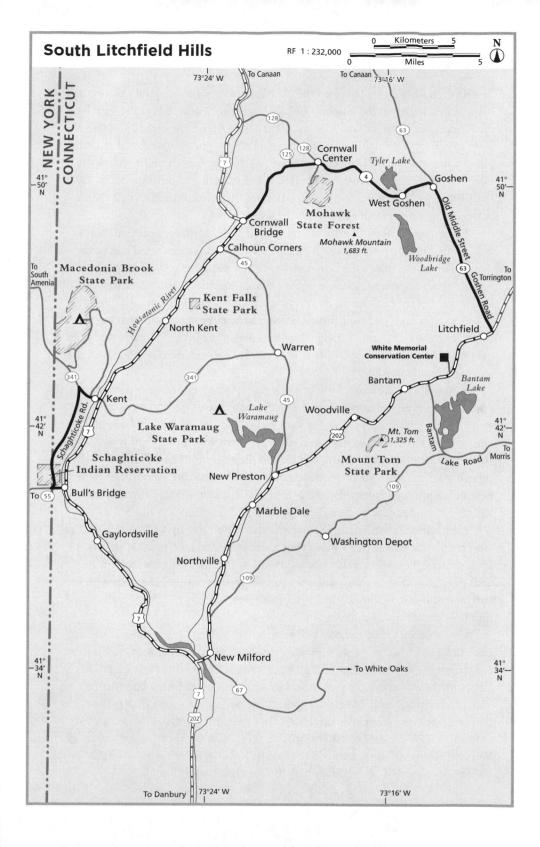

South Litchfield Hills

RF 1 : 232,000

New Milford to Lake Waramaug

The drive, readily accessible from the New York metro area and the Connecticut River Valley, begins at the junction of U.S. Highways 7 and 202 on the west bank of the Housatonic River in New Milford, 12 miles north of Interstate 84's exit 7 in Danbury. Turn east (right), cross the river on a steel girder bridge, and enter the historic center of **New Milford.** This town, anchoring the southern end of the Litchfield Hills, is the largest in Litchfield County with a population of 28,000. Established in 1707, it was built on land bought from local Indians in 1703 by enterprising settlers from Milford on the south coast.

The expansive New Milford Green, one of the area's largest, runs a quarter-mile along Main Street. Grand colonial homes bound the green, including the Town Hall. Its site marks the home of Roger Sherman, the only man to sign all four of America's founding documents—the 1774 Articles of Association, the 1776 Declaration of Independence, the 1777 Articles of Confederation, and the 1787 U.S. Constitution. The **New Milford Historical Society Museum,** in an eighteenth-century house at the end of the green, offers a glimpse into the town's past with historic portraits, furniture, china, and silver. Nearby are antiques shops, art galleries, and restaurants.

Follow US 202 through New Milford past old homes and bear northeast. The highway passes an old cemetery and quickly takes leave of the town as it passes into a broad, rolling valley studded with farms and houses. After a few miles The Silo at Hunt Hill Farm, an easily recognizable farm with a couple of houses, large barns, and twin silos, lies on the east side of the highway. The Silo offers changing monthly art exhibits and an acclaimed and popular cooking school. The highway next passes through Northville and Marble Dale, a pair of small towns with a handful of homes, and reaches the edge of New Preston after 8 miles.

Turn left on Connecticut Highway 45 here and drive up a hill into **New Preston** itself. This village offers numerous, excellent antiques shops along with an array of cafes, boutiques, galleries, and the New Preston Congregational Church. This delightful church with a tall, thin steeple was erected in 1853, although its congregation was established nearly a century earlier, in 1757. A red abandoned mill lies on the far side of town.

Continue up CT 45 to **Lake Waramaug,** the second-largest natural lake in Connecticut; its Indian name supposedly means "place of good fishing." The lake is surrounded by several inns and ninety-five-acre Waramaug State Park. On the lake's northwest corner, the park offers seventy-seven campsites, boating, fishing, and a swimming beach. Nearby Hopkins Vineyard offers wine samples in an old barn and vineyard tours. The Litchfield Hills are an important Connecticut viticultural area. A few miles farther north on CT 45 lies the picturesque hamlet of Warren. This small town, named for General Joseph Warren, who was killed at the Battle of Bunker Hill, is dominated by its Congregational Church.

Mount Tom to Litchfield

Return south on CT 45 to US 202 to continue the scenic drive. The highway runs northeast through Woodville and dips sharply into a wooded valley. It climbs steeply, swings across a hill, and after 14 miles reaches the entrance to **Mount Tom State Park.** The 232-acre state park, sitting on the east side of spring-fed Mount Tom Pond, includes a beach for swimming, water for nonmotorized boating, picnic tables alongside the lake and in the woods above, and an excellent mile-long trail that winds through dense woods to a three-story lookout tower atop 1,325-foot-high Mount Tom. The lookout, perched above the tall trees below, yields a superlative view of the Litchfield Hills. The forested hills roll away below the peak, their green flanks broken by grass and the glint of occasional lakes. Mount Frissel, Connecticut's highest mountain at 2,380 feet, rises to the northwest, while the white church spires of Litchfield lift above the green hills on the northeast horizon.

US 202 skirts the west edge of Mount Tom Pond and shortly afterward reaches Bantam. This small town is bordered by the **White Memorial Foundation,** a unique woodland reserve that protects more than 4,000 acres. Turn off US 202 at the woodland reserve's sign and follow a gravel road 0.5 mile to a parking area at the museum and gift shop. This privately administered preserve, the state's largest wildlife refuge, was established by a brother and sister of a wealthy family that summered in nearby Litchfield in the late nineteenth century. Remembering their formative summers here, Alain and May White acquired the land between 1908 and 1912 and set up a land trust in memory of their parents. The foundation preserves the area's unique woodlands and wetlands, providing environmental education, recreational opportunities, and research facilities.

More than 35 miles of nature trails lace the parkland, winding through woodlands of black cherry, Canadian hemlock, white oak, and large white pines. Other trails explore swamps and peatlands on boardwalks, passing characteristic marsh plants that include skunk cabbage, bulrush, turtlehead, and ferns, and provide great birding opportunities. The trails are also used for horseback riding and, in winter, cross-country skiing. Boating and fishing are popular pastimes along the Bantam River and Bantam Lake here, where a campground is available for overnight visitors. Inquire at the visitor center for the current schedule of nature programs, field trips, and lectures.

Litchfield

The highway rolls through Bantam past antiques shops and reaches **Litchfield** in a scant 3 miles. Litchfield, considered one of the best-preserved late eighteenth-century New England villages, makes a cluster around the expansive Town Green. The town is split by two principal residential thoroughfares, named, with Yankee brevity, North and South Streets. William Adam described the streets in 1897:

North Street "is a magnificent way, broad and straight, with ample plats of grass, bordered by fine old houses with spacious yards, the ideal of a New England street, while its southern continuation curves gently past houses of much the same sort and once the homes of distinguished men and women." The streets haven't changed much in the last hundred years.

Sprawling across a rounded hilltop some 1,200 feet above sea level, Litchfield is part of old New England and abounds in historical nuances. The town, named by its first English settlers for the old country's Lichfield, was settled in 1720. As surrounding hills were cleared and farmed, Litchfield grew into the county seat by 1751. The village thrived in the late eighteenth century as a freighting and passenger crossroads between the upper New England cities and New York and the Hudson River settlements.

The American Revolution thrust Litchfield into an infant nation's arms. Its relative isolation made Litchfield an ideal place to confine royalist prisoners, including the royalist mayor of New York, David Matthews, and William Franklin, the royal governor of New Jersey. The town's advantageous location on the main highway between Hartford and New York made it an ideal supply depot and storehouse for George Washington's Continental Army. A statue of despised British King George III was shipped here from New York in 1776 and melted into 42,088 bullets to help expel the British soldiers from the new nation. The war gave Litchfield a decidedly military atmosphere with numerous generals, including Washington and Lafayette, visiting the town.

Litchfield continued to prosper after the revolution and by 1810 was Connecticut's fourth-largest municipality. Industry and manufacturing fueled this now-quiet town, with eighteen sawmills, forges, nail and comb factories, a paper mill, and five tanneries. The town's boots and shoes were renowned for their quality and superb workmanship. By the 1830s, however, Litchfield's fortunes began to decline as the Industrial Revolution's burgeoning web of railroads bypassed the hill-bound town and spread its industry into the Connecticut Valley and along rivers that provided hydropower. This decline was a blessing in disguise, preserving Litchfield's historical treasures and ambience for late twentieth-century historians and travelers.

The three-centuries-old **Town Green** is the first of Litchfield's historic sites encountered along US 202. The long, undulating green, studded with benches and sidewalks and shaded by towering trees, was created in 1723 at the town center. The rest of Litchfield, a historic district composed of almost 500 buildings and listed on the National Register of Historic Places, surrounds the green and the residential side streets. Begin a good walking tour of old Litchfield by parking near South Street and the green.

The 1721 **First Congregational Church,** the town's most noted landmark, soars to the north above the green and its trees with a white facade, bell tower, and conical steeple. Rumor says this is the most photographed church in New England. Nearby is the **Litchfield History Museum,** housed in a brick library that dates from 1900. The museum's galleries offer portraits of early Litchfield luminaries by eighteenth-century painter Ralph Earl, early American toys, furniture displays, and exhibits detailing the area's history. Across the street from the museum is a narrow cobblestone alley that leads to Cobble Courtyard, a brick nineteenth-century livery stable that now houses shops.

A block down South Street sits the **Tapping Reeve House and Law School.** The nation's first law school was established by Tapping Reeve in 1775. After several years of teaching in his house, Reeve moved the school in 1784 into a one-room building next door. The small unheated school, so cold in winter that ink froze in the wells, taught law to some of early America's finest legal and political minds. Graduates included Reeve's brother-in-law and vice president Aaron Burr, educator Horace Mann, western painter George Catlin, inventor Sydney Morse, and statesman John C. Calhoun, as well as three Supreme Court justices, two more vice presidents, twenty-six senators, six cabinet members, more than a hundred members of Congress, and sixteen governors, including six of Connecticut's. The school closed in 1883.

After a stroll around the green and the surrounding spacious streets, turn north onto Connecticut Highway 63 on the north side of the green. The highway, following North Street, passes numerous historic homes, notably the Pierce Academy and the Beecher House. The Sarah Pierce Litchfield Female Academy was established in 1792 to cultivate the intellectual and cultural potential of young American women. More than 3,000 students enrolled in the school during its forty-one-year history. **The Beecher House** was home to Litchfield's most prominent family. Pastor Lyman Beecher landed here as a country preacher in 1810. His offspring became two of the nineteenth century's most noted and influential Americans—Reverend Henry Ward Beecher and Harriet Beecher Stowe, author of the anti-slavery novel *Uncle Tom's Cabin*. Other famed Litchfield residents include Revolutionary War officer Benjamin Tallmadge, patriot Nathan Hale, the Wolcott family, and a prolific Mary Buel, "wife of Dea. John Buel, Esq." Her 1768 gravestone notes her death at age ninety after "having 13 children, 101 grandchildren, 247 great-grandchildren, and 49 great-great-grandchildren; total 410. Three hundred and thirty-six survived her."

The drive's next leg runs northwest to **Goshen** along CT 63. The highway quickly leaves Litchfield and passes forests, pastures, and occasional houses tucked among trees. In Goshen the highway intersects Connecticut Highway 4 at a small rotary. Turn west (left) on CT 4 at the rotary.

Goshen owns a large fairgrounds, which hosts the annual Connecticut Agricultural Fair in late July and a Scottish festival in October. Another well-tended colonial village, Goshen preserves its history at the **Goshen Historical Society Museum,** a white colonial building on CT 4.

Outside Goshen the road passes a cemetery and reaches West Goshen after 2 miles. The highway then rolls west past Tyler Lake, through deep woods, and after a few miles reaches the turnoff to Mohawk State Forest. Turn south onto Allyn Road and go 1.6 miles to the forest parking area and headquarters.

Mohawk State Forest

Mohawk State Forest, one of Connecticut's best woodland preserves, spreads across the slopes of 1,683-foot Mohawk Mountain. The 3,351-acre parkland protects some unique ecosystems, including a two-acre black spruce bog. Although similar bogs are common in northern New England, they are rarities this far south. A short boardwalk trail explores the bog, initially passing through a forest of tall red pines before reaching the bog's edge. The dominant tree in the bog is black spruce, a boreal tree that reaches heights of 30 feet. These stunted, spindly trees are well-adapted to the bog's harsh and acidic peat, a mass of undecayed organic material deposited in the bog. Sphagnum moss is another common plant found here along with sheep laurel, dwarf huckleberry, and sundew, a carnivorous plant that digests insects trapped in sticky hairs on its round leaves. Other trails venture through the forest, climbing to lookouts and winding through dense woods.

Mohawk Ski Area, also in the state forest, is Connecticut's largest ski and snowboard area. It offers twenty-four groomed trails and slopes, snowmaking equipment, night skiing, and a lodge.

Past the state forest turnoff, the highway drops steeply downhill and reaches the junction of Connecticut Highways 4, 128, and 43. Keep left on CT 4. The road passes the turnoff to Mohawk Ski Area and drops down another hill to Cornwall Center, a township established in 1740. All the Cornwalls in the vicinity are somewhat confusing—Cornwall, Cornwall Bridge, Cornwall Center, Cornwall Hollow, West Cornwall, and East Cornwall. The area's famed Cornwall covered bridge lies to the north in West Cornwall, not in Cornwall Bridge. (See Scenic Drive 3, North Litchfield Hills.)

A good Cornwall side-trip ventures to the famous **Cathedral Pines Preserve.** Turn left on Pine Street at the junction of CT 4 and Connecticut Highway 125 in Cornwall. The road leads to the Cathedral Pines, a once-immense old-growth white pine forest that was decimated by a rare tornado on July 10, 1989. The stand of 200-year-old pines, one of the few in all New England untouched by nineteenth-century land clearing and charcoal cutting, was a stunning sight before its destruction. The Nature Conservancy, which manages the forty-two-acre property, has allowed nature to take its course and has left the mangled trees as testimony to nature's wild caprices.

Along the Housatonic River

The drive continues southwest from Cornwall on CT 4 for 4 miles to **Cornwall Bridge,** the Housatonic River Valley, and a junction with US 7. Turn south (left) on US 7 toward New Milford for the last 23-mile segment of the drive. At Swift Bridge, 1 mile south, US 7 intersects CT 45. This 11-mile road, running southeast to New Preston, makes a good side excursion. It climbs over hills and dips through broad valleys broken by woods, farms, and stone fences. The scenic drive, however, runs southwestward along the eastern edge of the broad Housatonic River Valley on a designated Connecticut Scenic Road.

The **Housatonic River,** paralleling the scenic drive from here to New Milford, is a part-wild/part-workhorse river that once powered industry along its banks. The river, with an Indian name meaning "place beyond the mountains," originates in the Berkshire Hills and wanders 132 miles southward across Connecticut before emptying into Long Island Sound.

Four miles from Cornwall Bridge, the drive reaches **Kent Falls State Park.** This idyllic spot, popular with picnickers and hikers, is a broad, grassy expanse framed by thick woods and the 250-foot-high cascade Kent Falls. Kent Falls Brook, fed by springs high in the Litchfield Hills above the valley, riffles and tumbles over a series of rocky steps. A 0.25-mile trail climbs 250 feet from the falls' base to a higher viewpoint. The area also offers picnic tables and restrooms.

The highway runs along the valley edge past houses, occasional farms, and an old cemetery. St. John's Ledges, accessed via the famed Appalachian Trail, are on a

Flanders Cemetery, south of Kent Falls, has numerous gravestones that date back to the Revolutionary War.

scruffy cliff poised 500 feet above the rural valley. The cliff, composed of ancient metamorphic gneiss deposited billions of years ago as volcanic debris, yields superb views of the valley from its summit as well as good slab routes for rock climbers. The cliff and trail are accessed from Skiff Mountain Road on the west side of the river.

Flanders Cemetery, south of the falls, offers a clean vista of St. John's Ledges and the broad river valley. The cemetery is worth a look too. The grave of thirty-nine-year-old Captain Jirah Smith, who was killed in the Revolution, boasts the inscription: "I in the Prime of Life must quit the Stage, Nor see the End of all the Britains Rage."

South on US 7 is the **Flanders Historic District,** a cluster of eighteenth-century homes that are part of the original Kent. One home, now the Flander Arms bed-and-breakfast, dates from 1738. Across the highway is Seven Hearths, the former home and studio of portrait artist George Laurence Nelson. The 1754 house, operated by the Kent Historical Society, displays Nelson's prolific works and is open for tours on weekends in July and August.

Kent to New Milford

The Sloane-Stanley Museum, on the northern outskirts of Kent, lies west of the highway along the riverbank. This interesting museum houses a large collection of early American tools and implements collected by Eric Sloane, an artist and writer who resided in nearby Warren. The museum was established in 1969 after Sloane donated his collection to the building erected by Donald Davis, president of the tool-making Stanley Works on the site of the old Kent Iron Furnace. The collection includes an astonishing number of ingenious wooden and iron tools fashioned by early settlers to eke a life out of New England's wilds. Excellent interpretative displays illustrate the uses of these arcane, unrecognizable tools. Sloane's studio and workshop, recreated from his home, are also displayed along with a furnished replica of an early American house and an 1826 pig iron furnace. After his death in 1985, Sloane was buried under a spreading maple on the property.

Kent, founded in 1731 and once a bustling iron center, is a charming old town reputed for its wide selection of antiques shops, galleries, and craft stores. Its streets are lined with fine homes, shops, and a white, turreted First Congregational Church established in 1741 and built in 1849. Turn right in the town center on Connecticut Highway 341 to visit **Macedonia Brook State Park** and St. John's Ledges. The state park offers fifty-one campsites, fishing, and hiking trails.

The highway continues south from Kent across the green valley floor. Occasional views open onto the mirrorlike Housatonic River and green pastures and farms. Bull's Bridge is reached after 4 miles. Turn west to its covered bridge, dam, and an abrupt rocky gorge. The bridge, one of two remaining covered bridges of

Kent's First Congregational Church was built in 1849.

the eighteen that once spanned the Housatonic, was originally built in 1842 for $3,000. The bridge was used on a route that hauled iron products from Jacob Bull's furnace to New York markets. The bridge was later raised 20 feet after the Connecticut Power & Light Company built a power plant at the site. Just west of the bridge and river is a parking area for hikers, fishermen, and picnickers. The Appalachian Trail travels north from here along the river and over St. John's Ledges en route to its Maine terminus.

An excellent side-trip runs north from here on Schaghticoke Road on the west bank of the river. The road narrows to rough one-lane pavement and gravel as it winds through tall sycamores along the narrow west bank of the Housatonic River. The Schaghticoke Indian Reservation, the remnant of a once-great Indian nation, huddles along the road. The old burying ground sits alongside the road among shady trees. One stone is engraved "Eunice Mauwee, a Christian Indian, 1756–1860." Farther north the road passes Kent School, a private academy, before rejoining CT 341 just west of Kent.

The drive continues by heading back south on CT 341 to Bull's Bridge. From here the highway rolls south along the river's east bank for 7 miles to **Gay-lordsville,** a pleasant riverside town founded in 1725. Nearby sits the last one-room schoolhouse in Connecticut. It opened in 1765 and held classes for two centuries until closing in 1967. The road swings over the river and meanders another 7 miles south through quiet, wooded countryside broken by glimpses of the river and secluded homes. Past a power plant, the drive ends at the girder bridge at the drive's starting point and the busy junction of US 7 and US 202 in New Milford.

3

North Litchfield Hills Scenic Drive

General description: A 56-mile loop drive that wanders across wooded hills and up the Housatonic River in northwestern Connecticut's scenic Litchfield Hills.

Special attractions: Housatonic Meadows State Park, West Cornwall Covered Bridge, Housatonic State Forest, Appalachian Trail, Norfolk, Yale School of Music, hiking, camping, fishing, canoeing, nature study.

Location: Northwestern Connecticut.

Drive route numbers: U.S. Highways 7 and 44, Connecticut Highways 41, 272, and 4.

Travel season: Year-round. A good time to visit is May through October. Summers are pleasant, but can be hot. Autumn brings warm weather and spectacular fall colors. Winters are cold and snowy.

Camping: Macedonia Brook State Park, west of Kent and just south of the drive, offers fifty-one sites April through September. Lake Waramaug near New Preston south of the drive has seventy-eight sites from April through September. Housatonic Meadows State Park at Cornwall Bridge on US 7 offers ninety-five sites April through September. Several private campgrounds are found along or just off the drive.

Services: All services in most towns along the drive, including Winsted, Canaan, Sharon, and Cornwall Bridge.

Nearby attractions: Sloane-Stanley Museum, Kent Falls State Park, Litchfield Historic District, Mount Tom State Park, Lake Waramaug State Park, Mohawk State Forest, Mohawk Ski Area, White Memorial Conservation Center, Bartholomew's Cobble, Berkshire Hills.

The Drive

The North Litchfield Hills scenic drive explores the rural northwestern corner of Connecticut, traversing west from Winsted across rolling hills studded with occasional towns before turning south along the New York border and driving up the narrow valley of the Housatonic River to end at Canaan just south of the Massachusetts border.

The drive begins on the west side of Winsted at the junction of U.S. Highway 44 and Connecticut Highway 183. **Winsted,** the second-largest town in Litchfield County, is a busy old mill town that reflects its working-class roots in stark contrast to surrounding rural communities. Lying almost midway between Winchester and Barkhamsted, Winsted draws its name from the first syllable of one and the last syllable of the other. The town was a clock-making center during the early nineteenth century. Later, during the Industrial Age, its factories manufactured wire, electrical products, and twelve million stickpins a day. The town offers a

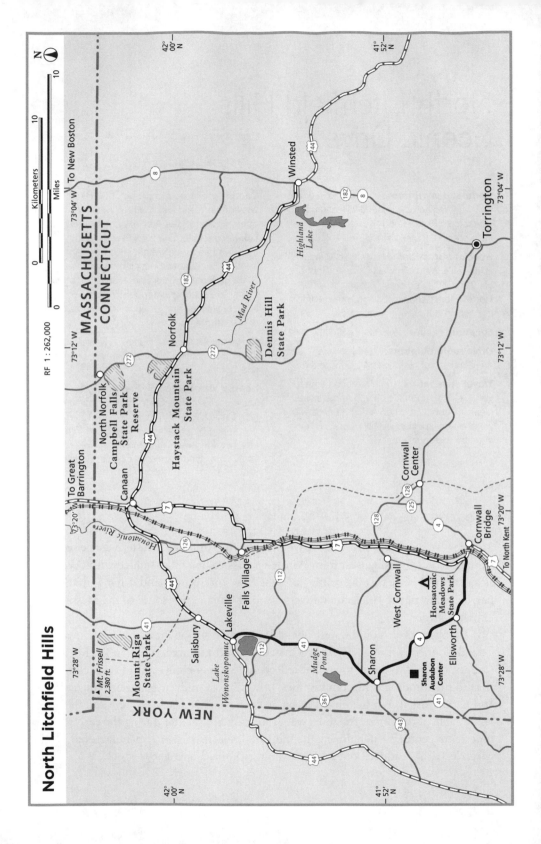

North Litchfield Hills

good selection of restaurants and shops, retaining its industrial heritage with old brick factories lining its congested streets.

Winsted to Canaan

Head west on US 44 from Winsted to take the scenic drive's first leg, which runs 16 miles northwest to Canaan. The highway leaves Winsted, climbs out of its sprawling valley, and enters the Litchfield Hills. These hills, the southern end of the Green Mountains–Berkshire Hills range in Vermont and Massachusetts, are composed of a rolling upland broken by valleys. After 1 mile the highway passes Mad River Dam, and after 6 more miles enters Norfolk. This stretch of road offers pleasant, wooded country interrupted by small hill farms and occasional open pastures with good views to the south.

Compared to some of its Puritan neighbors, **Norfolk** is a relative latecomer. This isolated town, spread across stony, rolling hills, was originally settled in 1744 and incorporated fourteen years later by the town's forty-four voters. Norfolk sat along the old Albany-to-Hartford turnpike, a busy overland route that carried coastal goods inland to the upper Hudson River frontier. When the American Revolution began at Lexington in Massachusetts, twenty-four local men took up arms and marched to Boston to begin the fight for freedom. After the war the town's hilltop isolation and hardscrabble terrain kept Norfolk from becoming an agricultural center. Instead the townspeople built an industrial economic base in the early 1800s, relying on nearby forests for lumber and the Blackberry River for hydroelectric power.

When its manufacturing era declined, Norfolk used its country charm to flourish as a summer resort for the well-heeled. The town's wealthy ambience stems from this period in the late nineteenth century. Immense homes, many of them now elegant bed-and-breakfasts, line Norfolk's streets. Interesting buildings include the handsome Norfolk Library built in 1889 by Isabella Eldridge, and the Norfolk Historical Society, housed in the 1840 Norfolk Academy on Main Street, which offers exhibits about three prominent Norfolk families, the Battells, Eldridges, and Stoeckels, as well as local relics. The Eldridges built the library and also commissioned Stanford White to design a three-tiered fountain with watering troughs for dogs, horses, and people near the village green. The Battell and Stoeckel families established a lasting legacy in Norfolk by leaving their rich estates to the Yale School of Music. The town hosts a renowned summer music festival in the school's music shed.

The scenic drive and US 44 intersect with Connecticut Highway 272 in Norfolk's center. A short run south on CT 272 leads to **Dennis Hill State Park,** a small parkland that offers room for picnicking and walking. The area's centerpiece is a stone observation pavilion atop Dennis Hill, providing spacious views of the surrounding hills.

A mile north from the highway junction on CT 272 is **Haystack Mountain State Park.** This scenic area yields an excellent hiking trail that winds through shady woods to the summit of 1,716-foot Haystack Mountain. A round stone tower with a spiral staircase offers spectacular vistas above the treetops of Connecticut's Litchfield Hills, the Berkshire Hills in Massachusetts to the north, and the Taconic Mountains in New York to the west. This long, thin range of mountains straddles New York's eastern border from here north to central Vermont.

A third state park, **Campbell Falls State Park Reserve,** lies another 6 miles north of Norfolk off CT 272. Lying near the Massachusetts border, it is named for a series of cascades that tumble over rock ledges here. The park includes opportunities for hiking, picnicking, nature study, and photography.

Crossing the divide that separates the Connecticut and Housatonic river drainages just west of Norfolk, the scenic drive continues northwest along US 44 for 7 miles from Norfolk to Canaan. After crossing this nondescript divide, the highway drops into the broad valley of the westward-flowing Blackberry River. The river swings in wide meanders across the valley floor, its banks lined with black locust and cottonwood, a poplar more commonly found in the Midwest. High mountain ridges hem the valley to the south, forming a long, forested wall. Occasional farms and homes dot the pastoral scene.

Canaan

The blacktop runs through East Canaan and, 2 miles later, enters the village of **Canaan.** A crossroads town in the wide Housatonic River Valley at the junction of U.S. Highways 44 and 7, Canaan sits a scant 2 miles south of the Massachusetts state line. Like other northwestern Connecticut villages, it thrived with the area's early iron industry. The remains of abandoned iron forges are scattered throughout the Canaan area; most, however, are on private property. The **Beckley Iron Furnace,** listed on the National Register of Historic Places, is the best preserved site to visit. Reach it by turning from US 44 onto Furnace Hill Road east of town. Head right at the stop sign and drop to the furnace ruins along the banks of the Blackberry River. East of the turn on US 44 is Lone Oak Campground, one of the state's largest private campgrounds with 500-plus sites.

The **Canaan Union Station,** built in 1872 and listed on the National Register of Historic Places, sits in the center of town. The yellow station, one of the oldest in continuous use, is home to the Housatonic Railroad. The railroad runs excursion trains south to West Cornwall alongside the Housatonic River.

Salisbury, Lakeville, and Sharon

From here, the scenic drive makes a 40-mile loop southwest of Canaan along US 44 and Connecticut Highways 41 and 4 to Cornwall Bridge, returning on US 7 along the Housatonic River. Head southwest out of Canaan on US 44. The highway leaves town, crosses the Blackberry River, and after a mile reaches the Housatonic. The highway is a designated Connecticut Scenic Highway for the next 8 miles, as the tree-lined river, descending gently southward, slowly unwinds across the broad valley. After another mile the road crosses the river, works west over a ridge, passes private Salisbury School, and tilts down into a wide valley and Salisbury.

Salisbury, founded in 1741, and neighboring Lakeville, 2 miles south, were major iron ore centers in the eighteenth century. The almost pure iron smelted and forged in these communities proved crucial to the colonial effort in the American Revolution, supplying cannons, shot, and balls to George Washington's Continental Army. The iron industry here was so important to the Revolution that the ironworkers were supplied with meat and plentiful rum to sustain their work. The town's iron industry also produced war materiel during the War of 1812, and later provided iron used in the growing rail network that spread across the United States in the nineteenth century. Salisbury is now a quiet community dominated by a white Congregational Church built in 1800 and the stone Scoville Memorial Library. The Appalachian Trail, the long-distance footpath from Georgia to Maine, threads across the north side of town before heading into the Berkshire Hills to the north.

To take a good side-trip, travel north on CT 41 a few miles to the Massachusetts border. The road traverses a countryside of fields and occasional grassy pastures framed by dense woodlands. The Under Mountain Hiking Trail is reached 3 miles north of the junction of US 44 and CT 41. This trail meanders west to the top of 2,355-foot Bear Mountain, one of Connecticut's highest summits.

Back on the main scenic route, **Lakeville** sits 2 miles southwest of Salisbury. This once-flourishing iron town is now a peaceful rural community dotted with spacious colonial homes, including the Holley-Williams House. The house, built in 1768 and enlarged in 1808 by ironman John Milton Holley, was inhabited by five generations of the Holley family until 1971 when it was deeded to the town. This unique house museum offers a glimpse into daily nineteenth-century life with period furniture and portraits, as well as an iron furnace model and tool displays in the adjoining Carriage House. One of Lakeville's most famous residents was patriot Ethan Allen, who lived here before his Green Mountain Boys captured Fort Ticonderoga from the British in May 1775. Allen was an owner of the Lakeville Forge between 1762 and 1765. The forge became a cutlery factory in the mid-1800s. Lakeville was also renowned for the excellent knives produced by the Holley Manufacturing Company in Pocketknife Square.

In Lakeville, turn south (left) onto CT 41, then drive 7 miles south to Sharon. The road runs past Lake Wononskopomuc and the Hotchkiss preparatory school grounds before entering a mixed woodland of pine and hardwoods interrupted by occasional marshy fens, dairy farms, and colonial houses. You'll get good views of

The West Cornwall Covered Bridge, built in 1837, spans the Housatonic River.

the rolling hills from fields and pastures east of the highway. South of the highway's junction with Connecticut Highway 112, the blacktop undulates along a broad ridge crest. Mudge Pond, a long glimmering lake, nestles in a valley below.

The village of **Sharon,** like so many other Litchfield towns, is quintessential New England with a picturesque village green dating from 1739, a spired white Congregational Church, and broad streets lined with handsome homes. Town attractions include the Gay-Hoyt House, where the Sharon Historical Society displays local artifacts and paintings. Sharon's landmark is the 1884 cut-stone Hotchkiss Clock Tower on the south side of the green.

At the junction of Connecticut Highways 343, 41, and 4, continue southeast on CT 4 for 8 miles to Cornwall Bridge. The highway climbs away from the town into the hills to reach the **Sharon Audubon Center,** sprawling across the valley floor, in a couple of miles. This 1,147-acre nature preserve offers almost 12 miles of hiking trails that explore surrounding forests and meadows, as well as a Children's Adventure Center, a bookstore, and nature exhibits.

The road ascends the broad crest of the hills and rolls southeast past old farmhouses dating from the 1700s and overgrown stone fences dividing pastures. After a few miles it twists into a narrow canyon, passes a small roadside picnic area, and weaves steeply downhill through dense woods to the Housatonic River Valley and the junction with US 7 at Cornwall Bridge. A wealth of Cornwall-named locations are found in the immediate vicinity—Cornwall, West Cornwall, East Cornwall, and Cornwall Bridge. The area's covered bridge is not found in the town of Cornwall Bridge, but farther north on the scenic drive in West Cornwall.

Up the Housatonic River

Turn north (left) on US 7 for the drive's last 17 miles back to Canaan. The highway runs north along the narrow west bank of the Housatonic River through a spectacular canyon lined with steep, wooded slopes broken by occasional rock steps. **Housatonic Meadows State Park,** a 451-acre area, straddles the river for the first few miles. It offers excellent fly fishing for trout, picnic tables for lunch, the 2.5-mile Pine Knob Loop Trail, which climbs to a 1,160-foot viewpoint, and a ninety-five-site campground. Canoes and kayaks are available for rental from a roadside outfitter to anyone willing to brave the river riffles.

The canyon narrows past the campground and 0.5 mile later reaches **West Cornwall** and its long covered bridge. The village on the river's east bank is reached via the sturdy, one-lane, red covered bridge built in 1837. Clatter across the bridge and park in the narrow streets of West Cornwall. This picturesque village offers several interesting craft shops, including a pottery shop and Shaker furniture maker.

The drive continues north along the deep canyon floor, passing dense woods in 9,543-acre **Housatonic State Forest.** The forest, covering steep hillsides on both sides of the river, is broken into a dozen tracts of wooded land. The valley opens and widens as the road runs north. A few miles past the highway's intersection with Connecticut Highway 112 and the Appalachian Trail, the road crosses the river and enters Falls Village. Named for the nearby Great Falls on the Housatonic River, Falls Village was once part of Canaan. The town, like its neighbors, prospered with the iron industry, along with a busy lumber mill and hydroelectric dam. The frothy **Great Falls** are easily viewed from overlooks reached from the village center.

The scenic drive continues north on US 7 from Falls Village, following a broadening river valley for 6 miles to the route's terminus at the junction of US 7 and 44 in Canaan. This segment traverses a lovely valley flanked by lofty ridges to the east and dense thickets of trees and shrubs that choke the placid river's banks. Near Canaan, the highway crosses the Blackberry River and enters a residential area before this scenic drive ends at US 44.

4

Rhode Island Coast Scenic Drive

General description: A 61-mile scenic drive along Rhode Island's coast and Narragansett Bay between Westerly and Newport.

Special attractions: Watch Hill, Misquamicut State Beach, Burlingame State Park, Ninigret National Wildlife Refuge, Ninigret Conservation Area, Fort Ninigret, Charlestown, Trustom Pond National Wildlife Refuge, Point Judith, Silas Casey Farm, Gilbert Stuart Birthplace, Conanicut Island, Fort Wetherill State Park, Newport attractions, Cliff Walk, scenic views, hiking, birding, fishing, historic sites.

Location: Southern Rhode Island.

Drive route numbers: U.S. Highways 1 and 1A, Rhode Island Highways 108 and 138.

Travel season: Year-round. The weather along the coast is generally very pleasant. Warm summer temperatures are moderated by sea breezes.

Camping: Burlingame State Park north of US 1 has 755 campsites with water, washrooms, showers, toilets, and picnic tables. Charlestown Breachway offers seventy-five sites for self-contained units. Fisherman's Memorial State Park at Galilee has 147 trailer/RV sites and thirty-five tent sites.

Services: All services in Westerly, Watch Hill, Charlestown, Wakefield, Narragansett Pier.

Nearby attractions: Providence attractions, Lincoln Woods State Park, Connecticut coastline, Mystic seaport, Cape Cod National Seashore.

The Drive

This 61-mile excursion begins in Westerly on the Connecticut border and roughly follows the Rhode Island shoreline east to Narragansett. Here it works north along Narragansett Bay, crosses the bay to Conanicut Island, and finishes in the famed city of Newport at the southern tip of slender Aquidneck Island. The drive offers pleasant scenery, historic sites and mansions, dense woodlands, rock-rimmed peninsulas, long sand spits and beaches, salt marshes, and a maze of inlets, coves, and harbors.

Rhode Island, nicknamed the Ocean State, is the nation's smallest state, measuring only 48 miles long by 37 miles wide. More than 20 percent of Rhode Island is consumed by Narragansett Bay, a wide slice of water reaching across the state. The bay encompasses 12 miles of water on the south, narrows to 3 miles in the north, and extends 28 miles inland. Three major islands—Aquidneck, Conanicut, and Prudence—split the bay into two rough halves. The twisting shoreline of the bay, which is the state's premier natural feature, totals more than 300 miles. The ocean front between Point Judith and Watch Hill is a long, straight stretch of sand beaches, lagoons, and salt ponds.

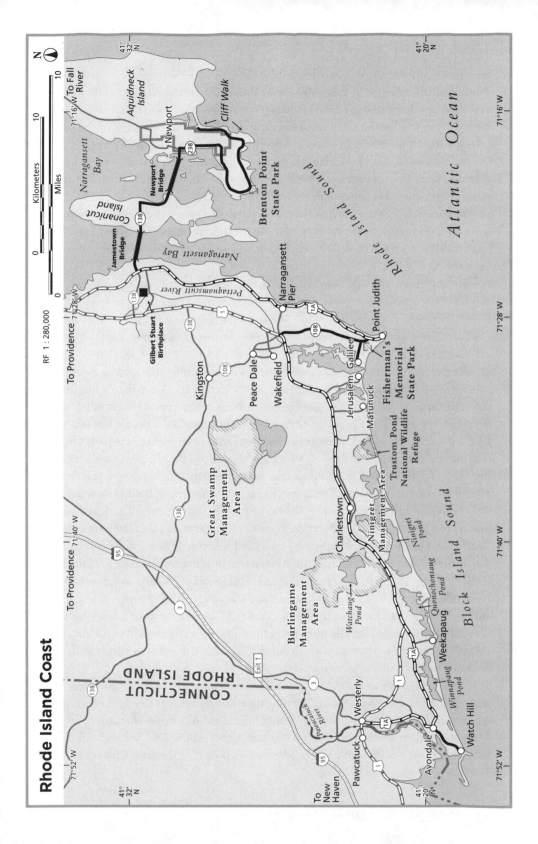

Rhode Island Coast

Westerly to Watch Hill

The scenic drive begins in **Westerly,** a few miles south of Interstate 95. Take exit 1 and drive south on Rhode Island Highway 3 into the downtown area. The city, as its name suggests, lies in far western Rhode Island along the west bank of the Pawcatuck River, opposite the Connecticut border. It's a pretty town with tree-shaded streets, elegant homes, and a long history. Besides sharing the placid river with Pawcatuck, its Connecticut twin, Westerly shares the same post office and railroad station. The town was supposedly founded by settlers John Babcock from Plymouth Colony and Mary Lawton from Newport. The lovers eloped from Newport in 1648. Other immigrants followed, settling on this riverbank purchased from local Indians. To tame the wild surroundings, a bounty of 20 shillings was given for every wolf killed in Westerly in 1687.

In later times Westerly flourished with a diverse industrial base, including shipbuilding, granite quarrying, and wool and cotton textile mills. The huge White Rock Company cotton mill, built in 1849 and purchased in 1874 for Fruit of the Loom, still testifies to this prosperity. Westerly's claims to fame now are the *Westerly Sun*, the only Sunday evening newspaper in the United States, and the world's oldest operating automatic telephone system. The city's downtown has a distinct small town flavor, dominated by eighteen-acre Wilcox Park. More than a hundred tree and shrub species, an herb garden, flower beds, a large pond filled with goldfish, statuary including a marble Christopher Columbus, and a Braille-marked trail are found here. The **Wilcox Park Historic District** surrounds the park, with charming old buildings and stately Victorian residences. Buildings of note here are the 1872 Old Town Hall, the Romanesque-style Westerly Public Library, and the 1732 Babcock-Smith House. The house, open in summer with limited hours, is a well-preserved pre–Revolutionary War home furnished with period antiques that once belonged to Dr. Joshua Babcock, a member of the state's General Assembly, chief justice of the colony's Supreme Court, and a friend of Benjamin Franklin.

From Wilcox Park the scenic drive begins by heading south on Beach Street (U.S. Highway 1A), following signs to Watch Hill. Solid old Victorian houses line the shaded street. The road passes River Bend Cemetery, with many monuments and gravestones of blue Westerly granite, and rolls south over worn granite hills covered with secluded homes. After almost 4 miles, bend right on Watch Hill Road. The asphalt twists southwest through hills for a few miles to **Watch Hill,** one of New England's oldest seaside resorts.

This small town at the state's far southwestern corner is surprisingly unpretentious and quiet. Parking is limited, however, and once the available spots are filled, it's hard to find anywhere to stop. Watch Hill received its unusual name during the Revolution when soldiers perched on this point and watched for British raiders. Later it became a fashionable resort. Many of its homes and estates with ornate hedges date from the nineteenth century. Bay Street, Watch Hill's business district, is lined with shops and restaurants. A statue of Ninigret, a 1630s chief of the Niantics, greets visitors on the street.

The Flying Horse Carousel, found at the end of Bay Street, is the oldest continuously operating merry-go-round carousel in the United States. The carousel, also called the Watch Hill Carousel, was built in 1867, spent a dozen years traveling with a carnival, and was finally set up permanently in Watch Hill in 1879. The carousel, unlike modern ones, has no wooden deck. The 140-year-old, hand-carved, hand-painted horses are suspended from above and give the illusion of flying as the central shaft rotates. The horses were carved from single pieces of wood, decorated with agate eyes and genuine horsehair tails and manes, and have leather saddles. Adults are not permitted to ride the carousel; only children whose feet do not touch the ground when seated are allowed. The ride operates through the summer.

Another Watch Hill spot of interest is its popular sand beach facing the Atlantic Ocean. The bathhouse is near the carousel, and beach access is granted to those who have paid the bathhouse fee. A good short walk goes to the 1856 Watch Hill Lighthouse, an excellent example of a nineteenth-century lighthouse. The light is closed to visitors, but nearby is the Watch Hill Lighthouse Museum.

A longer hike is out to Napatree Point Beach and Conservation Area. The 1.5-mile walk to the very western end of Rhode Island follows a long spit of sand that juts into Little Narragansett Bay. It's a charming hike, with the emerald surf breaking on packed sand, a litter of shells sprinkled on the beach, and the wheeling of gulls on the sea breezes. Protected nesting sites of terns and ospreys are found on the point. Beach houses once lined this long, narrow stretch of land until a disastrous hurricane struck in 1938 and erased them. At the end of Napatree Point are the tumbled ruins of old Fort Mansfield, built during the Spanish-American War.

Watch Hill to Charlestown

To continue the scenic drive, follow Watch Hill Road back to US 1A and go east (right) on Scenic Route 1A, also called the Shore Road Highway. Just down the road is the turnoff to **Misquamicut State Beach,** and a couple of miles later the turn to Weekapaug. Down this lane is this small village to the east of Winnapaug Pond, a large lake and tidal marsh dotted with wading birds. Farther along the road is Westerly Town Beach. East of the town of Weekapaug is a good bluff viewpoint that overlooks the coastline and Block Island, a large offshore island that appears to float on the horizon.

Burlingame State Park, a 2,160-acre public area, sits on the left a few miles down the road. The park is a popular summer spot, with its 755-site campground and 600-acre Watchaug Pond. Boating and fishing are popular pursuits, and the

Atlantic beaches are only a few miles to the south. The forested area also includes the Audubon Society's twenty-nine-acre **Kimball Wildlife Sanctuary,** a popular stopover for migrating birds and waterfowl including wood ducks, mallards, and teal. A nature center offers ongoing interpretative programs and displays.

Farther east, **Ninigret National Wildlife Refuge** and Ninigret Park border the highway on the south. Farther out along the coast is Ninigret Conservation Area. These three areas flank Ninigret Pond, a huge 1,700-acre salt pond separated from Block Island Sound by a long barrier beach. The wildlife refuge, on the site of an abandoned airport, offers rich habitat for migrating birds and waterfowl with deciduous forest, freshwater ponds, and salt grass. The refuge bird checklist includes 289 regular species (most of those found in the state) as well as twenty-one accidental species. The spring and fall migration seasons offer the best viewing, with the warbler migration peaking in May. Almost 3 miles of footpaths loop through the refuge. **Ninigret Park** is exactly that, a park owned by the town of Charlestown with swimming beaches, lifeguards in summer, a playground, bike course, and tennis and basketball courts. Ninigret Conservation Area fronts the ocean along the 2-mile-long stretch of barrier beach. Although it can be crowded, it is less busy than other nearby beaches because of parking limitations. When the area parking lot reaches its one-hundred-car capacity, it is closed.

From the refuge the road becomes a four-lane, limited-access highway, and bends north to the site of Fort Ninigret on Fort Neck Road. The bare outlines of this Dutch trading post from the early 1600s sit on the grassy north bank of sheltered Ninigret Pond. A large, irregular stone at the site is a memorial to the Niantic and Narragansett Indian tribes. The drive then enters **Charlestown.** Exit the highway for a quick stop in Charlestown center. The town, named for England's King Charles II, separated from Westerly in 1738. It grew as a mill village, grinding grains into flour and meal. An interesting stop here is the Charlestown Historical Society Schoolhouse on the grounds of the public library. The restored 1838 one-room school is austerely furnished with old desks, a potbelly wood stove, an old map, and blackboard. The school was used until 1918 in nearby Quonachantaug before being moved here. If you have time to explore the area, the local chamber of commerce has an information center that can point you in more directions.

A good detour drives south from town on Charlestown Beach Road. Charleston Beach State Park and Charlestown Breachway lie at road's end, where swimming and other water activities are the norm. The breachway also offers a seventy-five-site campground for self-contained units.

Rhode Island's rich landscape was long inhabited by Native Americans, including the powerful Narragansetts. Today, the Narragansett Nation's tribal land covers more than 1,800 acres in the Charlestown area. The Narragansetts, whose place names are scattered across the region, have a historic village north of Charlestown off Rhode Island Highway 2/112. Here is the reconstructed Greek

Revival Narragansett Indian Church. Samuel Niles, the first native minister, was buried here in 1785. To the east, off Narrow Lane, is the Royal Indian Burial Ground, a twenty-acre undeveloped site with the peaceful graves of Sachem Ninigret and his family from the 1700s. The Narragansett Longhouse and Cultural Center is the site of annual tribal celebrations. Nearby are the Cup and Saucer Rocks. These large boulders, balanced on a ledge, were rolled together to send rumbling messages.

Charlestown to Point Judith

Back on the drive, four-lane U.S. Highway 1 runs east from Charlestown through lush, deciduous woodlands broken by occasional pastures, farms, and houses. The next exit allows access to sandy **Green Hill Beach** and 800-acre **Trustom Pond National Wildlife Refuge.** The 160-acre pond here, the state's only undeveloped salt pond, is an important nesting and resting habitat for migratory birds. The refuge and pond, separated from Block Island Sound by sand barrier Moonstone Beach, offer diverse habitats for more than 300 identified birds and forty mammals, including deer, red fox, mink, and otter. An information station is found on Matanuck Schoolhouse Road with directions for nature trails. The refuge is a serene oasis far removed from the nearby bustling shoreline and beaches. The Perryville State Trout Hatchery is just north of the highway.

Farther along the route is Matunuck Beach Road, which leads south to three popular beaches—Roy Carpenter's, South Kingston, and Mary Carpenter's—and the famous shore attraction, Theater by the Sea. Summer theater has been performed in this old barn, listed on the National Register of Historic Places, since 1933. **East Matunuck,** a fine state beach, sits at the end of Succotash Road, accessed just up the drive. Nearby is Jerusalem and the Block Island Ferry Dock.

The highway arcs north around Point Judith Pond, a narrow bay, and passes **Wakefield.** This town and its neighbors to the north, Kingston and Peace Dale, are lovely, quiet villages set among verdant, rolling forests. Some excellent points of interest lie north of the drive here. Beginning in 1800, Wakefield thrived with the Narragansett and Wakefield mills. The village of Peace Dale, named by the village founder Rowland Hazard for his spouse, Mary Peace Hazard, is an old mill town on the Saugatucket River next to Wakefield. Hazard built several cotton and textile mills here that brought prosperity to Peace Dale through the nineteenth century. The mills contributed to the Civil War effort by weaving blankets for Union soldiers and by making khaki for World War I uniforms. The town houses the Museum of Primitive Art and Culture with its small but fascinating collection of Rhode Island Indian artifacts, as well as items from other Native American tribes and world primitive cultures.

A few miles north of Peace Dale is **Kingston.** The town, originally part of a land tract purchased from the Narragansetts in 1658, was named Little Rest until 1825. Kingston has a charming historic district with numerous old buildings and homes, including the 1820 Kingston Congregational Church; the 1710 John Moore House, the oldest here; the 1820 George Fayerweather House, built by an Afro-Indian blacksmith who was the son of a slave; the 1792 Washington County Jail; and the landmark Kingston Railroad Station. The University of Rhode Island's campus is also in Kingston.

Just west of Kingston is the 3,349-acre **Great Swamp Management Area,** the site of the Great Swamp Fight. This bloody, decisive battle fought on December 19, 1675, was a turning point in King Philip's War. The Wampanoag Indians and their chief, King Philip, tried to force settlers off Indian lands. Colonists marched on a Wampanoag Indian encampment set on a frozen island in the Great Swamp and set fire to an Indian fort, killing more than 500 people, including warriors, women, and children. King Philip, however, was not at the camp and continued to fight until his capture and death in August 1676. A hard-to-find historical marker in the woods commemorates the battle.

The scenic drive route exits from US 1 just past Wakefield and turns south (right) on Rhode Island Highway 108, the Old Point Judith Road. The drive follows RI 108 past houses, cottages, and businesses for 4 miles to US 1A (Ocean Road). Cove Road, just before the highway intersection, goes west to the active fishing village of Galilee, some good seafood restaurants, and Salty Brine and Roger W. Wheeler Beaches. Another side road makes a jaunt over to **Fisherman's Memorial State Park,** a popular camping area.

From the junction of RI 108 and US 1A, a right turn leads drivers a short distance to **Point Judith** and its lighthouse poised on the land's jutting tip. The lighthouse and adjoining Coast Guard station are surrounded by a low wall and a beach of broken boulders. The 51-foot-high, octagonal lighthouse, built in 1816, sits on a strategic site overlooking the entrance to Narragansett Bay. Not only was this point an important lookout in the Revolution, but its lighthouse beacon has warned sailors of impending peril since first placed here in 1810. So many ships have wrecked off Point Judith that it acquired the nickname "Cape Hatteras of New England." Spectacular views of the ocean wrapping around this windswept, rocky point are seen from a nearby hillock. This is a great spot to watch the endless waves breaking on the shoreline. Fishing boats dot the undulating water; the white cliffs of Block Island puncture the southwestern horizon; and large container ships sail slowly towards New York.

Along Narragansett Bay

From Point Judith the scenic drive runs north on US 1A for 6 miles to Narragansett Pier. Cottages and beachfront homes line the highway. Several great sand beaches lie along Narragansett Bay and the road. The best is **Scarborough State Beach,** a 300-yard stretch of beach and dunes that is very popular in summer with swimmers and tanners. The 3,000-car parking area is usually full on weekends. On the southern outskirts of Narragansett Pier is the Ocean Road Historic District.

US 1A wends slowly through the resort town of **Narragansett Pier.** The town was a fashionable resort in the late nineteenth century, with luxurious hotels and the famed Narragansett Casino. This ornate casino was built in 1883, but was destroyed by fire in 1900. A stopover for the well-heeled, traveling between Newport and New York, the grand casino offered bowling alleys, billiard halls, tennis courts, a rifle range, theater, and ballroom. All that remains of it today is The Towers, a local landmark spanning Ocean Road. The local chamber of commerce is housed in the base of the twin stone turrets. On the north side of town are a couple of beaches, including crescent-shaped Narragansett Town Beach, and the Narragansett Indian Monument. This mammoth 23-foot-high sculpture weighs 10,000 pounds and is carved from the trunk of a huge Douglas fir. South County Museum, sitting on US 1A north, details the area history with artifacts, tools, and exhibits including a country kitchen, cobbler's shop, tack shop, children's nursery, general store, and antique vehicles such as a horse-drawn hearse and fire engines.

US 1A, here called Boston Neck Road, runs north and crosses the broad Pettaquamscutt River before entering a lovely stretch of countryside. Farms and old houses, stone walls, swampy lowlands, and dense forests cover the land. This area along the west coast of Narragansett Bay was the site of many of the large Rhode Island plantations that flourished in the 1600s and 1700s. The Silas Casey Farm, on the left, was once a plantation and is still a working 350-acre farm surrounded by stone walls. The house, built in the mid-1700s, is furnished in period pieces from the Casey family. During the Revolutionary War, an encounter between colonial patriots and British sailors led to a musket shot. The hole still pierces the parlor door.

The **Gilbert Stuart Birthplace** is just north of the farm and a mile west of the highway on Snuff Mill Road. Stuart, America's most famous eighteenth-century portrait painter, was born here in 1755 in a red colonial house above his father's snuff mill. After showing an early aptitude for art, Stuart went to England and studied. He returned to America in 1792 and painted famed Americans, including Presidents John Adams, John Quincy Adams, Thomas Jefferson, James Madison, and, most notably, George Washington. The best known of Stuart's 124 portraits of the first president is the unfinished Athenaeum Head, which appears on the face of the one-dollar bill. After painting more than a thousand portraits, Stuart died in 1828.

The drive continues north and in less than a mile reaches Rhode Island Highway 138. Turn right on RI 138 and drive over the sweeping 1.5-mile Jamestown Bridge to Conanicut Island. The highway dashes across the island, but a loop drive around the island on East Shore, North, and Beavertail Roads makes a good interlude. The roads thread through a bucolic countryside, passing old farms, lush forests, and green pastures. Several interesting stops are found along the way.

Conanicut Island

The island, named for the Narragansett Sachem Canonicus, stretches almost 9 miles from Conanicut Point on the north to Beaver Tail on the south. Conanicut, acquired from the Indians in 1657, sits at a strategic location at the entrance to Narragansett Bay. Quaker farmers settled the island, tilling its fertile soil and raising sheep. During the American Revolution, the British captured and occupied the island in 1776 until 4,000 French soldiers overran it in 1778 and forced the British and Hessian troops to retreat to Newport.

Conanicut Island points of interest include the Watson Farm, Sydney L. Wright Museum, Fort Wetherill State Park, and Beavertail Lighthouse and State Park. The Watson Farm, now owned and operated by the Society for the Preservation of New England Antiquities, was a family farm founded in 1798. Five generations of Watsons lived here over 183 years. Today the farm is run as a living history site. Nearby is the old Jamestown Windmill. The Wright Museum, tucked into a corner of the Jamestown library, is an interesting collection of Native American artifacts. Many were recovered from the West Ferry archaeological site.

Fort Wetherill, perched atop a rocky crag opposite Newport, has long protected this narrow strait called East Passage. The first fort was installed in 1776. Later forts were equipped with powerful guns to protect the harbor in the Civil War and both world wars. Nearby Pirate's Cove is the possible burying place of a treasure belonging to the notorious buccaneer Captain Kidd, who often visited fellow pirate Captain Thomas Paine in Jamestown. Fort Getty sits on the opposite site of the island. **Beavertail State Park,** encompassing the island's rocky tip, offers what is perhaps Rhode Island's best ocean view. The surf endlessly pounds against the cliffs and boulders along the shoreline here, and sunsets are usually spectacular. The nearby Beavertail Lighthouse has guided mariners through these treacherous channels since 1749. A small museum details the colorful history of Rhode Island lighthouses.

Newport

The last drive segment begins on the east side of the island. Get back onto RI 138 east and follow the traffic over the Newport Bridge, a towering suspension bridge arcing over the East Passage. The view from this lofty span is stunning, with the whole bay and its islands spreading out below. After a couple of miles, the bridge gently descends and enters the famed resort and sailing city of Newport.

Stately nineteenth-century summer "cottages" line the Cliff Walk in Newport.

Spread across a J-shaped promontory at the southern end of Aquidneck Island, **Newport** is one of America's most beautiful and historic cities. History lurks at every turn. Rather than being encased in a museum, the town wears its past like an opulent cloak. It was settled in 1639 by religious dissenters from Massachusetts. The city acquired a reputation as a haven for tolerance, welcoming Quakers, Jews, and religious outcasts from the more rigid northern colonies. Newport, with its ocean-edge location and good, deep-water harbor, flourished as a trade center and major port that shipped goods and livestock from the American colonies to Europe, including horses, wool, other agricultural products, and rum. It was rum that put this bastion of tolerance at one corner of the infamous Triangle Trade between Newport, west Africa, and the West Indies. Newport rum was traded for black slaves in Africa, who in turn were traded in the Caribbean for sugar and molasses to make more rum in Newport. As many as sixty ships based out of Newport participated in the slave trade. Newport was also a popular port for privateers, ships that were licensed by the state to destroy competing enemy ships. The rum trade established the pineapple as the Newport symbol for hospitality. A returning seaman, when he was ready to receive visitors, would place a pineapple outside his door.

Newport's strategic location and trade also made it an important site in the Revolution. The British captured and occupied the city from 1776 to late 1779, when the colony's French allies liberated it. The occupation, however, decimated the city's population and destroyed many of its buildings. It wasn't until around 1830 that Newport began recovering from its war wounds when southerners began summering here. By the late nineteenth century, Newport was recognized as "America's First Resort" and became the summer playground for the rich and famous. During this gilded age the country's robber barons and wealthy industrialists, with immense profits and no income tax, bought the city's beaches and clifftop properties as sites for their "cottages." These cottages, numbering almost sixty, were huge, extravagant mansions and estates that are reminiscent of the chateaux and castles of European royalty. Some cost as much as $10 million to build and furnish. Their owners, who came only for, at most, eleven weeks of the year, spent hundreds of thousands of dollars entertaining during the summer season, and thought that because they had money they were the American aristocracy. One society matron went so far as to call the local townspeople "footstools." Taxes and the Great Depression brought this lavish age to a grinding halt, and the summer cottages became too expensive for even the very rich to maintain. By 1950 only a few remained in private hands.

Today Newport, one of the world's yachting capitals, is a charming and attractive city with lots of historic attractions, festivals, and events. The scenic drive winds through the city's downtown. After crossing the bridge, head south on Rhode Island Highway 238 (Farewell Street). Farther along turn left on Memorial

Boulevard, which becomes RI 138A. Drive eastward on the tree-lined street and park on the east side of Newport along a breakwater that separates Easton Pond on the left from the ocean waters. The famed Cliff Walk footpath begins on the south side of the road.

The **Cliff Walk** is a 3-mile trail that winds along the cliff top between the breaking waves of Rhode Island Sound and a long row of seaside mansions. Six of the best mansions, managed by the Preservation Society of Newport County, are open for public viewing. The society began acquiring these mansions, including The Breakers, Rosecliff, and The Elms, in 1945. These huge palaces are Newport's single most popular attraction, visited by more than a million people annually. The Cliff Walk and a visit to at least a couple of the mansions is a requisite for any Newport visitor.

The trail winds above the broken cliffs, offering marvelous views of the surf breaking on the rocks below. The mansions, facing the ocean, line the path. All the mansions open for tours are on Bellevue Avenue, paralleling the Cliff Walk to the west. One of the best and the largest is **The Breakers,** the 1893 summer home of railroad magnate Cornelius Vanderbilt. The four-story limestone mansion, surrounded by an eleven-acre manicured estate, contains seventy rooms. It took hundreds of craftsmen two years to build, with entire rooms built in Europe and shipped over to Rhode Island.

To continue the drive, head south from Memorial Boulevard on Bellevue Avenue past the mansions to Ocean Avenue and the Ocean Drive along the south coast of the island. This route yields inspiring scenic vistas of Rhode Island Sound and the rocky shoreline, passing Brenton Point State Park, Hammersmith Farm, and Fort Adams State Park. The drive follows Ridge Road, Harrison Avenue, Wellington Avenue, and Thames Street back to Memorial Boulevard and the drive's end in downtown Newport.

Lots of other activities and attractions are available for Newport visitors. Museums include the International Tennis Hall of Fame, Museum of Newport History, Newport Art Museum, Newport Historical Society, and the Museum of Yachting. There is Colonial Newport; the old Common Burial Ground; the 1687 White House Tavern, thought to be the oldest tavern in the United States; and many stores, shops, and restaurants. Popular events include the annual Newport Music Festival in July, the Newport Folk Festival in August, and the Classic Yacht Regatta over Labor Day weekend. Newport, the City by the Sea, makes a fitting climax and busy ending to Rhode Island's magnificent coastal drive.

Western Rhode Island Scenic Drive

General description: A 31-mile open loop drive across rolling, forested hills in western Rhode Island.

Special attractions: Arcadia Management Area, Tomaquag Museum of the American Indian, Parker Woodland Wildlife Refuge, Swamp Meadow Covered Bridge, Scituate Reservoir, Clayville National Historic District, Prinster-Hogg Park, hiking, birding, boating, fishing.

Location: Western Rhode Island between Interstate 95 and Slatersville.

Drive route number and name: Rhode Island Highway 102 (Victory Highway).

Travel season: Year-round.

Camping: No campgrounds along the drive. George Washington Management Area west of Chepachet has a forty-five-site camping area.

Services: Limited services on the route at Clayville and Chepachet. Full services, including gas, food, and lodging, in Slatersville at the northern terminus.

Nearby attractions: Blackstone Gorge State Park, Providence attractions, Snake Den State Park, Lincoln Woods State Park, Diamond Hill State Park, Slater Mill Historic Site, Narragansett Bay area, Newport, Cliff Walk, Great Swamp Fight Monument.

The Drive

The 31-mile-long Western Rhode Island Scenic Drive, following Rhode Island Highway 102, slices across the west side of the state through a rural, hilly region far removed from the glamour and glitz of Newport. Rhode Island, smallest of the fifty states, covers a scant 1,210 square miles, an area only slightly larger than half the size of Delaware, the next smallest state. The state, however, is densely populated. Its 925 people per square mile are exceeded only in areas of New Jersey. Nine-tenths of the Rhode Island population lives in urban areas such as Providence, New England's second-largest city. This scenic drive crosses a more sparsely populated region of low rolling hills, part of what's called the Eastern New England Upland by geographers. The state's high point, 812-foot Jerimoth Hill, rises west of the drive near the Connecticut border.

I-95 to Clayville

Easily accessed from Providence, the drive route begins at exit 5 on Interstate 95. Turn onto RI 102 north. The two-lane road runs north through rolling hills

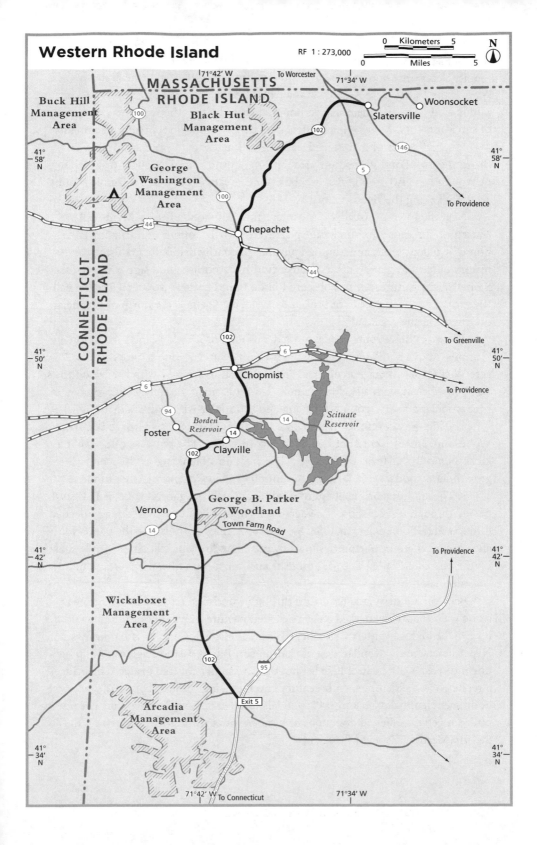

Western Rhode Island

RF 1 : 273,000

Kilometers
0   5
Miles
0   5

N

71°42' W   To Worcester   71°34' W

MASSACHUSETTS
RHODE ISLAND

Buck Hill
Management
Area

100

Black Hut
Management
Area

Woonsocket

Slatersville

102

146

41°
58'
N

George
Washington
Management
Area

5

To Providence

100

44

Chepachet

44

102

To Greenville

41°
50'
N

6

Chopmist

To Providence

6

94

Borden
Reservoir

14

Scituate
Reservoir

Foster

14

41°
50'
N

102

14

Clayville

George B. Parker
Woodland

Vernon

Town Farm Road

14

41°
42'
N

To Providence

41°
42'
N

Wickaboxet
Management
Area

102

Arcadia
Management
Area

95

Exit 5

41°
34'
N

41°
34'
N

71°42' W   To Connecticut   71°34' W

CONNECTICUT
RHODE ISLAND

thickly matted with white pine and hardwoods, including oak, hickory, beech, and maple. Occasional homes break the forest solitude. Southwest of the highway sprawls the 13,817-acre **Arcadia Management Area,** the state's largest reserve of public lands. The irregular-shaped unit, managed by the Rhode Island Department of Environmental Management, offers numerous outdoor opportunities along its more than 30 miles of maintained trails, including canoeing and swimming on Browning Mill Pond Recreation Area, birding, hunting, and excellent trout fishing in Wood River. Two good hikes are the 6-mile Arcadia Trail and the 3-mile Mount Tom Trail along the river.

Near the town of Arcadia is the interesting **Tomaquag Indian Memorial Museum.** The museum, run by the Narragansett tribe, offers an intriguing collection of artifacts, tools, and photographs that primarily detail the prehistory and history of New England's diverse native cultures. Another good side trip is to Step Stone Falls, a picturesque but obscure Rhode Island natural wonder. Here the Fall River cascades over a series of broken rock ledges. The falls are north of Escoheag on rough Falls River Road.

The main drive route runs past the University of Rhode Island's Alton Jones Campus. About 3 miles west of the highway off Plain Meeting House Road is 678-acre Wickaboxet Management Area. Low, rolling hills covered with hardwood trees and dense brush, with a trickling brook, lie in this small, rarely visited preserve. This woodland area is good for birding and is popular with hunters in autumn.

The highway continues north and a few miles later reaches **George B. Parker Woodland,** an 860-acre Audubon Society nature area. The preserve offers what a kiosk sign calls "historic archaeology." The area, now blanketed with second-growth hardwoods, was a farming community called Coventry Center in the 1700s. The land was originally purchased from the Narragansett tribe in 1642 and passed through a succession of owners until George Parker acquired it and deeded it to the Audubon Society in 1938. More than 7 miles of trails lace the parkland, allowing excellent opportunities to study the area's flora and fauna or simply soak up the peace and quiet. The area protects an almost pure fifteen-acre stand of chestnut oak.

Back on the drive, the road runs through woods interrupted by overgrown stone walls that once marked a farm's cleared pastures. Five miles from the wildlife refuge, the highway enters **Clayville,** a National Historic District of old houses. Foster lies a couple of miles west of Clayville on Rhode Island Highway 94. Just north of Foster off Central Pike is Rhode Island's only covered bridge. The bridge, a replica of a classic nineteenth-century covered bridge design from 1820, was first built over Hemlock Creek in 1992. Vandals torched it the following year. The town pulled together, solicited donations of lumber, money, and time, and rebuilt the Swamp Meadow Covered Bridge in 1994.

Clayville to Slatersville

The highway twists through Clayville and drops northeast to the Ponaganset River branch of massive Scituate Reservoir. The Y-shaped reservoir, built in 1915 for Providence's drinking water supply, covers 13,000 acres in the Pawtuxet River drainage and is the state's largest freshwater lake. The lake here is a narrow arm, fringed with tall trees. After crossing a bridge over the water, RI 102 and Rhode Island Highway 14 intersect. Keep left on RI 102. Prinster-Hogg Park, with picnic tables and grills, sits at this lonely intersection. The park is named for two pilots who landed a burning airplane on the reservoir in 1982, saving themselves and twelve passengers.

The road heads over rolling hills blanketed with woodlands and occasional farms with open fields for the next 6 miles to the town of **Chepachet.** This charming town, the largest along the drive, sits at a crossroads of three highways. It's a pleasant, rural town with antiques shops and historic homes and buildings lining its main street. The Job Armstrong Store houses a small museum, run by the Gloucester Heritage Society, which displays local artifacts and lore every Saturday. Of particular interest are the details of the Dorr Rebellion, a suffrage revolt led in 1842 by local resident Thomas Dorr.

Ned the cat at an old wooden barn along the Western Rhode Island Scenic Drive.

Dorr had been elected governor of Rhode Island, but the incumbent governor Samuel King refused to concede the reins of government. The state militia entered the fray and put down the rebellion. The failed revolt, however, led to a new state constitution and liberalized voting rights in 1843. Rhode Island at that time was still governed by its original 1663 charter, which allowed voting only by landholders or their eldest sons. The balance of power in the state government had been slanted toward rural areas, whereas most of the population lived in cities and was denied voting rights. The Dorr Rebellion helped remedy that situation by allowing the vote to native-born men who paid $1.00 or more in taxes annually or served in the state militia.

The drive continues north on RI 102 for its last 10 miles. It passes an old cemetery and Sucker Pond before arcing northeast through thick forests in the hills west of the Chepachet River. A few large natural areas lie in the northwestern corner of the state, west of the highway. **Buck Hill Management Area** is an undeveloped 1,300-acre tract in the state's extreme corner. Reached via Rhode Island Highway 100 and Buck Hill Road, it offers some fine hiking and lots of wildlife and waterfowl. **George Washington Management Area**'s 3,200 acres lie west of Chepachet. This hilly parkland, with some points reaching as high as 770 feet, is broken by rocky outcrops, large Bowdish Reservoir with a beach and boating, and a fifty-five-site campground. The area also has hiking trails, swimming, ski touring, fishing, and hunting in season. **Black Hut Management Area** sits just north of the drive and Glendale. The 1,290-acre area, managed by the state Division of Fish and Wildlife, is a quiet woodland reserve spread over low hills. More than 5 miles of trails thread through the forest. Nearby is Spring Lake, a popular fishing and boating pond.

Houses and businesses abut the pavement as the drive nears Slatersville and its end at four-lane Rhode Island Highway 146. **Slatersville,** along with other northern Rhode Island towns situated along rivers, was a birthplace of America's Industrial Revolution, the far-ranging economic transformation that changed the country from a nation with a rural, agrarian base to an industrial, urban power.

In 1793 Samuel Slater opened the Slater Mill along the Blackstone River at Pawtucket southeast of here. This was the first modern textile mill in the United States to be powered by water. An English textile machinery expert, Slater had departed England disguised as a farm laborer. The English, after inventing power spinning and weaving, had restricted emigration of textile workers to keep trade secrets from rival countries. Slater, however, reinvented the machines from memory after arriving in America, setting the stage for the complete transformation of the U.S. textile industry from a home craft to mechanized, mass production.

The town of Slatersville, a pleasant old town founded in 1807, was a planned community built around a mill that was overseen by John Slater, Samuel's brother. The Slaters erected houses, churches, and schools for the mill workers. Points of interest include the triangular village green with the circa 1838 Greek Revival–style Congregational Church alongside, the William Slater Mansion, and the Slater Mill.

Northeast of town is the hard-to-find **Blackstone River State Park.** The Blackstone River has excavated an impressive little gorge through the bedrock here, offering scenic views and the state's only whitewater canoeing. Ask at Slatersville for precise directions. Otherwise, the drive dead-ends against RI 146, a four-lane, divided highway that quickly leads south to Providence and its numerous attractions.

Cape Cod Scenic Drive

General description: A 63-mile scenic route along the historic south shore of Cape Cod Bay and up the Outer Beach along the Atlantic Ocean in Cape Cod National Seashore to Provincetown at the Cape's northern tip.

Special attractions: Heritage Plantation, Sandwich Historical Museum, Crocker Tavern, Cape Cod Museum of Natural History, Nickerson State Park, Cape Cod National Seashore, Nauset Beach and Light, Marconi Beach and Station Site, Race Point, Salt Pond Visitor Center, Province Lands Visitor Center, Old Harbor Life Saving Station, Three Sisters Lighthouse, trails, hiking, picnicking, beaches, biking, birding, fishing, children's programs.

Location: Southeastern Massachusetts.

Drive route numbers: Massachusetts Highway 6A, U.S. Highway 6.

Travel season: Year-round.

Camping: Nickerson State Park offers 420 campsites. Shawme-Crowell State Forest, near the Cape Cod Canal, has a 285-site campground. Call (877) 422–6762 for reservations at any Massachusetts state forest and park campground. Otherwise, there are several private campgrounds available on Cape Cod.

Services: All services in Sandwich, West Barnstable, Barnstable, Yarmouth, Dennis, Brewster, Orleans, Eastham, South Wellfleet, Wellfleet, Truro, and Provincetown.

Nearby attractions: Woods Hole, Martha's Vineyard, Nantucket Island, Monomoy National Wildlife Refuge, Aptucxet Trading Post, Myles Standish State Forest, Plymouth Rock, Plymouth Plantation, Boston attractions.

The Drive

Like a flexed, muscular, 60-mile-long arm, Cape Cod bends far out into the Atlantic Ocean from the southeastern corner of Massachusetts. This long, crooked peninsula, bordered by 585 miles of shoreline and 310 miles of sand beaches, is a quintessential New England landscape. When anyone talks of the great natural wonders of the Northeast, the Cape is always the first one mentioned—and for good reason. Here lies a magnificent landscape shaped by the earth's most basic elements: storm and sunlight; the unceasing wind constantly resculpting sand dunes; and the restless North Atlantic pounding against the outer edges.

This 63-mile scenic drive, beginning at the Cape Cod Canal and ending at the tip of the Cape, follows a spectacular transition zone between land and sea, skirting salt marshes and cranberry bogs; passing quiet estuaries, ponds, inlets, and coves; running along one of New England's longest sand beaches; threading through miniature forests of pitch pine and scrub oak; and crossing sand dunes anchored by beach grass. Be warned, however, that much of the Cape has succumbed to tacky strip malls, fast-food joints, factory outlet stores, and other businesses out to separate travelers from their money. Fortunately it's easy to look

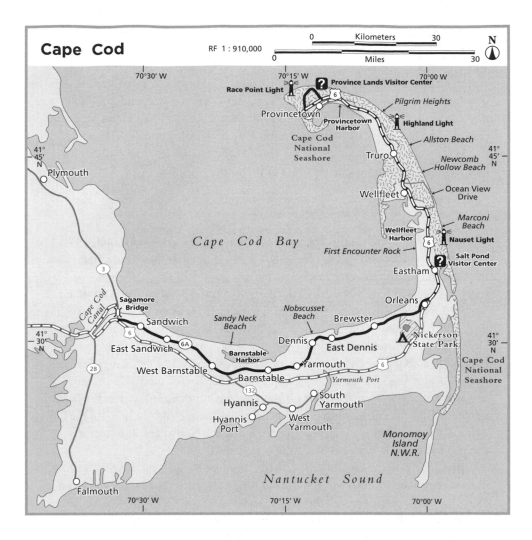

Cape Cod

RF 1 : 910,000

Kilometers
0   30

Miles
0   30

N

70°30' W   70°15' W   70°00' W

Race Point Light

Province Lands Visitor Center

Provincetown

Provincetown Harbor

Pilgrim Heights

Highland Light

Cape Cod National Seashore

Truro

Allston Beach

Newcomb Hollow Beach

Wellfleet

Ocean View Drive

Marconi Beach

Wellfleet Harbor

Nauset Light

First Encounter Rock

Salt Pond Visitor Center

Eastham

Cape Cod Bay

Sagamore Bridge

Orleans

Sandwich

Sandy Neck Beach

Nobscusset Beach

Brewster

Nickerson State Park

Cape Cod Canal

East Sandwich

Dennis

East Dennis

Cape Cod National Seashore

West Barnstable

Barnstable Harbor

Yarmouth

Barnstable

Yarmouth Port

Hyannis

South Yarmouth

Hyannis Port

West Yarmouth

Monomoy Island N.W.R.

Nantucket Sound

Falmouth

Plymouth

70°30' W   70°15' W   70°00' W

41° 45' N

41° 30' N

beyond the T-shirt shops and see the enduring beauty of this outermost land.

The Cape offers a year-round travel climate, with each season lending a distinct flavor to the journey. Summers are the traditional beach season, with vacationers flocking onto the beaches and filling the campgrounds and trails. Weather is generally mild in summer with daily highs rising into the 80s, sunny skies, and warm water. The ocean is generally warmest in August and September. Autumns are superb. Daytime temperatures range from 50 to 70 degrees with brisk nights, little precipitation, and fewer folks to share the beach. Winter, with its heavy seas, cold temperatures, and windy conditions, might not seem like an ideal time to travel Cape Cod, but stalwart visitors will have the place to themselves. Snowfall is usually moderate. Spring is a short, fickle season. Expect cool to warm temperatures, occasional foggy or rainy days, and wind.

The scenic drive follows Massachusetts Highway 6A to U.S. Highway 6 at Orleans. This route, called the King's Highway, is one of the oldest roads in the United States. US 6 offers a quick return trip from Orleans to Sagamore and the mainland on a limited-access, four-lane highway. The highways usually offer easy driving with localized congestion. Be advised, however, that weekends and holidays, particularly in summer, are entirely different. Cape Cod's highways are then clogged with legendary stop-and-go traffic jams in morning and evening. Only two bridges cross the Cape Cod Canal, choking the arteries leading to them. It's best to time your trip for quieter times of the week.

Cape Cod Canal and Sandwich

The scenic drive begins at the Sagamore Bridge over the **Cape Cod Canal,** a 17.4-mile-long, 500-foot-wide ditch (the widest sea level canal in the world) that severs the Cape's arm from the mainland at its narrow shoulder joint. The canal, used by more than 20,000 vessels annually, effectively makes the peninsula into an island. The idea for a trans-Cape canal originated back in 1624, when Pilgrim Myles Standish realized a canal would increase trade between the Plymouth Colony and the Dutch at New Amsterdam. George Washington later ordered a survey and saw plans drawn up for the canal, but the project was shelved. The first canal, financed by millionaire August Belmont, opened in 1914 after almost forty years of work. The narrow, one-way canal, slicing off more than a hundred miles from the Boston to New York connections, didn't begin generating revenue and traffic until the U.S. Army Corps of Engineers widened and deepened it. The two graceful steel spans, the Sagamore and Bourne bridges, were completed in 1935.

Begin the drive by crossing the arched Sagamore Bridge on US 6 then exiting immediately at exit 1 onto MA 6A, the old King's Highway. The road swings east along the canal, passing under the bridge, and heads onto the Upper Cape, the section nearest the mainland. The Mid Cape is exactly what it sounds like—the midsection between the biceps and elbow of the flexed "arm." The Lower Cape is the outer forearm section, which extends northward.

Just past the bridge the drive enters the quaint 1637 town of **Sandwich,** the oldest settlement on Cape Cod. The area was originally settled in 1627 when Pilgrims built the Aptucxet Trading Post as a commerce center for Indians and Dutch and English colonists west of today's town. Ten years later, Edmund Freeman and some followers moved here from Saugus on the coast north of Boston. By 1669 the town had grown enough to become incorporated and was named after a village in Kent, England, where many of the pioneer families had originated. Quakers later settled in Sandwich, but were persecuted by the Puritan majority. Eventually they were tolerated, and the town now boasts the oldest continuous Quaker meeting in America, begun in 1657.

The lack of a harbor kept Sandwich from growing as a maritime center, so the town relied instead on whaling and local farming for sustenance. In the early nineteenth century, Sandwich began a glass-making tradition, using the abundant local sand or silica and sodium chloride, which is now preserved in the Sandwich Glass Museum. The Boston & Sandwich Glass Company created a wide range of glass objects that today are coveted by collectors. The factory, founded in 1825, was shut down during an 1888 labor dispute and never reopened.

Sandwich now retains much of its old charm and history in the **Town Hall Square Historic District,** a collection of forty-seven houses, some dating from the 1600s, and the elegant 1834 Town Hall. The village offers a potpourri of classic New England architecture, including saltboxes from the 1700s, Federal and Gothic Revival–style houses and buildings, and the famed and often imitated Cape Cod cottages. The town's 1847 First Church of Christ now houses one of New England's oldest congregations. It was initially gathered in 1637 by the first Pilgrim settlers.

A host of interesting museums and domiciles are found in the immediate environs of Sandwich. Some of the best surround Shawme Lake, a pond created by early residents to generate power for milling. The Hoxie House, built in 1637, has thick timbers and recessed windows, and is reputed to be the oldest house still standing on the Cape and, outside the Pueblo and Hopi villages in the Southwest, among the oldest dwellings in the United States. This classic saltbox, once the home of whaling captain Abraham Hoxie, has been restored and furnished to the 1680 era. It is open for tours in summer.

Nearby is **Thomas Dexter's Grist Mill,** used from the 1650s until the late 1800s and now restored to grind grain the old-fashioned way. The Thorton Burgess Museum honors a local naturalist and children's author with a collection of his memorabilia and natural history exhibits. Also near the pond is the old Sandwich burying ground, with some slate gravestones from the 1680s. A headstone of interest sits atop the 1677 grave of Sandwich founder Edmund Freeman in a grove of pines on Wilson Road. Freeman is buried under a saddle next to his wife, Elizabeth, who lies under a pillion, a chair attached to a saddle so two people can ride side by side. In this case, that ride went into eternity.

The last attraction of note at Sandwich is the **Heritage Plantation,** off Massachusetts Highway 130. This fascinating place, covering seventy-six landscaped acres, includes gardens, woods, ponds, and several diverse museums. The area was once the private estate of industrialist Charles Breeder, who indulged in creating hybrid rhododendrons during his twenty-two-year retirement. The blossoms in May and June are simply stunning, and worth a visit for that alone. The plantation offers a slew of other sights, however. A replica of the round Hancock Shaker Barn from the Berkshires houses a collection of thirty-four antique and classic autos, including Gary Cooper's 1931 custom yellow Duesenberg and President Taft's 1909

Church spires in Barnstable rise above a salt marsh along the Cape Cod Scenic Drive.

White Steamer, the first official presidential limo. A Military Museum houses antique weapons, more than 2,000 miniature figures, and flags that have flown over the United States. Other collections include artworks, Currier & Ives lithographs, American folk art, and Indian artifacts.

Just north of town is the Sandwich town beach, a lovely and quiet beach reached by a boardwalk across a salt marsh. On the southwest shore of Cape Cod Bay, both the beach and the marsh are popular birding areas.

Barnstable, Yarmouth, and Dennis

The drive heads southeast from Sandwich, rolling through low, undulating hills dotted with houses. Two large salt marshes, fed by seawater that floods Scorton Creek, flank the asphalt. Down the road lie the towns of West Barnstable and, in just a few miles, Barnstable. **West Barnstable** is a small village with an assortment of shops and restaurants. The village's 1717 West Parish Congregational Church is considered the denomination's oldest church building. Its half-ton bell was cast by patriot Paul Revere. Sandy Neck Road, just west of the town, leads northeast to the excellent barrier beach of Sandy Neck. The 8-mile neck, built of beach sand and dunes, separates Cape Cod Bay from Barnstable Harbor. The small parking lot charges a fee and fills quickly on weekends, since it offers easy access to this quiet beach.

Barnstable, encompassing the communities of Barnstable, Hyannis, Cotuit, Santuit, Osterville, Centerville, and Cummaquid, is the Cape's largest town. This was the Cape's second village, established in 1639 by a separatist Puritan parish that had originally landed at Scituate in 1634. By the 1700s the town and its protected harbor flourished as a rum trading and whaling port. The Sturgis Library, named for local trading tycoon William Sturgis, is the oldest public library building in the United States. Part of the library is a 1644 house. In addition to such rich history, the Barnstable area also offers bed-and-breakfasts, restaurants, and shops.

Three miles past Barnstable MA 6A runs through **Yarmouth,** the third village established on the Cape. Settled in 1639, Yarmouth and its neighbor Yarmouth Port thrived in the mid-nineteenth century as seafaring towns. The 1740 Captain Bangs Hallet House, run by the local historical society, preserves a slice of this heritage. Several botanical trails begin at the house and thread across fifty-three nearby acres. Other preserved Yarmouth houses are the Bray Farm, an old shipyard and farm, and the Winslow-Crocker House, which was built in 1780 in Barnstable but taken down and reassembled at Yarmouth in 1935. Hallet's Store, a turn-of-the-last-century drugstore and soda fountain in Yarmouth Port, is a nostalgic stop. Grey's Beach, a municipal beach on the warm-water bay, is about the only town beach here that doesn't charge a daily fee.

The drive continues to **Dennis,** the next classic old Cape village, and East Dennis. The town was originally part of Yarmouth but separated in 1793, taking the name of Reverend Josiah Dennis, the popular pastor of its first meeting house. Like Yarmouth, Dennis was a seagoing village. The Shiverick Shipyards at Sesuit Harbor built many clipper ships, schooners, and packet boats in the early 1800s. In 1837 the town boasted more than 150 captains basing vessels out of Dennis. The Josiah Dennis Manse, the 1736 home of the village's namesake, offers free tours of the restored, furnished house. Other points of interest are the Cape Museum of Fine Arts, the Cape Playhouse, and the 1801 Jericho House and Barn Museum. The 28-foot-high Scargo Hill Observatory, just off the highway, is a stone tower that yields superb views of Cape Cod Bay, the long sandy Cape peninsula, and Provincetown with its tall Pilgrim Monument on a clear day. Just east of town near Scargo Lake and the tower is the Nobscusset Indian burial ground.

Brewster and Orleans

The scenic drive leaves East Dennis and enters **Brewster,** the last of the historic towns on the Mid Cape. Brewster, settled in 1656 and named for William Brewster from the Plymouth Colony across the bay, is a lovely, rural town spread along elm-lined MA 6A. Despite its lack of a port, Brewster was a thriving sea captains' village. One of its more famed seamen was Captain Dave Nickerson, whose adopted son René Rousseau was, legend has it, the Dauphin. The child, supposedly the son of French King Louis XVI and Marie Antoinette, was given to Nickerson by a veiled woman in the war-torn streets of revolutionary Paris in 1789 to save him from certain death. Brewster's captains also defied the American trade embargo with the British in the unpopular War of 1812 by continuing their shipping business. After the war the sailors brought vast wealth from around the world to their Brewster home base, making immense fortunes and building huge houses. The private Dillingham House, built about 1660 by Captain John Dillingham, is possibly the Cape's second-oldest existing house.

A host of visitor attractions scatter across Brewster. One of the best is the restored 1873 **Stony Brook Grist Mill and Museum.** The picturesque, water-powered mill, set along Stony Brook Pond, offers milling demonstrations through summer. An annual spawning run of herring, or alewives, going from Cape Cod Bay to inland freshwater ponds passes the mill via a fish ladder in late spring. Other attractions include the Cape Cod Museum of Natural History, with displays on the Cape's ecology and history, a weather station, and three trails; Drummer Boy Museum, illustrating scenes from the Revolution; and the fascinating New England Fire and History Museum. This interesting museum exhibits a great collection of fire equipment, including hand- and horse-drawn fire engines, old fire helmets, a diorama detailing Chicago's 1871 fire, and an old fire house.

Nickerson State Park sprawls along the eastern edge of Brewster. The inland park, covering 1,955 acres, is a pitch pine and oak woodland dotted with eight ponds and threaded with trails. The ponds are glacial features called "kettle" ponds that formed when large chunks of a melting glacier dropped into the ground and were blanketed with other debris. Later the ice melted, leaving these small ponds in the resulting depressions. The park's bayside section, north of MA 6A, has a large salt marsh, coastal dunes, and tidal flats. The park offers a wide assortment of outdoor recreation, including boating on Cliff Pond, picnicking, hiking, biking on the Cape Cod Rail Trail, trout fishing in the stocked ponds, and camping in the 420-site campground. This campground also makes a great base camp for exploring the upper parts of Cape Cod.

From Nickerson State Park the drive continues east and in 1.5 miles reaches US 6 and the town of Orleans. Turn left (north) onto US 6 to continue the drive. The highway runs through piney sand hills west of Orleans and a couple of miles later reaches a rotary. Continue north on US 6.

Orleans, bypassed by the scenic drive route, is the busy gateway to Cape Cod National Seashore. Lying on the southwest shore of Town Cove, the town was settled in 1693 and called Nauset, but was later renamed for the exiled Duke of Orleans, Louis Philippe de Bourbon, who visited here in 1797. As the commercial hub for the Lower Cape, Orleans offers numerous accommodation choices, restaurants, and shops. A few points of interest here include the Orleans Historical Society's collection in the 1834 Greek Revival–style Meeting House, and the French Cable Museum with cables and transmission equipment from the 1879 trans-Atlantic telegraph system between Orleans and Brest, France. Orleans has a dual coastline, with its Rock Harbor and Skaket Beach opening onto placid Cape Cod Bay to the west. Nauset Beach, accessed from Beach Road, is a gorgeous swath of sandy beach that stretches south from here to Chatham.

The highway bends northeast after bypassing Orleans, running along Town Cove. The right turn to the Fort Hill area in Cape Cod National Seashore is 1.5 miles from the rotary. The road runs back to parking lots on a low rise above Nauset Marsh. The 1.5-mile Fort Hill Trail begins across from the Penniman House, dropping across fields with old stone walls and house sites to some good views of Nauset Marsh before following the Red Maple Swamp Trail back to the parking area. The landmark Empire-style Penniman House was built in 1868 by whaling captain Edward Penniman. The fort at the end of the road was the apparent site of an earthen breastworks fort erected in 1653 during a Dutch-English conflict. Later the area was cleared and tilled as part of Reverend Samuel Treat's farm.

Cape Cod National Seashore

Back on the drive, the highway runs north to the national seashore's **Salt Pond Visitor Center** in Eastham. The center, open daily, is a great place to pick up maps, visitor information, and a schedule of Salt Pond interpretative programs. Displays on the Cape's natural history, geology, and history as well as an introductory video educate visitors to this seaside world. The Nauset Marsh Trail also begins at the center. Since 1961 most of Cape Cod north from here to the tip has been protected in 43,608-acre Cape Cod National Seashore, the nation's first designated seashore administered by the National Park Service. This 40-mile stretch of land, fronted by the chilly North Atlantic Ocean, is a much different and wilder landscape than that traversed by the first section of this scenic drive along the south shore of Cape Cod Bay. This is a place of open beaches, flanked by sand dunes and marshes, and fewer villages. The parkland offers a wealth of natural areas, historic sites, and things to do.

Cape Cod boasts a long and colorful history that began as the 3,500-year-old homeland of the Wampanoag Indians, although earlier archaeological sites date to nearly 9,000 years ago. The Algonquin-speaking Wampanoags, living in villages on the Cape, survived by fishing and farming. Explorer Samuel de Champlain noted in 1605 that the Indians grew corn, squash, beans, and tobacco, and stored corn in buried grass sacks. European exploration of Cape Cod possibly began in A.D. 1003 when mariner Leif Ericson and his Viking crew landed on Nauset, calling it "Wonderstrand." The Cape was the first landfall for later explorers, including English-man Bartholomew Gosnold, who named it Cape Cod in 1602 for "the great store of cod fish."

This cape was also the first landing site of the Pilgrims in early November 1620 after a sixty-five-day journey from Holland. Although they intended to sail south to the Hudson River, they decided to look at this area for possible settlement. The *Mayflower* anchored off today's Provincetown; the Pilgrims drew up and signed the Mayflower Compact to govern themselves then set about exploring the Cape and the bay. Near Eastham, a party led by Myles Standish was attacked by Indian arrows at First Encounter Beach. Musketfire was returned, and both sides retreated with no injuries. A plaque marks the spot today. By mid-December the Pilgrims finally decided to settle across the bay at Plymouth, finding Cape Cod, in one Pilgrim's words, "a hidious and desolate wildernes."

Eastham to Wellfleet

Eastham, one of the original towns on Cape Cod, was settled in 1644 by forty-nine Pilgrims from the Plymouth Colony. The village grew as an agricultural center, despite the damage that blackbirds and crows did to crops. A 1667 law forced every household to kill twelve blackbirds or three crows a year. The stakes were upped in 1695 when another ordinance forbid any bachelor from marrying unless his annual bird quota was fulfilled. Later Eastham become a fishing, whaling, and trading port. The town's past is displayed by the local historical society in the 1869 Eastham Schoolhouse Museum. The building, across from the Salt Pond Visitor Center, has an entrance framed by the jawbones of a great whale. Just south on US 6 is the 1680 Eastham Windmill, the oldest windmill on Cape Cod. It was built in 1680 in Plymouth and subsequently moved to Truro and then Eastham in 1793. The octagonal tower was used to grind grain for flour. The town's Old Cove Cemetery is the burial ground of many early Eastham settlers, including three of the *Mayflower* Pilgrims, who died in 1620.

US 6 heads north from Eastham along haphazard strip development to Wellfleet. Both Doane and Nauset Cable Roads lead east to Coast Guard Beach and Nauset Light Beach along the shore. **Nauset Light,** possibly the Cape's most spectacular lighthouse, perches on a bluff above the beach. Three stone towers topped with lights, called the Three Sisters by sailors, were first built here in 1838 but collapsed as sand was eroded from their base. The lighthouse warns mariners of the many offshore dangers that lurk along Cape Cod's Atlantic coast. Dense fog, fierce storms, and hurricanes have conspired with hidden sandbars, shoals, and rip tides to sink more than 3,000 ships in these treacherous waters since the *Sparrowhawk,* an English ship, ran aground off Orleans in 1626. The worst wreck occurred in 1898 when 175 people went down off Truro on the steamship *Portland* in a terrible gale. After the Cape Cod Canal opened in 1914, shipping losses went down dramatically. Radar, sonar, and other navigational equipment have further reduced underwater dangers. The historic lighthouse was moved 300 feet west of an eroding cliff in 1996.

Continuing the drive, the highway passes the 1,100-acre Audubon Society's **Wellfleet Bay Wildlife Sanctuary** along a cove on the bay side. A right turn leads to **Marconi Beach** and **Marconi Station Site.** Marconi Station is the site of the first wireless trans-Atlantic radio broadcast. When Italian engineer Guglielmo Marconi experimented with radio communication, he selected this remote high point above the beach to build four 210-foot towers and a transmitting station. On January 18, 1903, he succeeded in sending a Morse code message from President Theodore Roosevelt to England's King Edward VII. Soon afterwards the wireless became the chosen mode of communication, especially between ships. The Marconi Station picked up the 1912 distress call from the luxury liner *Titanic* after it struck an iceberg. The station was closed in 1917 and dismantled four years later. Little remains at the site today, except two of the four tower foundations. Marconi's towers, now on the edge of cliffs, were originally set back 165 feet from the sandy edge. The restless surf has eroded the bluffs in the intervening years so that this historical site sits on the edge of the sea.

The Atlantic White Cedar Swamp Trail begins on the opposite side of the Marconi Station parking area. This 1-mile footpath is an excellent hike through some diverse woodlands. The trail initially passes through a pygmy forest of bear or scrub oak, beach heather, crowberry, and stunted pitch pines. The trees, including white and black oaks, become taller farther inland. Finally a boardwalk loops through a swampy peatland in a kettle pond left by a retreating glacier. Here grows a magnificent stand of Atlantic white cedar, a light, rot-resistant wood that was prized for lumber in colonial New England.

The drive continues north to **Wellfleet,** a splendid town centered around its harbor on Wellfleet Bay. Incorporated in 1763, the town was named for the Wellfleet oyster beds in England. It prospered early from its own oyster beds and as a fishing port. In 1606 passing explorer Samuel de Champlain dubbed it Oyster Port. Even today Wellfleet is a working fishing town, with its shellfish industry generating more than $10 million annually. Wellfleet is also the hometown of the United Fruit Company, an enterprise started by sea captain Lorenzo Dow Baker in the 1870s as a banana importer. The Wellfleet Historical Society Museum displays items from the area's past, including farm tools, weapons, and everyday household items. The town also offers numerous shops and art galleries along with the usual assortment of dining establishments and hotels.

A good side-trip leads west from town on Chequesset Neck Road to Great Island, part of the national seashore. A trail begins from a picnic area and heads south onto Great Island, a thin peninsula that stretches its sandy spit south into

Atlantic waves break on sandy Marconi Beach at Cape Cod National Seashore.

Cape Cod Bay. East of Wellfleet is Ocean View Drive. Reach it by turning east on Le Count Hollow Road. The drive runs along the dramatic coastline atop sand cliffs. A number of town-managed beaches lie below the asphalt. Beyond the road spreads the great expanse of ocean, with its frothy surf pounding against the shore.

Truro

Farther north on the drive is **Truro.** This village, probably the least commercialized of the towns on the Lower Cape, sits amid sand dunes on the Pamet River. The Truro area boasts an early Pilgrim association. Myles Standish discovered a buried cache of Indian corn on what is now known as Corn Hill. The hungry men took the corn, and Standish eventually paid its rightful owner the following year for its use. The town was first settled by a group of Pilgrims called the Pamet Proprietors in 1689, and took the name Truro at its incorporation in 1709 because of its similarities to a Cornish seaside area in England. Truro, like Wellfleet, was a longtime fishing village that harvested cod and whales. A ferocious storm in October 1841 decimated its population by killing fifty-seven town fishermen. Most were caught while fishing on Georges Banks or making the desperate journey home. The next day more than a hundred bodies were recovered along the Cape's sandy shores.

The Truro area offers many points of interest. Two good hikes are the 0.5-mile Pamet Cranberry Bog Trail, exploring an abandoned cranberry operation, and the 0.75-mile Pilgrim Spring Trail, which leads to the spring where the Pilgrims drank their first freshwater in New England. The 66-foot-tall Highland Light or Cape Cod Light is the oldest lighthouse on Cape Cod. The first light was erected in 1798 to steer ships away from this treacherous stretch of beach. Today's automated lighthouse, perched atop 120-foot cliffs of sand, gravel, stones, and boulders, was built in 1857. The Coast Guard maintains a radio beacon here to orient passing ships. Nearby is the Highland Golf Course, built in 1892, and the Highland House Museum, housed in an old inn, with a collection of artifacts from shipwrecks, whaling relics, old guns, and Sandwich glass.

Cape Cod Geology

As the drive heads north from the developed part of Truro, the Cape narrows and appears more desolate than the wooded southern parts. Out here this becomes a place defined first and foremost by the ocean. The Cape, the easternmost point of American land in the Atlantic Ocean, is rocked by the full fury of the famed nor'easter storms. In late fall the prevailing winds gradually shift to the north and east, and the resulting violent winter gales begin to erode away the cliffs, beaches, and barrier dunes. The average rate of cliff erosion on the outer Cape escarpment above the beaches is between 2 and 4 feet a year. Since the Pilgrims landed almost 400 years ago, the alterations to the shoreline have been momentous and closely linked to the Cape's tenuous relationship with water, tides, wind, and weather.

Cape Cod is, in a sense, a momentary landscape, a transitory hook on the edge of North America. The world's largest glacial peninsula, the Cape is one of our newest landforms and will likely be one of the first erased from the continent. It was deposited a scant 25,000 years ago by an immense, retreating ice sheet that reached a thickness of some 10,000 feet. During that glacial period much of the world's water was encased in ice and the ocean level was about 400 feet lower than today. As the climate warmed, the glacier began melting and retreating northward. The ice sheet departed 17,000 years ago, leaving huge moraines—vast deposits of broken rock debris and glacial till or a rough assortment of sand, pebbles, cobbles, and boulders—and outwash plains on a now-submerged coastal surface that became Cape Cod, Martha's Vineyard, and Nantucket Island.

The drive continues north, following the northwest bend of the Cape's bent wrist. At Pilgrim Heights are the Pilgrim Spring and Small Swamp trails, along with a picnic area. Past that is brackish Pilgrim Lake, a large body of water edged by the highway on the south and a sizable region of parabolic sand dunes on the northeast. The lake is separated from the harbor by a long dike constructed in 1869 to protect the harbor and its fishing industry from the ocean. The highway runs into Provincetown, a picturesque town rimming Provincetown Harbor, one of the Cape's best anchorages.

Provincetown

Provincetown, or P-town to locals, is a busy, crowded town with narrow streets crammed with shops, restaurants, and hotels. The town, the first landing place of the Pilgrims, has been a whaling and fishing port, trading hub, and artists' colony. On November 11, 1620, the *Mayflower,* navigating through sandy shoals around Race Point, anchored in "ye Capeharbor wher they ridd in saftie." A party of Pilgrims came ashore here that day and "fell upon their knees and blessed ye God of heaven, who had brought them over ye vast and furious ocean" five weeks before they decided to settle across the bay in Plymouth. P-town locals and Cape Codders always want to set the record straight—the Pilgrims came here first, and Plymouth was merely an afterthought. The 250-foot-high granite **Pilgrim Monument,** built in 1907 and supposedly the tallest granite building in the world, commemorates the Pilgrims' landing here and their subsequent colonization of Massachusetts. The top of the tower, 352 feet above sea level, affords a marvelous view of the ocean, the bay, the sandy Province Lands at Race Point, and, on a clear day, a glimpse of the mainland.

The town, with its protected harbor, is a superb fishing port. It flourished through the nineteenth century with great catches of cod from the fertile offshore banks. Many Portuguese fishermen migrated here from the Azores Islands and the Lisbon area for the good fishing a century ago. Their descendants make up much of the town's permanent population. The town has also been a famed artists' colony, beginning with the founding of the Cape Cod School of Art in 1901 by portrait painter Charles Hawthorne. Painters, writers, and playwrights have flocked here ever since to experience the airy, translucent light of this village by the sea.

Colorful Provincetown is Cape Cod's most popular and fascinating town, and is usually bustling—particularly in summer, when it fills to capacity with a week-end population of 100,000. Overnight reservations are a must. Commercial Street, the main thoroughfare, jams with tourists and locals. Many boutiques and shops offer hours of browsing. An eclectic selection of eateries including chowder bars, seafood, and Portuguese cuisine keep the hungry amused. The Cape's greatest number of art galleries line the streets. Points of interest include the Provincetown Heritage Museum and MacMillan Wharf, where the town fishing fleet anchors and whale-watching cruises originate.

The Province Lands

The last part of this scenic drive enters Provincetown on US 6 and turns right (north) onto Race Point Road. This road winds through grass-covered dunes and beech and oak forests to Race Point and the northern edge of Cape Cod. **Province Lands Visitor Center,** offering information and maps, has a great observation deck with sweeping panoramic views of Provincetown, the dunes, and the ocean. The center has exhibits on the Cape's natural and human history, and naturalist-led walks and talks. Several trails for hikers and bicyclists begin here and wander out into the dune field, passing through stunted woods and exploring the Province Lands. At Race Point Beach is the Old Harbor Life Saving Museum housed in a life saving station transported here from Chatham in 1977. The museum displays artifacts and relics from the nineteenth U.S. Life Saving Service.

The Province Lands, the Cape region lying north of Provincetown, make up the newest part of Cape Cod. The area is a post-glacial deposit about 5,000 years old, formed of sand and alluvial material shifted from the Atlantic side of the Cape to the long sand spit southwest of Provincetown. Most of this young area is composed of sand dunes that are swept by wind and held mostly in place by beach grass, heather, and occasional woodlands. When the Pilgrims landed here, trees and shrubs anchored the sand. After settlement, however, the dunes were laid bare when the forest was cut for building and firewood, and cattle were let loose to graze the fragile ecosystem.

The great beach at Race Point is a fitting climax to Cape Cod. This long beach, edged by sand dunes and rimmed by the cold expanse of the North Atlantic, feels like the watery edge of the continent. Stand here in the wind and sun, where the relentless surf washes against your feet. A seagull wheels against the azure sky. A fishing boat slowly disappears beyond the ocean horizon. This is an elemental place, far removed from the clamor of nearby Provincetown. All that matters here is the lonely sea and sky.

Return to Provincetown from Race Point via the Province Lands Road, which runs down onto the west side of the tip, passes Herring Cove Beach, and bends inland back to Provincetown. Retrace US 6 back to the Cape Cod Canal to complete the journey.

Berkshire Hills Scenic Drive

General description: A 132-mile loop drive through the scenic Berkshire Hills in western Massachusetts.

Special attractions: Hancock Shaker Village, Great Barrington State Forest, Albert Schweitzer Center, Monument Mountain Reservation, East Mountain State Forest, Bidwell House, Otis Ridge Ski Area, Beartown State Forest, Mount Greylock State Reservation, Berkshire Museum, Arrowhead, Pittsfield State Forest, Chesterfield Gorge, camping, hiking, historic sites, scenic views, fishing.

Location: Western Massachusetts. The drive begins and ends at exit 1 on the Massachusetts Turnpike.

Drive route numbers: U.S. Highway 20, Massachusetts Highways 41, 23, 112, 116, 8, and 41.

Travel season: Year-round. Snow and ice can close or slicken roads in winter.

Camping: Beartown Mountain State Forest east of Great Barrington off MA 23 has a twelve-site campground. Tolland State Forest, south of MA 23 near Otis has a ninety-two-site campground alongside Otis Reservoir. Chester Blandford State Forest, north of Blandford, has a fifteen-site campground.

D.A.R. State Forest north of Goshen, off MA 112, has a fifty-site campground. Windsor State Forest, off Massachusetts Highway 9 south of MA 116, has a twenty-three-site campground. Mount Greylock State Reservation, west of Adams, has a thirty-five-site campground. Pittsfield State Forest, northwest of Pittsfield and US 20, offers thirty-one campsites. October Mountain State Forest, southeast of Pittsfield, has a forty-six-site campground. Mount Washington State Forest, southwest of Great Barrington, has a fifteen-site campground.

Services: All services in Adams, Pittsfield, and Great Barrington. Limited or seasonal services in the many small towns along the drive.

Nearby attractions: Bartholomew's Cobble, Colonel Ashley House, Bish Bash State Forest, Berkshire Opera, Tanglewood, Lenox, Stockbridge, Chesterwood Museum, Norman Rockwell Museum, Berkshire Theater Festival, Williamstown, Clark Art Institute, Williams College Museum of Art, Taconic Trail State Park, Western Gateway Heritage State Park, Natural Bridge State Park, William Cullen Bryant Homestead, Bennington (VT), Litchfield Hills (CT).

The Drive

The 132-mile Berkshire Hills Scenic Drive makes a wide loop across the wooded hills and valleys of western Massachusetts, avoiding all the main thoroughfares such as U.S. Highway 7 and the tourist towns. Instead, the drive follows rural highways and quiet back roads through some of the region's loveliest countryside. Every New England landscape is found here—thick woodlands punctuated by serene ponds and lakes; ancient, worn hills gentled by time and erosion; bucolic villages topped by slender church spires; open pastures and farms interrupted by stone fences, silver silos, orchards, and grazing Holsteins; rivers that wander between grass-lined banks; and tumbling brooks that shatter to foam over cliffs.

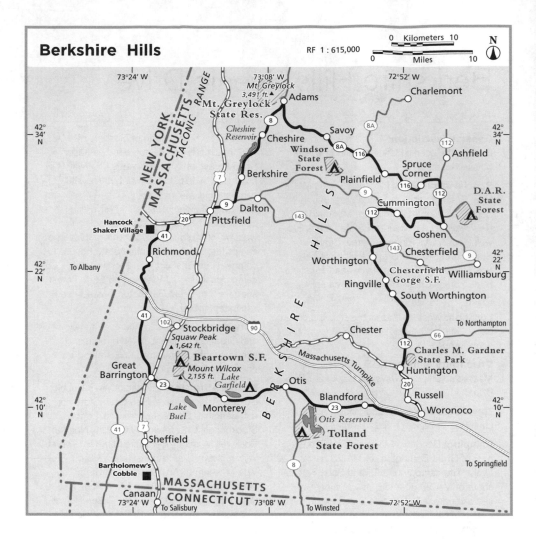

RF 1 : 615,000

0   Kilometers 10

0   Miles   10

N

The drive, with its many natural wonders (including Mount Greylock) and marvelous historic sites (including Hancock Shaker Village), easily takes a full day to enjoy.

The Berkshire Hills cover the western third of the Bay State, forming a high barrier that long impeded westward travel and settlement. The hills are the southern extension of Vermont's Green Mountains, the eroded roots of an ancient mountain range that rose here some 440 million years ago. Erosion slowly leveled the once lofty peaks down to an almost flat plain studded with occasional mountains, including Maine's Mount Katahdin, New Hampshire's Mount Monadnock, and Massachusetts's Mount Greylock, formed of hard, erosion-resistant rock. Geologists estimate that erosion has since carried some 6 miles of rock off today's mountains. The Berkshires are part of the uplifted New England peneplain, the old erosional mountain surface that was later lifted and then dissected by water erosion and smoothed by long episodes of glaciation. The hills rise gently on the east from the Connecticut River Valley to a wide plateau atop the range. The western edge of the Berkshires is an abrupt escarpment that drops as much as 1,000 feet to the broad valley that separates the hills from the Taconic Mountains along the New York border.

Because of this mountain barrier, the Berkshire Hills towns and people have historically been isolated, set apart from busy eastern Massachusetts and Boston. The New York Dutch, who settled the lower Hudson Valley by the 1630s, failed to traverse the Taconic Mountains and settle the fertile Berkshire vales. The English, likewise, were unable to penetrate this mountain stronghold from their East Coast colonies, finding the high granite barrier almost impassable. It wasn't until 1725 when Matthew Noble erected a log cabin in today's Sheffield that settlement began. Pioneers eager for new lands came and built houses and villages in the rich river valleys on the west side of the hills.

Towns here prospered during the nineteenth-century Industrial Revolution, when railroads connected them to burgeoning markets. Industry eventually migrated to the bigger eastern cities, and farmers migrated farther westward in search of new and better lands, leaving the Berkshire Hills again quiet and unspoiled. These attributes have since attracted visitors who now come to sample the area's pastoral silence as well as its splendid cultural events and festivals. Still, this underpopulated sector of Massachusetts feels ignored by the state government far to the east in Boston. One *Berkshire Week* editorial called for secession from Massachusetts, saying: "Citizens of Berkshire, the time has come to throw off the chains and shackles that bind us to uncaring masters. Let us withdraw from the cesspool of Massachusetts politics and declare that we are the great and sovereign State Of Berkshire."

Stockbridge to Great Barrington

The scenic drive begins at exit 1 on the western end of the Massachusetts Turnpike ("Mass Pike"), which is also Interstate 90. Turn south from the exit onto Massachusetts Highway 41. The road runs south through a wide valley shaded with thick woods. A few miles east of here lies the old village of **Stockbridge,** which was settled in 1739 as an Indian mission. Stockbridge, coupled with its sister city Lenox to the north, has long been a bastion of wealth and culture—a Newport in the Berkshires. Some great points of interest in the Stockbridge area include Norman Rockwell's art studio; the Berkshire Playhouse; Chesterwood, the home and studio of Lincoln Memorial sculptor Daniel Chester French; and famed Tanglewood, the summer home of the Boston Symphony Orchestra for more than fifty years.

MA 41 is a pleasant, narrow road winding through woods west of the meandering Housatonic River. Old stone walls line occasional green pastures, and hills embrace the edges of the broad river valley. To the east looms humpbacked Monument Mountain, one of the more famed hills in the southern Berkshires. This craggy peak is not only a superb hiking spot, but also a local literary landmark. On an August afternoon in 1850, writers Herman Melville and Nathaniel Hawthorne were introduced to each other on a hike organized by Oliver Wendell Holmes. The writers and the party's eight other hikers were caught in a torrential thunderstorm just below the mountain's narrow, rocky summit. The party waited the storm out under a granite outcrop, drinking champagne and reciting local poet William Cullen Bryant's tragic poem "The Story of the Indian Girl," an old legend that takes place on the mountain's slopes. The Indian maiden was flung from the summit for loving an enemy warrior. Hawthorne and Melville became fast friends after the incident. Hawthorne returned to Boston not long afterward, while Melville stayed in the Berkshires for ten more years, writing *Moby Dick,* his masterpiece novel, which he dedicated to Hawthorne.

To retrace the novelists' ascent, drive north about 6 miles on US 7 from Great Barrington and park. The marked 1.25-mile Indian Monument Trail begins here and ends atop the 1,642-foot summit, called Squaw Peak, an hour later. Stunning views of the surrounding Berkshire and Litchfield Hills and the Taconic Mountains unfold beyond the summit.

The first section of the scenic drive ends after 10 miles in **Great Barrington,** the largest town in the southern Berkshires. Incorporated in 1761, the town has long been a haven for poets and philosophers. When attorney William Cullen Bryant, town clerk here in 1816, published his poem "Thanatopsis" at age twenty-three, he was hailed as a literary genius in Europe. His poetic potential never reached beyond those initial accolades, however, and Bryant marched south to New York City and became the influential editor of the *New York Post* newspaper.

Great Barrington, an excellent base camp for exploring the area of this scenic drive, is a working, everyday kind of place that is relatively busy for the Berkshires. The town was the first American locale to be lit by electric lights. Inventor William Stanley, founder of the General Electric Company, tested his electrical transformer here by wiring the downtown for streetlights in 1886. The Albert Schweitzer Center, a museum and educational facility dedicated to the great doctor, is also located here.

Great Barrington has harbored a large black population ever since slavery was abolished in Massachusetts in 1781. Mum Bet, a servant in Ashley Falls just south of here, filed the 1783 test case that led to her freedom under due process of law and the subsequent abolition of slavery. Fugitive slaves from the south journeyed through the area on the Underground Railroad during the Civil War. Black scholar and pioneering civil rights leader W. E. B. Dubois was born here in 1868.

Other fascinating points of interest are found in the larger Great Barrington region. Sheffield, the oldest town in Berkshire County, has two covered bridges. The Colonel John Ashley House is in Ashley Falls off US 7 south of town. The restored 1735 house, the oldest in Berkshire County, is a museum that details colonial history and was the site where the Sheffield Declaration was signed in 1773. This document affirmed that all men were created equal and had rights to property.

Nearby is **Bartholomew's Cobble,** a superb 294-acre nature preserve along the Housatonic River near the Connecticut border. The area, with 6 miles of trails, offers diverse habitats for plants and animals near two cobbles or cliffs of marble and quartzite along the glassy river. More than 240 bird species have been identified here, along with 740 plant species that include forty-five different ferns— more than in any other similar-sized area in the continental United States.

Great Barrington to Woronoco

The next scenic drive segment runs 30 miles east along Massachusetts Highway 23 to Woronoco. The road follows a section of the old stage route between Boston and Albany, as well as the Knox Trail, a route followed by Colonel Henry Knox during the Revolution. Knox and his men pulled more than sixty tons of weaponry, including forty-three cannons and sixteen mortars, captured by Ethan Allen at Fort Ticonderoga in 1775. Using ox-drawn sledges, they hauled the arms almost 300 miles in midwinter, giving General George Washington the firepower to enforce the siege of Boston and drive the British out.

Turn east on MA 23 on the north side of Great Barrington. The road initially runs past houses, and after 1.5 miles leaves town and heads up a flat valley flanked by hills. A mile later is the turn to Ski Butternut, an intermediate area with a 1,000-foot vertical drop and 8 kilometers of groomed cross-country ski trails. The highway climbs eastward to a forest section uprooted by a violent and rare tornado in 1994. After 4 miles the road crosses the long-distance Appalachian Trail, a footpath that runs from Georgia to Maine. Farther along lies Lake Buel, half-hidden behind trees.

The turnoff to 10,879-acre **Beartown State Forest** is at 6 miles. This large state parkland encompasses a mostly unspoiled upland region of undulating hills with 1,865-foot Beartown Mountain and 2,155-foot Mount Wilcox the forest high points. Trout streams lace the valleys, while ponds, including thirty-five-acre Benedict Pond, are tucked against wooded ridges. The park offers swimming, fishing, boating, and hiking—5 miles of the Appalachian Trail traverse the park. It also has twelve campsites.

The pretty little village of **Monterey** nestles among hills after 8 miles of the MA 23 drive. The town, settled in 1739 and incorporated in 1847 during the Mexican-American War, was named for the site of an American victory at Monterrey, Mexico. Monterey is strung along the highway, with houses, summer cottages, and a lovely church. A 1927 stone monument honors General Knox and his men for their incredible 1775 winter trek to Boston with Fort Ticonderoga's captured guns. The Bidwell House, listed on the National Register of Historic Places, is a restored 1750 mansion that is open for tours in summer. Past Monterey, Lake Garfield sits just north of a screen of trees. The large lake, named in 1881 for assassinated President James Garfield, offers fishing, boat rentals, and campsites.

The highway continues east, dipping through valleys filled with swamps and beaver ponds and edging over rounded hillsides. The vacation town of **Otis,** sitting at the highway's junction with Massachusetts Highway 8, is one of the area's oldest villages. It was named for Harrison Gray Otis, a Massachusetts senator, Speaker of the House of Representatives, and mayor of Boston. The 1828 St. Paul's Church, built in Gothic Revival style, is one of the most picturesque churches in the southern Berkshires. The first nudist colony in the Berkshires was founded near Otis in 1933. Just west of town is Otis State Forest and Otis Ridge Ski Area.

Continue the drive by zigzagging through Otis on MA 23 then escaping into the hills. The road dips and rolls for the next 10 miles, descending sharply through moist ravines colored with mountain laurel and passing Benton Pond and Otis Reservoir. **Tolland State Forest,** lying south of the highway, is a 4,893-acre area wrapping around Otis Reservoir. The lake offers fishing for bass, bluegill, perch, pickerel, and trout, along with swimming and boating. The forest also has a ninety-two-site campground, with thirty-five sites along the lakeshore. Past Blair Pond, a small lake on the north named for Hiram Blair, the road scales a long, steep hill to Blandford.

Straddling a high ridge, **Blandford** is a town with a view. As the road descends through town, astounding vistas of the Pioneer Valley spread out to the east. It was incorporated in 1741 by a group of Scottish immigrants, who dubbed their village Glasgow for their hometown. However, the provincial governor, who had recently arrived from England on the ship *Blandford,* denied their request and named it for the ship. In the early 1800s Blandford became a leading dairy center in western Massachusetts.

Past Blandford the highway runs alongside the Mass Pike, beginning a steep descent down the eastern side of the Berkshire Hills. The road drops into a broad valley, crosses the turnpike, and winds down a steep, curvy road for another mile to its junction with U.S. Highway 20 near Woronoco. Turn left or north onto US 20. The next drive section runs north on US 20 and Massachusetts Highway 112 for 21 miles to Worthington Corners.

Into the Berkshire Hills

The highway twists northwest in a broad valley above the west bank of the Westfield River, passing through a spectacular roadcut that illustrates the uptilted layers of

Otis Reservoir is the centerpiece of Tolland State Forest in the southern Berkshires.

metamorphic rocks on the eastern edge of the Berkshire Hills. The town of Russell, a paper mill town, is a couple of miles up the road. Huntington, settled in 1769, quickly follows. A picnic area sits along the river. Angle right onto MA 112 in town. The road passes some churches and the Huntington Country Store, leaves the village, then bends up a narrow valley alongside the small river. **Charles M. Gardner State Park,** a small twenty-nine-acre roadside area shaded by white pines, is 3 miles from Huntington. The park includes a picnic area and a great swimming hole.

The highway passes a junction with Massachusetts Highway 66, crosses the river, and threads up into hilly countryside. At 5 miles is a view of Knightville Reservoir and dam. The road crests a ridge and turns through a thick woodland of cedar, pine, and birch along a bouldery creek. Farther along is an unmarked pulloff for South Worthington Cascade, a gentle 50-foot waterfall over ledges.

The scenic drive next runs through the Worthingtons—first South Worthington, then Ringville, Worthington Center, and Worthington Corners, the largest of the villages. The latter crossroads town is set atop a high plateau, surrounded by houses and hill farms. Another of the region's ubiquitous Congregational Churches is here, adorned with stained glass windows. The highway passes a small pond and a golf course built in 1904 before intersecting Massachusetts Highway 143. Turn right onto MA 112/143.

The next 14-mile segment of the scenic drive follows real back roads through a rural landscape in the heart of the Berkshire Hills. The highway heads north through wide fields and heads down a steep hill into a broad valley. Keep north (left) on MA 112 at the highway junction. MA 143 goes east to Chesterfield, a short jaunt that makes a rewarding side-trip. The classic hilltop village of Chesterfield holds an 1835 Congregational Church and a small local museum. Like this one, most of the colonial villages in the Berkshires are situated atop hills that, with more sunlight, allowed a longer growing season and were immune from lowland flooding.

Three miles from the highway junction at West Chesterfield is a deep valley carved by the East Branch of the Westfield River. Turn right just before the bridge on River Road and drive almost a mile south to **Chesterfield Gorge,** one of the Bay State's lesser known geologic wonders. Protected in a 166-acre reservation, Chesterfield Gorge is an abrupt 1,000-foot-long chasm incised by the Westfield River into ancient Devonian-age metamorphic bedrock. A trail leads from the parking area along the rim of the 30-foot-deep canyon. In spring the river roars through the narrow aperture, swollen water filling the gorge, while in summer and autumn the river quietly tumbles over worn boulders. Look for long grooves in the cliffs that glaciers etched by dragging boulders encased in ice across the rock surface.

Old hemlocks line the clifftop and cling to the steep walls. Other trees shading the gorge and trail include American beech, white ash, red oak, paper birch, and yellow birch. One yellow birch, the largest of its species in Massachusetts, is at least 14 feet in circumference and 79 feet tall. Ferns fill moist cracks and cover the damp gorge cliffs. The gorge was saved by the Trustees of Reservations in 1929 when some boaters noticed loggers preparing to clearcut the east side of the gorge. The Trustees stopped the cutting and were able to purchase and preserve the property. Note the stone abutment on the canyon wall from the 1739 High Bridge on the old Boston-to-Albany Post Road.

Back on the main scenic drive route, head north on MA 112. The next 5 miles follow this classic country lane. Old colonial homes, tree-lined fields, and a long row of maples lie along the asphalt. The road bends east, drops through a shallow ravine dense with trees, and wends through open pastures with dairy cows. The road joins Massachusetts Highway 9 in Cummington, a small village that was a flourishing industrial town in the nineteenth century with textile mills, paper mills, and tanneries. Stop by the restored Kingman Tavern, which is also the general store and local post office, for a look back at the past.

To go on, turn right on MA 9/112. The next 7-mile stretch runs east alongside the Swift River in a shallow valley for a few miles before climbing through low hills to the highway's junction with MA 112 North. Turn north (left) on MA 112 and enter Goshen, a small dairy town with homes, a red barn, and the village cemetery.

A mile out of town is the right turn to 1,770-acre **D.A.R. State Forest.** This parkland is one of western Massachusetts's most popular recreation areas, with visitors filling its fifty-site campground, 9 miles of trails, and two lakes every summer weekend. The hilly terrain is studded with rocky tors, including 1,713-foot Moor's Hill and its five-state view from a fire lookout. The forest also has a nature center with programs through the summer.

MA 112 continues north a few miles over hill and dale to its junction with Massachusetts Highway 116. Turn west (left) on MA 116. For a side-trip head north on scenic MA 112 toward the Mohawk Trail, dashing down a broad valley amid low hills. The beautiful village of **Ashfield,** a mile north of this remote highway intersection, is worth a quick visit. The 1812 Town Hall, originally a church, is a stunning edifice topped with a weather-vaned steeple. Many well-kept colonial homes line the village streets. But unlike most New England villages, Ashfield has no village green.

Over the Hoosac Range

The main drive route heads west on MA 116 for 23 miles over the plateau crest of the Hoosac Range, a sub-range of the Berkshire Hills, to Adams. This section of highway crosses a superb landscape, threading across scenic, rolling hills punctuated by occasional distant views broken by picturesque villages and farms. The road runs west for 8 miles to Plainfield, passing fields, farms, and barns. Spruce Corner, at 3 miles, holds the small, white clapboard, 1874 Spruce Corner School House. **Plainfield** is another classic hill town, settled relatively late (1770), which flourished with industry in the mid-nineteenth century. It is now an agricultural and tourist center. Stone walls and towering maples line the village streets. The Plainfield Congregational Church, with a gold-domed steeple, dominates the skyline.

The highway rolls west through the wooded hills. The Kenneth Dubuque Memorial State Forest, with 7,882 acres, lies north of the drive off Massachusetts Highway 8A. This rugged area, part of a mostly wild block that also includes Savoy and Mohawk Trail state forests, has 7 miles of designated hiking trails, several ponds, and a thick northern hardwood forest. Stone walls, heaped up by long-ago farmers clearing their rocky fields, edge the tar road. Farther along is a wide valley with a left turn to **Windsor State Forest.** The forest, 3 miles south, offers twenty-four campsites, hiking trails, and opportunities for fishing. The small settlement of Savoy, dominated by an old schoolhouse and Baptist Church, is reached after 15 miles.

The highway continues west over this high, upland region to a lofty ridge crest. Here it begins the long descent down the western escarpment of the Hoosac Range to the industrial town of Adams. Mount Greylock, the 3,491-foot high point of Massachusetts, looms to the west. The road drops down steep, wooded vales and past open fields. A few miles later it begins the final abrupt descent into Adams and the broad and fertile Hoosac Valley.

Adams to Pittsfield

Adams is a good-sized industrial town that spreads along the Hoosic River's banks in the afternoon shadow of towering Mount Greylock. The town was founded in 1766 as East Hoosuck but was later renamed for Samuel Adams, the Revolutionary patriot who led irate citizens to a "tea party" in Boston Harbor in 1773. West Hoosuck is today's Williamstown. The main part of East Hoosuck was later divided into North Adams and Adams. The two naturally became rivals, although Adams always asserted it was the original settlement. After the Mohawk Trail highway opened, North Adams erected a sign that read: "This is the City of North Adams, the Mother of the Mohawk Trail." The Adams citizenry, feeling slighted after being ignored in the dedication festivities, put a sign on its north boundary that said: "You are now leaving Adams, the Mother of North Adams and the Grandmother of the Mohawk Trail."

Adams grew as a Quaker settlement in the 1700s, and its 1782 Quaker Meeting House is still a local historic landmark. The nineteenth century brought industrial prosperity to the town. Textile and paper mills, powered by the river, fueled the boom alongside their looming smokestacks. An immense statue of President William McKinley in the town center was erected after his 1901 assassination. Today the town economy relies on industry and a large quarry. Susan B. Anthony, the famed woman suffrage leader, was born here in a simple two-story frame house.

MA 116 and MA 8 intersect in downtown Adams. To continue the drive, turn south (left) onto MA 8. The road winds through the town's southern outskirts and finally breaks away from the development after 1.5 miles, then runs up the Hoosac Valley. Lofty wooded ridges on Mount Greylock tower to the west. This 3,491-foot mountain, the state's high point, is the focus of the 12,500-acre Mount Greylock State Reservation. The peak is a spur of the Taconic Mountains, a long, narrow range that straddles the New York border.

After 5 miles the drive enters **Cheshire.** This village has long been a dairying center. The Cheese Press Monument, sitting on the corner of Church and School Streets across from the town post office, testifies to its economic and historic importance. It's also one of the stranger monuments in New England, whose towns usually display Revolutionary or Civil War statues on the village green. The monument, a concrete reproduction of a cheese press, says: "Near this spot was made in 1801 the great Cheshire Cheese weighing 1235 lbs. One day's product of the town's dairies, moulded in a cider press. It was drawn by oxen to Hudson, N.Y. and shipped to Washington. It was presented at the White House to President Thomas Jefferson as a token of regard from the citizens of Cheshire." The cheese was well received in the nation's capital, and slices were dispensed to the president, his cabinet, his advisors, and foreign dignitaries. Later the town sent a 100-pound cheese to President Andrew Jackson, who responded with a letter that can be seen in the town's historic Cole House. Built in 1804, the Cole House also has an eight-panel door that forms a double cross to protect it from witchcraft.

Cheshire Lake, a long, thin reservoir, is tucked among hills south of Cheshire. The highway runs along its eastern shore, bordered by lots of roadside development and houses. About 12 miles from Adams, the drive meets MA 9. Turn right on MA 9 and enter Pittsfield, the largest town and commercial center in western Massachusetts. A small city with a population of almost 45,000, Pittsfield sits along the upper Housatonic River, which has long provided power for its diverse industries.

Pittsfield, the Berkshire County seat, was settled in 1752 and quickly became a trading and agricultural hub. The town figured in the American Revolution, having declared independence from British authority three months prior to the signing of the Declaration of Independence. After the war agriculture could not support the town, so Pittsfield turned toward industrialization and thrived. Mechanized textile mills, using cheap river power, helped fill the nation's demand for clothing during the War of 1812. Paper mills and the establishment of General Electric by William Stanley, who first successfully used alternating current and lit the streets of Great Barrington with electric lights, brought further prosperity.

Today Pittsfield is a busy, working-class town that seems out of place amid the pastoral Berkshire Hills and their small, scattered villages. The town offers travelers not only a wide variety of services, but also some interesting points to visit. The **Berkshire Museum** on Main Street is a superb regional museum with eighteen galleries that include a collection of Hudson River School landscapes, mobiles by Alexander Calder, and a natural history collection of shells, fossils, an aquarium, and local fauna. Arrowhead is a stately eighteenth-century house that was home to writer Herman Melville for thirteen years in the mid-nineteenth century. It was here in 1850 and 1851 that Melville penned his classic novel *Moby Dick* about Captain Ahab and his obsession with a great white whale. The spartan house is still furnished with some of Melville's belongings and is open for viewing in summer and fall.

The Berkshire County Historical Society is also located here. East of town off MA 8 is the **Crane Museum of Papermaking,** with displays on papermaking and paper money. The Crane Paper Company is the supplier of paper for U.S. currency.

The drive jogs through Pittsfield. From the junction of MA 8 and MA 9, go west on Dalton Avenue to Tyler Street. Take a left on South Street (US 7), drive through the downtown with its old brick buildings, and in a few blocks go right on US 20. Follow this road, Housatonic Street, through a residential area for just over 4 miles to the intersection of US 20 and MA 41. Go left or south on MA 41.

Hancock Shaker Village

Hancock Shaker Village, one of the most fascinating and popular Berkshire attractions, sits immediately west of this highway junction. To visit it, continue west from the junction on US 20 for 0.5 mile to the village entrance and parking area. The Shaker Community at Hancock, now preserved as a living museum, was the third of nineteen Shaker colonies established between 1778 and 1836 in the eastern United States. The village was established in 1790, fourteen years after Mother Ann Lee and her disciples came from England as dissident Quakers. The group, calling themselves the United Society of Believers in Christ's Second Appearing, received their later name from their ecstatic worship practices. As they prayed, the spirit moved them with trembling, whirling, dancing, and shaking. The Shakers believed Mother Ann to be the female personification of the Messiah after her vision in an English jail when Christ appeared to her and became one with her.

After Mother Ann's death in 1784, the Shakers codified their lifestyle and beliefs in the Millennial Laws, which governed how their utopian communities were run and served as a code of conduct for believers. They dedicated themselves to God; established complete equality of the sexes, although men and women lived apart; held only common property; were pacifists; kept separate from the outside world; and found God and perfection in work. The Shakers were also celibate, which allowed their church to grow only through new believers and adopted orphans.

The Hancock Shaker Community was one of the largest in the United States by the 1850s, with a population of more than 300. The thriving village boasted at least twenty buildings along with fertile gardens, herds of livestock, and prosperous craft workshops. The Shakers, with their meticulous craftsmanship and attention to detail, marketed vegetable seeds, invented things such as the clothespin, circular saw, and flat broom, and made simple chairs and ovoid wooden boxes. As the Industrial Revolution gathered steam, however, traditional Shaker markets were flooded with inferior but cheaper goods, turning community reliance to agriculture.

As the Shaker faith emerged into the twentieth century, its population of converts slowly ebbed and by the 1950s only a handful remained here. In 1960 the remaining buildings were to be sold by the last Shaker sisters and razed to make room for a racetrack. Local residents raised funds, however, and bought the community and 1,000 acres to preserve the Shaker heritage as an outdoor museum. Today visitors can explore the grounds and brick and wood buildings, delving into the Shaker lifestyle. The visitor center sells tickets, has a cafe and gift shop, and dispenses information, including a map of the village.

The herb garden, staffed by knowledgeable herbalists, is where the Shakers grew seeds and raised medicinal herbs. The most interesting building and one of

A worn millstone leans against a stone barn at historic Hancock Shaker Village.

the great masterpieces of American folk architecture is the round stone barn built in 1826. Erected in a functional round design, this three-story dairy barn housed fifty-two milk cows that one man, standing in the middle, could feed at once. Other buildings of note include the laundry and machine shop; the brick dwelling that housed nearly a hundred Brothers and Sisters in separate quarters; the 1795 Brethren's Workshop, where round wooden boxes are still made by carpenter-interpreters; the replica schoolhouse; and the austere 1793 Meetinghouse. Hancock Shaker Village offers a wonderful glimpse back at a little known but intriguing chapter in American religious history. Much of the positive energy and simplicity that the Shakers brought to their unusual community still remains for today's visitors to reflect back on. Remember the old Shaker hymn that begins: "'Tis a gift to be simple, 'Tis a gift to be free."

The last 8 miles of the scenic drive head south from the Shaker Village on MA 41 to West Stockbridge and exit 1 on the Mass Pike. This section runs through open countryside on the east flank of the forest-clad Taconic Mountains. Corn fields, farms, and occasional homes fringe the road. The highway runs through Richmond, now a housing community but once a busy iron ore center. West Stockbridge is a small town with an active downtown area that includes restaurants and shops. Its old 1830 Shaker Mill on the Williams River is the site of the world's first hydroelectric dam. The drive ends on the south side of West Stockbridge where MA 41 meets exit 1 on I–90.

8

Mohawk Trail Scenic Drive

General description: This 57-mile route follows the Mohawk Trail, one of the country's first designated scenic drives, through the northern Berkshire Hills between Greenfield and Williamstown and ends by climbing to the summit of Mount Greylock.

Special attractions: Shelburne Falls, Mount Mohawk Ski Area, Catamount State Forest, Deerfield River, Berkshire East Ski Area, Mohawk Trail State Forest, Savoy Mountain State Forest, Florida State Forest, Natural Bridge State Park, Western Gateway Heritage State Park, Mount Greylock State Reservation, Clarksburg State Forest, Williamstown, Sterling and Francine Clark Art Institute, Williams College Museum of Art, scenic views, rafting, kayaking, hiking, camping, fishing.

Location: Northwestern Massachusetts, west of Interstate 91.

Drive route number and name: Massachusetts Highway 2, Notch Road.

Travel season: Year-round.

Camping: Public camping is found in several state forests on or just off the drive. Mohawk Trail State Forest has fifty-six sites; Savoy Mountain State Forest has forty-five sites; Mount Greylock State Reservation has thirty-five sites; Clarksburg State Park has forty-nine sites.

Services: All services in Greenfield, Shelburne, Shelburne Falls, North Adams, and Williamstown.

Nearby attractions: Deerfield Village, Mount Sugarloaf State Reservation, Hancock Shaker Village, Bennington (VT), Pittsfield State Forest, Berkshire Museum, Stockbridge, Taconic Trail State Park, Beartown State Forest, Bish Bash Falls.

The Drive

This 57-mile scenic route follows the Mohawk Trail, the first designated scenic road in New England, from Greenfield in the Connecticut River Valley to the quaint college town of Williamstown in far northwestern Massachusetts. The drive also makes a 9-mile detour south to the airy summit of Mount Greylock, the state's highest peak. One of New England's most beautiful and famed scenic roads, the Mohawk Trail is a drive to be savored and enjoyed time after time, season after season.

The drive follows a centuries-old footpath blazed by Indians, traverses deep valleys floored by rivers, high wooded ridges and mountains, white farmhouses surrounded by grassy pastures, apple orchards, colonial villages, and a blaze of autumn colors during prime leaf-peeper season. The paved highway is open year-round, although the Mount Greylock spur road closes in winter.

The route also crosses the Berkshire Hills, a southern extension of Vermont's Green Mountains. The Berkshires, comprising a high, rolling plateau without a definite mountain spine, are a remnant of the uplifted New England peneplain. A handful of steep river valleys slice deeply into the range, but nowhere do the rivers

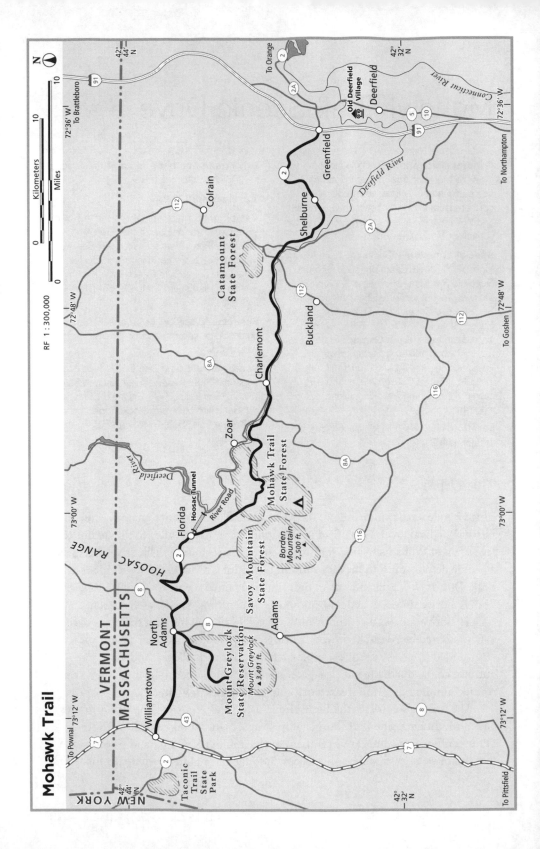

cut completely across the formidable Green Mountain–Berkshires upland barrier. This mountain barrier was long an impediment to westward travel, expansion, and settlement. The Mohawk Trail carves a path across an interesting cross-section of the Berkshire uplift. It traverses the Deerfield River Valley before following the deep gorge of the tributary Cold River to the top of the plateau. At the western edge of the plateau, the escarpment drops abruptly 1,000 feet to North Adams and the Hoosic River Valley. Across the wide valley towers Mount Greylock, one of the highest peaks in the Taconic Mountains, a long range that stretches along New York's eastern border from northern Connecticut to central Vermont.

The drive begins on the west side of Greenfield at the rotary intersection of Interstate 91 and Massachusetts Highway 2. Go west on MA 2. The actual designated Mohawk Trail begins 20 miles to the east in Orange.

Greenfield and Deerfield

Greenfield, the seat of Franklin County, spreads among green and fertile fields on the west bank of the wide Connecticut River at its confluence with the Deerfield River. The old town, originally settled as part of greater Deerfield in the 1680s, incorporated in 1753 and drew its name from the verdant grasslands blanketing the valley. The town, with a population of about 18,000, has long prospered as an agricultural and industrial center. The country's first cutlery factory opened here in the early 1800s. It retains an interesting Main Street with an eclectic assortment of buildings. A few of these include the Greenfield Public Library and St. James Church, an 1847 reproduction of an English church. The local historical society has a small collection of local artifacts, furniture, photographs, and paintings on display at 3 Church Street.

Before you go much farther, a worthwhile side-trip is **Historic Deerfield** village just south of Greenfield on U.S. Highway 5. Deerfield, established in 1663 on the lush river plain, is considered the best-preserved colonial village in New England. Along The Street, Deerfield's main avenue, sit sixty-five eighteenth- and nineteenth-century houses and buildings with thirteen of them open to the public. For years after its settlement, Deerfield was a remote and dangerous outpost on the edge of the great western wilderness. Two major Indian raids in the years just after its founding decimated the settlement, including the Bloody Brook Massacre on September 18, 1675, when sixty-four men, most of the village's male population, were killed in an Indian ambush during King Philip's War.

An even worse event occurred one cold February dawn during Queen Anne's War in 1704 when the French led a contingent of 350 Indians into the Deerfield stockade, killing forty-nine residents, burning much of the village, and capturing 112 prisoners who were promptly marched 300 miles north in the dead of winter to Canada. One eyewitness who survived the attack later recalled, "not long before the break of day, the enemy came in like a flood upon us; our watch being unfaithful." Within three years the town was resettled by many of the same families, and flourished through the 1700s as an agricultural center.

Over time neighboring Greenfield usurped Deerfield as the commercial and business center of the upper Pioneer Valley, which kept Deerfield from destroying its old colonial heritage. Now its historic district stands as a charming, elegant reminder of the richness of American life in the eighteenth century. Almost 6,000 acres of prime farmland surrounding the village have also been acquired and removed from modern development. Historic Deerfield is hard to see in a single day—there is so much to explore. Begin by stopping at the visitor center in Hall Tavern in the heart of Deerfield. Maps, interpretative information, a short film, and admission passes to the buildings are here. Admission to all the dwellings is by guided tour with a costumed interpreter only.

Since it's hard to visit all the interesting sights here, it's best to pick a few and come back another day to visit others. Some of the best buildings include the 1717 Wells-Thorn House, once owned by tavern owner Ebenezer Wells; the 1733 Ashley House inhabited by Reverent Jonathon Ashley; the 1799 Federal-style Asa Stebbins House, a brick home built by a wealthy farmer and decorated with scenic French wallpaper that depicts the South Sea voyages of Captain Cook; and the Memorial Hall Museum, which includes a door hacked by Indian hatchets in the terrible 1704 ambush along with a textile museum, silver and metalware collection, and a nineteenth-century printing office.

Greenfield to Shelburne

The scenic drive begins by heading west on MA 2 from I–91 and Greenfield. The road quickly passes through a business strip mall and bends north into woods and out of town as it arcs around Greenfield Mountain, a high knoll perched above the broad valley. After about a mile is Shelburne Summit, with an observation tower that yields a spacious view east across the Connecticut River Valley and north to New Hampshire and Vermont. Continuing westward, the highway swings around the mountain to enter the Deerfield River Valley at Shelburne. The river lies below the highway in a deep, steep-walled valley. The Mohawk Trading Post, the first in a series of "trading posts" along the route that vend American Indian crafts, sits alongside the drive with its prominent totem pole (a Northwest Coast Indian symbol) and teepees (the traveling lodge of the Plains tribes). Farther along are a couple of maple sugar houses, including Gould's Maple Farm, which offer sap-to-syrup demonstrations in early spring.

Low hills composed of ancient granites and metamorphic rocks rise beyond the valley and highway. A diverse woodland of white pine, poplar, sugar maple, black locust, American elm, and red oak blankets the hillsides, while willow and sycamore trees shade the riverbanks. After almost 8 miles a spur road, MA 2A, turns south (left) and leads 0.5 mile into the tidy hamlet of **Shelburne Falls.** This 1768 village, named for Salmon Falls and the second Earl of Shelburne, straddles the Deerfield River. It once had a hill-farm economy, but now relies on tourism along with local dairy farms and maple sugaring houses for sustenance. Linus Yale constructed his first Yale locks here in 1851. Its Victorian-style downtown, relatively unchanged since the turn of the last century, is lined with attractive shops, art galleries, and restaurants.

The unusual **Bridge of Flowers** is the main attraction that every Mohawk traveler wants to see at Shelburne Falls. An abandoned 398-foot-long, five-arch trolley bridge, now reserved for pedestrians, is decorated with more than 500 flower species that bloom from spring to fall. The local Shelburne Women's Club cultivates the beautiful and prolific gardens as a war memorial with an ingenious use of the defunct bridge. The bridge actually links Shelburne Falls with the neighboring township of Buckland.

The town's other major attraction is the glacial potholes chiseled into the bedrock by the swirling Deerfield River. The symmetrical potholes, ranging from a few inches to more than 40 feet in diameter, formed over thousands of years when the river, laden with melted glacial water and sediments, scoured and polished holes into the metamorphic rock with tumbling cobbles and boulders. The smooth bedrock here is a popular sunning and swimming area on hot summer days.

Back on the drive, the highway reaches its junction with Massachusetts Highway 112 just past Shelburne Falls. A left turn on MA 112 leads to the placid 1779 village of Buckland, with a classic church, some lovely 1700s houses, and a small museum. A right turn on MA 112 winds up a pretty valley lined with apple orchards and rolling farms to Colrain. This small village, basically a church, post office, and town hall with a scattering of homes, is the site of the first school to fly the American flag, an old foundry, and a small covered bridge on Lyonsville Road (one of four nineteenth-century bridges in Massachusetts). Catamount State Forest, a 1,125-acre parkland, lies north of here. This hilly country offers streams, marshes, a forty-seven-acre pond, and 5 miles of hiking trails.

Along Deerfield River

From here, the scenic drive route heads west up the deepening valley. The Deerfield River runs deep and still through this section, its calm waters reflecting trees, sky, and clouds. About 7 miles from Shelburne Falls, the drive reaches Charlemont, a snug town along the river's fertile floodplain. This largely rural village was first settled in 1749, when it was known as Chickley's Town and, later, Charley Mount. The Charlemont Historical Society Museum in the town hall displays local memorabilia. The A. L. Avery & Son General Store has been open since 1861.

The Cold River flows over cobbles in Mohawk Trail State Forest.

White clapboard homes with grassy yards studded with snowball bushes line the highway. Nearby is the rebuilt Bissel Covered Bridge over the Deerfield River. The hills across the valley harbor Berkshire East Ski Resort and its 1,180-foot vertical drop, forty-five trails, and plenty of beginner and intermediate terrain. The Deerfield River in this area offers some of Massachusetts's best trout fishing as well as a challenging 10-mile raft run over Class II and III rapids.

Just past Charlemont, the drive intersects Massachusetts Highway 8A, which heads south into the heart of the Berkshire Hills. The road continues west past an old farm amid cornfields and, a mile later, a roadside rest area with picnic tables beside the river. A historical marker here remembers the Shunpike, the nation's first toll-free "interstate" road, which followed the river. The site is dedicated to "the thrifty travelers of the Mohawk Trail who forded the Deerfield River here in 1797 rather than pay a toll at the turnpike bridge." This protest helped win the battle for free travel on Massachusetts roads by 1810. Adjacent to the marker is an old cemetery with the remains of many area pioneer families.

The highway crosses the river on the Mohawk Indian Bridge and reaches **Mohawk Park** and its landmark bronze sculpture of a Mohawk with upraised arms on the opposite bank. The statue, placed atop a nine-ton boulder in 1932, honors the five Indian nations that regularly used the Mohawk Trail. An arrowhead-shaped tablet at the base reads: "Hail to the Sunrise—In Memory of the Mohawk Indian." The valleys that the highway now follows through the northern Berkshire Hills were once traversed by a centuries-old Indian trail leading from the fertile Connecticut Valley to the Mohawk and Hudson River Valleys in New York. This trail was used in 1663 by a warring party of Pocumtuck Indians who invaded Mohawk territory in today's New York. Dutch settlers in Albany forged an uneasy peace between the sides, but when Mohawk Chief Saheda was murdered on the trail en route to signing the treaty, the enraged Mohawks retaliated by killing all the Pocumtuck warriors and thus eradicating the tribe.

Later pioneers traversed the Mohawk Trail from the Massachusetts Bay Colony to the Dutch settlements in New York. Their trail grew into a wagon route and then the toll-free Shunpike Road. The Mohawk Trail highway opened on September 1, 1914, and was the first designated scenic auto route in the United States.

Across the Berkshire Plateau

The highway continues west, leaving the Deerfield River and entering a narrow gorge carved by the Cold River through **Mohawk Trail State Forest.** The 6,457-acre forest, straddling river and highway, adjoins 10,500-acre Savoy Mountain State Forest to the west, forming the largest slice of undeveloped land in Massachusetts. A mile into the park is a forty-five-site campground on the north side of the river. Several hiking trails also begin here. The highway follows the narrowing valley, twisting alongside the river as it tumbles and pools over cobbles and boulders.

A dense canopy of trees, including maple, birch, and beech, clots the steep mountain slopes and encloses the asphalt in a green embrace. An abundant understory of azalea, raspberry, wild rose, and mountain laurel blankets the forest floor. Occasional pullouts allow access to the river for trout fishermen and photographers. The Black Brook Road twists south from the canyon and, after a couple of miles, intersects Tannery Road. It then tracks west into Savoy Mountain State Forest and a 0.5-mile, blue-blazed trail that leads to Tannery Falls. This beautiful falls, tucked into a narrow defile, cascades and drops 80 feet over cliffs and ledges to a placid pool.

After a few miles the highway leaves the Cold River Valley and begins steeply climbing northwest onto the broad, wooded flank of Hoosac Mountain. The road ascends 1,200 feet in the next couple of miles to Whitcomb Summit, the highway's 2,173-foot high point. Here, along with an inn and cottages, is a bronze elk statue and a stone tower that offers far-ranging views. To the north stretch Vermont's Green Mountains. Mount Monadnock, an isolated New Hampshire landmark, sits on the northeast horizon. The rolling Berkshire Hills unfold to the south, and Mount Greylock looms to the west.

The drive, now atop the Berkshire plateau, next runs through Florida. This small village, ironically one of the state's coldest places, was founded in 1805 just after the United States purchased Florida from Spain. To reach a great viewpoint north of the drive, go 1 mile past Whitcomb Summit. Turn north (right) on Tilda Hill Road and follow it to a sign that says "Raycroft Lookout." A one-lane track leads down to a short trail, which in turn leads to a lofty and sweeping viewpoint perched high above the Deerfield River Valley.

Just up the highway is Central Shaft Road, which goes south for 4 miles to Savoy Mountain State Forest. Below the drive route is the **Hoosac Railroad Tunnel,** one of the great engineering feats of the nineteenth century. The 4.7-mile railroad tunnel, completed in 1873, opened an easy rail route from Boston to Albany and points west by boring through Hoosac Mountain's solid rock base. The epic construction of the tunnel, nicknamed "Bloody Pit," required twenty-four years of labor, the lives of 196 men, $15 million dollars, and the new explosive nitroglycerin.

Back on the Mohawk Trail, continue to **Western Summit.** Here is the third lookout tower on the route and a marvelous aerial view of Mount Greylock towering above the green valley of the Hoosic River and the patchwork quilt of farms surrounding North Adams. From the overlook the highway bends north and sharply descends from the 1,000-foot-high escarpment on the western edge of the northern Berkshire Hills. Almost 4 miles from Whitcomb Summit, the highway wheels slowly around the famed and scenic Hairpin Turn and a restaurant at its head. The road edges 3 more miles down the Hoosac Mountain wall to North Adams, the bustling commercial hub of northwestern Massachusetts.

North Adams and Mount Greylock

Settled in 1737 and incorporated in 1878, **North Adams** has long been a busy blue-collar town with paper and textile mills along the Hoosic River. The factory town, part of the state's industrial backbone, thrived after the completion of the Hoosac Tunnel, connecting it with Boston and its port. More than 60 percent of Boston's trade came through North Adams and the tunnel by 1895, causing the town to proclaim itself "the western gateway." Most of that industry and its jobs have now passed, and the city relies on a diverse economic base. Fort Massachusetts, a frontier outpost built in 1745, sat just west of today's town and protected the area from marauding Indian attacks—and kept Hudson River Dutch settlers from living in the area. The French and Indians torched the fort in 1746, but it was rebuilt the next year.

The drive enters North Adams, passing old brick mills and warehouses built in the nineteenth century and the tall spires of churches, including the brick St. Francis of Assisi Church. Beaver Mill, an 1833 mill on Beaver Street, is a historic landmark. The Western Gateway Heritage State Park, just south of MA 2 in the old city railroad yard, offers a glimpse into local railroad and industrial history. A large display details the construction and economic impact of the Hoosac Tunnel and includes a replica of a tunnel section complete with dripping water, the sounds of picks against stone, and the deafening explosion and flash of nitroglycerin. Other basic tools used in the tunnel's excavation are seen, including plumb bobs and sighting transits. Amazingly, when the two ends of the almost 5-mile tunnel met midmountain, the alignment error was less than 1 inch. The museum is housed in old railroad buildings and surrounded by renovated shops and restaurants.

North Adams also boasts the **Massachusetts Museum of Contemporary Art,** usually called MASS MoCA, in the nineteenth-century former Sprague Electric Works Factory building. The museum, with art and sculpture galleries and performing arts venues, is considered one of the largest and finest contemporary art museums in the world.

The highway passes the North Adams downtown area and a junction with MA 8. A right turn on MA 8 leads north a short distance to **Natural Bridge State Park,** a forty-eight-acre parkland with a marble natural bridge arching over a narrow, 60-foot-deep chasm. The road twists through the western side of town, passing old houses with steep yards and a sprawling cemetery holding the remains of some of the Hoosac Tunnel fatalities.

Look for Notch Road on the edge of town, which is the turnoff for this scenic drive's summit side-trip. Turn south (left) on the road and work uphill through houses. The road quickly leaves town and begins a meandering, 9-mile course up the north and west flank of **Mount Greylock,** the 3,491-foot rooftop of the Commonwealth of Massachusetts.

Greylock is a magnificent mountain standing high and aloof over verdant river valleys and towns that skirt its wooded slopes. The isolated peak, separated from the Berkshire Hills by the Hoosac Valley, sits on the eastern edge of the narrow Taconic Mountains. This distinct range runs along the New York border from northern Connecticut to the midsection of Vermont. The centerpiece of the 12,500-acre **Mount Greylock State Reservation,** the mountain has its own climate because of its height and exposure. Fog and clouds often shroud its windy summit, while heavy rain and snow storms sweep across its wooded slopes.

The road to the top is hemmed in by hardwood forest and climbs steeply. Occasional glades of grass and wildflowers break the woods. After a mile the road enters the park and passes through a beautiful forest of birch floored with ferns. A drive up Mount Greylock is like a telescoped journey to northern Canada's boreal forests. The woodland is initially composed of the northern hardwoods, including yellow and paper birches, and American beech with some hemlock and white pine. Mountain maple, ash, and small shrubs grow higher, above the 3,000-foot level. And finally, near the summit, is the taiga conifer forest of red spruce and balsam fir.

As the narrow lane works its way upward, you may get glimpses of the lower mountains and valleys between tree trunks. The road crosses the white-blazed

Dense woodlands surround the narrow road to the top of Mount Greylock, Massachusetts's highest point.

Appalachian Trail and a day-use parking area for hikers before spiraling up to the mountaintop. A pygmy forest of windswept balsam fir, its branches flagging east away from the prevailing westerly wind, borders the road near the summit. The road emerges at last on the broad summit and a one-way loop. Paved parking areas here allow access to viewpoints, trails, Bascom Lodge, and the War Memorial Tower. The stone lodge, built in 1937, welcomes overnight visitors and hikers. The 92-foot War Memorial Tower, honoring the state's men killed in wars, pokes high above the summit plateau. A clear day offers a startling view of five states.

A road continues south from the top, dropping 2 miles to a thirty-five-site campground and 7 miles to the park visitor center. The reservation comprises more than 35 miles of trails, including an 11-mile segment of the long-distance Appalachian Trail. This drive section is open only from May through October, depending on snowfall and snowmelt.

Williamstown

To continue the main scenic drive, return back down Notch Road to MA 2 in North Adams and turn west (left). The last section of the drive runs 4 miles from North Adams to the colonial village of Williamstown. The highway passes through the western outskirts of North Adams, a strip of houses, an old mill, and factory outlets. Outside town it rolls across the broad Hoosac Valley and enters **Williamstown,** the ideal New England college town and home of prestigious Williams College.

Williamstown was established in 1753 by soldiers from nearby Fort Massachusetts, who named it West Hoosuck. Settlers were required to own five acres and to build a house that measured at least 15 by 18 feet. Colonel Ephraim Williams, the fort commander and one of the first settlers, wrote a bequest in his will in 1755 to found a free school stipulating that it was in the Massachusetts Bay Colony and the town be renamed for him. Two months later he was ambushed and killed during the French and Indian War, but the terms of his will and the establishment of the college couldn't be carried out until 1791 when a forty-year border dispute between Massachusetts and New York was finally settled. The college and town were then named for their early benefactor. Williams College has since acquired a reputation as one of the nation's finest liberal arts schools with a beautiful campus and a small student body. The college's fine Federal and Georgian-style buildings, many dating from late colonial times, surround the town's village green at the end of the drive.

Williams College is the cultural center of western Massachusetts with two excellent art museums. The free **Sterling and Francine Clark Art Institute** is one of the best small museums in the entire United States, with an extraordinary collection that rivals most big-city museums. The institute harbors the nation's largest collection of nineteenth-century French paintings, including eight works by Corot, eight by Monet, and thirty by Renoir. Medieval works include the exquisite *Virgin and Child Enthroned with Four Angels* by Piero della Francesca. The American canvas collection boasts a dozen works by John Singer Sargent as well as work by Frederic Remington, Mary Cassatt, John Kensett, and ten paintings by renowned Maine artist Winslow Homer. The diverse collection came to Williamstown in the 1950s after the Clarks felt that the town and their art would be safe in the event of nuclear war. Nearby is the Williams College Museum of Art, another free museum, with a permanent collection of some 11,000 pieces.

The Williamstown village green, surrounded by the college buildings, is the end point of this scenic drive. It is a good place to park and roam around town. A nearby tourist office can provide maps and brochures. On Main Street is a 1753 house, built to the original zoning specifications for settling in West Hoosuck and constructed with the period tools and materials. The Williamstown Theatre Festival, one of New England's great summer theaters, offers more than 200 performances every July and August in the 521-seat Adams Memorial Theater. West of town is Taconic Trail State Park and the college's Hopkins Memorial Forest, a 2,500-acre nature reserve laced with trails. The Hoosic River offers both canoeing and fishing opportunities. To connect up with the Berkshire Hills Scenic Drive to the south (see Scenic Drive 7), head out of Williamstown on U.S. Highway 7 and follow this scenic road south to Pittsfield.

9

Southern Green Mountains Scenic Drive

General description: This 69-mile drive explores the southern Green Mountains, the northern Taconic Mountains, and the Vermont Valley.

Special attractions: Green Mountain National Forest, Big Branch Wilderness Area, Hapgood Pond Recreation Area, Batten Kill River, Long Trail, Bromley Ski Area, Manchester villages, Hildene, American Museum of Fly Fishing, Southern Vermont Arts Center, Dorset, Dorset Playhouse, Merck Forest and Farmland Center, Pawlet, Danby, fly fishing, hiking, camping, bicycling, downhill skiing, cross-country skiing, picnicking.

Location: West-central Vermont.

Drive route numbers: U.S. Highway 7, Forest Road 10, Vermont Highways 11, 30, 315, 153, and 133.

Travel season: The lower-elevation roads are open year-round. Expect snow and icy conditions in winter. Most of FR 10 is closed in winter. Avoid during the spring mud season.

Camping: Emerald Lake State Park off US 7 between Manchester and Danby offers 105 campsites. Hapgood Pond Campground north of Peru has twenty-eight campsites. Several private campgrounds are found along the drive.

Services: All services in Danby, Manchester area, Dorset, and Pawlet. Limited and seasonal services are found in other towns along the drive.

Nearby attractions: Emerald Lake State Park, Mount Equinox Sky Line Drive, Bennington, Shaftsbury State Park, Coolidge Homestead, Middlebury, Middlebury Gap, Lake Champlain, Stephen Douglas birthplace, Quechee Gorge, Mount Ascutney State Park, Gifford Woods State Park, Woodstock.

The Drive

The two-part, 69-mile Southern Green Mountains Scenic Drive explores a remote slice of the Green Mountains before dipping across the Vermont Valley at Manchester and driving a series of pastoral back roads through the northern Taconic Mountains along the New York border. The roads traverse a wide variety of topography, including broad valleys, intimate vales, and densely wooded mountains. Foliage season is excellent along this drive. The first drive segment, a narrow dirt road in Green Mountain National Forest, is passable only during the summer and autumn months. The rest of the drive is open year-round.

Danby to Devil's Den

The drive begins at **Danby,** a crossroads village between Manchester and Rutland. This quaint village nestles at the northern end of the Vermont Valley along U.S.

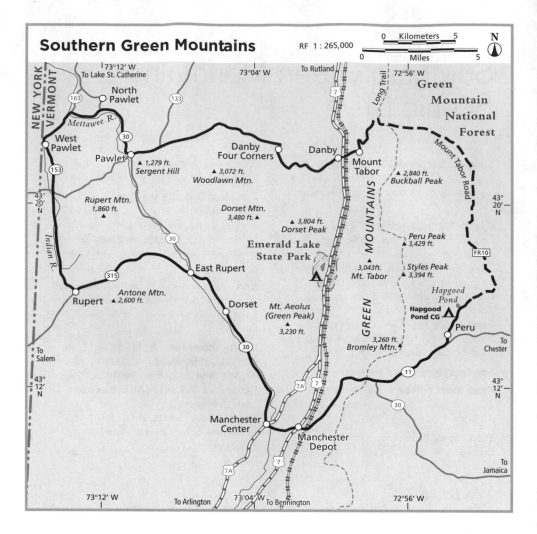

RF 1 : 265,000

0   Kilometers   5

N

0   Miles   5

NEW YORK

VERMONT

73°12′ W
To Lake St. Catherine

73°04′ W

To Rutland

72°56′ W

163

North
Pawlet

133

Mettawee R.

7

Long Trail

**Green
Mountain
National
Forest**

West
Pawlet

30

Danby
Four Corners

Danby

Mount Tabor Road

Pawlet

▲ 1,279 ft.
Sergent Hill

▲ 3,072 ft.
Woodlawn Mtn.

Mount
Tabor

▲ 2,840 ft.
Buckball Peak

153

43°
20′
N

Indian R.

Rupert Mtn.
1,860 ft.
▲

Dorset Mtn.
3,480 ft. ▲

▲ 3,804 ft.
Dorset Peak

43°
20′
N

30

**Emerald Lake
State Park**

Peru Peak
▲ 3,429 ft.

FR10

315

East Rupert

▲
3,043ft.
Mt. Tabor

Styles Peak
▲ 3,394 ft.

GREEN

MOUNTAINS

GREEN

*Hapgood
Pond*

Rupert

Antone Mtn.
▲ 2,600 ft.

Dorset

Mt. Aeolus
(Green Peak)
▲
3,230 ft.

Hapgood
Pond CG

Peru

To
Salem

30

3,260 ft.
Bromley Mtn. ▲

To
Chester

43°
12′
N

7A

7

11

43°
12′
N

30

Manchester
Center

Manchester
Depot

To
Jamaica

7A

7

73°12′ W

To Arlington

73°04′ W
To Bennington

72°56′ W

Highway 7, and offers antiques stores, an inn, and a general store. Settled by Quakers in the 1760s, Danby prospered with the dairy industry, lumbering, and marble quarrying, but now relies on tourists for its trade. The town boasts Vermont's first home-grown millionaire. Native son Silas Griffith, born here in 1837, amassed a fortune as a lumber baron after selling his Danby store. His sprawling empire included more than 55,000 acres of timber, twelve sawmills, and holdings in Kansas, Washington, and California. Part of Griffith's local legacy still includes Christmas gifts for town children. Nobel Prize–winning novelist Pearl S. Buck settled here in the 1960s, buying local properties and renovating them after US 7 bypassed the town center.

The scenic drive begins by turning east from US 7 at Danby onto Forest Road 10. The road bumps across railroad tracks, crosses Otter Creek, and after 0.5 mile passes a few homes in the tiny village of Mount Tabor at the base of the Green Mountains. This town, the story goes, was called Griffith for wealthy landholder Silas Griffith between 1891 and 1905 after mail coming to town listed its name as Griffith. It was originally a center for Griffith's charcoal industry before becoming a marble center. Even today, Vermont's largest marble quarry operates at nearby Mount Tabor.

The drive's first segment traverses 19 miles along FR 10 (Mount Tabor Road), a narrow paved and dirt track that climbs to the crest of the Green Mountains before dropping south along rounded ridges to Peru and Vermont Highway 11. This scenic road, flanked by Big Branch and Peru wilderness areas, runs through some of Vermont's most rugged and remote landscapes. The still-paved road exits Mount Tabor at the base of the mountain range and begins a long uphill ascent. Signs warn motorists to be alert for logging trucks. After a mile the road enters 36,400-acre **White Rocks National Recreation Area,** where a roadside kiosk offers information and a locator map.

The road swings across Big Branch Creek, a rushing stream that tumbles over worn boulders and cobbles, then begins a steady switchbacking ascent up a steep hillside blanketed with birch trees. Eventually the road bends onto the northern flank of Big Branch's deep gorge and edges northeast above abrupt dropoffs. **Big Branch Picnic Area** perches on the hillside at 2.7 miles. The area offers stunning views of Big Branch Valley below and the high peaks of the southern Green Mountains. A trail drops south into the canyon from here, enticing anglers with some of Vermont's best trout-fishing opportunities.

The narrow paved road continues to climb above the gorge before beginning to flatten at 3 miles. The Appalachian/Long Trail crosses the road here, and a small parking area for hikers lies just past the trail crossing. At 3.4 miles the pavement ends and the narrow road becomes dirt and gravel. Watch for mud and slippery sections during wet weather for the road's duration. The road rises over rounded ridges dense with conifers and hardwoods and dips through shallow valleys filled with beaver ponds, trickling brooks, swamps, and moose stomps. An abandoned apple orchard that gave fruit to some early homesteader sits alongside the road at 6.4 miles. Early Vermont was heavily populated with hill farmers who decimated the state's original forests for building material, firewood, and arable land. Foresters say 75 percent of Vermont's forests were cut then. Today, 75 percent of the state is forest again.

Steep, bouldery slopes and roadcuts rear above the road as it slowly descends southeastward. One of the best is **Devil's Den**—broken rocky outcrops in a narrow saddle just past the 8-mile mark. Occasional views of surrounding knolls are seen from open valleys.

Looking down into Big Branch Valley near the crest of the Green Mountains.

Hapgood Pond and Peru

The drive leaves the national recreation area at 8.4 miles and drops south alongside Mount Tabor Brook, a small brook riffling over boulders. The road leaves Green Mountain National Forest at 13.1 miles, passes some beaver ponds, then reaches homes and open fields. Beyond a right turn and an old cemetery, the drive swings through the small, picturesque village of 1,300-foot-high North Landgrove. The townsite was originally settled by William Utley in 1769. At 14.8 miles the road makes a sharp right turn, crosses Utley and Griffith Brooks in a shallow, open valley and rises into a dense forest.

The road becomes paved again at 16 miles, near where **Hapgood Pond Recreation Area** sits off to the right in the woods. This area, acquired in 1931 for the infant Green Mountain National Forest, offers swimming, boating, and fishing on seven-acre Hapgood Pond. A picnic area and twenty-eight-site campground also accommodate visitors. A couple of miles north of here is Wild Wings Ski Touring Center with plentiful snow atop the range crest and more than 25 kilometers of trails.

The road runs southwest into **Peru,** a serene and graceful town on the eastern flank of 3,260-foot Bromley Mountain. The town was established in 1773. Neat white houses line the road here. Peru's square-towered Congregational Church was built in 1846. Another point of interest is the J. J. Hapgood Store, built in 1827. The first drive section ends at FR 10's junction with VT 11. Turn west (right) on VT 11 toward Manchester for the next 8-mile segment of this scenic drive.

The highway rolls southwest, traversing rounded ridges to Bromley Ski Area. Begun in 1937, the ski area is one of New England's oldest ski resorts. Its mountain offers forty-three trails with a vertical drop of 1,334 feet, snowmaking capabilities, and lots of amenities. Hapgood State Forest perches atop Bromley Mountain north of the ski area and highway. Allowing far-reaching views to the south, the drive climbs west to the crest of the Green Mountains before beginning a long, steep descent into the Vermont Valley and Manchester. A scenic viewpoint partway down yields great views of the valley below. The highway quickly drops to cross US 7 and enters Manchester.

Manchester

Manchester has long been Vermont's most exclusive and trendy resort. The town is itself a collection of several villages, including Manchester Center, Manchester Depot, and Manchester Village. The area's gorgeous mountain scenery, sparkling rivers and brooks, winter snowfalls, clear air, and mineral springs began attracting visitors in the mid-nineteenth century, although the town was chartered in 1761. Urbanites flocked to Manchester to bathe in the salubrious, sulfuric waters for good health and long life. The posh, white-pillared Equinox House hotel became

one of the East's fashionable spas in the nineteenth century and today is the refur-
bished centerpiece of the Manchester Village Historic District on the town's southern outskirts.

This genteel, historic town with colonial mansions and marble sidewalks is
also a booming, upscale shopping center with dozens of outlet shops for shrewd
bargain hunters. Visitors flock here to dine in trendy restaurants and cruise
designer stores for labels such as Ralph Lauren, Izod, Timberland, and Calvin
Klein. A couple of fine bookstores—Northshire Bookstore and Johnny Appleseed
Bookshop—offer plenty of material to peruse.

The Manchester area is renowned for its superb trout streams. The town itself
is the home of the Orvis Company, a famed manufacturer of fly-fishing rods and
tackle begun in the 1850s by Charles Orvis, whose brother Franklin founded
Equinox House. The store, located on US 7A, offers split bamboo rods, reels, flies,
and other equipment. Buyers can test gear in a pool out back. The shop also offers
the Orvis Fly Fishing School from April through August. Manchester is also home
to the **American Museum of Fly Fishing,** displaying historic rods and reels from
famed Americans including President Dwight D. Eisenhower, Daniel Webster,
Ernest Hemingway, and Bing Crosby, as well as colorful hand-tied flies. The Batten
Kill River, considered by many anglers to be Vermont's and perhaps New England's

The village of Manchester nestles against Vermont's Green Mountains.

prime trout stream, meanders south down the Vermont Valley through Manchester and Arlington.

Manchester's many other attractions include Hildene, the spacious estate of Robert Todd Lincoln, Abraham Lincoln's only surviving son, and the Southern Vermont Arts Center. Hildene is an impressive, twenty-four-room Georgian Revival manor on 412 valley acres. The historic mansion was bought after Mary Lincoln Beckwith's death in 1975 and preserved as a museum. Visitors can tour the house and its formal gardens, and perhaps hear a demonstration of its thousand-pipe organ. Robert Todd Lincoln first came here as a boy before the president's death and later returned to build this splendid summer retreat during his career as an attorney, diplomat, and Cabinet member. He died here in 1926.

An excellent side-trip from Manchester is the 5-mile **Sky Line Drive** toll road up 3,825-foot Mount Equinox in the Taconic Mountains southeast of town. The summit offers stunning views of southern Vermont, New Hampshire, Massachusetts, and New York.

Dorset and Rupert

The main scenic drive route winds through Manchester, turns north on Vermont Highway 30, then quickly leaves homes, churches, and outlet stores behind. The highway runs northwest along the West Branch of the Batten Kill River up a broad valley past pastures filled with grazing sheep, horses, and geese. High, wooded mountains flank the valley, with 2,535-foot Owls Head looming to the east and 3,290-foot Mother Myrick Mountain and Bear Mountain rising to the west in the main Taconic Range.

The road runs through South Dorset before entering **Dorset,** a charming village at an elevation of 962 feet that could be rightly called the birthplace of Vermont. Originally settled in 1768, the town was the meeting place of the Green Mountain Boys in 1776 when they declared their independence from New York, the New Hampshire Grants, and England. Meeting at Cephas Kent's tavern, these founding fathers of the state agreed at their first convention "to defend by arms the United American States against the hostile attempts of the British fleets and armies until the present unhappy controversy between the two countries shall be settled."

Mount Aeolus above the town is the site of the first commercial marble quarry in the United States, established by Isaac Underhill in 1785. Dorset is a picturesque, well-preserved village with an affluent population. The Dorset Inn, a national historic site, is reputed to be Vermont's oldest operating hostelry, and the Dorset Playhouse is one of New England's most popular summer theaters. The drive quickly swings through town, passing large homes, the town center, and a golf course.

Outside town the road crosses the wide, flat valley to East Rupert. Turn west (left) off VT 30 here onto Vermont Highway 315. The next 6-mile leg of your route heads west up a narrowing valley flanked by wooded hills. Slowly the road narrows and climbs through dense forest past occasional houses. After 3 miles it crests a ridge. The turnoff to the **Merck Forest and Farmland Center** is here. This pristine 3,130-acre nature center offers trails, picnic sites, a spring-fed swimming hole, interpretive talks, a visitor center, a farming museum, and a working sugarhouse. The visitor center lies 0.5 mile south of the highway.

From the ridge the highway drops steeply. Antone Mountain, a 2,600-foot wooded knoll, looms to the south above open fields. Slowly the degree of descent lessens. A couple of miles later, the road enters the town of Rupert. Nestled in a peaceful valley near the New York border, **Rupert** is famed as the site of Vermont's first and only mint. When Vermont was still an independent republic before joining the United States, the legislature gave Ruben Harmon exclusive permission to mint copper coins. The mint, built on Mill Brook, smelted copper, rolled, cut, and stamped the new coins. The first coins were pressed with the words "Vermontensium Res Publica," the date 1786, and images of a plow and a mountain sunrise. Rupert remains a tidy town with old white homes and the simple Congregational Church.

Rupert to Danby

Turn north (right) on Vermont Highway 153 in Rupert. The highway runs north for 7 miles up the Indian River in a shallow valley. The broad valley floor holds open pastures and cornfields flanked by low wooded hills. After a few miles the road winds into the hills and through farmland to West Pawlet, a small village perched on the New York border. The town center is marked by a flagpole atop a granite marker. Deep slate quarries lie in the hills just east of town, surrounded by slag heaps or filled with water. The highway bends northeast out of West Pawlet and crosses open pastures before dropping down to the lovely Mettawee Valley where, 2.5 miles later, it rejoins VT 30.

Turn right on VT 30 and drive south up the valley past prosperous farms. Hills embrace the valley. Among these is rugged 1,919-foot Haystack Mountain with dark cliffs banding its flank. A few miles later the drive reaches **Pawlet.** This village nestles in Flower Brook's narrow valley at its confluence with the Mettawee River. Town Hill (to the north) and Sargent Hill (to the south) hem the town and valley. This now quiet town once rivaled Rutland as an industrial center. As far back as 1830, Pawlet bustled with mills and factories, including Vermont's first cheese factory. Before that the town was a hive of rebellion in the Revolution. Herrick's Rangers, the "Terror of the Tories," were organized here in 1777. Stop in at the General Store for a look through a glass-topped counter at Flower Brook beneath the floorboards. The brook is harnessed to a turbine to generate the store's electricity.

Follow the last 11 miles of this scenic drive by heading east from Pawlet on Vermont Highway 133. The highway heads up a broadening valley floored by dairy farms, hayfields, and pastures. At an intersection reached a mile east of Pawlet, continue straight on a narrow road instead of turning left on VT 133. The road climbs gently eastward on the south side of the Flower Brook valley. Lofty 3,072-foot Woodlawn Mountain, a northern outpost of the Taconic Mountains, rises to the southeast, while low wooded knolls block the northern horizon. The road dips and rolls over low ridges, running alternately through forest and field to the residential village of Danby Four Corners. This small settlement lies on a sloping plateau studded with farms. The village churchyard keeps many interesting old tombstones dating back to the American Revolution.

Turn right in town and follow the road southeast through thick woods for a mile into Mill Brook's narrow canyon. The high, rounded knob of 3,804-foot Dorset Peak towers to the south. The drive's last 2 miles wind down the steep narrow gorge before entering Danby. The road then drops through town to US 7 and the drive's terminus. Emerald Lake State Park, with 105 campsites, lies a few miles south.

10

Quechee-Coolidge Scenic Drive

General description: A 61-mile open loop that passes through picturesque villages and hilly countryside in the Piedmont of central Vermont.

Special attractions: Quechee Gorge State Park, Woodstock, Billings Farm and Museum, Coolidge State Park, Calvin Coolidge Homestead and Birthplace, Plymouth Notch Historic District, Plymouth Cheese Corporation, Killington Ski Area, Gifford Woods State Park, White River National Fish Hatchery, historic sites, shopping, hiking, old-growth forests, downhill skiing, cross-country skiing, camping, autumn foliage.

Location: East-central Vermont.

Drive route numbers: U.S. Highway 4, Vermont Highways 100A, 100, and 107.

Travel season: Year-round.

Camping: Mid-May to Columbus Day only. Quechee Gorge State Park on US 4 has forty-seven campsites and seven lean-to sites. Coolidge State Park offers twenty-five campsites and thirty-five lean-to sites. Gifford Woods State Park has twenty-seven campsites and twenty-one lean-to sites. Silver Lake State Park, 10 miles north of Woodstock off Vermont Highway 12, has forty campsites and seven lean-to sites mid-May through Labor Day.

Services: All services in White River Junction, Quechee, Woodstock, and Sherburne Center. Limited and seasonal services in other towns along the drive.

Nearby attractions: Green Mountain National Forest, Batten Kill River, Manchester Center, Hildene, Mount Ascutney State Park, Saint-Gaudens National Historic Site (NH), Middlebury, Middlebury Gap, Joseph Smith Monument, Thetford Hill State Park, Connecticut River.

The Drive

The 61-mile Quechee-Coolidge Scenic Drive passes through some of Vermont's finest landscapes. This land, part of the New England Uplands or Piedmont, is a plateaulike region of low, rolling hills incised by river valleys. The drive offers not only superb scenic views but also a good look at rural Vermont and its sleepy country villages, the abrupt Quechee Gorge, gentrified Woodstock, historic Plymouth and the birthplace of President Calvin Coolidge, and the central Green Mountains.

Quechee Gorge

The drive begins off Interstate 89 in the White River Valley just upriver from White River Junction and the Connecticut River. Take U.S. Highway 4 at exit 1 on the interstate 3 miles west of Interstate 91. US 4, running west from here to Rutland, is

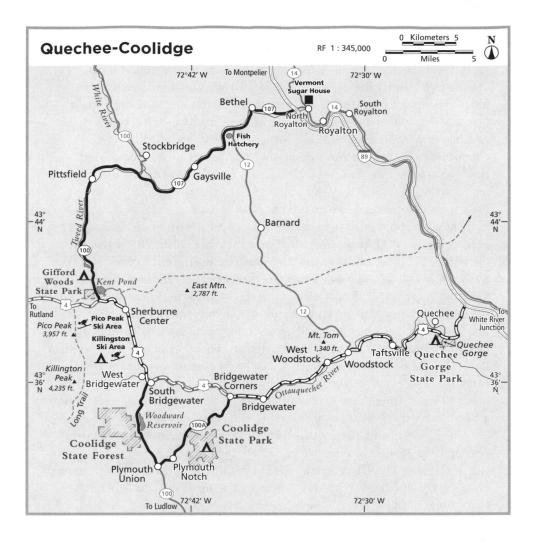

Quechee-Coolidge

RF 1 : 345,000

0 Kilometers 5

0 Miles 5

N

To Montpelier 14
Vermont Sugar House
72°42' W 72°30' W

Bethel 107
North Royalton
Royalton
South Royalton 14

White River

100
Stockbridge
Fish Hatchery

89

Pittsfield 107 Gaysville 12

43°44' N

Tweed River 100

Barnard

43°44' N

Gifford Woods State Park
Kent Pond
East Mtn. 2,787 ft.

To Rutland 4
Pico Peak 3,957 ft.
Pico Peak Ski Area
Sherburne Center
Killingston Ski Area

Quechee
To White River Junction

12

Mt. Tom 1,340 ft.

4

Quechee Gorge

Killington Peak 4,235 ft.
4
West Bridgewater
South Bridgewater
Bridgewater Corners 4
West Woodstock
Woodstock
Taftsville
Quechee Gorge State Park

43°36' N

Long Trail
Woodward Reservoir
100A
Bridgewater

Ottauquechee River

43°36' N

Coolidge State Forest
Coolidge State Park

Plymouth Union
Plymouth Notch

100
72°42' W 72°30' W
To Ludlow

Vermont's principal east-west thoroughfare and one of its busiest highways. Semi-trucks laden with goods, skiers' cars topped with gear, leaf-peeper buses, and local farm traffic all conspire to overload the narrow highway. Use care and caution on the US 4 section of this drive. The highway closely follows the old right-of-way of the Woodstock Railroad between White River and Woodstock. Operating from 1875 to 1933, the railroad carried vacationers to posh Woodstock until diminishing traffic, a flood, and the new highway forced its closure.

The highway bends south away from the White River Valley and after 4 miles reaches **Quechee Gorge State Park,** one of Vermont's best-loved natural wonders. The abrupt 165-foot-deep gorge, nicknamed "Vermont's Little Grand Canyon," is a mile-long chasm excavated by the Ottauquechee River. The gorge's cliffs and slabs, densely blanketed with trees and foliage, are formed by greenschist and quartzite in the Devonian-age Gile Mountain Formation. Quechee Gorge began forming a mere 13,000 years ago at the end of the Wisconsin glaciation when an immense ice sheet that covered New England began to melt. As the ice melted, the water drained into Lake Hitchcock, a long lake formed by a gravel moraine-dam near today's Hartford, Connecticut. Later the gravel dam was breached and the lake drained. The Ottauquechee River, instead of following its ancestral course to the east, began cutting through soft lake bottom sediments and soon became entrenched in the erosion-resistant metamorphic bedrock. The trapped river slowly gnawed away at the formidable bedrock with the powerful rush of meltwater, excavating Vermont's deepest and most spectacular river gorge. The gorge's present level was reached about 6,000 years ago.

The gorge is protected in Quechee Gorge State Park. An overlook lies near a parking area at the **Quechee Gorge Bridge,** a 1911 steel railway bridge that spans the ravine. A popular and airy view can be seen by walking out to the bridge's center. Another lookout and picnic area sit on the gorge's west rim. A pleasant 1.25-mile trail threads along the gorge's east rim and descends to the canyon floor to the south. A variety of plants and trees are seen in the gorge, including beech, red maple, sugar maple, white pine, and hemlock, the dominant tree that thrives in this cool, wet climate. A series of small waterfalls and scoured potholes lie south of the bridge. Hikers entering the gorge should be very careful since the riverbank rocks can be slick and treacherous. Anglers often trek into the gorge seeking rainbow and brown trout in the river's furious whitewater. A pleasant state-run campground with sixty sites sits among towering white pines just east of the bridge.

The highway bends northwest away from the gorge and runs through strip development—houses, antiques shops, motels, and gas stations—outside the village of Quechee. The village is now mostly a mish-mash of condos and vacation homes in the Quechee Lakes resort. The best attraction here is the Simon Pearce Glass Works in an old mill run by hydroelectric power. Stop by and watch a glassblower shape the vases, jugs, goblets, and other functional glassware sold in the showroom. Look for "seconds," sold at a discount.

Woodstock

Past Quechee, US 4 meanders west through green hills along the south bank of the river for 6 miles to Woodstock. Along the way, at the small village of Taftsville, lies the red **Taftsville Covered Bridge** spanning the Ottauquechee River at a small waterfall and dam. The picturesque bridge, with two spans totaling 190 feet, was built in 1836 by Solomon Emmons. The scenic drive arcs around Blake Hill and almost 3 miles later enters the famed town of Woodstock.

Woodstock is a genteel and elegant town that straddles the river valley between the rounded knobs of Mount Tom and Mount Peg. It's a sophisticated, almost aristocratic place that works hard at preserving and protecting its storied past from the onslaught of unrefined twenty-first-century businesses, and as a result remains one of New England's prettiest towns. This charm comes with a price of course; the town attracts droves of tourists and celebrities who come to eye Woodstock's pristine colonial architecture.

The townsite was granted in 1761 by Benning Wentworth and settled four years later by Timothy Knox. It became the Windsor County seat, or shire town, in 1786 and a leading publishing center in the 1800s with bookbinders, publishers, and five newspapers. The town attracted many prosperous bankers, merchants, scholars, and craftsmen who built the handsome Federal-style homes that encase the elliptical village green. In 1818 more than 10,000 Vermonters gathered on the green to watch the hanging execution of Samuel Godfrey, convicted of killing the state prison warden. The state's first medical school was housed here between 1827 and 1856.

Many of Vermont's most distinguished residents and native sons lived in Woodstock. These luminaries include Jacob Collamer, postmaster general and U.S. senator who was a close confidant and advisor to President Lincoln. Collamer once remarked, "The good people of Woodstock have less incentive than others to yearn for heaven." George Perkins Marsh, a European diplomat, congressman, scholar, and scientist who helped found the Smithsonian Institution, lived on a farm outside town. Marsh's 1864 pioneering book *Man and Nature*, regarded as the ecologist's bible, detailed man's destruction of natural habitats and called for efforts to mitigate and curb further damage.

Frederick Billings, born in 1823 up the road in Royalton, was one of the town's most influential residents. Billings trekked out to California with his sister and her husband and set up the first law office in San Francisco. He prospered, made a fortune, and returned to Woodstock in 1869 where he bought the 270-acre Charles Marsh farm. He also invested in the Northern Pacific Railroad and took charge of its transcontinental construction. One of the towns along its route through Montana was named for him. Billings also ordered more than 10,000 trees planted on Woodstock hillsides denuded by timber cutting. Billings's influence continues today through his granddaughter Mary French's marriage to Laurance S. Rockefeller. The Rockefellers' generosity has included opening the Billings Farm and Museum to the public and burying the town powerlines.

Park in central Woodstock near the town green and roam around a bit. Most of the town is listed on the National Register of Historic Places, with almost all of its buildings dating from the nineteenth century. The Chamber of Commerce booth at the green offers daily walking tours. Highlights of any tour should include the Woodstock Historical Society's 1807 Dana House with its collection of antiques and resident ghost; the Romanesque Norman Williams Public Library; and the 1806 First Congregational Church. The **Vermont Institute of Natural Sci-**

ence, lying 1.5 miles southwest of town, offers nature exhibits, a rare herb collection, nature trails, and a raptor center with more than forty raptors on display.

Two covered bridges are in town. The **Middle Covered Bridge** near the town center was built in 1969. Its lattice structure spans 125 feet. The 1865 Lincoln Covered Bridge in West Woodstock extends 136 feet across the Ottauquechee River. The **Billings Farm and Museum,** north of town off Vermont Highway 12, is a restored, living museum that details Frederick Billings's 1890s farm where even today workers plant and harvest crops, make cheese and butter, and run a dairy with prize-winning Jersey cows. The farm, Woodstock's most popular attraction, is open daily from May through October.

The drive leaves Woodstock along a strip of houses and motels on US 4 and heads west along the north bank of the Ottauquechee River for 7 miles to the junction of US 4 and Vermont Highway 100A. Just before the turn is the old mill town of Bridgewater. The Long Trail Brewing Company, located in the Marketplace at the renovated three-story Bridgewater Mill, brews small but tasty batches of Long Trail beers. Stop by for tours and tasting in their pub. Turn south or left onto VT 100A a mile past town.

The next lovely 7-mile road segment, running from US 4 to Plymouth Union, offers marvelous mountain scenery and a slice of real Americana. The road crosses the river on an old girder bridge and runs southwest up a broad valley filled with farms. After 1.4 miles the highway bends west up a side valley. The narrow road winds up a verdant hollow alongside Pinney Hollow Brook. After a short distance it passes the turnoff for **Coolidge State Park,** a 500-acre parkland located within Coolidge State Forest. The park includes sixty campsites, hiking trails, a small museum, and trout fishing. The drive continues to wind up the valley and after 6 miles reaches **Plymouth Notch National Historic District,** the birthplace and burial site of Calvin Coolidge, the thirtieth U.S. president.

Plymouth Notch

The tiny white-clapboard village of **Plymouth Notch,** still a functioning community, forms a cluster on a grassy hillside on the eastern edge of the Green Mountains. This quiet, off-the-beaten-track hamlet gave the nation Calvin Coolidge, a stoic, laconic, and reserved Yankee president who helped maintain a national sense of decorum and simplicity during the boisterous Roaring Twenties. Casual visitors, unacquainted with Coolidge, will wonder if they should bother stopping here. But those who do make the effort to visit Plymouth Notch find not only a fascinating glimpse into the late president's life, but also a nostalgic look back at New England's rural history.

Plymouth Notch was originally settled in 1771 as Saltash, but changed its name in 1797. The area, like so much of New England, prospered with industry in

President Calvin Coolidge is buried at his hometown cemetery in Plymouth Notch.

the early nineteenth century, with iron foundry work and stove manufacturing. A gold boomlet occurred in the 1850s, but things quieted down and the area reverted to its agrarian roots. It was from these roots that Calvin Coolidge was born on July 4, 1872, to John and Victoria Coolidge, Yankees from way back. John Coolidge's English ancestors landed in America about 1630.

Cal grew up, went to school, and launched his political career from this austere, no-frills town. His father, a state representative and senator, passed a sense of public service, political shrewdness, and self-restraint on to Calvin. After graduating from Amherst College, Coolidge entered the law profession and was elected to the city council of Northhampton, Massachusetts, in 1898. He went on to become city solicitor, a state representative and senator, mayor of Northhampton, lieutenant governor, and governor of Massachusetts. In 1920 Coolidge received the Republican vice-presidential nomination to run with Senator Warren G. Harding. The pair was elected easily, and Coolidge, at Harding's invitation, regularly attended Cabinet meetings, the first vice president to do so.

History was made at Plymouth Notch on the night of August 3, 1923. The vice president, in Vermont to help his father with haying, was awakened from a sound sleep and given the news of Harding's death. Coolidge telegraphed Washington for the oath of office, and at 2:47 A.M. was sworn in as president of the United States by his own father, a notary public, by the light of a kerosene lamp. Afterward, Coolidge went back upstairs to bed. The Coolidges' simple family room, now called the Oath of Office Room, remains much as it did that August night with a Bible, stacks of papers, a pen, and a lamp.

As president, Coolidge tidied up the mess left by Harding's Teapot Dome scandal, presided over a booming economy, established a summer White House at Plymouth Notch, and was easily re-elected in 1924 with the slogan "Keep Cool with Coolidge." After five years in Washington, he decided against running in 1928, citing the heavy strain on First Lady Grace Coolidge. Perhaps, some pundits conjecture, he foresaw the ruinous 1929 stock market crash. On leaving the capital, he told reporters, "Good-bye. I have had a very enjoyable time in Washington."

Coolidge retired to an estate in Northhampton, where he wrote his autobiography and a series of newspaper columns entitled "Thinking Things Over with Calvin Coolidge." He died suddenly of a heart attack at age sixty and was buried beside six generations of the Coolidge family in the Plymouth Notch cemetery, only a few hundred yards from his birthplace. His tombstone on a terraced hillside differs from those of his relatives only by the Great Seal of the United States above his name. The cemetery sits just south of VT 100A past the entrance to the town parking area.

Plymouth Notch remains a nineteenth-century village, touched only by preservationists. Its centerpiece is the Coolidge family compound with its houses and barns. The president's birthplace and boyhood home is a modest, five-room frame house attached to the back of the general store operated by his father. Displays in a small stone visitor center detail Coolidge's life history and achievements. Other buildings include the Wilder Barn with farm exhibits; the yellow 1830 Wilder House; the Union Christian Church, built in 1849; the Plymouth Cheese Factory, owned by the president's son John Coolidge; and the nostalgic General Store with lots of old-fashioned things for sale. Visit the cemetery on the south side of town. Other interesting graves in addition to those of the Coolidge family are found here, including twenty-four-year-old Barton Billings's stone. Engraved on it is his dying request in Kansas: "Carry me back to old Vermont, Where the rills trickle down the hills. There is where I want to lie when I die."

When strolling around Plymouth, remember President Coolidge's words from a 1928 speech: "I love Vermont because of her hills and valleys, her scenery and invigorating climate, but most of all because of her indomitable people. They are a race of pioneers who almost beggared themselves for others. If the spirit of liberty should vanish in other parts of the Union and support of our institutions should languish, it could all be replaced from the generous store held by the people of this brave little state of Vermont." The historic district and museum is open daily from late May through mid-October.

Plymouth Union to Sherburne Center

Past Plymouth Notch, the highway climbs sharply to a ridge and drops down a steep wooded valley to VT 100 in Plymouth Union. Turn right (north) on VT 100. The drive runs north for 5.5 miles alongside the Black River below the Green Mountains. Northan Road turns west from the highway to a large section of Coolidge State Forest a couple of miles up the highway, just before Woodward Reservoir. The 16,166-acre forest is composed of several irregularly shaped blocks encompassing several high peaks and a wide swath of pristine hills.

This forest section protects a pair of natural sites—Tinker Brook Natural Area and Shrewsbury Peak Natural Area. The forty-five-acre **Tinker Brook Natural Area,** lying about a mile up and just south of rough Northan Road, is a small and lovely preserve blanketed by an undisturbed, old-growth stand of tall red spruce and hemlock. The brook tumbles down a steep, narrow ravine lined with virgin forest. The 150-year-old trees here reach heights of 100 feet and have trunks more than 20 inches in diameter. Mosses, ferns, painted trillium, starflower, lily of the valley, and violet grow along the moist sides of the ravine. Bug repellent is handy when visiting in summer.

Continue up Northan Road (1.9 miles from the highway) to the Shrewsbury Peak trailhead. The 1.8-mile trail winds north through an excellent spruce-fir boreal forest to the lofty summit of 3,720-foot Shrewsbury Peak, one of the forest's highest points.

The drive continues on the highway past Woodward Reservoir. A fishing boat access area can be found on the lake's west shore. Past the lake, the valley narrows. Killington Peak towers to the west, its 4,235-foot summit wreathed in clouds. The peak, the second highest in Vermont, offers a superb view of the surrounding mountains and valleys. It was this view that supposedly gave Vermont its name—Reverend Samuel Peters from Connecticut surveyed the surrounding countryside below Killington Peak in 1763 and called it *Verd Mont*, or *Green Mountain* in French. Sunrise Ski Area, part of the famed Killington Ski Resort, is reached just before the junction of VT 100 and US 4 at West Bridgewater.

US 4 climbs north from the small village up the Ottauquechee River Valley. Bear Mountain at Killington Ski Area is a mile up the road on the left. The drive continues up the rounded glacial valley, its flat, marshy floor densely matted with willows. After 4 miles the highway reaches Sherburne Center and begins steeply climbing out of the valley and bending west. Pico Peak looms to the west, its sides creased with ski runs. At 6.4 miles VT 100 (your route) turns right, while US 4 continues straight to Rutland.

Killington Ski Area, the East's largest ski resort, lies a few miles south of this junction. With seven mountains, including Pico, the resort encompasses the longest ski run and ski season in New England, the longest gondola in the United States, and the world's largest snowmaking facilities. The area opened in 1958 with three lifts on Snowden Peak. Today it boasts more than 200 trails and slopes with a vertical drop of 3,050 feet. Numerous ski lodges line the highways and back roads around these ski areas, with accommodations for more than 11,000 visitors. Killington also offers four-season activities with an alpine slide, mountain bike rentals and trails, an eighteen-hole golf course, and tennis courts and schools. In summer you can ride the Killington Peak chairlift to the mountain summit and a restaurant. Many riders elect to hike back down.

Gifford Woods to Bethel

To continue the scenic drive, turn north (right) on VT 100, which drops down a hill into **Gifford Woods State Park.** This 114-acre park offers forty-eight wooded campsites, picnic areas, and hiking trails, including the Appalachian Trail, which crosses the park. The park, built in the 1930s, houses some impressive northern hardwoods in its developed area, but a hidden stand across the highway from the campground on the western shore of Kent Pond is even more thrilling. Somehow this virgin forest, today a state natural area, escaped the wholesale clearing of timber for firewood and construction that stripped 75 percent of Vermont by 1850 as well as today's rampant ski development to the south.

This climax forest alongside Kent Brook is one of the few remaining, untouched sugar maple–beech forests in the northeastern United States. The maples tower as high as 300 feet, while the trunks of eastern hemlocks are as thick as 3 feet. The understory of this small, primeval, forest remnant counts nineteen fern species and sixty-four species of flowering plants. This small forest is vulnerable to human impact and damage, so use care when hiking not to leave any sign of your passage. Ask at the park headquarters for directions to the old-growth forest.

VT 100 next runs north from the woods down a widening, glacier-carved valley on the eastern slope of the Green Mountains. The Tweed River riffles over boulders and hides behind woods alongside the asphalt. Pittsfield, 7 miles from Gifford Woods, was established in 1791 by settlers from Pittsfield, Massachusetts. The road runs through town past a private covered bridge (signed DO NOT ENTER) and the long village green bordered by the town hall and immaculate white houses. Nearby are several ski lodges.

Past the village, the drive and river bend east and run past farms and cornfields on the river bottomlands. Almost 3 miles from Pittsfield, VT 100 intersects Vermont Highway 107. Turn right on VT 107. For a side-trip to historic Stockbridge, go a mile farther north on VT 100.

The main scenic drive's last 13 miles follow VT 107 and the White River northeast to I–89. The road reaches the wide river's south bank after a mile and traverses the long, narrow valley. Dense woods line the highway. The road dashes through Gaysville, passes the White River National Fish Hatchery, and continues to Bethel at the confluence of the White River and the Third Branch. Bethel was the first town chartered by the State of Vermont in 1778. The small village once thrived as a cutting and shipping center for granite quarried from area hills. Today's town of Bethel sits on the site of old Fort Fortitude, erected in 1780 to protect Bethel's early settlers from hostile Indian war parties that traveled down the White River Valley from Canada. Two months later nearby Royalton was burned by Indians, but Bethel was ignored because of its armed fort.

At Bethel the highway crosses an old girder bridge to the river's north bank and climbs onto terraces above. In 2 miles the highway reaches I–89 and the end of this scenic drive. Continue straight past the interstate to North Royalton, Royalton, and South Royalton. At the junction of VT 107 and Vermont Highway 14 is the Vermont Sugar House, a maple sugar–theme restaurant and gift shop decorated with chain-saw wood carvings. Interstate travelers can quickly reach Barre and Montpelier by driving north, and southbound travelers can head down the four-lane highway back to White River Junction.

11

Middlebury Loop Scenic Drive

General description: An 81-mile loop drive through Middlebury and Brandon Gaps in the Green Mountains and across open farmland in the Champlain Valley.

Special attractions: Middlebury College Center for the Arts, Sheldon Museum, Vermont Folklife Center, Middlebury College Snow Bowl, Robert Frost Wayside Area and Trail, Middlebury Gap, Texas Falls Recreation Area, Green Mountain National Forest, Long Trail, Chittenden Brook Recreation Area, Brandon Brook Recreation Area, Brandon Gap, Vermont Ski Museum, Lake Champlain, apple picking, bicycle touring, fishing, hiking, downhill and cross-country skiing.

Location: North-central Vermont.

Drive route numbers: Vermont Highways 30, 74, 73, 100, and 125, and U.S. Highway 7.

Travel season: Year-round. Expect snow and icy conditions in winter.

Camping: Branbury State Park offers forty-five campsites from Memorial Day weekend through Columbus Day. Chittenden Brook Campground, with sixteen sites, lies 2.5 miles south of VT 73 on the east side of Brandon Gap.

Services: All services in Middlebury and Brandon. Limited and seasonal services in other towns along the drive.

Nearby attractions: D.A.R. State Park, Fort Ticonderoga (NY), Mount Independence State Historic Site, Crown Point State Historic Site (NY), Chimney Point State Historic Site, Branbury State Park, Silver Lake Recreation Area, Lincoln Gap.

The Drive

The 81-mile Middlebury Loop Scenic Drive, beginning in the college town of Middlebury, crosses the Green Mountains via Middlebury and Brandon Gaps and runs across rolling farmland on the eastern side of the Champlain Valley. This scenic drive incorporates two of Vermont's geographic regions—the state's rugged spine formed by the Green Mountains, and the Champlain lowland, the broad basin holding Lake Champlain that separates the Green Mountains from New York's Adirondacks. The drive's diverse scenery samples farmland and orchards, the Lake Champlain waterfront, superb mountain views, and a host of picturesque country villages and towns.

Middlebury

The drive begins in **Middlebury,** a classic New England town of 8,000 people that straddles Otter Creek in the morning shade of the Green Mountains. Although chartered in 1761, the town was not permanently settled for almost twenty years

Middlebury Loop

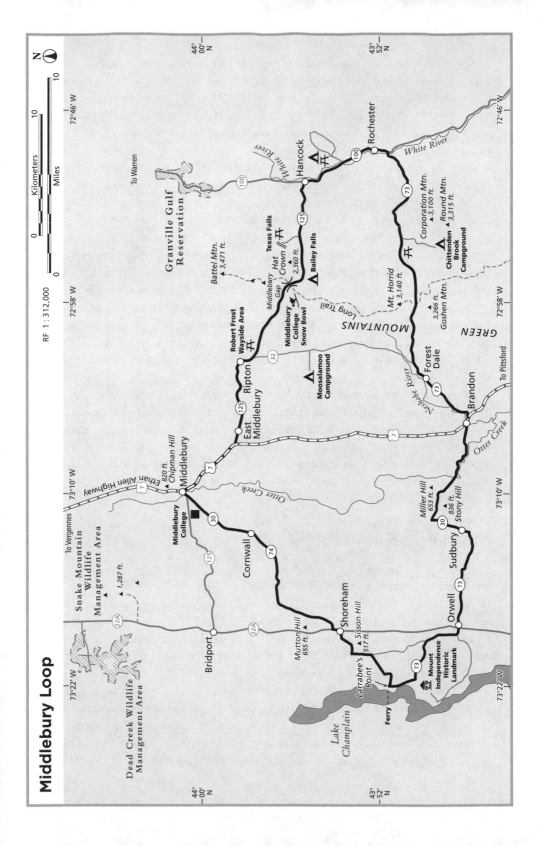

RF 1 : 312,000

until the local Indians were subdued. It received its name because it sat midway between Salisbury and New Haven on an old military road. Middlebury is home to prestigious Middlebury College. Founded in 1800, the college contains many excellent historic buildings, including the 1815 Painter Hall made from locally excavated marble. A college office is in the Emma Willard House National Historic Landmark, site of the 1814 Middlebury Female Seminary. The Johnson Gallery at Middlebury offers a collection of Vermont artists as well as work by Rodin and Rosso. Despite its more-famous marble neighbors Rutland and Proctor to the south, Middlebury boasted Vermont's first large marble quarry, opened in 1803. The town sits on a bedrock of Ordovician limestone, marble, and quartzite.

To really see and appreciate Middlebury, it's best to park your car and walk the tree-lined streets. The Middlebury Common sits in the town center. A pretty white Congregational Church, completed in 1809, dominates the green. The church's tall Ionic columns were each hewn from a single tree trunk. Just down from the town common spreads the Frog Hollow Historic District, along tumbling Otter Creek. The waterfalls along Otter Creek powered numerous nineteenth-century textile mills when wool processing was one of Middlebury's dominant industries. The district's buildings date from the 1700s and 1800s and have been renovated into shops and galleries.

One of the best stores here is the **Vermont State Craft Center,** with exhibitions, classes, and lots of Vermont crafts for sale, including stained glass, jewelry, and pottery. The **Vermont Folklife Center** in the Gamaliel Painter House near the green promotes folk art and traditions through special events and revolving exhibitions. The **Henry Sheldon Museum,** located on Park Street in an 1829 house, displays everyday nineteenth-century artifacts including furniture, tools, and household utensils, in period settings.

Through the Champlain Valley

The scenic drive starts at the Middlebury Common at the junction of U.S. Highway 7 and Vermont Highway 30. Turn southwest on VT 30, dropping past Frog Hollow Historic District, and pass Middlebury College on the outskirts of town. In less than a mile, the two-lane highway has left Middlebury far behind and entered a bucolic, rolling land. Good views of the lofty Green Mountains along the eastern horizon are to the highway's left. After 4 miles the road passes a church and cemetery and enters Cornwall. Turn west here onto Vermont Highway 74.

The drive follows VT 74 for the next 13 miles to Larrabee's Point on the eastern shore of Lake Champlain. This rural highway stretch yields pleasant views west to the Adirondack Mountains in New York as it meanders past cornfields, apple orchards, silos, barns, and white farmhouses on the gently tilted plain. Occasional hillocks poke above the farmland. Among these is 655-foot Mutton Hill and 517-

foot Sisson Hill near the small village of Shoreham. Most of these hills are stream-lined, elongated knobs called "sheepbacks," oriented north to south by thick ice sheets that scoured the land during long episodes of glaciation.

The lowland topography here in the Champlain Valley was first excavated by the glaciers and later filled by thick sediment deposits beneath the ancient Lake Vermont and Champlain Sea waterways. Lake Vermont was a huge inland lake that covered all of the Champlain basin when the drainage to the St. Lawrence River to the north was icebound during glacial melting at the end of the Pleistocene Epoch. The lake also featured fjordlike fingers that poked east through the Green Mountains into today's Winooski, Lamoille, and Missisquoi River Valleys. The numerous hills in today's Champlain Valley were islands in the ancient lakes. Terraces of wave-deposited sediments are still visible on some hills here.

A few miles north of Shoreham, just off the drive, is **Dead Creek Wildlife Management Area,** at 2,858 acres the largest state waterfowl refuge in Vermont. The Dead Creek wetlands, created by water-control dams, offer excellent birding opportunities. Canada and snow geese, various species of ducks, wading birds such as bitterns and herons, and songbirds bring flocks of birdwatchers, particularly in spring and fall. Northeast of the wildlife area is the landmark promontory of 1,287-foot Snake Mountain, with a fine hiking trail up its long ridge to good sum-mit viewpoints.

Past Shoreham, VT 74 zigzags south and west to **Larrabee's Point.** This quiet village named for John Larrabee, who built a warehouse on the shore here in 1823, was once a busy commercial port and center for shipping quarried stone, lumber, and textiles. The railroad network that spread across the northeast by the mid-1800s reduced the point's attractiveness as a shipping hub. Historic structures here include not only Larrabee's original warehouse but also the town's ferry dock, still in use.

The Fort Ticonderoga Ferry runs from Larrabee's Point to Fort Ticonderoga in New York from May through October. The fort was originally built by the French and later captured by the British. In 1775 Vermonter Ethan Allen and his Green Mountain Boys surprised the then-British garrison, capturing the fort and its guns. These weapons were eventually used to free Boston. British General Bur-goyne recaptured the fort from the colonials in 1777, but lost it again with inde-pendence. The restored stone fort, open mid-May through mid-October, displays weapons, uniforms, and artifacts in its museum.

Mount Independence, just south of Larrabee's Point, is another Revolution-ary War site, Vermont State Historic Site, and National Historic Landmark. The 400-acre site on a peninsula jutting into Lake Champlain was largely ignored by preservationists until 1975 when restoration, archaeological, and interpretative work was undertaken. Four trails lace this key military complex that faced Fort Ticonderoga. The fort, linked to Ticonderoga by a floating bridge, was built in

1776 to house 12,000 soldiers intended to protect the northwestern flank of the American colonies. It was captured by the British in July 1777 along with Fort Ticonderoga. The Continental Army, after abandoning the two forts, retreated southeast to Hubbardton where the army's rear-guard, including Seth Warner and the Green Mountain Boys, fought the British army to a standstill on July 7 in the only Revolutionary War battle fought on Vermont soil. The 1,200 Vermonters held the select British units off for two hours before scattering when Hessian reinforcements arrived. Their action, however, delayed the British enough so that the main American column was able to escape southward. The battlefield, 12 miles south of Sudbury off VT 30, is commemorated by a marble spire.

Larrabee's Point to Brandon

The second segment of the scenic drive runs 20 miles from Larrabee's Point to Brandon on Vermont Highway 73. Head southwest from the lake and pass a picturesque barn painted with a large-scale imitation of Grant Wood's *American Gothic*. The road dips and rolls past hilly farms and the turnoff to Mount Independence State Historic Site. After 5 miles it crosses Vermont Highway 22A and enters the hamlet of Orwell. The highway then heads east toward the Green Mountain wall, crossing beautiful farmland broken by wooded hills. About 5 miles from Orwell, the drive intersects VT 30. Turn north here on VT 30/73 to enter Sudbury. This small town perches atop a hill and offers good views of the Champlain Valley and the rounded Adirondack Mountains to the west. Continue north on VT 30 for a couple of miles to its junction with VT 73. Turn east (right) here.

A marker designating the Crown Point Military Road is found by going west for a mile from the crossroads. This 85-mile road reached the farthest outposts of the American colonies when it was built in 1759. The road connected the Connecticut River Valley with the Lake Champlain region and eased travel for British army units and early settlers.

The scenic drive route runs southeast from VT 30 through low hills and along Otter Creek for 6 miles to Brandon. As VT 73 the road climbs sharply up through a gap between Miller Hill on the left and 836-foot Stony Hill on the right before it drops to meandering Otter Creek, the longest river entirely within Vermont. The highway runs along the flat valley floor through swampy Brandon Swamp Wildlife Management Area, passing fields of corn punctuated by dense woodlands. After turning away from the creek at last, the asphalt enters Brandon.

A busy town of 4,000, **Brandon** sits on low hills between Otter Creek and the Neshobe River. It offers two village greens, an 1861 town hall, and a good selection of nineteenth-century Federal and Victorian homes. The town, chartered in 1761 as Neshobe, was rechristened Brandon in 1784 after the Revolution. It flourished after iron deposits were discovered nearby in 1810. John Conant's furnace cast Ver-

The Seth Warner statue and monument at Mount Independence honor the only Revolutionary War battle fought on Vermont soil.

mont's first cookstoves. The Forestdale Iron Furnace, dating from 1810, preserves this heritage. Other industries included the Howe Scale Company, which moved to Rutland in the late 1860s, and marble-cutting mills powered by the Neshobe River. Thomas Davenport invented the electric motor here in 1834 and used his new invention to operate a newspaper press in New York City. In an editorial, he foretold the future when he wrote that electricity "must and will triumphantly succeed."

Brandon was also the 1813 birthplace and childhood home of Stephen A. Douglas, the "Little Giant" who became a powerful Democratic senator from Illinois. Regarded as a potential president, he debated Abraham Lincoln in the famed Lincoln-Douglas debates during the 1858 Senate race in Illinois and was elected. The tables turned two years later when Lincoln, the Republican nominee, defeated Douglas for the presidency. Douglas, Vermont's native son, received only 19 percent of the state's vote and died shortly afterward in 1861.

Over the Green Mountains

The drive meets US 7 in downtown Brandon. Drive past the intersection and the 1785 Baptist Church and turn east (left) on VT 73 after 0.25 mile. The road runs past stately houses and exits Brandon in 0.5 mile. Two miles later the highway passes through modest Forest Dale and climbs eastward into the Green Mountains in a narrow valley alongside the Neshobe River. This meager river, hemmed in by dense woods, tumbles over a rocky streambed. As the highway steepens, glimpses of high ridges and peaks, including 3,266-foot Goshen Mountain on the right and 3,140-foot Mount Horrid on the left, stretch ahead. The drive enters 383,000-acre Green Mountain National Forest 6.5 miles from Brandon and climbs more steeply up the final grade to **Brandon Gap,** a pass between the two peaks. A picnic area, the Long Trail crossing, and Brandon Gap trailhead all lie near the gap's summit.

Marvelous views unfold upon cresting the gap. Mount Horrid and its precipitous **Great Cliff** loom dramatically above a roadside overlook and reflective beaver ponds on the valley floor. The top of the granite cliff lies 700 vertical feet above Brandon Gap and is reached by a spectacular 0.6-mile trail (part of the Long Trail traversing Vermont's Green Mountain crest). The hike begins in a small pullout near the gap summit. The short, steep, forty-five-minute hike leads to a superb viewpoint atop the cliffs. The Champlain Valley lies below, floored by the glistening lake, and the rugged Adirondacks stretch to the western horizon. The forested spine of the Green Mountains, punctuated by lofty peaks, stretches to the north and south, and a maze of hills lies to the east. Besides hiking, the Great Cliff area offers some of Vermont's rare rock-climbing opportunities and wildlife watching. Peregrine falcons, re-established by the Forest Service, are slowly making a comeback here. They can be seen soaring high above the cirque.

The Mount Horrid Great Cliff and the deep U-shaped valley of Brandon Brook east of the gap clearly illustrate the effects of glaciers on the Green Mountains. The cliff itself was formed by a glacial process that geologists call "quarrying" or "plucking." This occurs on the leeward side of the mountain, away from the direction in which the glacier came. As the ponderous glacial ice slowly crept across the exposed rock surfaces, it froze to the rocks then "plucked" them out along fracture lines as it moved downslope. Many thousands of years of glacial activity sculpted these lofty cliffs and excavated the deep valley below.

The drive drops eastward alongside Brandon Brook, passing Brandon Brook Picnic Area and, a few miles later, the turnoff for Chittenden Brook Campground. This seventeen-site campground, open Memorial Day through Labor Day, lies 2.5 miles south up a dirt road and offers fishing and several good hiking trails. The highway and brook join the broad valley of the West Branch of the White River a mile later, and follow it east past cornfields and farms for 4 miles to the White River and the junction of VT 73 and Vermont Highway 100. Turn north (left) on VT 100 and enter Rochester 0.1 mile later.

Rochester is a pleasant village that once thrived with logging, talc mining, and dairying but now offers a diverse business base that includes a New Age book publisher, a greeting-card company, and Liberty Hill Farm, a working guest farm.

A prosperous farm along Vermont Highway 100 north of Rochester.

Rochester is a good place to stop, sit back on the village green, and watch the world go by. Visit the Rochester Ranger Station on the south side of town for hiking, camping, and fishing information and maps of Green Mountain National Forest.

From Rochester the highway runs north across corn-covered, flat bottomlands along the White River, passing a small picnic area 0.5 mile north of town. The drive enters the lumber village of Hancock 4.5 miles from Rochester, turning west in Hancock on Vermont Highway 125. An excellent side-trip continues north a few miles on VT 100 to 1,200-acre Granville Gulf Reservation. Dense forest lines the road as it ascends into Granville Gulf, an immense rock-lined cirque. Moss Glen Falls State Natural Area includes a marvelous waterfall that plummets over abrupt cliffs.

Middlebury Gap

The main drive route heads west up VT 125 alongside the Hancock Branch of the White River. This last drive segment over Middlebury Gap is a designated Vermont Scenic Highway. The highway leaves Hancock and runs west up the narrowing valley. The turnoff to **Texas Falls Recreation Area** is reached after 3.1 miles. Turn right and drive a short distance north to the falls parking lot and small picnic area with thirteen sites. Texas Falls is a spectacular series of waterfalls sharply sliced into ancient metamorphic bedrock. The walls of the small gorge here are festooned with dense mats of moss and ferns. A short footbridge spans the gorge and gives a great view of the dashing water. Texas Falls Nature Trail, an easy 1-mile hike, begins at the bridge and explores Texas Brook.

The highway continues westward up the glacier-carved valley through a thick forest of hardwoods, pine, and spruce. After a couple of upward miles, the road climbs steeply into leafy 2,149-foot Middlebury Gap. Like the other east-west passes in the Green Mountains, Middlebury Gap was initially excavated by streams before the Wisconsin glaciation completed the final sculpting. The Long Trail, a 265-mile pathway along the main crest of the Green Mountains between Massachusetts and Canada, crosses the highway atop the gap.

Past Middlebury Gap, the drive begins a steep descent down a broad valley flanked by mountain ridges. Less than a mile from the summit, the road passes **Middlebury College Snow Bowl Ski Area,** a popular winter destination. The ski area has three chairlifts, fifteen trails, a ski school, a rental shop, and a restaurant. The highway descends more gradually below the ski area and, in a mile, reaches the rolling bottomland along the South Branch of the Middlebury River.

The drive dips and rolls north of the river, past occasional cleared fields, before cutting through the campus of Middlebury College's famed Bread Loaf School of English. This collection of dun-colored buildings houses the college's

The Champlain lowland and the Adirondack Mountains from the summit of Middlebury Gap.

esteemed summer writer's programs. Forest Road 59, which turns north just past the campus, leads to trailheads at the edge of Bread Loaf Wilderness Area.

Past the campus, the drive enters Robert Frost country. The highway runs west through woods past an old cemetery to the **Robert Frost Wayside Area.** The area, offering picnic sites in an open red pine forest, is enclosed by a ragged stone fence. Robert Frost, the famed Poet Laureate of Vermont, summered in a farmhouse near here between 1939 and 1962. After his death in 1963, the Vermont Division of Historic Sites dedicated this wayside area and a nearby nature trail to the poet's memory. This highway section is the Robert Frost Memorial Drive. A small, unmarked dirt road just before the wayside area leads to the white-washed Homer Noble Farm and Frost's small cabin there. Pilgrims can park in a designated lot and walk to the unassuming cabin, although it's not open to the public. The cabin, owned by Middlebury College, is maintained exactly as it was upon Frost's death in 1963. Just down the highway on the left side is the **Robert Frost Interpretative Trail.** The mile-long path treks out along a boardwalk through a marsh and open fields. Some of Frost's famous poems are mounted on placards along the trail. Stop and linger at each one and feel the power of his interpretations.

Robert Frost is one of America's most beloved poets. Using simple language tempered by irony, this Yankee bard penned numerous stanzas about his adopted homeland. His poems evoke the character of this harsh countryside, reveling in its hard-won joys and stern sorrows and the plethora of emotions in between. Frost employed this powerful landscape to explore and delineate the relationships between poet, landscape, season, and fellow man. His poems speak to us not as if we are New Englanders but as Americans. They look forward, they look toward the future. They offer a promise of spring, a promise that miracles do happen amid the toil and grim overcast of winter. In plain English the poems show the land as we see it as well as the underlying landscape of our hearts and consciences.

It's important to remember that Frost was not a native of New England, but rather a traveling poet who came to love this land and people. He chose the intimate geography and humanity of New England for his life's work. Born and bred in California (of all places), Frost moved here at the age of twenty-six to live with his family on a small New Hampshire farm while he mastered the art of poetry. His most famous poem, "The Road Not Taken," tells of that choice:

> I shall be telling this with a sigh
> Somewhere ages and ages hence:
> Two roads diverged in a wood, and I—
> I took the one less traveled by,
> And that has made all the difference.

Beyond the trail site the scenic drive bends northwest along the river. Forest Road 32 turns south here and runs 4 miles to Moosalamoo Campground in the national forest. The highway parallels the river's rocky streambed and enters the quiet town of **Ripton.** The town, chartered in 1781 and organized in 1828, is one of Vermont's largest townships with 31,599 acres and a population hovering at 550. Sights here include the usual white clapboard churches and the old Ripton Country Store.

The drive crosses the river upon leaving Ripton and twists along the rocky south bank. The river tucks into a small roadside canyon that quickly deepens and becomes **Middlebury Gorge,** an abrupt defile slicing through Precambrian layers of fine-grained gneiss and fractured quartzite. The highway drops steeply down the edge of the gorge, passes a good viewpoint, and crosses the river on a bridge 3 miles from Ripton. Look up-canyon from the bridge for a good view of the gorge.

At East Middlebury the road enters a more sedate countryside on the eastern fringe of the Champlain plain. Continue west through residential East Middlebury, taking care to angle right on VT 125 at its junction with Vermont Highway 116. East Middlebury offers many bed-and-breakfasts, including the now famous Waybury Inn. The exterior and front porch of the inn were used as the locale for the long-running television show *Newhart.* Even today fans of the series stop for a glance at the inn.

After leaving the village, the highway crosses farmland and joins US 7. Turn right on US 7 and head northwest across pastures dotted with grazing cattle and farms. Good views of the Green Mountain escarpment stretch across the eastern horizon. After a couple of miles, the highway passes Middlebury Ranger Station and enters the town of Middlebury. Continue on to the green at the town center, the end point of this scenic drive.

Barre to Danville Scenic Drive

12

General description: A 49-mile drive through rolling hills and picturesque country villages in Vermont's upland region.

Special attractions: Barre, Rock of Ages Quarry, Groton State Forest, Peacham, country churches, quaint villages, trout fishing, cross-country skiing, hiking.

Location: North-central Vermont.

Drive route numbers and name: U.S. Highway 302, Vermont Highway 25, Minard Hill Road.

Travel season: Year-round. Expect snow and icy conditions in winter.

Camping: Groton State Forest, with four state park campgrounds and 223 sites, is open Memorial Day through Labor Day.

Services: All services in Montpelier, Barre, and St. Johnsbury. Limited services elsewhere along the drive.

Nearby attractions: Montpelier, Vermont Statehouse, Vermont Historical Society Museum, Stowe, Stowe Ski Area, Smugglers Notch, Mount Mansfield Toll Road, Mount Mansfield State Forest, Middlebury Gap, Green Mountain National Forest, St. Johnsbury attractions, Lake Willoughby, White Mountain National Forest (NH), Franconia Notch (NH).

The Drive

Beginning in Barre, just east of Montpelier, this 49-mile drive runs southeast along U.S. Highway 302 and Vermont Highway 25 before turning north along a back road to Danville. The route crosses rolling, wooded hills and dales and passes through picture-postcard villages. This area, encompassing Orange and southern Caledonia Counties, is quintessential Vermont. Its lovely landscape is a verdant tapestry broken by modest pastures and farmhouses tucked against hills clad in hardwoods and dark evergreens. Tidy, well-preserved villages crowned by white-spired churches sit atop humped ridges and nestle in shallow valleys.

Although Vermont offers some wild, inspiring vistas of snowy mountains and rugged defiles, it is this peaceful corner of the state that attracts visitors and photographers with simple grace and beauty. The land and villages here are the image of a utopian rural America. While driving down these country lanes, it's easy to imagine the horse-and-buggy days, the mule-drawn plow, the backbreaking labor of clearing a field and building a stone fence. That's what this drive offers—a glimpse into the forgotten heart of agrarian America and the practical values that sprang from this simple countryside.

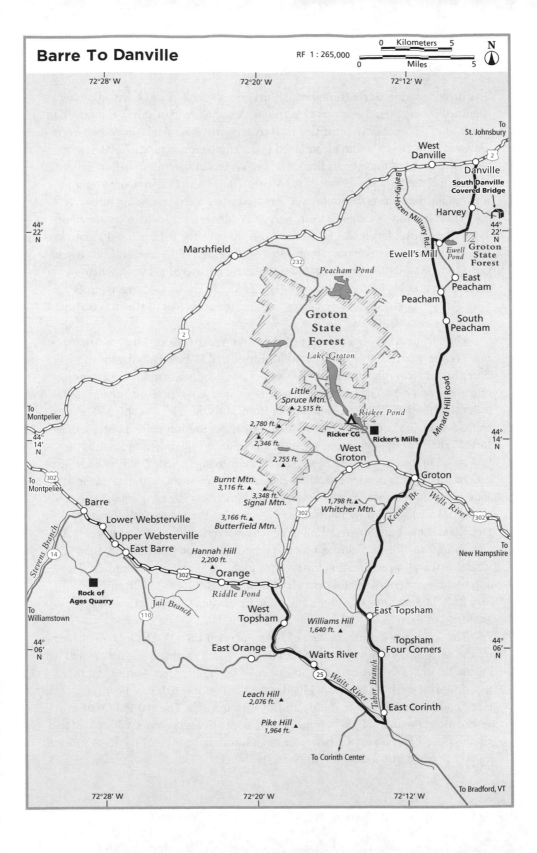

Barre To Danville

RF 1 : 265,000

Kilometers 0 — 5
Miles 0 — 5

N

72°28' W   72°20' W   72°12' W

To St. Johnsbury

West Danville

Danville

South Danville Covered Bridge

Harvey

44° 22' N

Marshfield

Bayley-Hazen Military Rd.

Ewell's Mill

Ewell Pond

Groton State Forest

East Peacham

232

Peacham Pond

Peacham

Groton State Forest

South Peacham

Lake Groton

Minard Hill Road

2

Little Spruce Mtn.
▲ 2,515 ft.

2,780 ft. ▲

Ricker Pond

Ricker CG ⛺

Ricker's Mills

2,346 ft. ▲

44° 14' N

To Montpelier

2,755 ft. ▲

West Groton

Groton

302

Burnt Mtn.
3,116 ft. ▲

3,348 ft. ▲
Signal Mtn.

302

Keenan Br.

Wells River

302

To Montpelier

302

Barre

Lower Websterville

Upper Websterville

East Barre

1,798 ft. ▲
Whitcher Mtn.

3,166 ft. ▲
Butterfield Mtn.

To New Hampshire

14

Stevens Branch

Hannah Hill
2,200 ft. ▲

Orange

302

To Williamstown

Rock of Ages Quarry

Jail Branch

Riddle Pond

110

West Topsham

East Topsham

Williams Hill
1,640 ft. ▲

44° 06' N

East Orange

Waits River

Topsham Four Corners

25

Waits River

Tabor Branch

Leach Hill
2,076 ft. ▲

East Corinth

Pike Hill
1,964 ft. ▲

To Corinth Center

To Bradford, VT

72°28' W   72°20' W   72°12' W

Barre to East Corinth

The drive begins in **Barre** (pronounced "berry"), a rough-edged town adjoining dignified Montpelier, the capital of Vermont. A 4-mile strip of stores and fast-food joints lines US 302 between the two rival cities. Barre is actually two cities—Barre City and Barre Town—with a combined population approaching 17,000. It sprawls along the banks of the Stevens Branch of the Winooski River in a shallow valley. Nicknamed the "Granite Center of the World," Barre was, like so many Vermont towns, famed for the excellent granite quarried from the surrounding hills.

The Barre towns were originally part of Wildersburgh, a village chartered in 1793. The first settlers held a town meeting to rename the village. Local legend says two Massachusetts emigrants, Thompson from Holden and Sherman from Barre, came to blows over the town's new name. Sherman battered his way to victory, then stood over his inert opponent and declared, "There, by God, the name is Barre." Historians dispute the colorful account but agree that the town was named after Barre, Massachusetts.

Granite quarrying began here in 1813 at the Wells-Lamson Quarry, America's first granite quarry. Other quarries on Millstone and Cobble Hills southeast of Barre began excavating granite for millstones, foundations, window and door lintels, and fenceposts. The granite vein here is as wide as 4 miles and as deep as 10 miles. The flawless light and dark granite from Millstone Hill was shipped by ox teams for use in the construction of the state capitol in Montpelier between 1833 to 1837. Barre's population and fortunes soared after 1880, when thousands of low-paid European stonecutters worked in the thriving quarries. This volatile mixture of immigrants from Scotland, England, Germany, Spain, Scandinavia, and Italy successfully struck for higher wages and benefits in the early 1900s. They also elected a socialist mayor, supported the Communist Party during the Great Depression, and built Socialist Hall to benefit workers.

Granite remains a mainstay of Barre's modern economy, with more than 1,000 workers excavating and milling the rock for use as monuments, sculptures, floors, and building exteriors. Visitors can view the nearly 600-foot-deep, twenty-seven-acre Rock of Ages Quarry and the adjoining Craftsmen Center in Graniteville, southeast of Barre.

The scenic drive route travels east from Barre on US 302. The highway heads up the narrow, wooded valley of the Jail Branch River, passing a few homes and businesses in Lower Websterville and Upper Websterville. After 3 miles and the junction with Vermont Highway 110, the road dashes through East Barre and climbs out of the valley into rolling, thickly forested hills. The town of Orange, spread along the roadside, is dominated by a white Congregational Church. Atop a rise just west of Orange, look back west for an impressive view of the Rock of Ages Quarry notched into a distant hillside.

The highway runs east for the next 4 miles through thick evergreen woods and past rounded, 2,000-foot hills. At Riddle Pond the asphalt drops into a narrow valley with a shallow, meandering creek to the junction of US 302 and VT 25. Turn south (right) onto VT 25 and head down the broad Waits River Valley.

A couple of miles down VT 25 lies West Topsham, a small hamlet perched above the river. Beyond the village the highway drops steeply down the picturesque valley, past green hayfields hemmed in by Sanborn Ridge to the east. The road bends southeast after the turn to East Orange and follows the broadening Waits River Valley downstream. After a short distance the drive passes through the tiny village of Waits River. The village and river, as well as the town of Waitsfield, were named for General Benjamin Wait, a veteran of both the French and Indian Wars and the American Revolution.

East Corinth to Groton

The highway continues down the pastoral valley another 4 miles to its junction with a narrow country lane that runs north. Turn north (left) at this intersection. The next 28-mile drive segment runs north from here to Danville through a lovely swatch of Vermont's Piedmont country, that area of rolling hills between the Green Mountains and the Connecticut River on the state's eastern border. The drive runs alongside trickling Tabor Branch through a scenic valley with hayfields, occasional cattle, and large farmhouses. In 0.5 mile the road climbs through **East Corinth,** a small village dominated by the lovely East Corinth Congregational Church. The road quickly passes through **Topsham Four Corners,** a small collection of houses, and continues up the valley to East Topsham. This quaint cluster of homes is set on grassy knolls above the creek. The town's whitewashed church lifts its steeple above tin roofs and wood piles.

The drive leaves East Topsham and the Tabor Branch to climb steeply along Powder Spring Creek in a densely wooded draw. Rolling hills, some as high as 1,900 feet, rise above the road. Beaver ponds in the forest reflect a sky of steely clouds. Occasional moose stomps, trampled mudflats, lie alongside the narrow roadway. After 4 miles the road tops a rise then begins a northward descent past stubblefields fenced in by thick woods. Bending northeast around 1,798-foot Whitcher Mountain, the asphalt meets Keenan Brook in a shallow vale before descending gently into the broad valley of Wells River. This section of road yields superb views eastward across rolling hills to the snowcapped Presidential Range in northern New Hampshire.

The road enters **Groton** and drops to another junction with US 302 and the town center. Groton, named by early Scottish settlers for Groton, Massachusetts, straddles the Wells River in a wide valley amid forested hills. **Groton State Forest,** Vermont's largest state recreation area, sprawls across 25,625 acres northwest of town. This immense swath of wild forest is topped by numerous peaks that reach higher than 2,500 feet. Signal Mountain, a 3,348-foot-high summit, lies just south of the park's boundary. More than 40 miles of developed trails lace the forest, scaling the peaks and exploring lakes, ponds, and streams. Lake Groton, a 3-mile-long reservoir, and nearby Ricker Pond offer the bulk of the area's recreational opportunities. Most visitors come to fish and swim in the lakes, hike the trails, hunt in the forests, and ski-tour and snowmobile in winter snow. The state forest also offers four campgrounds in four state parks for summer campers.

Like most of New England's forests, Groton State Forest was heavily logged in the nineteenth century. Ricker's Mills, just outside of Groton, is one of the nation's oldest continuously operating sawmills. The area is also rife with lumberjack history, including the Old Lake House, a boardinghouse that was the hangout of bank robber Bristol Bill Darlington from Bristol, England. The famed outlaw was finally captured here in 1850, and in a final desperate act during his sentencing at St. Johnsbury, he killed the prosecutor with a knife.

Peacham and Danville

On reaching Groton, turn east (right) on US 302 and drive 0.3 mile to Minard Hill Road. Turn north (left) here toward Peacham. The narrow, paved road climbs steeply out of Groton and drops into a broad swale. The drive runs north alongside Tannery Brook up the narrowing valley. Dense woods interrupted by occasional farms and hayfields line the blacktop. After a few miles the road crests an open ridge. Superb views of the distant White Mountains and the Vermont Piedmont unfold beyond the rise. The road gently descends into open farmland, crossing South Peacham Brook and sliding past a few houses in South Peacham. A mile later it enters Peacham.

Nestled among green hills at the relatively lofty elevation of 1,908 feet, **Peacham** is one of Vermont's most charming villages. This isolated community was chartered in 1776 by Deacon Jonathon Elkins and flourished after the Bayley-Hazen Military Road pushed through the region. This 55-mile route was begun in 1776 for launching possible attacks on British Canada and opened northern Vermont to settlers after the Revolution. The Peacham Academy, founded in 1795 as the Caledonia County Grammar School, operated for well over a hundred years until closing in the 1920s. A stone monument marks its former site. The impressive Congregational Church, recognized as one of America's most beautiful country churches, presides over the town, lifting its tapered white spire above surrounding trees, barns, and houses near the village green. The church was built in 1806 and moved to its present location in 1843.

Notable Americans who grew up in Peacham include the violent abolitionist Thaddeus Stevens and George Harvey, an influential journalist and editor of

A farm nestles among the rolling hills on the Barre to Danville Scenic Drive.

Harper's Weekly who was nicknamed "The President-Maker." Harvey engineered Woodrow Wilson's rise to political power as governor of New Jersey. He later pushed Warren G. Harding's nomination and supported fellow Vermonter Calvin Coolidge for vice president. Herbert Hoover also consulted with Harvey before his election.

Peacham is a good place to stop and stretch your legs. Walk west from the four corners up a side street past the village church to a cemetery with spacious views of the surrounding countryside. Lovely green hills punctuate the skyline, among them New Hampshire's White Mountains to the east. The town is also graced by several stately historical homes and the Peacham Store, which vends fresh croissants and Vermont crafts and quilts while at the same time serving as a bed-and-breakfast.

Leave Peacham and travel north out of the valley over rolling ridges and shallow vales. At Ewell Pond, a large lake hemmed in by trees, the road bends northeast and passes a detached section of Groton State Forest. Turning north again the road rolls through a small collection of houses at Harvey and 1.5 miles later enters **Danville.** The scenic drive ends at the road's junction with U.S. Highway 2 in Danville. This lovely village, spread across a humped hill, was northern Vermont's largest town some 200 years ago. Today it is home to the American Society of Dowsers. Interstate 91 and St. Johnsbury lie 7 miles east.

13

Smugglers Notch Scenic Drive

General description: This 23-mile drive climbs to the summit of Mount Mansfield, Vermont's highest point, and threads through 2,162-foot-high Smugglers Notch, an abrupt cleft chiseled into the Green Mountains. Cars pulling trailers and recreational vehicles should not attempt the road section through Smugglers Notch.

Special attractions: Smugglers Notch State Park, Mount Mansfield State Forest, Mount Mansfield Toll Road, Bingham Falls, Mount Mansfield Ski Area, Smugglers Notch Ski Area, Stowe, hiking, rock climbing, ice climbing, downhill skiing, cross-country skiing, alpine tundra, Long Trail.

Location: Northern Vermont.

Drive route number and name: Vermont Highway 108 and Mount Mansfield Toll Road.

Travel season: May through October. The highway usually opens sometime in May and closes by November, depending on snowfall.

Camping: Smugglers Notch State Park, open late May to mid-October, offers thirty-four sites with flush toilets, showers, phone, picnic tables, and lean-tos. A one-hundred-site private campground is just south of Stowe off Vermont Highway 100.

Services: All services in Stowe and Jeffersonville.

Nearby attractions: Elmore State Park, Little River State Park, Burlington, Shelburne Museum, Lake Champlain, Chester A. Arthur birthplace, Montpelier attractions.

The Drive

Mount Mansfield, Vermont's highest point at 4,393 feet above sea level, towers above the surrounding Green Mountains and forms a distinctive landmark for travelers. The mountain's 5-mile-long summit ridge resembles a reclining human profile, with four fanciful bumps defining the forehead, nose, chin (actual summit), and Adam's apple. American Indians saw the peak's unique features differently, calling Mansfield *Moze-O-Be-Wadso* or "mountain with a head like a moose." The mountain dominates northern Vermont, looming over the broad Stowe Valley and casting an alpine presence on the otherwise pastoral landscape.

The Smugglers Notch Scenic Drive follows Vermont Highway 108 for 18 miles on a short but spectacular outing that runs northwest from the Stowe Valley into the abrupt defile of Smuggler's Notch below Mount Mansfield. The road drops past the notch to Jeffersonville along the Lamoille River. An excellent side-trip is a 4-mile toll road that leaves the drive and climbs to the peak's windswept summit.

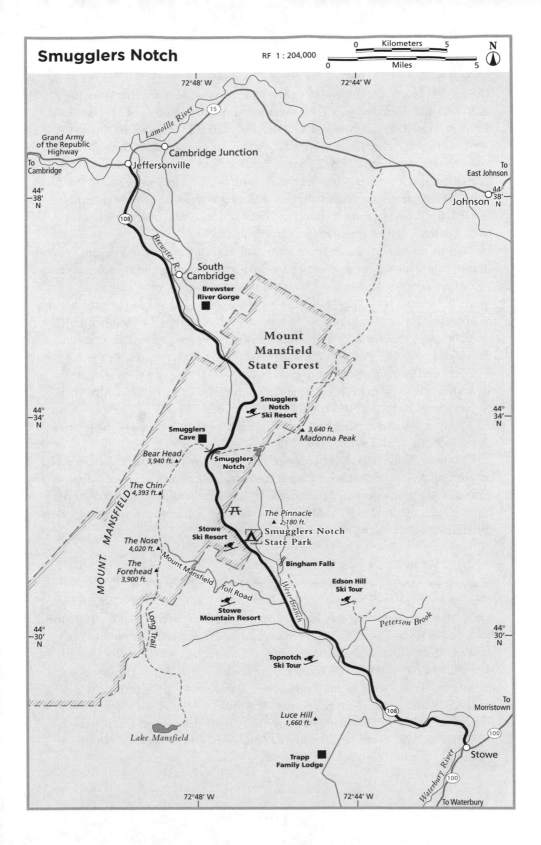

Stowe

The drive begins in downtown Stowe at the junction of Vermont Highways 100 and 108. Head northwest on VT 108. **Stowe,** lying at an elevation of 723 feet along the Waterbury River in Stowe Valley, nestles between the Green Mountains to the west and the Worcester Range, a subsidiary range of the Greens, to the east. The town, the self-proclaimed "Ski Capital of the East," owes its ski fame to the prodigious amounts of snow that blanket the surrounding mountains. The town itself is old, with its charter granted by Governor Benning Wentworth of New Hampshire in 1763. It received its name from several early residents who hailed from Stow, Massachusetts. The "e" appeared in the name in 1838.

Despite its bustling resort atmosphere, Stowe retains a quiet and elegant charm. Before the ski boom, the town languished as a logging and farming center. Then southern New Englanders discovered its superb winter snow and snow sports in the mid-1800s. The town's history is preserved in its 1864 Stowe Community Church; a museum run by the local historical society; the Bloody Brook Schoolhouse, a restored 1828 one-room school that was moved here in 1909; and the Helen Day Art Center, with exhibits by Vermont artists, housed in an 1861 high school. The town offers travelers more than 5,000 beds in a wide range of accommodations, from rustic to elegant, including the Trapp Family Lodge, built on 2,000 acres by the real von Trapp family after their *Sound of Music* escape from Nazi Austria. Another famous spot is the Green Mountain Inn, one of the town's oldest hostelries with roots back to 1833.

Visitors will find a broad selection of fine restaurants in Stowe. The town and the immediate area also afford numerous recreational opportunities, including downhill skiing, cross-country skiing, hiking, horseback riding, golf, tennis, and fishing. A popular option is the Stowe Recreation Path, a scenic 5.5-mile trail through a greenway along the West Branch River.

Stowe to Mount Mansfield

The drive winds through Stowe and bends up the West Branch of the Waterbury River. After 4 miles the highway leaves most development behind and heads up the broad valley toward looming Mount Mansfield and its famed facial profile. The Stowe Country Club and its eighteen-hole golf course, open to the public, sit on the right just out of town. The Trapp Family Lodge, one of the area's more popular attractions, is still owned by the Trapp family. Reach the lodge by taking the well-marked left turn just past the golf course. The lodge, rebuilt after the original one burned in 1980, sits in the shadow of Luce Hill. The Baroness von Trapp, buried here after her 1987 death, settled with her family in Stowe because the Green Mountains resembled her beloved Austria.

Rock walls loom above the Smugglers Notch Scenic Drive.

The highway and valley bend northwest following a broad valley floored with gravel glacial deposits. After 7 miles the drive begins to climb. Three ski touring centers lie along this stretch of highway—Edson Hill (30 miles of trails), Topnotch (20 miles of trails), and Stowe Mountain Resort (60 miles of trails). The signed turn for the **Mount Mansfield Toll Road** is on the left as the road climbs.

The 4.5-mile dirt toll road, open from late May through October, makes a spectacular scenic detour. This popular route finishing on Mansfield's summit ridge, and the roof of Vermont offers spectacular views and Vermont's most extensive alpine tundra—the cold, windswept land above timberline. The road dates back to 1858 when a carriage road was hacked onto the peak's slopes and a modest hotel built in the saddle between The Nose and The Chin. The first 3 miles wind up through a forest of northern hardwoods, including beech, sugar maple, and paper and yellow birches. Above, the road steeply climbs and switchbacks through a life zone akin to that of northern Canada with its forest of balsam fir, mountain ash, and paper birch. The auto trip ends at a parking area below The Nose, a 4,020-foot promontory on Mansfield's long summit ridge.

A worthwhile hike treks northwest from here along the Long Trail for 1.4 miles to The Chin, Mount Mansfield's 4,393-foot high point. The trail wends through a pygmy forest of balsam fir *krummholz,* the crooked trees twisted and stunted by relentless high winds, and finishes atop 250 acres of tundra covered with rare and endangered plant species. The plants here are like those species found in the Arctic more than 1,000 miles to the north, including turflike Bigelow's sedge, alpine bilberry, crowberry, and mountain cranberry. These small but hardy plants, adapted to a frigid world of snow, high winds, and a three-month growing season, occur on only a handful of New England summits. Despite the harsh conditions, life not only survives but flourishes here on this land above the trees.

The vegetation, however, forms a very delicate ecosystem that is easily damaged by thoughtless walkers. Tundra has almost no carrying capacity, and any human use quickly impacts the plants. Trampled areas take hundreds of years to recover. Stay on the rock-surfaced paths and boardwalks to preserve this unique alpine grassland from being loved to death.

Mount Mansfield's summits also yield some of Vermont's best far-reaching views on a clear day. Low hills roll westward to the glistening expanse of Lake Champlain. Farther west, New York's Adirondack Mountains recline above the lake. To the east loom the Worcester Mountains above the broad Stowe Valley. Beyond them stretch the high peaks of the White Mountains in New Hampshire, their lofty summits studding the distant horizon. Mount Ascutney's solitary summit looms to the south above the Connecticut River Valley, while the long crest of the Green Mountains marches southward past prominent 4,083-foot Camels

Hump. The pleasant valley of the Lamoille River unwinds to the north, and in the hazy distance beyond it lie domed peaks in southern Quebec, including Mont Royal overlooking Montreal.

Up to Smugglers Notch

Past the turnoff to Mount Mansfield, VT 108 steadily climbs upward through the narrowing U-shaped glacial valley. A roadside parking area on the right just past the toll road leads to a short trail that drops down to Bingham Falls, a cascade tucked into a shallow gorge. After 9 miles the road enters 38,000-acre Mount Mansfield State Forest. Only 0.25 mile later is the main turn to Stowe Ski Resort.

On the northeast slope of Mount Mansfield, **Stowe Ski Resort** is one of America's oldest ski slopes and one of the largest east of the Rockies. Skiing began here as early as 1912. A ski jumping event at a winter carnival drew more than a thousand spectators in 1921. Albert Gottlieb designed and built, with the help of a Civilian Conservation Corps crew, one of America's first ski trails—the famed Nose Dive Trail—here in 1933. The mountain's and the East's first chairlift opened in 1940. The National Ski Patrol, a skier's rescue squad, was organized here in 1938. Today Stowe Ski Resort spreads over two mountains—Mount Mansfield and Spruce Peak. Its 39 miles of slopes and forty-eight trails are served by twelve lifts. The gondola climbing Mount Mansfield's steep flank offers summer travelers a good alternative to a drive to the summit.

Smugglers Notch State Park sits across the highway from Stowe Ski Resort. The park offers thirty-four campsites, including fourteen lean-tos, and hiking trails. The Spruce Peak section of the ski area is also accessed from here. An alpine slide, a popular summer attraction for kids, twists down the mountainside.

Past the state park and ski area, the highway climbs steeply upward for 2 miles to Smugglers Notch. A picnic area lies along a tumbling creek about a mile past the state park. Above here the valley funnels visitors toward the precipitous notch. Steep, forested slopes are littered with massive moss-covered boulders and broken by soaring moist cliffs. Small gurgling creeks tumble over cascades and boulders in the thick forest. The last 0.5 mile, a winding, narrow road of sharp hairpin turns, slows traffic to a crawl, and the shoulderless road gives scant room for oncoming cars to pass. **Cars pulling trailers and recreational vehicles should not attempt to drive this road section.**

Near the top the road threads through immense moss-covered boulders before leveling off and reaching a parking area atop the 2,162-foot pass. One huge boulder, King Rock, is designated by a plaque that notes the 6,000-ton block rolled from the cliffs above in 1910. Park at the rest area atop the notch and walk around. A trail climbs the opposite hillside to good viewpoints of the abrupt defile. Rock climbers enjoy scaling the scattered boulders on the notch summit.

Smugglers Notch is a narrow, leafy cleft filled with damp air. A canopy of trees encloses the road and summit parking area in a shroud of cool shadow, while sunlight glints off broken cliffs of metamorphic rock high above. The twisted rock, belonging to the Camels Hump group from the Cambrian Age some 550 million years ago, is green schist (colored by the mineral chlorite) interspersed with layers of erosion-resistant quartzite. The rocks were folded, faulted, then thrust westward from their original position and slowly uplifted. As the mountains rose, erosion, particularly glaciation, attacked and sculpted them into the mountain range seen today. As much as 6 miles of rock layers were stripped off the old peaks, leaving only stumps of the once-mighty range.

Periodic episodes of glaciation excavated the Green Mountains over the last two million years, but it was the last great advance, called the Wisconsin glaciation, that put the finishing touches on the scenery. This ice sheet surged across New England some 20,000 years ago, burying Vermont under mile-thick ice. During the early part of the Wisconsin glaciation, valley glaciers filled the valleys on either side of Smugglers Notch. Later the advancing ice sheet overrode Mount Mansfield and locked the land in an icy grip. The ice gouged deep U-shaped valleys and scraped their sides into cliffs and steep slopes. The ice further contoured the landscape, softening and smoothing its rough edges and erasing all traces of previous glacial periods.

The cliffs and forests of Smugglers Notch, like the summit of Mount Mansfield, harbor a selection of rare and hardy plants found almost nowhere else in New England. The cliffs host an arctic flora superbly adapted to harsh living conditions—cool, moist summer weather, deep winter snows, and frigid temperatures of spring and fall. Plants found here include mountain saxifrage and butterwort, a carnivorous plant that snares insects in its sticky leaves. Common trees found on the pass are sugar maple and yellow birch. The notch is famed for its numerous fern species, however. Vermont boasts more than eighty species of this graceful, shade-loving plant, including the rare green spleenwort. This beautiful fern was first discovered in the notch by botanist Cyrus Pringle in 1876.

Smugglers Notch received its colorful name in the tumultuous period just before the War of 1812 broke out between the fledgling American republic and the British Empire. Trade with Canada was prohibited at that time by President Thomas Jefferson's Embargo Act. Businessmen, however, were quick to see the opportunity to make a few dollars by smuggling goods along the old Indian trail through this notch in Vermont's remote backcountry. Contraband, including herds of cattle to feed hungry British soldiers, passed through the mountain fastness on its way to markets in Boston and Quebec. A small, damp cave tucked into a cliff west of the notch is where the smugglers supposedly stashed their cargoes.

Down to Jeffersonville

The highway drops away from the pass, swings onto the northeast flank of a deep amphitheater drained by the Brewster River, and edges across steep, wooded slopes. The road plunges almost 1,700 feet in 8 miles from the notch to the drive's end in Jeffersonville. The first 3 miles are the steepest. After 0.5 mile the highway sweeps past a roadside waterfall, its frothy water cascading over rock ledges. **Smugglers Notch Ski Resort** lies another mile downhill. This self-contained resort offers over 50 miles of ski trails on three mountains with a 2,610-foot vertical drop. The area also has accommodations, indoor tennis, a skating rink, a ski shop, and other resort amenities.

Past the resort, the road leaves Mount Mansfield State Forest and begins to flatten out, paralleling the Brewster River as it tumbles over worn cobbles and ponds behind beaver dams. A picnic area sits on the roadside at 16 miles. The **Brewster River Gorge,** with cascades and riffling rapids in a steep rocky canyon, lies off the road near here. The drive route descends along the riverbank, passes the small hamlet of South Cambridge, and swings onto a high gravel terrace west of the river in the broadening valley. It then runs along the terrace for 1.5 miles before dropping steeply into the river canyon. About 0.5 mile later the drive enters Jeffersonville and ends at the junction of VT 108 and Vermont Highway 15.

At road's end **Jeffersonville** is a placid old town spread along the south bank of the Lamoille River, one of Vermont's few east-west trending rivers. The town, named after Thomas Jefferson, once boasted a bustling lumber industry. Now it's a quiet place with a peaceful nineteenth-century ambience. Attractions include the Mary and Alden Bryan Memorial Gallery with its superb New England landscapes; the Windridge Bakery, a former dry goods store converted to a bakery and cafe (try their maple-syrup bread); and the elegant Le Cheval d'Or French restaurant next door to the bakery. The local chamber of commerce on Main Street dispenses lodging, dining, and visitor advice. From here, travelers can retrace their paths to Stowe via the scenic drive for a second look at the spectacular scenery or head southwest on VT 15 to Burlington.

Lamoille River Scenic Drive

14

General description: A 34-mile drive over rolling hills and along the placid Lamoille River between St. Johnsbury and Morrisville.

Special attractions: St. Johnsbury, Fairbanks Museum and Planetarium, Maple Grove Maple Museum and Factory, St. Johnsbury Athenaeum, American Society of Dowsers (Danville), Fisher Covered Railway Bridge, trout fishing.

Location: Northern Vermont.

Drive route numbers: U.S. Highway 2, Vermont Highway 15.

Travel season: Year-round. Expect snow and icy conditions in winter.

Camping: Elmore State Park, south of the drive and southeast of Morrisville off Vermont Highway 12, offers sixty sites from late May to mid-October. Includes showers, toilets, phone, tables, but no hook-ups. A private campground is south of Hardwick.

Services: All services in St. Johnsbury, Danville, Hardwick, and Morrisville.

Nearby attractions: Lake Elmore State Park, Moss Glen Falls, Stowe attractions, Stowe Ski Resort, Mount Mansfield Toll Road, Smugglers Notch, Green Mountain National Forest, Lake Willoughby, Connecticut River Valley, Crawford Notch (NH), Franconia Notch (NH), White Mountain National Forest (NH).

The Drive

The Lamoille River Scenic Drive runs through pleasant countryside west of St. Johnsbury to the Lamoille River Valley. It continues along the river to Morrisville at the northern base of the Worcester Mountains.

The 34-mile drive begins at the intersection of Interstate 91 (exit 21) and U.S. Highway 2 just west of St. Johnsbury. The town lies east of the junction on the other side of The Knob, a 1,120-foot-high bluff, among high hills at the confluence of the Sleepers, Passumpsic, and Moose Rivers. **St. Johnsbury,** affectionately nicknamed "St. J" by locals, is a surprisingly elegant and cultured town in Vermont's mostly rustic Northeast Kingdom. Built along the riverbanks and terraces, the town retains its industrial roots and prosperity shown by Victorian mansions along Main Street, stately stone and brick buildings (including a fine museum and the St. Johnsbury Athenaeum), and a bustling downtown.

St. Johnsbury

The area was first settled in 1786 after Jonathan Arnold and a group of fellow Rhode Islanders received a town charter. They named their farming community for French consul Michel Guillame Jean de Crevecoeur, a friend of Vermont Revolutionary War hero Ethan Allen who wrote under the pen name of J. Hector Saint

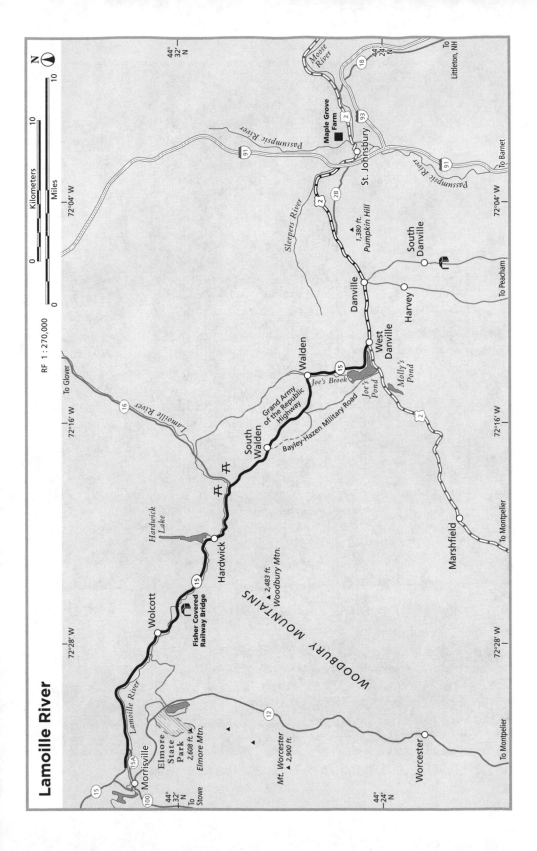

Lamoille River

RF 1 : 270,000

The Fisher Covered Railway Bridge is the only one of its kind left in Vermont.

John. Beginning as a farming center, St. J flourished in the nineteenth-century as a railway hub and industrial center. The Fairbanks family, early settlers and inventors, fueled the town's growth and provided an industrial and philanthropic legacy that remains.

Thaddeus and Erastus Fairbanks established an iron foundry here in 1823. Thaddeus, the family inventor, patented a cast-iron plow and later came up with the idea of a platform scale using a system of levers to reduce the weight needed to counterbalance a load of local hemp, which was sold to make rope. His ingenious idea became the Fairbanks Scale in 1830 and the family fortunes soon swelled as precision industrial scales were shipped around the world for measuring everything from doses of medicine to railroad cars. The scale factory still exists in St. Johnsbury. After the conglomerate ownership threatened to relocate the factory elsewhere in the 1960s, townspeople banded together and raised the funds to build a new plant.

The influence that the Fairbanks family and industry had on St. Johnsbury goes far beyond the factory. The Fairbanks brothers and their progeny became a nineteenth-century dynasty that produced not only a thriving business but two Vermont governors. The **Fairbanks Museum and Planetarium,** founded by Franklin Fairbanks in 1889, occupies a red sandstone building on Main Street. The museum's collection includes a natural history section with fossils; stuffed bears, moose, and 300 hummingbird species; Indian artifacts and stone tools; a Civil War exhibit; Fairbanks Scales; a Vermont wild plants exhibit in summer; a hands-on kids' nature center; one of the nation's oldest weather stations; and a fifty-seat planetarium.

The St. Johnsbury Athenaeum, built in 1871 by Governor Horace Fairbanks, is another Fairbanks legacy. It houses the town library and a fine art museum with a superb selection of American nineteenth-century landscapes. The collection centerpiece is Albert Bierstadt's grand *Domes of the Yosemite,* a huge 116-inch by 180-inch painting hung below a skylight on the gallery's back wall. Other notable town buildings are the Gothic-designed North Congregational Church with red granite pillars, the Neoclassical white clapboard South Congregational Church, the 1856 Caledonia County Courthouse, and the 1883 Canadian Pacific Railroad Depot.

Make sure to visit **Maple Grove Farm** just east of St. Johnsbury on US 2. The farm, Vermont's second most popular tourist attraction, is the world's largest maple candy maker. Owned by the Cary Maple Sugar Company, Maple Grove offers informative exhibits that detail the maple sugar to syrup process. A tour of the candy factory shows all facets of producing maple candy and associated products such as maple salad dressing. Visitors can sample some of the delights, as well as purchase almost any maple product imaginable in the gift shop.

St. Johnsbury to Hardwick

After visiting St. Johnsbury and its attractions, head west to the junction of I–91 and US 2 just west of town. The drive follows a two-lane, paved highway that runs northwest along the Sleepers River in rolling forested hills broken by occasional farms and fields. After a couple of miles, the highway bends southwest away from the river up a shallow valley, and after 6 miles it reaches a high plateau. A pullout on the south side of the highway yields an excellent view of the Vermont hills above the Connecticut River Valley stretching southeast to the looming White Mountains in northern New Hampshire. Snow crowns the high peaks much of the year. On clear days their white summits glisten in the sun like alabaster towers.

Past the overlook, the road dips through a vale and climbs into Danville after 7 miles. A pretty village spread across a rounded hilltop, **Danville** was northeastern Vermont's largest town some 200 years ago when it had a population of 1,500. The state legislature even met here in 1805. But St. Johnsbury eclipsed it in size and population, and in 1855 the Caledonia County seat was transferred from Danville to St. J. The town, built around an attractive tree-shaded green, was first settled in 1784 and named for French Admiral d'Anville. Much of the village was destroyed by fires in the 1880s, and from the ashes rose the library in 1890 and the imposing town hall in 1925. The Caledonia Bank, one of the state's safest banks, was last held up in 1935—such a rare occurrence in Vermont that it warranted national publicity. One of Danville's most famed citizens was Thaddeus Stevens, a grim, bitter abolitionist and congressman who served as chairman of the powerful House Ways and Means Committee. He opposed the post–Civil War reconstructionist policies of President Andrew Johnson, arguing for sterner measures to punish slave owners and secessionists.

Danville is now home to the 3,500-member American Society of Dowsers. A dowser is a valued New England resident, since he or she uses a forked stick (called a water witch or wand) or a pendulum to divine subterranean water. The society holds its colorful annual convention here every year in mid-September. The Dowser's Hall offers some informative displays and a dowsing video. Practitioners can purchase dowsing equipment and books or attend weekend workshops.

The drive route continues west on US 2 across the high plateau, with more views of the upland hills and New Hampshire's White Mountains. Drivers reach West Danville after 3 miles. Its main point of interest is **Hastings Store,** a genuine old-fashioned general store that appears unchanged since the 1850s. The drive turns north here at the junction of US 2 and Vermont Highway 15; turn north (right) on VT 15.

The road swings around the north shore of Joe's Pond, an L-shaped lake named for Indian Joe. This Indian guide and Revolutionary War scout is remem-

Wolcott and its cemetery flank the Lamoille River Scenic Drive.

bered with the lake that bears his name and a small memorial in West Danville. Joe's Pond, an old summer resort with a public beach, drains south to the Connecticut River and Long Island Sound, while neighboring Molly's Pond, named for Joe's wife, empties north into the St. Lawrence River.

The drive bends north past the pond and follows a wooded valley alongside Joe's Brook for 4 miles to Walden. This rural hamlet was originally built around a military blockhouse on the Bayley-Hazen Military Road and named for its commander. The 55-mile road, authorized by George Washington, was begun in 1776 for launching possible attacks on British Canada. After a month builder Colonel Jacob Bayley decided that the road would also make an ideal passage for British troops to march south into New England and suspended construction until 1779. After the Revolution the road opened northern Vermont to settlement. The road stretched from Newbury on the Connecticut River to Hazen's Notch at Westfield. Almost two-thirds of the route remains in use today.

The highway turns west and climbs into thickly forested hills, passing hayfields and farms. Good views of the Green and Worcester ranges to the southwest may be glimpsed through the trees. After a few miles the road descends through a gentle valley to South Walden, a small village with a handful of houses. The highway continues down the narrowing valley beside winding Haynesville Brook and reaches its junction with Vermont Highway 16 and the Lamoille River after 20 miles. Continue west along the river a few miles more to Hardwick.

A good-sized industrial town of 2,700, **Hardwick** is spread along the banks of the Lamoille River in a shallow valley. The town was first settled by Captain John Bridgam in 1797, as an agricultural center. It grew, along with neighboring Woodbury to the south, into one of the nation's leading granite centers after Henry Mack's 1868 granite discovery. As many as fourteen quarries cut mammoth blocks of Vermont granite and shipped it to Hardwick via the Hardwick & Woodbury Railroad. The railroad boasted the most hairpin turns and steepest grades of any eastern line until its abandonment in 1940. Skilled European stonecutters milled the stone, which was then shipped all over the world. The busy, prosperous town, nicknamed "Little Chicago," boasted five churches, numerous saloons, a couple of elegant hotels, and three creameries. Hardwick's fortunes and population ebbed after the 1920s, leaving the town a shell of its glorious past.

Along the Lamoille River

Continue through Hardwick on VT 15 past its junction with Vermont Highway 14. Follow the placid Lamoille River northwest out of town. The river, rising northeast of here at Horse Pond, is one of three Vermont rivers that flow east to west through the Green Mountains to Lake Champlain. The three rivers—the Lamoille, Missisquoi, and Winooski—are "antecedent" rivers in geologic terms, following courses established before the Green Mountains began uplifting some 430 million years ago.

A couple of miles past Hardwick, the highway bends west and crosses to the river's west bank. Just upstream of this crossing sits the 103-foot-long **Fisher Covered Railway Bridge,** a unique bridge spanning the river's slow currents. The wooden bridge, built in 1908 and reinforced with steel beams in 1968, is the only covered railway bridge still in use in Vermont. The weathered bridge features a full-length cupola that provided an escape for locomotive smoke. A pullout with restrooms allows travelers to view the bridge.

After crossing the river the highway runs along the river before recrossing and bending through Wolcott, a tiny hamlet founded in 1789 and named for General Oliver Wolcott, a signer of the Declaration of Independence. The drive continues down the broad valley, past wooded hills and occasional farms. A sign on a barn with a steep metal roof close to the road warns drivers to watch for sliding snow from the roof.

Farther west the road passes a private campground. Views of the Green Mountains unfold to the west, including the prominent escarpment of 3,715-foot White Face Mountain on the north end of the Mount Mansfield massif. The long, humpbacked ridge of 2,608-foot Elmore Mountain looms to the south. Elmore

State Park, 4.2 miles southeast of Morrisville on Vermont Highway 12, straddles the mountain's slopes and offers hiking, camping, and picnicking. A superb hike with great views of the Worcester Range, Green Mountains, and Lamoille Valley climbs 1,528 feet in a few miles from the park's parking area to the Elmore Fire Tower perched atop the mountain summit.

The scenic drive ends at the junction of VT 15 and VT 15A. VT 15 continues west along the twisting Lamoille River to Jeffersonville and Cambridge before turning southward. VT 15A bends south, crosses the river, and enters Morrisville, a lumber and dairy town spread across a gravel terrace south of the river.

15

Lake Willoughby Scenic Drive

General description: A 35-mile scenic drive in Vermont's Northeast Kingdom between Lyndonville and Derby Center.

Special attractions: Lake Willoughby, Willoughby State Forest, Great Falls of the Clyde River, scenic views, hiking, fishing, boating, ice and rock climbing.

Location: Northern Vermont.

Drive route numbers: U.S. Highway 5 and Vermont Highway 5A.

Travel season: Year-round. Winters are snowy and icy.

Camping: No public campgrounds are found along the drive. There are a couple of private

ones near Lake Willoughby, including White Caps Campground.

Services: All services in St. Johnsbury, Lyndonville, and Derby Center. Limited or seasonal services in other towns along the highways.

Nearby attractions: St. Johnsbury attractions, Connecticut River, Smugglers Notch State Park, Mount Mansfield State Forest, Stowe, Chester A. Arthur birthplace, Franconia Notch (NH), Crawford Notch (NH), White Mountain National Forest (NH), Mount Washington (NH), Dixville Notch (NH).

The Drive

The Lake Willoughby drive traverses a scenic and hauntingly beautiful section of northeastern Vermont, crossing 35 miles of the remote upland area nicknamed the "Northeast Kingdom." The drive, following U.S. Highway 5 and Vermont Highway 5A, begins in Lyndonville just north of St. Johnsbury and ends in Derby Center 5 miles from the border between the United States and Canada. Along the drive is fjordlike Lake Willoughby, a long, thin lake bounded by mountains, which is one of Vermont's most spectacular natural wonders.

Lyndonville and West Burke

Following paved roads and open year-round, the drive begins in Lyndonville just north of St. Johnsbury. To find the beginning of the drive, take exit 23 from Interstate 91 north of St. Johnsbury and follow US 5 north through bustling **Lyndonville.** The town was chartered to Jonathon Arnold in 1780, who named it for his son Josias Lyndon Arnold, but not settled until 1788. Spreading across the east bank of the Passumpsic River, Lyndonville prospered as a railroad hub, headquarters for the Passumpsic Division of the Boston & Maine Railroad in the

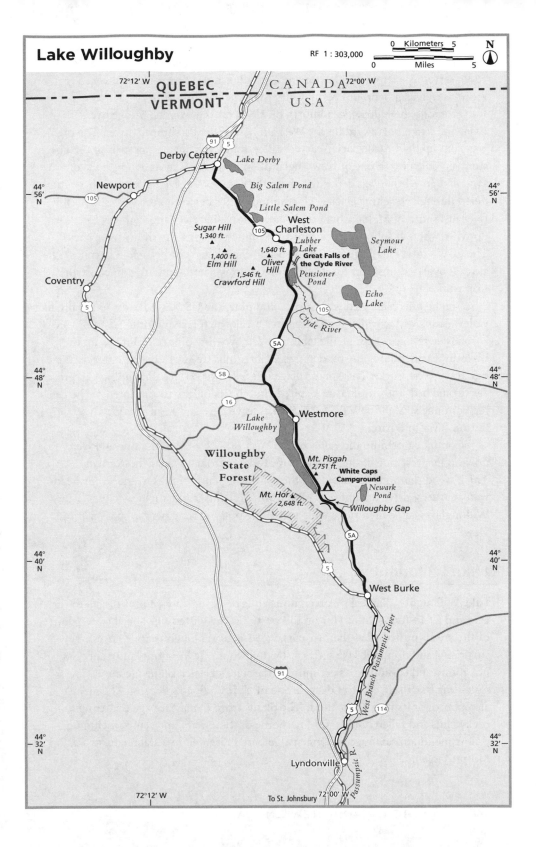

late nineteenth century. Today the town, site of the Caledonia County Fair since 1846, serves as a supply center for smaller villages and farms in northeast Vermont as well as a bedroom community for larger St. Johnsbury.

From the town green, head north on US 5, cross a wooden bridge over the river, and strike northward up the West Branch of the Passumpsic River. The highway runs up the broad, glacier-carved valley, following the west branch of the Passumpsic Valley esker, one of New England's longest. An esker is a long ridge of sand and gravel that was deposited along the course of a river or stream that tunneled through a melting glacier. This sinuous esker begins on the west side of the river just south of St. Johnsbury and snakes alongside river and highway to Lyndonville, where it splits into east and west branches along the river's two valleys. The esker's total length from start to end on the longer east branch is 24 miles. The esker is quarried in places for its clean mix of gravel and sand, used in construction work.

Rolling hills blanketed with spruce and pine line US 5 as it heads up the broad valley. Farms with cornfields and pastures break the forest and offer pastoral views. A roadside rest area with picnic tables shaded by white pines sits 3 miles up the highway. Farther along the road passes a Christmas tree farm before entering the hamlet of West Burke. This small village offers visitor services, including gas, groceries, and bed-and-breakfasts. A spired church sits off the town center. At the center, continue straight on VT 5A; US 5 takes leave here and heads west up the Sutton River to Barton.

Continue north up the valley of the West Branch of the Passumpsic River, now on the west side of the road as it meanders across a marshy bottomland. Thick woods hem in the valley and the road as it gently climbs to the river's headwaters. After a drive of almost 6 miles from West Burke, the highway crests Willoughby Gap, a high ridge with a roadside pullout. Stop here to marvel at the view.

Lake Willoughby

Lake Willoughby, flanked by precipitous cliffs on 2,751-foot Mount Pisgah to the east and 2,648-foot Mount Hor on the west, fills the glistening valley below. Much of the area is protected as the two-part, 7,682-acre Willoughby State Forest. The surprising and dramatic lake offers a startling view of a Vermont landscape that is not round and contoured as are most of the state's glacier-shaped features. The 5-mile-long lake itself, 308 feet deep, is one of New England's deepest. The area is also famed for its rare Arctic flora, relic plants from the last ice age that cling to the rocky cliffs and fallen boulders below. Some of these remnant plants, including yellow mountain saxifrage and green alder, are preserved in a state natural area on Mount Pisgah.

Mount Hor towers above Lake Willoughby.

Lake Willoughby, like most of Vermont's natural features, was formed by glaciation. During the last ice age, a glacier followed a river valley along a fault line in the granite bedrock here. After encasing the surrounding land in a sheet of white, the glacier slowly chiseled the U-shaped valley deeper and smoothed the granite mountains on either side. After the ice retreated, both the north and south drainages remained dammed with sand and gravel and formed today's lake.

An excellent hike begins from an inconspicuous trailhead just north of the gap. **The Mount Pisgah Trail** goes only a few miles to its rocky summit. Numerous lookouts are found along the yellow-blazed trail, offering great views of the lake below. The poet Robert Frost referred to the rocky flanks of Mount Pisgah as "the Devil's den." The trail, as it reaches the airy clifftops, is a great place to watch raptors. In fall, flocks of hawks and falcons catch rising air currents to drift over the mountains here. The area was also the last known nesting site in Vermont for the endangered peregrine falcon in the 1950s.

Lake Willoughby is popular with anglers, who come to cast for lake and rainbow trout and land-locked salmon. Sand beaches at both its north and south ends allow swimming, but a dip on all but the warmest summer days will quickly remind the bather of the lake's glacial origins.

The drive drops steeply from Willoughby Gap and reaches the lake's south shore in 0.5 mile. A small sand beach, a marina, houses, tourist cabins, and a private campground lie at the south end. The highway winds north along the lake's eastern edge, hemmed against the rocky shore by Mount Pisgah's abrupt flank of granite cliffs and slabs. This 1-mile shelf section offers spectacular views of the lake and cliffed Mount Hor to the west. Several pullouts give dramatic views of the choppy lake, the soaring cliffs, and cascading waterfalls.

Mount Pisgah's lakeside front above the highway is acclaimed as one of the nation's finest ice-climbing areas, with more than twenty-five ice flows on the cliff face during winter. Rick Wilcox, author of a New England ice-climbing guidebook, calls the ice climbs "unrivaled in sheer size, verticality and sustained difficulty." Since the mid-1970s the Lake Willoughby area has been a testing ground for those climbers who pursue the rigorous challenge of scaling frozen waterfalls. The first route here was established in 1974 at Twenty Below Zero Gully, named for the frigid conditions climbers encountered.

Past Mount Pisgah and the state forest, the highway passes a public boat ramp and enters an area of summer cottages, homes, and motels that reflect Willoughby's long-standing popularity as a summer resort. In the late nineteenth century, the area was filled with grand hotels, tearooms, and dance halls to entertain visitors. Today the activity is more subdued, with the small village of Westmore being the focal point for fishermen, snowmobilers, sailors, and windsurfers.

North to Derby

At the north end of the lake, VT 5A intersects Vermont Highway 16. Continue north (straight) on VT 5A. The last 16 miles of the drive run north from here to Derby Center. Vermont Highway 58 is reached after 1.5 miles. The drive runs over wooded hills broken by rolling farmland. Barns, silos, and farmhouses interrupt the brooding landscape. The road swings across the western edge of a broad valley. The slow Clyde River, named after the famed Scottish river, meanders through pastures and marshes on the valley floor. Upriver, the Clyde has such a low gradient that it sometimes reverses itself and flows backwards to its headwaters at Island Pond.

Pensioner Pond, a large lake surrounded by low hills, is 8 miles north of Willoughby. It received its name after a Revolutionary War soldier used his military pension to build a mill here. On the north end of this small lake, the highway meets Vermont Highway 105, which runs southeast through lovely country to Island Pond. VT 5A ends here. Continue north on VT 105. Just north of the highway intersection are the Great Falls of the Clyde River. Here the river narrows and plunges through a series of small falls and cataracts in a twisting gorge before emptying into Lubber Lake.

The road then curves through West Charleston, a small village that thrived before the local lumber-milling industry closed down, and continues northwest along the Clyde River past pastures and dairy farms. Big and Little Salem Ponds lie alongside the road and offer good salmon, bass, and northern pike fishing. The highway winds slowly downhill, dips to cross the river on an old bridge, and climbs into the town of Derby Center. Drive north past large white-clapboard homes and businesses along a wide green and, 0.5 mile later, reach US 5. Turn left here and drive a mile west to the drive's northern terminus at I–91, which you can take south to Lyndonville and St. Johnsbury. Quebec lies a scant 5 miles north.

16

Connecticut River Scenic Drive

General description: A 41-mile scenic route along the pastoral Connecticut River Valley between Claremont and Orford in western New Hampshire.

Special attractions: Cornish-Windsor Covered Bridge, Saint-Gaudens National Historic Site, Connecticut River, Dartmouth College, Hood Museum of Art, Orford Street Historic District, Appalachian Trail, scenic views, fishing, hiking, nature study.

Location: Western New Hampshire.

Drive route numbers: New Hampshire Highways 12A and 10.

Travel season: Year-round.

Camping: No campgrounds along the drive. Nearby campgrounds in Vermont include Mount Ascutney State Park (forty-nine sites) northwest of Ascutney (VT); Quechee Gorge State Park (fifty-four sites) just west of White River Junction and Lebanon; and Thetford Hill State Park (sixteen sites) west of East Thetford and Lyme.

Services: All services in Claremont, Lebanon, and Hanover. Limited services in towns along the drive including Plainfield, Lyme, and Orford.

Nearby attractions: Cardigan State Park, Sculptured Rocks Natural Area, Mount Sunapee State Park, Gile State Forest, White Mountains National Forest, Bedell Bridge State Park, Mount Ascutney State Park (VT), Quechee Gorge State Park (VT), Woodstock (VT).

The Drive

The 41-mile Connecticut River Scenic Drive explores some of New Hampshire's most charming scenery as it winds through hill country along the east bank of the mighty Connecticut River in the Upper Valley. The rural secondary roads along the drive pass not only superb views, but also some of New Hampshire's famed cultural and historic shrines including the home of Augustus Saint-Gaudens, perhaps the nineteenth-century's greatest American sculptor; the longest covered bridge in the United States at Cornish; and the beautiful Orford Street Historic District at the drive's northern end.

The Connecticut River, New England's longest and largest river, cleaves the region politically, forming the boundary between New Hampshire and Vermont, and geologically. Some geologists interpret the zone that the river follows as a tectonic boundary between two crustal plates—North American bedrock on the west and a slice of an exotic plate from Europe or Africa on the east. The river existed well before the long glacial episodes that have intermittently covered and shaped

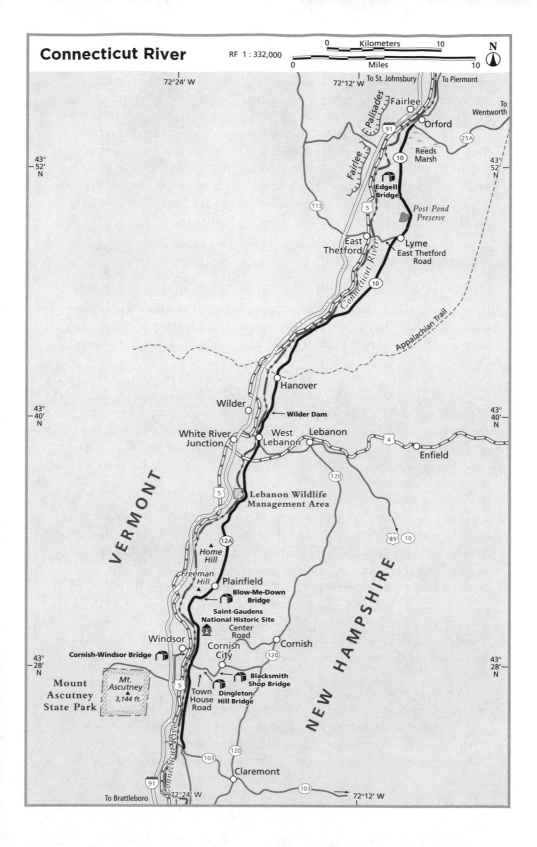

Connecticut River

RF 1 : 332,000

Kilometers 0 — 10
Miles 0 — 10

N

72°24' W 72°12' W To St. Johnsbury To Piermont

Fairlee

To Wentworth

Orford

91

25A

43°52' N

10

Reeds Marsh

Palisades

Fairlee

Edgell Bridge

113

5

Post Pond Preserve

43°52' N

East Thetford

Lyme
East Thetford Road

10

Connecticut River

Appalachian Trail

Hanover

Wilder

Wilder Dam

43°40' N

43°40' N

White River Junction

West Lebanon

Lebanon

4

Enfield

120

VERMONT

5

Lebanon Wildlife Management Area

89 10

12A

Home Hill

NEW HAMPSHIRE

Freeman Hill

Plainfield

Blow-Me-Down Bridge

Saint-Gaudens National Historic Site

Center Road

Windsor

Cornish-Windsor Bridge

Cornish City

Cornish

120

43°28' N

43°28' N

Mount Ascutney State Park

Mt. Ascutney 3,144 ft.

5

Town House Road

Blacksmith Shop Bridge

Dingleton Hill Bridge

103

120

Claremont

91

Connecticut River

103

To Brattleboro 72°24' W 72°12' W

New England's topography. The last episode, called the Wisconsin glaciation, choked the valley with ice and chiseled it deeper into underlying bedrock.

Later, as the glaciers melted, the valley was filled by Lake Hitchcock, a long, thin lake that stretched 200 miles north from the moraine that blocked the river's course near Middletown, Connecticut. Sediment and silt deposited in the lake by the melting glacier allow geologists to study the rate of glacial recession from New England. Studies of the distinctly laminated varved clays, each layer representing a single year's deposit, show that it took 4,300 years at an average of 245 feet annually for the glacier to recede from Middletown to St. Johnsbury, Vermont. Much of the drive crosses terraced floodplains above the riverbanks.

Claremont to Cornish

The drive begins just west of Claremont at the junction of New Hampshire Highways 12A and 103. This junction is on the east side of the Connecticut River opposite exit 8 on Interstate 91 and Ascutney, Vermont. The journey's first leg, following NH 12A, travels 18 miles north from here to the southern outskirts of West Lebanon.

The rural highway runs north along the river's east bank past orderly cornfields, apple orchards, and rich farmlands studded with strikingly plain barns and adjoining houses. Low, undulating hills border the riparian floodplain to the east. Pyramid-shaped Mount Ascutney, a 3,144-foot peak, looms above the valley to the west in Vermont. This dominating mountain, standing alone and aloof, is a monadnock or high point that towers almost 2,000 feet above the lower, older erosional surface that surrounds it. Ascutney's summit is reached by a 3.8-mile, paved toll road in Mount Ascutney State Park. The mountain is formed of igneous rocks that are part of the White Mountain magma series deposited some 200 million years ago. The mountain's commanding height along the Atlantic Flyway makes the peak a popular spot for birds and birders. The state park offers a forty-nine-site campground and an excellent trail to Mount Ascutney's apex.

At 4.2 miles the drive route passes the private Chase House, the 1808 birthplace of Salmon Portland Chase. Educated at nearby Dartmouth, Chase defended runaway slaves as a lawyer before becoming an Ohio senator and governor, helping found the Republican Party, and serving as Lincoln's Secretary of the Treasury and Chief Justice of the United States. Other old homes dating from the 1770s also line the road.

About 0.5 mile later the road enters Cornish. Two covered bridges lie just east of this village on Town House Road. The first, **Dingleton Hill Bridge**, is 78 feet long. The second, **Blacksmith Shop Bridge**, spans 96 feet across Mill Brook and was built in 1881. Back on the highway, the drive reaches New Hampshire's most famous covered bridge in another mile. The **Cornish-Windsor Bridge** (or the

The Cornish-Windsor Bridge, spanning the broad Connecticut River, is the nation's longest covered bridge.

Windsor-Cornish Bridge, depending on what side of the river you're on) is the longest covered bridge in the country. The 449-foot, two-span bridge, one of the most photographed bridges in America, was built in 1866 at the cost of $9,000. It was engineered and constructed by James Tasker, a construction genius who couldn't read or write. Tasker used heavy, squared timbers rather than thinner planks to form the lattice work, making a very strong design. Today's bridge, a designated National Historic Civil Engineering Landmark, is the fourth one on the site.

The bridge was the next-to-last Connecticut River bridge to charge a toll. The cost was two cents on foot, four cents for a horse, two cents for a cow, fifteen cents to tote a cord of wood across, and twenty cents for a four-horse carriage. A sign across the bridge entrance still says: WALK YOUR HORSE OR PAY TWO DOLLARS FINE. Over time the State of New Hampshire slowly bought out the bridge companies and opened them for free passage, a popular move to discontinue what was called "interstate holdup." The last toll on the Cornish Bridge was collected on May 31, 1943. The next day the bridge was ceremoniously opened for nonpaying customers.

The bridge is still open for traffic and is now a popular tourist stop. Pull off at the designated parking area just south of the bridge and walk up to have a look inside. Vendors across the highway sell postcards, drawings, and other bridge paraphernalia.

Windsor, the historic town on the other side of the river, is acclaimed as the Birthplace of Vermont. New Hampshire, as part of its boundary agreement with Vermont, owns the Connecticut River to its west-bank, normal high-water mark.

Saint-Gaudens National Historic Site

Two miles north of the bridge is another unique and important historic site. Turn right at a park sign and follow a short uphill road for 0.6 mile to **Saint-Gaudens National Historic Site.** The site, operated by the National Park Service from May through October, preserves the elegant hilltop home and studio of Augustus Saint-Gaudens, the premier American sculptor of the nineteenth century. Born in Ireland and reared in New York City, Saint-Gaudens worked as an apprentice cameo cutter as a teenager before studying in Paris. He returned to New York and in 1876 at age twenty-seven he received his first commission, the Farragut Monument in today's Madison Square Park. In 1885 he found this lovely spot above the Connecticut River and bought it as a summer residence. Here he executed some of his most famous works, including the Standing Lincoln, a Robert Louis Stevenson memorial relief, and the Shaw Memorial, a brilliant Civil War relief of Colonel Robert Gould Shaw and his Fifty-fourth Massachusetts Black Volunteer Regiment that took fourteen years of exacting work.

The site is scattered with various replicas of Saint-Gaudens's heroic works, sketches, drawings, and casting molds. Visitors can tour the sculptor's house, studio, and exhibition room along with 150 acres of manicured formal gardens and the small Greek temple where Saint-Gaudens is buried. From his deathbed on August 13, 1907, he looked out a window at sunset toward Mount Ascutney and said, "It's very beautiful, but I want to go farther away."

Cornish to Lebanon

Back on the drive, NH 12A passes a historic marker for the Cornish Colony. In the latter part of the nineteenth century, Saint-Gaudens's presence made the rural Cornish area into a thriving artist's colony. Some of the creative artists who lived at the Cornish Colony were the nation's most popular novelist, Winston Churchill (not the British prime minister), and painter Maxfield Parrish. One of Churchill's novels, *Richard Carvell,* sold more than a million copies. The writer hosted President Theodore Roosevelt's 1902 visit to Cornish. Parrish used the surrounding landscape in his colorful, fanciful illustrations for numerous books and magazine covers. Other luminaries who lived and worked here were sculptor Herbert Adams, poet Percy McKaye, architect Charles A. Platt, and artist Kenyon Cox.

The hilltop home and studio of sculptor Augustus Saint-Gaudens is preserved as a National Historic Site.

The highway continues north past small Freeman's Cemetery and a side road that leads to Tasker's Blow-Me-Down Bridge, a 90-foot covered bridge over Blow-Me-Down Brook. The bridge name is a Yankee corruption of the name Blomidon, an early settler. Past the turn, the roadway bends away from the river to the 1761 village of Plainfield. A red brick community church topped by a white spire dominates the residential town.

A series of low wooded hills—Freeman Hill, Stevens Hill, Home Hill, and Short Knoll—separate the highway from the river as it journeys northward. The road crests a low rise between two hills and drops through forest alongside Beaver Book to the river. Here it flattens and runs through thick pine and hardwood forests interrupted by occasional floodplain farms. Hills hem the road in on the east, keeping it along the riverbank. At Bloods Brook the highway passes Lebanon Wildlife Management Area, a swamp studded with cattails and twisted dead tree trunks. The road passes a gravel quarry and enters the southern outskirts of West Lebanon.

The next 6 miles are mostly developed. The drive continues along NH 12A under Interstate 89 and enters West Lebanon. In the town center, go straight on New Hampshire Highway 10 toward Hanover. For a short distance the drive emerges back into bucolic farm country. A roadside picnic area overlooks Wilder Dam and its accompanying hydroelectric plant. Nearby is the Pine Grove Rim Trail. After 3 more miles the highway enters Hanover.

Hanover

Hanover, home of Dartmouth College, remains a bastion of culture and diversity in what seems like the New Hampshire backwoods. The college motto, *Vox Clamantis in Deserto* or "A Voice Cries in the Wilderness," reflects this still-remote character. The college offers a classic Ivy League campus with a grassy quad surrounded by impressive buildings and spreading maple trees. The town of Hanover, originally a farming village, was granted in 1761. The college came eight years later when Eleazar Wheelock decided to move his Indian Charity School from Connecticut to New Hampshire "for the education of Youth of the Indian Tribes, English Youth, and any others." Hanover's citizens offered Wheelock 3,000 acres of land, free labor, and cash to move his school to their town. Governor John Wentworth gave a royal charter to officially establish the school, and the Earl of Dartmouth in England made a generous donation. In gratitude, Wheelock named his college after the Earl.

Dartmouth College and its town of 10,900 residents has since flourished. The college dominates both the town and region's economy and cultural life. Dartmouth itself boasts numerous beautiful buildings, including the famed Dartmouth Row on the east flank of the college green. These four Greek Revival buildings are the 1829 Wentworth Hall; Dartmouth Hall (a 1904 reproduction of the 1791 original destroyed by fire); Thornton Hall; and Reed Hall. The college's brick Webster Hall, fronted by tall columns, is named for Daniel Webster, its most famous alumnus. The 1928 Baker Memorial Library is modeled after Philadelphia's Independence Hall. In the library's basement is a spectacular, must-see series of frescoes called *The Epic of American Civilization,* painted by noted Mexican artist José Clemente Orozco in the early 1930s. The nearby Hood Museum of Art owns an interesting collection of African art, Assyrian bas-reliefs, and paintings by Italian, Dutch, and American artists.

The highway follows Main Street, leading right through Hanover to Dartmouth's campus before skirting around the quad on its east side. Stop and walk around the town and campus. Beside the classic buildings and museums are numerous bookstores, coffee shops, and interesting shops to browse through. During Winter Carnival in February, fantastic ice sculptures cover the quad.

The Appalachian Trail, running 2,140 miles from Georgia to Maine, crosses the river and threads through Hanover before bending north and tackling the White Mountains. The New Hampshire portion of the trail totals 157 miles.

Hanover to Orford

Back on NH 10, the road edges around the east side of campus before heading north. The scenic drive's next leg runs 17 miles from here to Orford along the terraced riverbank. Past the Hanover Country Club golf course is the Cold Regions Research and Engineering Laboratory, a U.S. Army Corps of Engineers research center on glaciers and polar conditions. The flat road passes a few homes and businesses before leaving town and re-entering the countryside. A few miles upstream is Hanover Boat Landing, a popular put-in spot for canoeists. The generally wide and placid Connecticut River offers superb canoeing on its flat water. There are lots of canoe rental places, some offering shuttle service between put-ins and take-outs on the river. As the tar road rolls north, good views unfold of the green Vermont hills to the west.

Almost 10 miles from Hanover, the drive edges the east side of Lyme Hill and enters the village of **Lyme.** This rural farming community is dominated by the narrow town green and its whitewashed, wood-frame Lyme Congregational Church topped by a spire with a small octagonal dome. The church still has twenty-seven numbered and painted horse stalls that were assigned in bygone days to Sunday parishioners. Nearby is a cemetery filled with old gravestones. The town, settled in 1761 and named for England's Lyme Regis, also offers the 1809 Lyme Inn and the excellent Lyme Country Store.

Past Lyme, the highway passes Post Pond Preserve, a town recreation area with good canoeing and fishing. The road then crosses a low gap and follows Clay

Brook north onto the flat river floodplain. Large cornfields and prosperous-looking farms with large barns spread across the fertile bottomland. The 132-foot-long **Edgell Bridge** crosses Clay Brook just west of the drive route. The bridge, built in 1885, was pre-constructed on Lyme Common and transported to the bridge site for assembly—a precursor of modern prefabrication. Farther north is sixty-four-acre Reeds Marsh, a state wildlife area that offers excellent birding on a swampy bend of the wide river.

Next the road gently turns northeast and enters the lovely old town of **Orford.** Set among green hills on the river's edge, Orford is one of those charming, unforgettable villages that travelers stumble across in rural New England. It boasts the Orford Street Historic District, a collection of stately white mansions dubbed Ridge Row, set back from the tree-lined highway. The houses, built in styles including Greek Revival and Federal, were erected between 1773 and 1839 for wealthy businessmen and professionals. They perch in a long row along a low ridge east of the road, fronted by wide, manicured lawns. The town also contains two churches—the 1854 Victorian Congregational Church and the Universalist Church. In the town center is the all-purpose Weeks General Store, established in 1804, and the Orford Social Library.

The scenic drive ends here in the town center where New Hampshire Highway 25A crosses the river to Fairlee, Vermont, and I–91. Fairlee is dominated by the Fairlee Palisades, a series of sheer precipices that offer sport for rock climbers. From I–91, travelers can easily go north to St. Johnsbury or south to White River Junction.

17

Bristol-Rumney Scenic Drive

General description: A 63-mile loop through scenic hills and valleys on the southern edge of the White Mountains.

Special attractions: Hebron Marsh Wildlife Sanctuary, Paradise Point Nature Center, Sculptured Rocks Natural Area, Newfound Lake, Wellington State Park, Sugar Hill State Forest, Cardigan State Park, Canaan Historic District, Lower Shaker Village, Rumney, Rumney Pound, Polar Caves, Mary Baker Eddy House, fishing, camping, swimming, rock climbing, wildlife observation, skiing.

Location: West-central New Hampshire.

Drive route numbers: U.S. Highway 4, New Hampshire Highways 3A, 104, 118, and 25.

Travel season: Year-round.

Camping: No public campgrounds along the drive.

Services: All services in Plymouth, Bristol, Danbury, Canaan, and Rumney.

Nearby attractions: Robert Frost Place, Sugar Hill Historical Museum, Polly's Pancake Parlor, Connecticut River Valley, Clark's Trading Post, Mount Washington, Conway Scenic Railroad, Echo Lake State Park, ski areas, Presidential Range Wilderness Area, Sandwich Range Wilderness Area, Pemigewasset Wilderness Area, Appalachian Trail, Madison Boulder Natural Area, White Lake State Park.

The Drive

This 63-mile loop drive, beginning and ending in West Plymouth just west of Plymouth and Interstate 93, traverses the unspoiled heartland of New Hampshire. Crossing rolling hills and following shallow valleys south of the White Mountains, the drive offers pleasant scenery, quiet back roads, a few quaint villages, and several backwoods natural areas.

West Plymouth to Bristol

The drive begins in West Plymouth, reached by driving 4 miles west on New Hampshire 25/3A from Plymouth and exit 26 on I–93. Turn south on NH 3A at the rotary in West Plymouth. The town is a small collection of homes and a few businesses. The highway heads south through fields below the east flank of broad-shouldered, 2,310-foot Tenney Mountain and Tenney Mountain Ski Area. The road ascends gentle slopes and dips through shallow valley bottoms before climbing out of the flat land onto thick forested hillsides. At 3.5 miles the road reaches a gap between Hoyt and Pike Hills and drops into a broad valley.

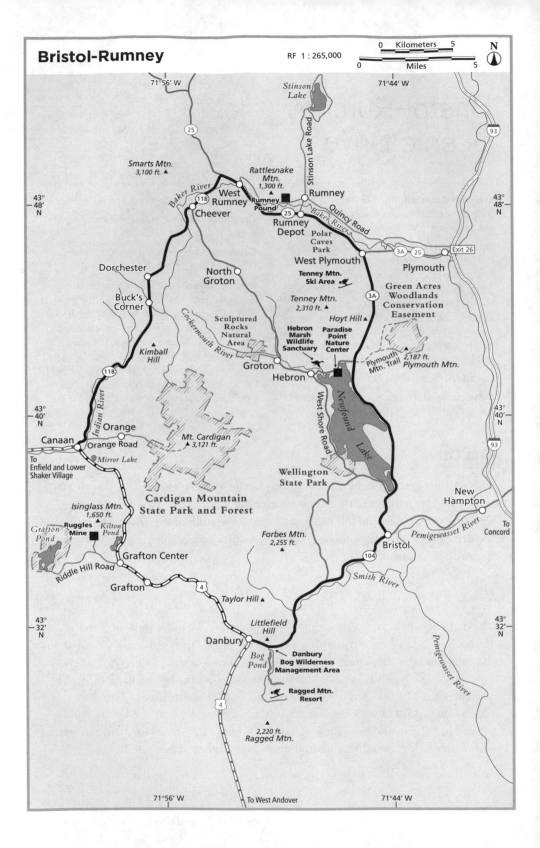

The highway reaches its junction with North Shore Road after 5 miles. Plymouth Mountain Trail begins off Pike Hill Road just east of the road and scales 2,187-foot Plymouth Mountain via a moderate 5.8-mile trail through lush woods. The north side of the mountain is protected by the Green Acres Woodlands Conservation Easement.

Turn west (right) on North Shore Road for a side-trip to several interesting natural areas. A mile down the road is **Paradise Point Nature Center and Sanctuary,** a forty-four-acre preserve that encompasses 3,000 feet of the pristine north shore of Newfound Lake. A mature forest of white pine, red spruce, and eastern hemlock blankets the area. Paradise Point Nature Center, open through the summer months, is an educational facility operated by the Audubon Society with three interpretive trails that explore the surrounding woodlands and lakeshore. Tupelo trees, rarely seen in New England, are found on the Elwell Trail. On other trails are abundant hemlocks, some as old as 150 years, that are probably remnants of virgin forest. Most of the area's mature white pine and red spruce were cut long ago as prized timber, but two tall, straight white pines along the Swamp Trail are estimated to be at least 175 years old.

The nature center offers excellent birding opportunities, particularly along the lake edge. Mergansers, diving under the water for food, dot the lake, while a host of woodland birds, including dark-eyed juncos, pileated woodpeckers, northern waterthrushes, and golden-crowned kinglets are seen among the trees. The nature center offers interpretive programs, hands-on displays, and a bird-viewing area.

Another mile down North Shore Road at the head of Hebron Bay on the northwest corner of Newfound Lake is **Hebron Marsh Wildlife Sanctuary.** This area includes open wetlands along the mouth of the Cockermouth River. Park at the refuge sign along the road and walk on a trail through woods to an observation tower. The platform atop the tower makes a great birdwatching vantage point. The swamp is an important stopover for migratory birds, including black ducks and mallards. Acute observers might also spot loons, grebes, ospreys, beavers, muskrats, and perhaps even a moose splashing through the marsh. This is also a good place to observe great blue herons as they gracefully hunt for small fish and frogs in the shallows.

A third point of interest on this side road lies a couple of miles farther west on Groton Road. Drive through the lovely village of Hebron with its whitewashed homes and two churches to Groton, then turn west off the main road to **Sculptured Rocks Natural Area.** After another mile park at a sign and step right to the Sculptured Rocks. Here the Cockermouth River chiseled under and through immense granite boulders that fill a narrow chasm, forming deep pools in immense potholes polished by swirling river water since the last ice age. A short trail walks past small cascades and more pools among the mossy boulders. After visiting the rocks, retrace your steps back to NH 3A and turn south (right).

The highway hugs the eastern shore of 4,106-acre Newfound Lake, a pretty lake set amid high hills. Almost all the shoreline is developed, with numerous homes, cabins, motels, inns, businesses, and private beaches. After 6 miles the highway reaches West Shore Road at the very southern tip of the lake. This road runs northwest along the lake a few miles to **Wellington State Park and Beach.** This small parkland offers one of New Hampshire's finest inland sand beaches. It also has picnic facilities, canoeing (but no boat launch), fishing for bass and trout, and hiking trails.

Past the lake, the highway runs a mile down the broad Newfound River Valley and enters Bristol, a medium-sized town on the banks of the Pemigewasset River. A long business strip backed by houses flanks the road. Keep an eye out for the highway's Y junction with New Hampshire Highway 104. Keep right at the junction and merge onto NH 104 for the next 9-mile segment of the scenic drive.

Danbury, Grafton, and Canaan

The highway leaves town and heads southwest, cresting a small rise then descending into the Smith River Valley. The road follows the slow, meandering river. Fields and blocks of forest lie along the asphalt. Low hills border the southern valley edge, while higher mountains, including 2,255-foot Forbes Mountain, block the northern horizon. The highway swings around Taylor Hill, crosses the river, climbs around Littlefield Hill, and passes the turn to Ragged Mountain Resort at 8 miles. On the western edge of long, thin Bog Pond is 246-acre Danbury Bog Wildlife Management Area. The ski area, with a 1,250-foot vertical drop, lies to the south on the northern slopes of 2,220-foot Ragged Mountain.

The drive crosses a low ridge and gently descends into Danbury. Its 1855 church, without a steeple, sits alongside the highway as it enters town. Go right on U.S. Highway 4 where it meets NH 104 at the village center. The next 14 miles travel northwest along the floor of the lovely valley of the Smith River. Low, undulating hills abut the U-shaped valley that was excavated and rounded by the ice sheet covering ancient New England. Old hill farms with cleared fields scatter along the fertile bottomland beside the twisting river. At 5.8 miles the highway passes the East Grafton General Store. About 1.5 miles later it reaches Grafton and Grafton Center. The village's 1812 burying ground sits on the left just past the Congregational Church.

In Grafton Center, turn left at the Village Green on Riddle Hill Road for an interesting side trip to Ruggles Mine. Sitting on the south slope of Isinglass Mountain, the mine is a popular visitor attraction. **Ruggles Mine** opened in 1803 and is the oldest mica, feldspar, and beryl mine in the United States. More than 150 different minerals have been found here, including amethyst, rose and smoky quartz, and garnet. The open-pit mine has interpretive rooms and tunnels that illustrate the formation of the surrounding mountains as well as a gift shop. Mineral collecting is permitted with a paid admission ticket. Other old mica mines are scattered across the surrounding hills. Mica was once used for transparent windows, but today is used on electrical equipment.

West of the mine is Grafton Pond, a beautiful and unspoiled lake that is considered one of New Hampshire's best wildlife viewing areas. Mammals seen here are moose, bear, otter, deer, and bear. The lake also hosts several nesting pairs of loons.

Back on the scenic drive route, the highway leaves Grafton and skirts sixty-eight-acre Kilton Pond, a good fishing and canoeing lake. A large beaver lodge lies at the pond's marshy north end. The tar road crosses the lower east flank of Isinglass Mountain then passes Tewksbury Pond and shining Mirror Lake, headwaters of the Smith River, before entering the historic village of Canaan.

Canaan sits on the banks of the Indian River in a wide valley surrounded by hills. The old village, incorporated in 1761, is preserved today in the Canaan Historic District. Handsome old buildings and houses line the highway, once called Broad Street. The Old Meeting House, built in 1793 and listed on the National Register of Historic Places, still has its original bell clock. Nearby is the 1828 Old North Church built in Gothic Revival style. The Canaan Historical Museum, built in 1840 as an academy and one of the nation's first integrated schools, displays local history including medical equipment, handmade tools, and Shaker farm and household artifacts. The museum is open June through October on Saturday afternoons. Old houses, some dating from the 1790s, line the maple-bordered streets.

Take an interesting side-trip from Canaan by journeying west a few miles to the **Lower Shaker Village** on Mascoma Lake. The Shakers, living in their own self-contained communities, were a Christian sect officially called The United Society of Believers in Christ's Second Appearing. During services the believers would enter trancelike stances to whirl and "shake" off sin and evil. The village here is one of New England's best preserved Shaker villages, and was an active Shaker community between 1793 and 1923. Among the thirteen buildings still on the site is the Great Stone Dwelling, the largest building ever constructed by Shakers, as well as the only remaining wooden Shaker cattle barn. Managed as a museum of Shaker life, the village also exhibits various artifacts, such as early sulfur matches invented by the Shakers, furniture, and wooden boxes. It also keeps Shaker songs, crafts, and gardening methods alive. The fee area is open mid-May through mid-October.

Canaan to Rumney

At Canaan, turn north (right) onto New Hampshire Highway 118 for the next 15-mile drive section, which leads to West Rumney. About 0.5 mile out of town is the

Wagon wheels and lupines lie near the historic village of Rumney.

turnoff to **Cardigan State Park and Forest.** This 5,655-acre natural area encompasses 3,121-foot Mount Cardigan, a popular hiking destination. The trailhead is reached by driving east through Orange on narrow Orange Road and continuing on the dirt road to the trailhead for West Ridge Trail. The 3-mile trail climbs 1,300 feet to the mountain's bald summit. The mountain is a huge mass of erosion-resistant rock called Kinsman Quartz Monzonite, formed when a great pluton (mass of molten rock) slowly cooled underground. This rock crowns the summit and is well exposed on the peak's upper slopes.

Just above timberline, the summit is an island of alpine plants that are seen more often on the highest New England peaks or the farther north reaches of Canada. A fire lookout atop the mountain offers one of central New Hampshire's best and widest views. To the east and south spread low, wooded hills, while the ragged mass of the White Mountains looms on the northern horizon. To the west stretch the Connecticut River Valley and the rolling crest of the Green Mountains, the spine of Vermont. Abundant blueberries are found along the trail by hikers in August.

The main scenic drive route heads north alongside the Indian River in a shallow, flat valley. The road slowly ascends past swamps and fields into rolling pine- and spruce-covered hills. Kimball Hill rises steeply to the east. After almost 7 miles the highway crests a ridge and good views spill north of the White Mountains, framed by the surrounding low hills. The road descends and crosses Bucks Brook before steeply rising again onto a shoulder of Streeter Mountain. Here the road begins a long descent through woods and across flattened terraces.

At Cheever is the pretty Cheever Union Chapel, a small white church with colorful stained glass windows. Below Cheever the drive steeply drops into the broad Baker River Valley. The highway ends at NH 25 just west of West Rumney. Turn east (right) on NH 25 toward West Plymouth for the last 9 miles of the scenic drive.

NH 25 follows a bench along the south bank of the Baker River, a small, meandering river that marks the southern edge of the White Mountains. The road runs through small West Rumney and, after a couple of miles, reaches the Nathan Clifford Memorial Rest Area, with picnic tables and tourist information, on the left. In 3 more miles the highway reaches Stinson Lake Road. Take a left here to **Rumney.** This historic village sits around a central town green. The metamorphic rock cliffs just west of here on the steep flanks of Rattlesnake Mountain are popular for their excellent rock-climbing opportunities, with hundreds of climbing routes on almost twenty different crags.

East of Rumney on Quincy Road is the unusual Rumney Town Pound. Most town pounds, used to enclose stray animals, were constructed of sturdy stone walls with a gate. The Rumney Pound used existing huge boulders to create the fence. These boulders are studded with small, delicate amethyst crystals. Also near Rumney, on Stinson Lake Road, is the Mary Baker Eddy Home. Eddy, founder of the Church of Christ, Scientist, lived here in the 1860s. The home is open for tours May through October.

The highway continues southeast past the Polar Caves, a popular attraction that includes a self-guided tour through chilly caves in the broken cliffs and boulder fields, a maple sugar museum, and other exhibits. The road heads down the broadening valley and, 3 miles from Rumney, enters West Plymouth where the drive ends. Travelers can continue east on NH 25 from the rotary to reach Plymouth and I–93.

18

Lake Winnipesaukee Scenic Drive

General description: An 81-mile loop around the Ossipee Mountains and the north shores of Lake Winnipesaukee and Squam Lake.

Special attractions: Squam Lake Natural Science Center, Squam Lake, Center Sandwich, White Mountain National Forest, Hemenway State Forest, Mount Chocorua Scenic Area, White Lake State Park, Ossipee Mountains, Wentworth State Park, Lake Winnipesaukee, Castle in the Clouds, hiking, historic villages, fall foliage, picnicking, fishing, boating.

Location: Central New Hampshire.

Drive route numbers: New Hampshire Highways 113, 113A, 16, 28, and 109.

Travel season: Year-round.

Camping: White Lake State Park offers 200 tent sites in three camping areas. Many private campgrounds are found near Lake Winnipesaukee and Squam Lake.

Services: All services in Plymouth, Ashland, Holderness, Center Sandwich, West Ossipee, Center Ossipee, Ossipee, Wolfeboro, and Tuftonboro.

Nearby attractions: White Mountains National Forest, Sandwich Notch, Sandwich Range Wilderness Area, Madison Boulder Natural Area, Conway, North Conway, Kancamagus Highway, Mount Washington, Crawford Notch, Franconia Notch State Park.

The Drive

The 81-mile Lake Winnipesaukee Scenic Drive follows a series of highways and back roads through scenic country on the north shores of Squam Lake and Lake Winnipesaukee and around the Ossipee Mountains in central New Hampshire. The lakes are the glistening centerpieces of the lovely Lakes Country, a region of rolling hills dotted with 273 lakes and ponds, including thirty that are more than one hundred acres in size. The largest, grandest, and most popular is sprawling Lake Winnipesaukee, New Hampshire's largest lake, covering 72 square miles with a convoluted 183-mile shoreline and 274 habitable islands. Squam Lake is considered by many to be New Hampshire's most beautiful lake with its forested islands, rocky shore, and stunning setting. The drive threads along the north and east shores of these two lakes and explores bucolic woodlands around the Ossipee Mountains. Open year-round, the route offers generally uncrowded roadways except for the busy stretch of New Hampshire Highway 16 between Ossipee and Chocorua.

Lake Winnipesaukee

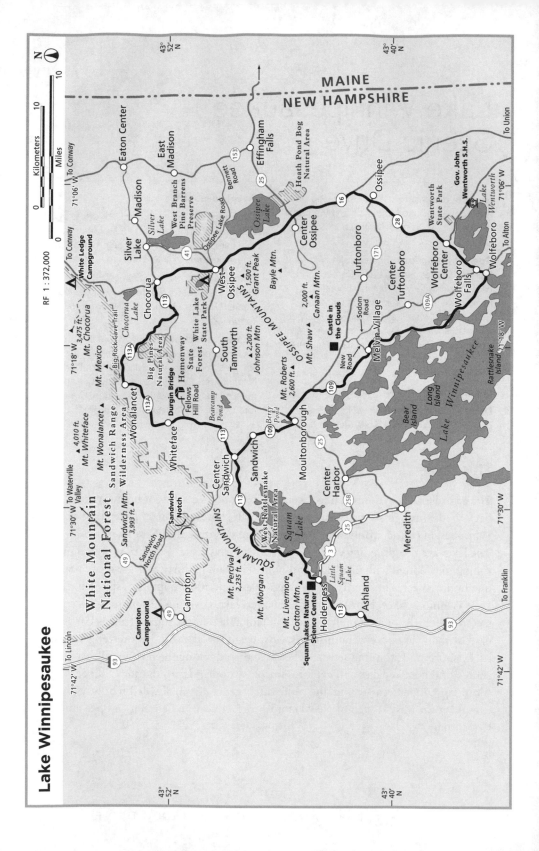

Along Squam Lake

The loop drive begins in Ashland just east of exit 24 on Interstate 93. Leave the interstate and drive east a short distance into town, then turn north on U.S. Highway 3 and head toward Holderness. **Ashland,** with lots of visitor services, has the Whipple Home Museum, birthplace of the 1934 winner of the Nobel Prize for medicine, George Hoyt Whipple. The highway runs northeast of town through commercial strip development along the north shore of 408-acre Little Squam Lake. A point of interest is the Squam River Bridge, a small covered bridge at the lake's west-side outlet. Built in 1990 by Milton Graton, the bridge is New Hampshire's newest covered bridge.

Just before the town of Holderness lies the **Squam Lakes Natural Science Center,** a 200-acre museum and wildlife sanctuary that interprets and explores New Hampshire's diverse native flora, fauna, and life zones. The center provides a 0.75-mile exhibit trail, Gordon Children's Center, field trips, lectures, and educational activities. The drive route turns north (left) on New Hampshire Highway 113 in Holderness.

The next 12-mile segment of the drive section from here to Center Sandwich winds along the north shore of Squam Lake past numerous summer cottages, then heads through pastures and dense woodlands below the southeastern slopes of the Squam Mountains. Quiet coves with anchored boats lie along Squam Lake's scalloped shoreline. Thick woods along the lower flanks of Cotton Mountain and Mount Livermore hem in the road. **Squam Lake,** covering 6,765 acres, is perhaps New Hampshire's loveliest lake. It is well-known as the locale for the 1981 movie *On Golden Pond,* starring Henry Fonda and Katharine Hepburn. "The loons! The loons are welcoming us back!" cried Hepburn's character in the film. The loons are still here, nesting on small isolated islands undisturbed by motorboats. The lake is renowned for its fishing—for salmon and lake trout along with smallmouth bass, perch, pickerel, and smelt.

After almost 4 miles the highway passes Bennett Cove and swings north around the low rise of West Rattlesnake Mountain. A roadside pullout marks the trailhead for the 1.8-mile round-trip Old Bridle Path Trail. The easy path ascends 450 feet to the mountain's 1,260-foot summit and a spectacular view south across Squam Lake. Another good trail begins just around the corner. The Morgan-Percival Loop climbs 5.8 miles north to the summits of Mounts Morgan and Percival in the Squam Mountains.

The highway bends northeast and travels through dense woods of white pine, oak, maple, and birch. Occasional cleared fields framed by overgrown stone walls interrupt the forest. After 11 miles, passing a large, marshy beaver pond and an old cemetery, the highway makes a steep descent into the Red Hill River Valley and reaches its junction with New Hampshire Highway 109 in Center Sandwich.

A farmhouse sits against foggy Mount Squam on the Lake Winnipesaukee Scenic Drive.

Center Sandwich to Chocorua

The village of **Center Sandwich** is one of those gorgeous New England villages often seen splashed across color postcards. This crossroads town is exceptionally well-preserved with three churches, a small museum, and many lovely Federal and Colonial-style homes dating from the early nineteenth century set on its tree-lined streets. The steepled First Baptist Church with a graveyard alongside is one of New Hampshire's best-looking churches. The Sandwich Historical Society Museum, housed in a shoemaker's 1850 home, displays kitchen and household implements and artifacts dating from the village's eighteenth-century birth. The League of New Hampshire Craftsmen arose in Center Sandwich at the Sandwich Home Industries, one of seven crafts shops run by the league. A stop here reveals the state's diverse crafts, including pottery, woven goods, furniture, woodwork, and jewelry. An excellent side drive heads northwest from town on Grove Street, which climbs northwest to beautiful and remote Sandwich Notch.

To continue the scenic drive, turn left on NH 113 in the town center and head northeast past the museum, town hall, and Quimby Barn Museum. Past the village, the quiet back road enters hills covered with dark woods occasionally broken by cleared fields and stone walls. The road twists through a forest and 3.7 miles later reaches North Sandwich. Continue straight north on NH 113A where NH 113 turns east. The highway runs over more low hills, passing a few homes. Mount Whiteface, a 4,010-foot peak in the 25,000-acre Sandwich Range Wilderness Area, looms to the north—white rocks crown its summit.

After a couple of miles, the road bends east and crosses Whiteface River, a pretty stream tumbling through a shallow rocky gorge. After 6.5 miles the highway leaves the woodland and enters a broad clearing flanked by high mountains. A white church nestles against the woods on the north side of the pasture in Wonalancet, a small rural village with a few houses tucked into the trees. A large farm occupies the clearing. Just past Wonalancet is the trailhead for Big Rock Cave Trail, a 1.6-mile trail that climbs over Mount Mexico en route to Big Rock Cave.

The highway bends south past a historic marker that details the Chinook Kennels, breeders of sled dogs used for numerous polar expeditions and explorations, and the Admiral Byrd Memorial "to all noble dogs whose lives were given on dog treks during the two expeditions to Little America, Antarctica." The asphalt winds through thick forest and past an old cemetery and, 10 miles from North Sandwich, reaches the Swift River. The road twists along the river's north bank and 0.5 mile later comes to the **Big Pines Natural Area** in Hemenway State Forest. The forest itself is a 2,106-acre reserve on the slopes of Great Hill southwest of the river. The 139-acre Big Pines Natural Area along the wild river protects a splendid grove of 150-year-old white pines, including one with a 42-inch diameter. Others exceed 150 feet in height.

The white pine, a magnificent straight tree, is one of New England's most beautiful and revered trees. The pine has long been important to the region's economy and history. White pine wood was often used by early colonists to build homes and furniture, and the British Royal Navy reserved all pines with diameters larger than 24 inches for use as masts and spars on ships. Towering pines shade the highway as it winds along the riverbank here.

After a few miles the road enters Tamworth, where it intersects NH 113. Tamworth is famed for the Barnstormers Theater, a summer theater group that has offered plays every summer since 1930. Turn east (left) on NH 113. The highway runs 2.6 miles northeast up a shallow valley on the north slope of Page Hill before descending gradually to Chocorua and NH 16. A mile north (left) on NH 16 is **Chocorua Lake.** The 222-acre lake perfectly reflects the bare, pointed summit of rocky 3,475-foot Mount Chocorua, a favorite subject of artists and painters. Birches and pines along the lakeshore frame this gorgeous view.

The peak, the second-most-climbed mountain in the state, is laced with trails. The Piper Trail, beginning a couple miles north of the lake, is the most popular summit route. The mountain is named for Chocorua, a 1760 Ossipee Indian chief who was killed near the summit after a feud with white settlers.

Chocorua to Wolfeboro

The main scenic drive route goes south (right) on NH 16 and passes through a thick commercial strip bordering the highway. After 1.4 miles the busy road leaves Chocorua and runs through gentle river-bottom land. **White Lake State Park** is reached after 3 miles. The popular 577-acre parkland surrounds White Lake, a good canoeing and fishing pond with a fine beach area graced with exquisite sand and warm water. The park offers a 200-site campground open from May through mid-October. Besides the lake and its recreational opportunities, White Lake State Park also protects the White Lake Pitch Pines, a seventy-two-acre National Natural Landmark on the northwestern shore of the lake. These old-growth pitch pines, relatively rare New Hampshire trees, grow tall and straight and give the air an aromatic, resinous scent on warm summer days. The fire-resistant pitch pines are more commonly seen on Cape Cod.

East of the highway and state park, off New Hampshire Highway 41, is the 341-acre West Branch Pine Barrens Preserve. This unique area is populated by white, red, and pitch pines and scrub oaks on a well-drained sandy glacial outwash plain. The area, protected by The Nature Conservancy, is one of New England's best-preserved pine barrens ecosystems.

Back on the scenic drive, continue south through West Ossipee into swamplands along the Chocorua River for 14 miles to Ossipee. The highway runs below the east flank of the Ossipee Mountains, a lofty granite range ringed by volcanic dikes. Geologists say the range is one of the best examples of a ring dike complex. This formed when the crust here drifted over a hot spot that welled up from the earth's mantle. Volcanic eruptions, including outpourings of ash and lava, covered the land. After the volcanic rock above was eroded away, the roots of the hot spot were left exposed.

A sign warns motorists that moose often cross the highway between the mountains and the lowlands to the east as the drive continues. After a few miles the highway runs through forest west of Ossipee Lake, a huge 3,092-acre lake that cannot be seen from the highway. Much of the lakeshore is rimmed by summer cottages and homes, except for the Ossipee Lake and Heath Pond Bog natural areas on the lake's south side. **Heath Pond Bog,** owned by the New Hampshire Division of Parks, is a superb example of a quaking sphagnum bog.

This distinctive ecological community, a designated National Natural Landmark, is accessed by a 0.5-mile loop trail that begins 2 miles east of Center Ossipee on New Hampshire Highway 25. Heath Pond's bog lies in a kettle hole, a deep depression formed when a chunk of glacial ice was embedded in the surrounding glacial till. After the ice block melted, the resulting cavity filled with water and formed a pond. The plants both in and around the bog community remain from a time when New England's climate was cooler. Trees surrounding the bog are mostly spruce and tamarack, both boreal species. The bog surface is dominated by sphagnum moss but also is home to other plants, including orchids, carnivorous pitcher and sundew plants, sedges, and laurel. Eventually the bog will fill with decayed vegetation, forming peat. Be prepared with bug spray for abundant black flies and mosquitoes when hiking here in spring and summer.

The scenic drive continues south from Center Ossipee on NH 16, passing a large glacial erratic boulder on the right before traversing a low ridge. The highway descends into a business area and, 14 miles from Chocorua, reaches its junction with New Hampshire Highway 28. Turn west (right) on NH 28 toward Wolfeboro, 10 miles away.

The highway rolls over low hills, passing swamps and moose stomps along the roadside before dropping down to Willey Brook. At 7.4 miles the road reaches Wolfeboro Center and a junction with NH 109. Wentworth State Park lies on the north shore of Lake Wentworth just east of NH 28 on NH 109. The small park offers a good swimming beach, picnic area, and bathhouses. Farther down NH 109 is the Governor John Wentworth State Historical Site. Here are the remains of the 1769 summer estate of the first of New Hampshire's royal governors. The house, now just a foundation, is considered by many to be the first summer vacation home built in America. The mansion was 100 feet long and two stories high. The keys to the front door weighed 1.5 pounds each. Manicured lawns with English-style gardens surrounded the house. During the Revolution Wentworth was exiled and became governor of Nova Scotia. This estate burned to the ground in 1820.

The First Baptist Church stands sentinel over Center Sandwich.

The main scenic drive route continues southwest from Wolfeboro Center along the forested north shore of the lake; in a couple of miles, travelers enter Wolfeboro Falls and Wolfeboro. Sitting on sheltered Wolfeboro Bay on the southeastern corner of Lake Winnipesaukee, **Wolfeboro** stakes its claim to being America's oldest summer resort town. The town arose after Governor Wentworth built his summer house on adjoining Lake Wentworth. By the early 1800s summer cottages began lining the shores of Lake Winnipesaukee at this village named in honor of British General James Wolfe, a French and Indian War hero. During the nineteenth century Wolfeboro flourished as a summer resort.

Not much has changed. Wolfeboro is still a premier summer destination, with lots of boating, fishing, and shopping. Numerous shops line the city streets. A good excursion here is a ride on the venerable M/S *Mount Washington* from Wolfeboro to Weirs Beach. The 230-foot-long boat, holding 1,250 passengers, cruises a 50-mile, three-hour trip daily from late May into October. The original *Mount Washington*, which burned in 1939, operated from 1888 to 1939. Historic points of interest in Wolfeboro include the 1778 Clark House Museum complex operated by the Wolfeboro Historical Society, with an 1868 schoolhouse and the replica of a nineteenth-century firehouse, and the Wright Museum of American Enterprise.

Along Lake Winnipesaukee

In Wolfeboro's business area is the junction of NH 28 and NH 109. Turn north (right) on NH 109 at the Civil War Memorial and village green. The road heads northeast past an old cemetery, homes, and businesses. A few miles out of town the highway passes the **Libby Museum.** The museum's collection, exploring the area's history and natural history, includes a 350-year-old dugout canoe, Abenaki Indian artifacts that date back almost 7,000 years, and artifacts found at the site of Governor Wentworth's nearby eighteenth-century summer home. The highway continues up the northeast side of Lake Winnipesaukee past numerous homes and summer cottages.

New Hampshire's largest body of water, **Lake Winnipesaukee** was, like most of New England's geographic features, formed by glaciation. When the great ice sheets crept across the land here, they scooped out an immense depression in this region of poor granite. Deposits of boulders left by the glacier at the southern end of the lake impeded drainage and allowed water to accumulate in the hollow, forming today's huge lake. Lake Winnipesaukee, covering 44,586 acres, is an irregular patchwork with a 183-mile shoreline, quiet coves and harbors, jutting forest-clad peninsulas, and 274 habitable islands.

The highway dips and rolls along the wooded lakeshore, with occasional glimpses of blue water glistening in the sun. Just past the highway's intersection with NH 109A is Melvin Village, a charming town perched on the north edge of Melvin Bay. The high, wooden Abenaki Tower yields great views of the lake and its many islands. The highway continues northwest and, a few miles later, joins New Hampshire Highway 171. A good side-trip tracks east down NH 171 to **Castle in the Clouds.** This famed mansion at the end of a narrow, one-way, 1.8-mile road perches on a hilltop above Lake Winnipesaukee. The castle was built in 1913 by shoe mogul Thomas Plant on his 6,000-acre estate on the lake's shores and the southern flank of the Ossipee Mountains. Plant brought more than 1,100 Italian stonecutters and masons to build the castle, which he called Lucknow. The place included uncommon conveniences for that time—an intercom, self-cleaning oven, central vacuum, and a clothes-drying system. Its eclectic architecture was influenced by Japanese, Swiss, Norwegian, Norman, and English architectural styles. The mansion, completed in 1914, cost more than $7 million. Plant, after some sour investments, died destitute in 1941.

Later the house was bought by Richard Robie and eventually opened to the public. Today visitors can tour the castle, ride horses or walk on more than 45 miles of trail, and sample the famous Castle Springs water. Views from the castle grounds are well worth the entry fee alone. Below spreads the crystal lake dotted with green islands and surrounded by wooded hills and mountains.

Back on the main route, the highway runs west from its junction with NH 171 to NH 25. Turn left at the intersection with NH 25 and jog 0.5 mile before turning northwest again on NH 109 in Moultonborough. The scenic drive's last 5 miles run northwest to Center Sandwich. The road passes marsh-edged Berry Pond and moves along through cleared fields lined with stone walls. Thick woods flank the asphalt. After 3 miles the highway dashes through Sandwich, a lovely small village with spacious old homes spread over the rounded top of Wentworth Hill. The highway drops steeply down the hill, passes an old burying ground, and a couple of miles later enters Center Sandwich and the drive's terminus at a junction with NH 113. Go left on NH 113 to head back to I–93 and Ashland, the drive's start.

19

Kancamagus Highway Scenic Drive

General description: A 58-mile paved highway that traverses the scenic heart of the White Mountains between Bath and Conway in northern New Hampshire.

Special attractions: Swiftwater Falls, Swiftwater Covered Bridge, White Mountain National Forest, Kinsman Notch, Lost River Reservation, Agassiz Basin, Sabbaday Falls, Rocky Gorge Scenic Area, Lower Falls Scenic Area, Swift River, hiking, backpacking, camping, fall foliage, rock climbing, swimming, picnicking, scenic views.

Location: North-central New Hampshire.

Drive route number: New Hampshire Highway 112.

Travel season: Year-round. Expect possible snow and winter driving conditions between November and April.

Camping: Seven national forest campgrounds—Big Rock (twenty-eight sites), Blackberry Crossing (twenty-six sites), Covered Bridge (forty-nine sites), Hancock (fifty-six sites), Jigger Johnson (seventy-six sites),

Passaconaway (thirty-three sites), and Wildwood (twenty-six sites)—with drinking water, tables, toilet facilities, and fireplaces are found along the drive. The campgrounds are open from late April to mid-October. Other national forest campgrounds are located within easy driving distance. Camping is available in Crawford Notch State Park (thirty sites) and Franconia Notch State Park (ninety-seven sites). Many private campgrounds are found in the White Mountains.

Services: All services in Conway, North Conway, Lincoln, and Bath.

Nearby attractions: Franconia Notch State Park, Robert Frost Place, Sugar Hill Historical Museum, Connecticut River Valley, Clark's Trading Post, Mount Washington, Conway Scenic Railroad, Crawford Notch State Park, Echo Lake State Park, ski areas, Presidential Range Wilderness Area, Sandwich Range Wilderness Area, Pemigewasset Wilderness Area, Appalachian Trail, Madison Boulder Natural Area, White Lake State Park.

The Drive

The White Mountains, encompassing northern New Hampshire, form a brooding highland creased with glacier-carved valleys broken by abrupt granite outcrops lorded over by knobby peaks. The range, including almost fifty peaks above 4,000 feet, was named by early sailors off the Maine coast who saw glistening white snowfields on the highest summits on clear spring days. The Whites, with eighty-six separate peaks and nine notches (passes), are divided into three subranges—the Presidential, Carter-Moriah, and Franconia ranges. These rumpled mountains, dark with woodlands, are often wreathed in clouds that swirl through amphitheaters and cirques. Capricious weather, characterized by high winds, rules these lovely, savage hills.

Kancamagus Highway

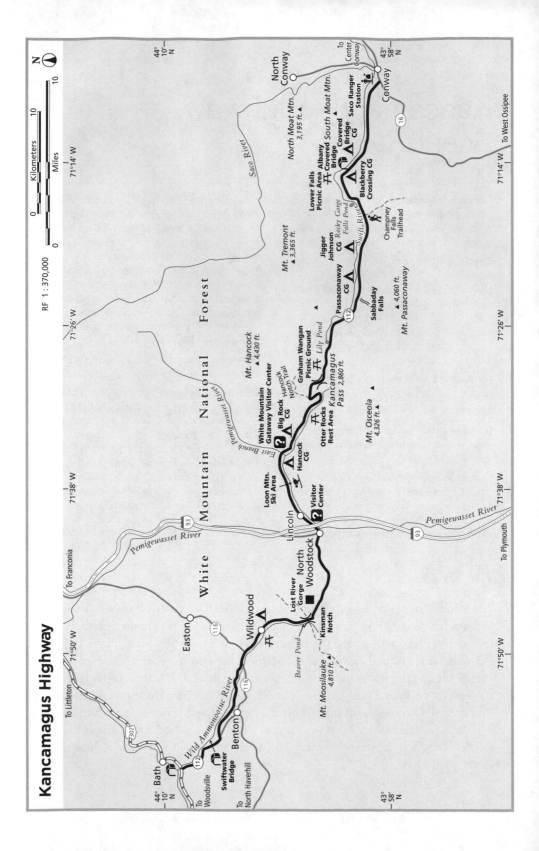

The dominant force that shapes the White Mountains and the lives that inter-mingle with them is climate. The range straddles an area where two storm tracks meet. Frigid masses of dry, subpolar air, sweeping down from the north and west, converge with warm, moist air pumped north from the subtropics and the Caribbean. This clash of weather systems brings a volatile mix of heavy rain and snow, sudden thaws, hard freezes, and quick temperature reversals that determines what plants and trees cling to these hills, which animals inhabit its forests, and how its human occupants cope with such weather vagaries.

The highest summits in the White Mountains experience extreme weather conditions and temperatures as well as some of the most powerful winds on the planet. On the summit of 6,288-foot Mount Washington, the range's high point, the thermometer regularly plunges below zero degrees Fahrenheit and the moun-tain hides behind clouds 55 percent of the time. Wind gusts over 100 miles per hour have been recorded in every month. The world wind record was set here on an April day in 1934 when the weather observatory atop Mount Washington's summit recorded one gust at an astounding 231 miles per hour. Another record is the 49.3 inches of snow that fell at the station during a twenty-four-hour period in February 1969. That two-day storm deposited a whopping 98 inches of snow on the summit.

The Kancamagus Highway Scenic Drive traverses the heart of the White Mountains, and is one of New England's premier scenic drives. Following New Hampshire Highway 112 for 58 miles, the drive runs from the Ammonoosuc River near Woodsville on New Hampshire's western border to Conway just west of the Maine boundary. In 1989 a 28-mile highway stretch between Lincoln and Conway became the Kancamagus Highway, one of the nation's first designated National Forest Scenic Byways. Until the late 1950s only two dead-end roads, one on each side of Kancamagus Pass, pointed at each other through the thick woods. Earlier trails were hacked out of the wilderness by settlers who built small farms on the fertile land along the Swift River west of Conway. With the advent of automobiles, the idea of a trans-mountain highway slowly grew. The land was surveyed in the 1930s, but the road wasn't completed until 1959. In 1964 the highway was paved, and it opened to year-round traffic in 1968. Today, more than one million vehicles traverse the highway annually.

The two-lane, paved highway has numerous scenic pullouts. Watch for heavy traffic, particularly in the busy summer months and in autumn when hordes of leaf-peepers descend on the White Mountains to view the fall foliage. The Kanca-magus is considered one of New England's premier foliage drives. Take your time and use the turnouts to view the scenery. The first drive section over Kinsman Notch is usually less traveled.

Expect variable weather along the byway. Snow can fall anytime between October and May, although the spring months are typically rainy. Summers are pleasant and balmy, with daily highs occasionally reaching into the 90s. Autumn days are usually perfect, with warm days and cool nights. Rainy spells that last for several days do occur. Winters are cold and snowy. Expect icy and snowpacked road conditions and plan accordingly.

Over Kinsman Notch to Lincoln

The drive description begins 3 miles east of Woodsville at the junction of U.S. Highway 302 and New Hampshire Highway 112. This start is easily accessed from Interstate 91 in Vermont. Take exit 17 and head east through Wells River and Woodsville to NH 112. Otherwise, begin the drive from Interstate 93 at exit 32 in Lincoln or from Conway on the east at the intersection of New Hampshire Highways 112 and 16.

The drive starts at the quiet highway junction of US 302 and NH 112 at the confluence of the Wild Ammonoosuc and Ammonoosuc Rivers near their larger junction with the Connecticut River in Woodsville. The Ammonoosuc, an Abenaki Indian word for "wide fishing place," originates at the Lake of the Clouds southwest of Mount Washington's summit. The rock-strewn river grows and tumbles almost 6,000 feet from its headwaters down to the Connecticut River. The first drive segment runs 21 miles from here to Lincoln via Kinsman Notch.

The highway heads southeast following the south bank of the Wild Ammonoosuc River, a tributary of the Ammonoosuc River, through low wooded hills. Tall white pines and hemlock abut the asphalt. Turn left at 2.2 miles to the 174-foot-long **Swiftwater Bridge,** an 1849 covered bridge spanning the Wild Ammonoosuc. At Swiftwater Falls the river rushes over rocky benches below the bridge, forming a picturesque scene and pleasant summer swimming hole. Park at a small lot on the north side of the bridge. Just past the bridge, the road enters the hamlet of Swiftwater, undoubtedly named for the frothy river, with a few homes and a general store. Past town, the drive plunges through thick woods punctuated by orderly Christmas tree farms and, after almost 7 miles, enters White Mountain National Forest.

Covering most of northern New Hampshire, the national forest protects 741,174 acres in New Hampshire and Maine—a larger land area than the state of Rhode Island. The forest, the largest single piece of public land in New England, lies within a day's drive of more than a quarter of the U.S. population and, as such, is an exceedingly popular recreation area. It covers more than 11 percent of New Hampshire, the highest percentage of federal land in any eastern state. Four wilderness areas here total 102,932 acres.

The forest was established after the lumber industry denuded the mountainsides of trees during the late nineteenth century. Many organizations, including the Appalachian Mountain Club and the Society for the Protection of New Hampshire

The Swiftwater Bridge occupies one of New Hampshire's most scenic settings.

Forests, joined with state governor Frank Rollins and U.S. Representative John Weeks for the passage of the Weeks Act of 1911. The act enabled the federal government to establish the national forest and protect its valuable watersheds and timberlands by buying back private property east of the Mississippi River.

The highway continues alongside the river, passing a junction with NH 116 at 10 miles. This is, historically, a great spot for moose sightings. In the nineteenth century, guests at Franconia-area inns would ride carriages to this intersection to be rewarded with evening moose viewings. Wildwood Campground and recreation area is reached at 12 miles. The campground offers twenty-six shaded campsites along the river.

Here the road bends south and begins climbing. Marvelous views of 4,810-foot Mount Moosilauke, the first grand mountain in the range, and its satellite peaks unfold through the windshield. Mount Moosilauke was first ascended in 1773, and offers a superb summit reached via the Appalachian Trail from Kinsman Notch. This beautiful trail section is a natural garden of wildflowers lined by waterfalls. As the highway climbs, roadside rock changes from the metamorphic Littleton Schist to the harder Kinsman Quartz Monzonite, a type of granitic rock. This well-exposed rock is a coarse-grained, gray rock flecked with gleaming bits of black biotite and white feldspar crystals. The road passes a small cascade and picturesque Beaver Pond with its single pine-clad island before reaching the summit of **Kinsman Notch** after almost 15 miles.

The notch was named after early settler and farmer Asa Kinsman who, with his wife, took the wrong track en route to their new home at Landaff in the 1780s. Instead of turning around, the pair hacked a new trail over this wild pass, which now commemorates their labor. The first road came through the notch in 1916. Beaver Brook Trail, part of the white-blazed Appalachian Trail, begins at the top of the notch. The trail climbs southwest to the summit of Mount Moosilauke along Beaver Brook, littered with flowers all summer, and after 0.33 mile reaches the start of a delightful chain of cascades. Continue up the trail past a dozen tumbling cascades in the steep ravine. Watch for many slick rocks while hiking alongside this steep section.

From the notch the highway bends east and drops down the sharp valley of the Lost River. About 0.5 mile down is **Lost River Gorge,** one of the most popular scenic attractions in the White Mountains. The 152-acre reservation, a preserve operated by the Society for the Protection of New Hampshire Forests, is a labyrinth of moss-covered boulders where the Lost River appears and disappears beneath the jumbled rocks. The gorge was formed, like most of New England's features, by glaciation. Some 15,000 years ago a great ice sheet crept over the mountains, excavating the notch and rounding the deep valleys. Later, as the climate warmed, the ice on the notch's north side lasted longer and drained its meltwater down the Lost River side. The frothy torrent sharply incised the gorge out of hard granite. The maze of boulders tumbled from the cliffs above, filling the gorge for today's sightseers. The Lost River Trail, beginning near the gift shop, explores the gorge and its tunnels on a system of walkways and stairs. Paradise Falls, a 20-foot waterfall, is near the base of the gorge. A fee area, Lost River Gorge is open from mid-May to mid-October.

The drive drops 6 miles and 900 feet from Kinsman Notch down a widening valley to Lincoln. About 2 miles from the pass, the road leaves the national forest. Farther east is a junction with scenic New Hampshire Highway 118. The lower part of the valley is called Agassiz Basin for Louis Agassiz, a Swiss geologist who was one of the first scientists to recognize that great ice sheets once covered North America and Europe. Evidence found here helped confirm his theories.

The highway continues east in the flattening valley alongside the Lost River as it riffles over bedrock and boulders. After 20 miles the road enters North Woodstock, crosses the Pemigewasset River, and passes exit 32 on I–93 to reach Lincoln. At the southern gateway of Franconia Notch in the broad Pemigewasset Valley, **Lincoln** is an old town that was named in 1764 for the Earl of Lincoln. This tourist town offers numerous facilities and services, including many accommodations and restaurants. Nearby is the North Woodstock–Clark's Trading Post covered bridge. The seventy-five-ton, 120-foot railroad bridge, originally built in Vermont, was taken apart and reassembled over the Pemigewasset River.

Up to Kancamagus Pass

The second drive section runs 37 miles from Lincoln to Conway over the famed Kancamagus Highway. The highway is named for Kancamagus, a native Abenaki Indian who was chief of the Penacook Confederacy of seventeen tribes in the late 1600s. Passaconaway, his grandfather, united the tribes in 1627. Kancamagus worked in vain to keep a fragile peace between the tribes and the English settlers moving into their valleys, but after being slighted by the colonial government, he gave in to the more inflamed factions and led several raids on the settlers. The 1689 raid on whites in Dover was particularly brutal. The colonists began a protracted campaign of retaliation that forced Kancamagus to disappear with his tribe into Canada.

A couple of miles past the interstate, NH 112 leaves Lincoln and heads east into White Mountain National Forest along the East Branch of the Pemigewasset River. Loon Mountain Ski Area scatters across the slopes of 3,073-foot Loon Mountain, to the south. The area offers a year-round gondola ride that yields impressive views and access to a nature trail atop the mountain. An informational kiosk, detailing the forest and its facilities, sits by the roadside another mile up the highway. Farther along is fifty-six-site Hancock Campground, a popular camp spot for trout fishermen, in a lovely birch forest on the river's north shore.

The **White Mountain Gateway Visitor Center** lies just north of the highway on the east side of the bridge over the river. Stop in for maps and information on the forest. It's also the trailhead for the popular Lincoln Woods Trail, which heads north along an old railroad bed beside the East Branch River into the Pemigewasset Wilderness Area, a trail noted for its logging relics and splendid waterfalls.

At the bridge over the East Branch, 5 miles from Lincoln, the highway bends southeast and follows the Hancock Branch. The asphalt gently ascends the valley, which closes in. Three lofty peaks—West Peak, Mount Osceola, and East Peak—loom to the south above wooded slopes. Big Rock Campground has twenty-eight riverside sites. Upper Lady's Bath, a swimming hole, is a five-minute walk from the campground.

At 7 miles is **Otter Rocks Rest Area,** with picnic tables and river access. Hancock Notch Trail begins another 2.4 miles up the road. Here the highway makes a hairpin turn and begins laboriously climbing out of the valley. **Pemi Overlook,** just past the second switchback, offers great views down the glacier-carved valley to the west and north to Mount Hitchcock and Mount Hancock with its obvious glaciated cirque. A mixed woodland of balsam fir, red spruce, and birch borders the highway.

Past the overlook, the highway steepens to an 8 percent grade and climbs almost 3 more miles to the summit of 2,860-foot **Kancamagus Pass.** A parking lot, viewpoint, and the Graham Wangan Picnic Ground sit just east of the pass summit. The picnic ground is the site of an ancient American Indian celebration. Stop here and take in the view. Marvelous vistas of the White Mountains surround this height-of-land. To the east stretches the wide, wooded Swift River intervale, and to the north sprawl the 45,000-acre Pemigewasset and 27,380-acre Presidential Range–Dry River wilderness areas. The mountains are composed of hard, erosion-resistant Conway Granite, a coarse, pink granite laced with pegmatite dikes.

The highway begins dropping east off the summit down a 7 percent grade. After a few miles it swings past elegant Lily Pond, a small lake surrounded by tall grass. Lily Pond is part of the Swift River's headwaters. The road, passing Sawyer River Trailhead and **Sugar Hill Overlook,** begins to flatten out 5 miles from the top of the pass. The overlook yields excellent views down the valley with the sharp edge of Greens Cliff and Owl Cliff to the northeast. Pointed 3,475-foot Mount Chocorua fills the southeast horizon. Farther along is the Sabbaday Falls parking area.

Sabbaday Falls to Conway

Park and take the short fifteen-minute hike south to one of the White Mountain's prettiest and most famous waterfalls. The trail strolls south alongside Sabbaday Brook through open forest. **Sabbaday Falls** is a series of three drops that funnel down a narrow gorge chiseled into soft basaltic dikes that were intruded into the

Sabbaday Falls, reached by a short trail, is a popular stop on the Kancamagus Highway Scenic Drive.

harder Conway bedrock. The first drop tumbles into a large basin; the creek then roars through a chute and pours down a 25-foot cliff into a deep chasm filled with spray, moss, and thundering whitewater. The trail leads to a crystalline pool at the base of the chasm before climbing a fenced walkway to a point above the falls. The trail is very popular in summer and autumn, so be prepared for company. Also remember that no bathing or swimming is allowed in the brook or falls area.

Sabbaday Falls were named, so the story goes, by early settlers who first came upon the frothy cascade on a Sunday or Sabbath. They returned every succeeding Sunday, their day off from work, to view the falls and picnic. They called it the "Sabbath Day" trip, which eventually became Sabbaday.

The drive continues east on the south side of the Swift River through second-growth forests punctuated by occasional clearings and moose stomps. This whole area was almost denuded by loggers in the late nineteenth century. The Swift River Railroad, running 20 miles up the valley from Conway, was completed in 1906 and brought wholesale decimation to the area's virgin forests. In 1912 forest fires and floods swept across the valley. The establishment of the White Mountain National Forest a few years later halted the clearcut tactics of the lumber industry and allowed the forest to grow again. Today's Kancamagus Highway follows much of the old railroad grade along the Swift River.

The highway passes several trailheads, and 3 miles from the falls reaches the **Russell-Colbath House,** an 1830s cabin staffed with guides in period clothes. The cabin offers information and displays on area nature and history. Thomas Russell built the small, wood-frame house in 1832 on a 2,000-acre homestead along the Swift River and ran a nearby sawmill. His son Amzi inherited the home and in turn passed it on to his daughter Ruth in 1887, the only one of his children who had not moved away.

Ruth lived here with her husband, a carpenter named Thomas Colbath, until one windy autumn day in 1891. Colbath went out for a walk, telling Ruth, "I'll be back in a little while." He didn't return in a little while, so she kept his supper warm and lit a kerosene lamp in the kitchen window. Colbath's "little while" turned out to be forty-two years. During that entire time the faithful Ruth placed the lamp in the window every evening. Nicknamed the "hermit woman," she maintained her vigil until her death at age eighty-one in 1930. A newspaper wrote of her: "No other woman in America leads such a lonely life during the bleak winters that shut in the valley of Passaconaway as this dear old lady of solitude." Her estate—land, house, and personal property—was sold. Tom Colbath returned three years later after wandering through Cuba, South America, and California and tried to obtain possession of the house. His claim was denied and he disappeared.

The house, listed on the National Register of Historic Places, is operated by the Forest Service and open to tours in the warmer months. Take note of the hops vines outside the cabin. Almost every rural New England homemaker had her own recipe for beer as well as bread, making the cultivation of these vines especially important.

Nearby is seventy-six-site Jigger Johnson Campground and the Rail and River Trail. This short hiking loop explores the area's trees and shrubs, including balsam fir, white pine, mountain maple, and black cherry. Bear Notch Road, beginning just past the campground, runs north 9 miles through scenic Bear Notch to Bartlett. It makes a good bike tour with gentle grades up, a steep but short grade down, and little competing traffic.

Back on the highway, continue east along the south bank of the Swift River. The Champney Falls Trailhead is on the right a mile down. It's only worth hiking the 1.5-mile trail during high-water season or after heavy rains; otherwise, the falls are meager. **Rocky Gorge Scenic Area** is reached after 3 more miles. Here the Swift River, dropping 10 feet over a ledge, slices down through bedrock granite to form an abrupt, narrow gorge. Swimming is prohibited in the Rocky Gorge area since currents here are treacherous and powerful. *Reader's Digest* magazine in 1949 reported the amazing story of a woman who attempted to wade the river above the falls and was swept downstream. She was found alive hours later, dangling upside down in an air pocket under the falls by an ankle wedged in the bedrock. A short path meanders down to the river and falls from the parking area and crosses the river on a footbridge. Continue a short distance to Falls Pond, a charming tarn below Bear Mountain. Look for carnivorous pitcher plants along the swampy shoreline in summer. The area forest includes mountain maple, paper birch, sugar maple, red oak, mountain alder, and shadblow, a shrub covered with white blossoms in May. The Rocky Gorge Scenic Area also offers picnic tables, restrooms, and drinking water.

The highway bends northeast past Rocky Gorge and runs above rapids in the rock-strewn river. The Rainbow Slabs and Painted Walls, both good climbing crags, stretch along the hillside north of the Swift River. The river's Lower Falls are a couple of miles from the Upper Falls at Rocky Gorge. This is another spectacular display of whitewater, particularly during heavy spring runoff when the river surges over bedrock ledges and boulders. During summer's low water the area teems with swimmers and sunbathers who jam the rocks and parking lots. The Moat Mountains dominate the skyline northeast of here. The mountain massif is the erosional remnant of an immense blanket of volcanic rock that covered New Hampshire during long episodes of volcanism some 175 million years ago.

At Lower Falls the highway turns south and passes a picnic area; twenty-six-site Blackberry Crossing Campground; forty-nine-site Covered Bridge Campground; and **Albany Covered Bridge** over the Swift River. This 136-foot span, dating from 1858, is of the Paddleford Truss design with graceful interior-arch trusses. The 2.5-mile Boulder Loop Trail leaves from Covered Bridge Campground and yields sweeping views of the Swift River Intervale and rocky, 3,475-foot Mount

Chocorua, an isolated and spectacular peak named for a Pequawket Indian chief who was killed on its slopes.

The last 6 miles of the scenic drive continue east along the Swift River. The road runs through woods, with occasional glimpses of the river and the mountains beyond. It leaves the White Mountain National Forest and passes the Saco Ranger Station, a good information stop with a visitor center, before dead-ending at NH 16 on the southern outskirts of Conway. Turn left to go into Conway and North Conway. The twin towns, settled in 1764, form the southern gateway to the White Mountains. They were named for Englishman Henry Seymour Conway. A historic artists' colony and resort, the town of Conway attracts visitors with more than 200 factory outlet shops, as well as numerous other shops and restaurants. Nearby is Echo Lake State Park, several ski areas, and Whitehorse and Cathedral Ledges, the best climbing cliffs in New England. Conway and North Conway offer all visitor services.

20

Crawford and Franconia Notches Scenic Drive

General description: A 55-mile scenic route through Crawford and Franconia Notches in the White Mountains.

Special attractions: Franconia Notch State Park, Profile Lake, The Flume, The Basin, Crawford Notch State Park, Arethusa Falls, Mount Washington Hotel, Appalachian Trail, Cannon Mountain, Cannon Mountain Ski Resort and Tramway, downhill and cross-country skiing, hiking, rock climbing, ice climbing, fishing, camping.

Location: Northern New Hampshire.

Drive route numbers: U.S. Highways 302 and 3, Interstate 93.

Travel season: Year-round. Expect possible snow and winter driving conditions between November and April.

Camping: Two national forest campgrounds are found on the drive—Zealand (eleven sites) and Sugarloaf (sixty-one sites). Other national forest campgrounds are located within easy driving distance on the Kancamagus Highway. Camping is available in Crawford Notch State Park (thirty-one sites) and Franconia Notch State Park (ninety-seven sites). Many private campgrounds are also found in the White Mountains.

Services: All services in Conway, North Conway, Glen, and Lincoln.

Nearby attractions: Robert Frost Place, Sugar Hill Historical Museum, Polly's Pancake House, Connecticut River Valley, Clark's Trading Post, Mount Washington, Conway Scenic Railroad, Echo Lake State Park, ski areas, Presidential Range Wilderness Area, Sandwich Range Wilderness Area, Pemigewasset Wilderness Area, Appalachian Trail, Madison Boulder Natural Area, White Lake State Park.

The Drive

This 55-mile scenic drive begins in Glen, climbs over Crawford Notch, and swings around the mountains to spectacular Franconia Notch. The drive traverses some of New England's best and most famous scenery in the notches, including Arethusa Falls, New Hampshire's highest waterfall. The White Mountains, stretching across northern New Hampshire, form a rough corduroy of rolling mountains and deep glacier-carved valleys. New England's highest range, the Whites are topped by 6,288-foot Mount Washington. Although people from the West consider these mere hills (even California transplant Robert Frost said, "The only fault I find with New Hampshire is that her mountains aren't quite high enough."), they remain the highest points east of the Black Hills and north of the Great Smoky Mountains.

The White Mountains tower almost 5,000 feet above the surrounding hills and are high enough that early sailors off the coast of Maine were amazed to see their snow-clad summits glistening in the sun. Florentine navigator Giovanni da Ver-

Crawford and Franconia Notches

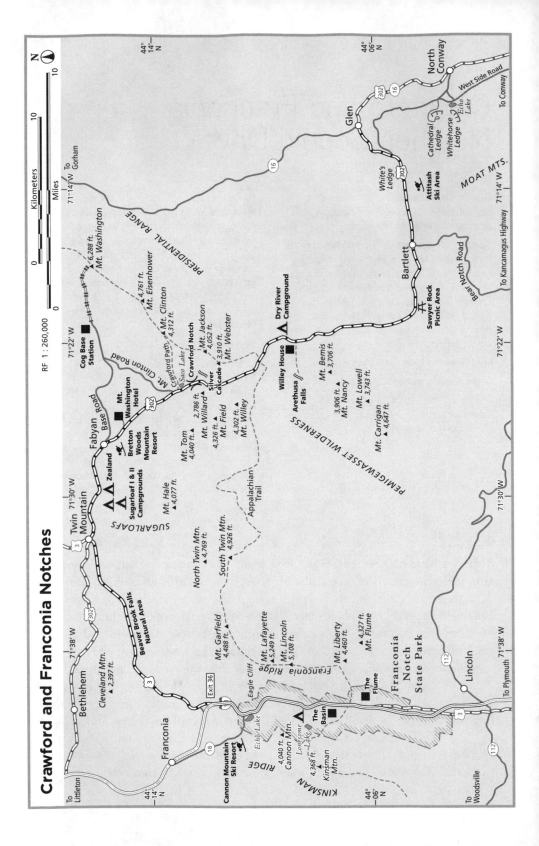

RF 1 : 260,000

N

Kilometers 0 · · · 10
Miles 0 · · · 10

To Littleton

Bethlehem

71°38' W

Franconia

Cleveland Mtn.
▲ 2,397 ft.

Beaver Brook Falls
Natural Area

302

Exit 36

18

Cannon Mountain Ski Resort

Echo Lake

KINSMAN RIDGE

4,040 ft. ▲
Cannon Mtn.

Lonesome Lake

Kinsman Mtn.
4,368 ft. ▲

Eagle Cliff

The Basin

Mt. Garfield
4,488 ft. ▲

Mt. Lafayette
▲ 5,249 ft.
Mt. Lincoln
5,108 ft.

Franconia Ridge

Mt. Liberty
▲ 4,460 ft.

The Flume

Mt. Flume
4,327 ft. ▲

Franconia Notch State Park

112

Lincoln

To Plymouth

71°38' W

To Woodsville

44°
06'
N

Twin Mountain

71°30' W

3

302

North Twin Mtn.
4,769 ft. ▲

South Twin Mtn.
4,926 ft. ▲

Appalachian Trail

PEMIGEWASSET WILDERNESS

71°30' W

SUGARLOAFS

Zealand ▲
Sugarloaf I & II
Campgrounds

Mt. Hale
▲ 4,077 ft.

Fabyan

Base Road

Mt. Washington Hotel

Bretton Woods Mountain Resort

Mt. Tom
4,040 ft. ▲

Mt. Field
4,326 ft. ▲

Mt. Willey
4,302 ft. ▲

Silver Cascade

Arethusa Falls

Willey House

Mt. Bemis
▲ 3,706 ft.

Mt. Nancy
3,906 ft. ▲

Mt. Lowell
▲ 3,743 ft.

Mt. Carrigan
4,647 ft. ▲

Cog Base Station

71°22' W

Mt. Clinton Road

Crawford Path

Saco Lake

Crawford Notch

Mt. Willard
2,786 ft. ▲

Mt. Jackson
4,052 ft.

Mt. Clinton
4,312 ft.

Mt. Eisenhower
4,761 ft. ▲

Mt. Washington
▲ 6,288 ft.

PRESIDENTIAL RANGE

71°22' W

Mt. Webster
3,910 ft. ▲

Dry River Campground

Bartlett

Sawyer Rock Picnic Area

Bear Notch Road

To Kancamagus Highway

71°14' W
To Gorham

White's Ledge

Attitash Ski Area

MOAT MTS.

71°14' W

302

16

Glen

16

302

North Conway

44°
06'
N

West Side Road

To Conway

Echo Lake

Cathedral Ledge

Whitehorse Ledge

44°
14'
N

44°
14'
N

razano wrote to the king of France in 1524 of "high mountains back inland, growing smaller toward the sea." And in 1628 Christopher Levett recalled "a great mountain called the Christall hill, being as they say one hundred miles in the country, yet it is to be seen at the sea side, and there is no ship arrives in New England, either to the West so farre as Cape Cod, or to the East so farre as Monhiggen, but they see this mountaine the first land, if the weather be cleere."

The scenic drive follows three highways—U.S. Highway 302, U.S. Highway 3, and Interstate 93—between Glen and Lincoln. The paved roads are open year-round, although drivers should expect winter driving conditions with icy and snowpacked roads during the colder months. The highways can be very busy on summer and autumn weekends. Autumn, a wonderful time to drive this byway, brings a spectacular display of color to the roadside, making the drive one of New Hampshire's best foliage tours. A good loop drive from either Conway or Lincoln combines this scenic route with the Kancamagus Highway scenic drive for a full day's adventure.

Glen and Bartlett

Begin the drive in Glen at the junction of US 302 and New Hampshire Highway 16, about 5 miles north of North Conway's commercial strip. Lying on the east side of the Mount Washington valley, Conway and North Conway form the eastern gateway to the White Mountains. Both are popular tourist towns, with bumper-to-bumper traffic along US 302/NH 16 and dozens of factory outlet shops that lure bargain hunters. Besides shopping, there's plenty to do and see in the valley. The Conway Scenic Railroad leaves from the 1874 North Conway Depot, offering a glimpse into the area's railroad past as it chugs along the Saco River. Echo Lake State Park, on the western edge of the valley, encompasses Echo Lake and Cathedral and White Horse Ledges. These two masses above the quilted valley offer some of New England's best rock-climbing adventures on their granite flanks. North of Glen on NH 16 is Pinkham North and the Mount Washington toll road. The Conway area also offers excellent and diverse downhill and cross-country skiing in winter.

In Glen, from the intersection of US 302 and north-south NH 16, go straight on US 302. Glen is a small tourist village with a strip of motels and services along the highway. The road crosses Ellis River on the west side of Glen and then the Rocky Branch a mile later. Past here, the highway bends south past Bartlett Covered Bridge (now a gift shop), a 167-foot span over the Saco River, before crossing to the river's south bank. White's Ledge, a slabby granite outcrop, lies on the north side of the valley. Attitash ski area, one of the East's best ski mountains, sits farther west on the north slopes of Attitash Mountain. The resort offers a vertical drop of 1,750 feet, with seventy trails mostly geared to advanced intermediate skiers and massive snowmaking capabilities. In summer it has an alpine slide and a chairlift to an observation tower with a grand view of the Whites. On the north side of the road, just before the ski area, is the Fields of Attitash, a well-known equestrian center with regular summer competitions.

The residential hamlet of Bartlett sits 2 miles up the road. Bear Notch Road, beginning in the middle of town, makes a good side-trip. The 9-mile road winds steeply south to scenic Bear Notch and drops gently to the Kancamagus Highway. After leaving the village the drive heads west alongside the Saco River up a textbook-example, U-shaped glacial valley. Looming mountains blanketed with a dense hardwood forest press in on the road. Their barren summits often scrape against sodden, gray clouds. These peaks form the southern end of the 15-mile-long Presidential Range, a major range in the White Mountains properly described by author Nathaniel Hawthorne as "majestic, and even awful, when contemplated in a proper mood, yet by their breadth of base and the long ridges which support them, give the idea of immense bulk rather than of towering height."

Mount Washington

Mount Washington, lying north of the Saco Valley, is the Whites' high point at 6,288 feet. It is also New England's most famous mountain. The broad peak, which includes New England's largest above-timberline ecosystem, was called *Agiocochook* by American Indians, a term loosely translated as "home of the Great Spirit." The Indians did not climb the sacred peak, so the first recorded ascent was by Darby Field in 1642. Hoping to find precious stones on the mountain, Field brought back a handful of diamonds that turned out to be quartz crystals. Today thousands of visitors reach the summit via a toll road, cog railroad, mountain bike, or foot. On the rare clear day, all of New England can be seen from this lofty perch.

The peak and range are famed for extreme weather conditions. Brutal combinations of wind and cold coupled with unsettled storm tracks give Mount Washington and the surrounding peaks the dubious distinction of having the world's worst recorded weather. The observatory atop the peak noted the highest wind gust ever recorded on earth, 231 miles an hour, on a windy April day in 1934. Gusts above 100 miles per hour have been recorded every month of the year, and the average wind-speed on the summit is 35 miles per hour. Snowfall averages 195 inches annually, with the average year-round temperature a frigid 26.9 degrees. Needless to say, area hikers need to be prepared for weather extremes and be skilled in the use of map and compass—and self-rescue.

Over Crawford Notch

Almost 9 miles from Glen, the highway enters White Mountain National Forest, the largest parcel of public land in New England, and passes Sawyer Rock Picnic

Area. The road and valley gently bend to the northwest toward Crawford Notch, one of the most storied passes in New England. The Notch was discovered accidentally in 1771 by Timothy Nash, a hunter tracking a moose. He climbed a tree to scout the way ahead and saw the dramatic notch that divides the Ammonoosuc and Saco Rivers. Since a good north-south route was needed to link new settlements in the northern Connecticut River Valley with southern New Hampshire, Nash reported his discovery to Governor John Wentworth. The governor skeptically offered Nash a tract of land in the notch if he could bring a horse through it and present the undamaged animal at Portsmouth. Nash took the challenge and, with the help of a friend, succeeded in transporting the horse through the rugged gap and delivering it. A block-and-tackle was used to lower the obliging animal over several cliffs en route. Nash received his grant, and the trail through Crawford Notch quickly gained traffic. It became a state turnpike in 1803, the precursor of today's US 302.

The pass was named for Abel Crawford, an early entrepreneur who capitalized on early tourism. Crawford and his son Ethan Allen Crawford blazed the Crawford Path in 1819, the first trail to the summit of Mount Washington; worked as tour guides; and established inns to accommodate visitors. Part of the Crawford Path, the 3 miles between the highway and Mount Clinton, comprise the oldest continuously maintained trail in the United States. The Crawfords settled here in 1792 and established Crawford House, the first hotel in the notch, in 1800. This famed hotel, in various incarnations, operated until 1977 when fire destroyed it.

The highway gently ascends the broad valley toward the notch. At 14 miles it passes Frankenstein Cliff, a tall crag named for George Frankenstein, an Ohio landscape painter. Major ice falls, attracting ice climbers, cascade down the cliff in winter. The **Arethusa Falls** trailhead is on the left at 14.7 miles. The 1.3-mile trail climbs 750 feet to secluded 176-foot-high Arethusa Falls, the tallest waterfall in New Hampshire. Coliseum and Bemis Brook Falls, both small but pretty, are also along the trail.

Crawford Notch State Park's boundary lies at the trailhead. This 5,775-acre reserve is a 1.5-mile-wide strip that runs up the valley floor to the crest of the Notch. The park's thirty-six-site Dry River Campground is just upvalley. The Appalachian Trail crosses the highway at mile 17. A mile past the trail is the **Willey House Historic Site,** site of one of the White Mountain's worst tragedies. The event, commemorated by a plaque on the house, occurred on Monday, August 28, 1826. Sam Willey, his wife, and five children, living in this lonely valley, were gripped in a torrential thunderstorm that raised the Saco River's level 24 feet in one night. They heard the terrible roar of a rock and mud avalanche loosened from the slopes above and ran, along with two hired men, for a nearby shelter but never made it. The slide struck a large boulder a scant 50 yards from the house and separated, sparing the frame building but burying the fleeing Willeys. A traveler stopped by several days later and found the dog barking and the house empty, but with a glass of toddy on a counter and Bible opened to the eighteenth Psalm— "Then the earth shook and trembled; the foundations also of the hills moved and were shaken." Three of the children's bodies were never recovered.

The aftermath of the fierce storm was described by Lucy Crawford, who wrote, "The whole valley, which was once covered with beautiful green grass, was now a complete quagmire, exhibiting nothing but ruins of the mountains, heaps of timber, large rocks, sand, and gravel. All was dismal and desolate." The slide area is still visible on the large rock slab and called, appropriately, Willey's Slide. The Willey House area makes a good road stop with marvelous views of the valley and surrounding mountains. The dam across the highway from the Willey House was used as a movie set one dreary November day for the New England film *Where the Rivers Flow North*.

Back on the scenic drive route, the highway continues ascending northward toward the gap. Its asphalt is flanked by several 4,000-foot peaks, including Mount Tom, Mount Field, and Mount Avalon on the south and the slabby Webster Brook Cliffs on the north. Mount Willard, a 2,786-foot peak, dominates the windshield view. The 800-foot-high southeast face, one of the tallest rock faces in New England, offers excellent rock climbs in summer and climbs up ice-choked gullies in winter. On the opposite valley wall is Silver Cascade, a silvery streak of water that tumbles almost 1,000 feet down the steep flank of Mount Webster. The road climbs steeply below the rock face, and after a total of 20 miles, the drive reaches the gap of Crawford Notch, an abrupt pass framed by cliffs and called the Gate of the Notch.

Crawford Notch is the most famous and most spectacular of all the White Mountains' notches. Like most of New England's geographic features, the pass was formed by glaciation. Immense valley glaciers squeezed through the narrow notch opening and down into the valley. Later the ice thickened and overrode the surrounding mountains, including Mount Willard to the south of the gap. The mountain's north slope was gently smoothed by the passing glacier, but the cliffed southeast flank overlooking the valley was formed by the ice freezing against the granite and plucking the rock away as the ice passed.

Abel Crawford's inn at the notch was visited by numerous dignitaries, including Presidents Pierce, Grant, Hayes, Garfield, and Harding. Novelist Nathaniel Hawthorne, who often wrote about the White Mountains, noted that the hotel was "the pleasure house of fashionable tourists and the homely inn of country travelers." The hotel burned several times and was rebuilt until the last fire in 1977. Still standing in the notch, however, is the old Victorian train station where guests arrived. The station, the Crawford Notch Depot, is now an Appalachian Mountain Club (AMC) information center with advice on trails and hiking, and hot drinks during foliage season.

A climber scales Mount Willard above Crawford Notch Highway.

The top of the notch is considered the headwaters of the Saco River, which gathers in tiny Saco Lake before cascading southeast into the valley. The west side of the notch is drained by Crawford Brook, an upper tributary of the Ammonoosuc River. A fine hike from the notch follows a 0.25-mile trail to the rounded top of Elephant Rock, an aptly named cliff on the north side of the gap. Another good trail gently ascends an old carriage road for 1.4 miles to the summit of Mount Willard. The AMC hiking guide notes, "From perhaps no other point in the mountains can so grand a view be obtained with so little effort." More intrepid hikers can tackle the trail along the crest of the Presidential Range, climbing ten peaks en route, on long summer days. Begin by following the Crawford Path up Mount Clinton.

To reach the **Mount Washington Cog Railway,** follow the Mount Clinton Road around the western edge of the Presidential Range to the base station. The spectacular railroad, the first cog railroad in the world, was completed in 1869. Coal-fired steam engines push passenger cars up 3.5 miles of track with an average grade of 25 percent. One steep stretch, called Jacob's Ladder, rises 37.41 percent, or more than 1 foot in 3. At this steep section the passengers in the front of the car are 16 feet higher than those in the rear.

Crawford Notch to I-93

Past the notch, the highway drops northwest down a broad valley floored by sparkling Crawford Brook. This road stretch is notorious for moose-caused accidents. Be alert for animals crossing the highway, especially in the evening. As the road flattens away from the gap, the entire 15-mile Presidential Range stretches along the eastern horizon—Mounts Jackson, Clinton, Eisenhower, Monroe, Washington, Jefferson, Adams, Quincy Adams, and Madison. A low ridge of mountains borders the drive on the west.

The Mount Washington Hotel, a huge twin-turreted inn, is reached 4 miles from the notch. This genteel hostelry, with its white stucco facade, red-tiled roof, Doric columns, and 900-foot-long veranda, is a renowned and luxurious resort set amid forested hills below looming Mount Washington itself. Built by railroad baron Joseph Stickney, the hotel was the last great resort built in northern New Hampshire and the only one still operating. It opened in 1902 after Italian craftsmen spent two years on its construction. The hotel's moment of fame, however, came in 1944 when the U.S. government reserved the entire hotel for the Bretton Woods Conference, which would shape world economics in the post–World War II period. Representatives from the United States and forty-three other countries met here and established the gold standard at $35 an ounce, made plans for the World Bank, and selected the dollar as the unit of international exchange. The hotel flourishes today as a three-season destination resort. It offers two golf courses, indoor and outdoor pools, tennis courts, horseback riding, and fishing.

The grand Mount Washington Hotel has the entire Presidential Range at its back door.

Past the hotel, the highway runs through the small village of Fabyan. The cog railroad station can also be reached by turning right here on a marked road and driving east for 5 miles. The Bretton Woods Mountain Resort is also here, with 101 trails, a 1,500-foot vertical drop, and night skiing on weekends. The area offers mostly beginner and intermediate slopes. A short distance away is a cross-country center with 100 kilometers of groomed trails.

The highway joins the Ammonoosuc River here and bends west down a broad valley. The river's name is an Abenaki Indian word for "wide fishing place." The river has long been a popular stream for anglers—among them Ethan Allen Crawford, who pulled out hundreds of pounds of trout and salmon to feed hungry guests. Just past Fabyan are the Lower Falls of the Ammonoosuc River. Here the river, forming a picturesque scene, slides over granite ledges. A short path, beginning at the large parking lot on the north side of the road, leads to the cascade.

Zealand Recreation Area includes an eleven-site forest campground along the south bank of the river. Follow Zealand Road south past Sugarloaf Campground, a lovely, secluded area by the Zealand River, and on to road's end where the Zealand Trail begins. The trail makes a good afternoon hike to two waterfalls and spectacular Zealand Notch. It heads south 2.7 miles to Zealand Falls and 4.8 miles to Thoreau Falls, a long cascade over rocky benches that was named for naturalist

Henry David Thoreau. This area was devastated by uncontrolled logging, then forest fires, and is only now being reborn.

Back on the main drive route, the scenic drive reaches the junction of US 302 and US 3, the Daniel Webster Highway, in the village of Twin Mountain. Turn left on US 3 for the next 9 miles of the drive. The road enters White Mountain National Forest again, passes Beaver Brook Falls Natural Area, and reaches the Mount Cleveland Scenic Vista after almost 7 miles. The view overlooks Beaver Brook and 2,397-foot Mount Cleveland to the northwest. The highway continues southwest, skirting the forested edge of the mountains. At 9.5 miles the drive reaches exit 36 on I–93. Continue straight for another mile and enter the southbound interstate lanes.

Franconia Notch

The last drive segment, running 11 miles from here to Lincoln, travels through Franconia Notch. Protected in a 6,692-acre state park, the notch offers breathtaking scenery and was home to New Hampshire's most famous landmark—the Old Man of the Mountain. Other natural features include The Flume, a deep stream gorge; The Basin, a glacial runoff–carved pothole; and Cannon Cliff, New England's tallest cliff. The interstate, here the Franconia Notch Parkway, narrows to two lanes as it zips down the valley. Several exits and parking areas give access to the area's special scenery.

Franconia Notch is a deep, narrow, 8-mile-long valley flanked by the lofty Franconia Range on the east and the Kinsman Range on the west. Several peaks over 4,000 feet cluster in these two ranges, making them the goals of many peak-baggers. Mount Lafayette, the 5,249-foot high point of the Franconia Range, was named in 1825 for the famed French general, the Marquis de Lafayette. The Pemigewasset River, originating at Echo Lake in the notch, dashes south along the valley floor.

The notch began as an ancient river valley some sixty million years ago. Later the land rose and the valley become deeply incised into the granite bedrock until glaciers began sculpting the land 60,000 years ago by carving out the U-shaped valley and forming abrupt cliffs on the mountain slopes.

The drive heads south on the interstate and in a mile enters **Franconia Notch State Park** at the notch itself. **Echo Lake** nestles in a hollow alongside the highway. Exit from the highway here and park. Artist's Bluff, a rounded rock dome north of the lake, gives a sweeping view of the lake, Cannon Mountain Ski Resort, and the glacier-carved valley to the south. A short trail climbs to the rock summit. In June, look for rare, protected white ladyslipper flowers here. The lake, reflecting the surrounding mountains, makes a good place to picnic, fish, boat, and swim. An 8-mile, tar bike path, bordering the interstate from Echo Lake down to The Flume, makes a fun and scenic way to explore the notch.

Although only 4,040 feet high, Cannon Mountain in the Kinsman Range dominates the western skyline. The bulky mountain is named for an oblong pile of immense boulders on its shoulders that resembles a cannon as seen from the highway. A tramway here ascends 2,022 vertical feet in six minutes, climbing from the lake to the summit for a marvelous panoramic view of Franconia Notch, five surrounding states, and Canada on a clear day. The tram operates in ski season and from mid-May to mid-October. Cannon Mountain Ski Resort, the largest ski mountain in New Hampshire, offers fifty-five trails on a 2,146-foot vertical rise. The New England Ski Museum, displaying old skis, bindings, boots, ski clothing, and trophies dating from the late 1800s, sits near the foot of the tramway.

The Old Man of the Mountain

At the far end of Echo Lake, a highway exit leads to a side road that drops south to the Profile Lake parking area and the Old Man of the Mountain. The Old Man, composed of five granite ledges that strikingly resembled a craggy human face in profile, was New England's natural version of Mount Rushmore until it fell into the cloudy night of May 3, 2003. The face, however, long inspired reverence in visitors with his jutting brow, sharp nose, pursed lips, and pointy-bearded chin. The 45-foot-high silhouette, poised 1,200 feet above Profile Lake on the brink of Cannon Cliff, not only looked human with its fine sculptural detailing and chiseled good looks, but also conveyed the flinty character of the classic New Hampshire Yankee.

The Old Man was immortalized in Nathaniel Hawthorne's short story "The Great Stone Face" when he wrote "all the features were noble, and the expression was at once grand and sweet, as if it were the glow of a vast warm heart, that embraced all mankind in its affection, and had room for more." Not everyone, however, waxed poetic at his visage. Swedish writer Frederika Bremer said the face "resembles an old man in bad humor and with a night cap on his head, who is looking out from the mountains, half inquisitive."

The Old Man remained unnoticed until 1805 when Luke Brooks and Francis Whitcomb, two surveyors plotting a road through Franconia Notch, saw the profile after stopping to wash up in Profile Lake. Earlier Native American residents had no records of the rock face, although one legend says they saw the features of the Great Spirit in it and the right to view it was reserved only for their chiefs. The face, seen only from a few vantage points near the lake, was a huge tourist attraction in the nineteenth century. A railroad stopped at the Profile House, an impressive 400-room hotel on the lake's edge. Circus-man P. T. Barnum was so impressed with the Old Man that he wanted, tongue-in-cheek, to buy him for his show. The area was bought by the state and preserved as a natural area in 1927. The Old Man became the official emblem of New Hampshire in 1946.

Franconia Notch's Old Man of the Mountain, as it appeared before falling.

The delicate formation, basically composed of several balanced, overhanging blocks of granite weighing more than 7,200 tons, was long considered unstable and subject to erosion by New Hampshire's severe climate. Geologists, as early as 1872 when a Boston newspaper reported the Old Man's instability, considered ways to forestall erosion's consequences and to secure the blocks to the main cliff. In 1916 a series of tie rods and turnbuckles were first installed on the Old Man's forehead. Over the ensuing years more rods and cables were installed and caretakers sealed cracks and fractures with epoxy and resin atop the head to minimize the infiltration of water, which levers out the granite blocks through repeated freeze-thaw cycles.

All efforts, however, were in vain. Sometime on the foggy night of May 3, 2003, the Old Man of the Mountain fell. State park official Mike Pelchat told reporters the next day, "We always thought it was the hand of God holding him up, and he let go." Geologist Brian Fowler and New Hampshire state geologist David R. Wunsch analyzed the collapse and determined "that the same geological processes that created the Old Man ultimately led to his demise. . . . Tenacious chemical weathering, frost-wedging, mechanical stress, and gravity all have conspired to send the Old Man down to the talus pile below." While the state mourned the loss of its "Great Stone Face," Governor Craig Benson formed a task force to determine if the face could be rebuilt or if a replica should be sculpted near Profile Lake. The Old Man of the Mountain Revitalization Task Force eventually recommended a sculpture-lined path around Profile Lake, a museum at the base of Cannon Mountain, and a life-size replica of the Old Man.

Past Profile Lake, the highway heads down a deep, wide gorge alongside the Pemigewasset River. *Pemigewasset* is an Abenaki Indian word for "swift current." The interstate highway through here, called the Franconia Notch Parkway, was the scene of a long standoff between development engineers and local environmentalists. The engineers wanted to continue the four-lane superhighway through the valley with shoulders and a wide median to accommodate high-speed traffic. Compromise was finally reached, and the result was today's excellent and scenic highway with two lanes, no passing, no left turns, and good access to the notch's wonders—the only such stretch of interstate highway in the nation.

As the highway descends, the towering eastern wall of Cannon Mountain hems in the valley on the west. The huge, vertical Cannon Cliff, reaching heights of 1,000 feet, is New England's tallest cliff. The 320-acre talus slope below the wall is the largest such area in New Hampshire. The cliff offers numerous rock-climbing adventures, ranging from short practice routes along the base to day-long affairs. Cannon Cliff was first climbed in 1928 via the Old Cannon route near the Old Man. Access to the crag is by trail from the Boise Rock parking area, named for woodsman Thomas Boise. Caught in a blinding blizzard at this overhanging boulder, Boise killed and skinned his horse to save himself, wrapping the warm, bloody hide around his body so that it encased him like a cocoon. The next day rescuers hacked him out of the frozen hide.

Lafayette Campground, with ninety-seven sites, lies along the riverbank farther along. A pleasant 1-mile hike up to Lonesome Lake on the southern shoulders of Cannon Mountain takes off from the campground.

The Basin, 3 miles south of Profile Lake, is a beautiful glacial feature below a large, marked parking area on the west side of the highway. This unusual geologic formation was created over the last 25,000 years as torrential runoff from melting glaciers spun through a circular basinlike cavity in the granite bedrock. The river funnels down a narrow chute and plunges into a deep, clear pool polished by tumbling cobbles and boulders. Below the pool the water funnels through narrow channels. Overhung by cliffs on its upstream side, The Basin is 30 feet in diameter and 15 feet deep at its center. An excellent hike follows the Basin-Cascade Trail up Cascade Brook west of The Basin. Numerous beautiful cascades, Kinsman Falls, and lovely Rocky Glen Falls are along the first mile.

This area also harbors a rare old-growth white pine forest, a remnant of forest untouched by the axe. One hardy specimen straddling the creek towers 100-plus feet with a trunk exceeding 4 feet in diameter. The pine, between three and four hundred years old, predates the American colonies. At that time every pine more than 2 feet in diameter and 72 feet tall was claimed, cut, and stamped with a crown for the Royal Navy as a "mast pine." The trail continues past Rocky Glen Falls another 1.4 miles to pretty Lonesome Lake in a cirque on the south slopes of Cannon Mountain.

The Flume, the last attraction in the notch, is reached a mile below The Basin. Exit the parkway and follow signs to the state park's Flume Visitor Center. The center, detailing the area's natural history with displays and a video show, makes a good introductory stop before visiting The Flume. Take the five-minute bus ride or walk the 0.7-mile distance to the site. The Flume is a fee area. Buy a ticket at the visitor center. A good 2.1-mile loop hike begins at the center and explores The Flume and The Pool.

The Flume is a spectacular fissure that stretches 800 feet through the lower slopes of Mount Liberty. The gorge ranges from 12 to 20 feet wide with vertical moss-coated walls rising 90 feet above frothy Flume Brook. This cool, refrigerated canyon (temperatures are usually 15 degrees cooler than outside) is accessed by trails and a boardwalk. A longtime tourist favorite, The Flume was discovered in 1808 by a ninety-three-year-old woman who was trout fishing near her homestead. The canyon was excavated by the stream, swollen with glacial snowmelt, as it ran along a soft basalt dike intruded into the more erosion-resistant Conway granite. The dike erodes much more quickly than the surrounding bedrock, resulting in the narrow, abrupt gorge.

Avalanche Falls, a 45-foot waterfall, sits at the head of The Flume. Atop the gorge, the trail threads northwest through woods to Liberty Gorge Cascade and another 0.1 mile to The Pool. This gorgeous spot on the Pemigewasset River is tucked into an immense basin 150 feet in diameter and 40 feet deep, surrounded by polished granite walls. The trail crosses a narrow covered bridge spanning the chasm, offering long views of The Pool and the valley. A grand, lone white pine once stood as guardian on a viewpoint above the pool, giving the name Sentinel Pine Point to the overlook. The path continues another 0.5 mile south to return to the visitor center. July hikers should keep an eye out for patches of delicious blueberries.

Back on the scenic drive, continue south by getting back onto I–93 or heading down parallel US 3. Either way the drive quickly leaves the state park and enters the tourist strip development of North Woodstock and Lincoln. The valley widens, and in a couple of miles, the drive ends at the junction of the interstate and New Hampshire Highway 112, the Kancamagus Highway. A white colonial visitor information center sits at that intersection. Travelers have numerous choices from here. The interstate continues south to southern New Hampshire and its cities, while the Kancamagus Highway heads east to Conway.

21

Upper White Mountains Scenic Drive

General description: An 89-mile scenic drive through deep glacier-carved valleys along the winding Androscoggin River, and through Dixville Notch in northern New Hampshire's White Mountains.

Special attractions: White Mountain National Forest, Pondicherry Wildlife Refuge, Moose Brook State Park, Weeks State Park, Androscoggin River, Dixville Notch State Park, The Balsams Hotel, Balsams Wilderness Ski Area, Colebrook State Park, hiking, backpacking, fishing, camping.

Location: Northern New Hampshire.

Drive route numbers and names: U.S. Highway 2, New Hampshire Highways 110, 110A, 16, and 26, North Road, Grange Road, Lost Nation Road.

Travel season: Year-round. Expect possible snow and winter driving conditions between November and April.

Camping: Moose Brook State Park (fifty-nine sites) is near the drive's start at Gorham. Coleman State Park (twenty-four sites) lies north of NH 26 west of Dixville Notch. Several private campgrounds lie along the drive.

Services: All services in Gorham, Jefferson, Groveton, Errol, and Colebrook.

Nearby attractions: Robert Frost Place, Sugar Hill Historical Museum, Connecticut River Valley, Mount Washington, Conway Scenic Railroad, Echo Lake State Park, ski areas, Presidential Range Wilderness Area, Appalachian Trail, Franconia Notch State Park.

The Drive

This 89-mile-long scenic drive follows a series of highways and back roads that thread through the upper White Mountains in northern New Hampshire. This mountainous area, north of the popular Presidential Range of the White Mountains, traverses a remote, untrampled section of New England far from the outlet shops and tourist traps. The region is a high, brooding upland broken by rumpled mountains and sliced by deep, glacier-carved valleys. Dense woodlands, interrupted only by occasional granite cliffs, blanket the hillsides. Travelers can expect excellent fall colors as well as frequent sightings of wildlife, especially moose, at dawn and dusk during autumn and spring. The year-round drive follows paved highways except for a narrow section between Jefferson and Groveton.

Gorham to Jefferson

The drive starts in Gorham at the junction of U.S. Highway 2 and New Hampshire Highway 16. This intersection is easily reached via scenic Pinkham Notch from Conway on NH 16. **Gorham,** in a breathtaking setting, is a working-class village

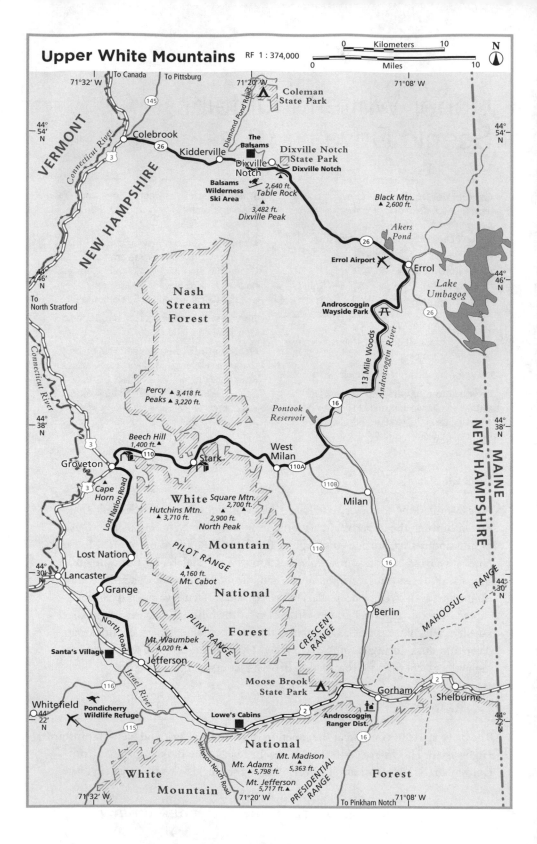

for paper mill employees. The town straddles the south bank of the Androscoggin River where it bends east to Maine. Settled in 1771, Gorham flourished after the railroad came in 1851 and made it the jumping-off place for White Mountain tourists. The old Victorian Railway Station on the town common is now a local museum that displays the area's railroad heritage. The Chamber of Commerce offers evening moose tours through the summer and early fall. A district ranger office in town has information and maps for White Mountain National Forest.

To begin the drive, head west on US 2 for 1 mile to the highway's junction with NH 16 north in Upper Village. Turn west on US 2. The highway heads west up the valley of the Moose River and, after a mile, reaches the turnoff to **Moose Brook State Park.** This area offers a pleasant fifty-nine-site campground, a swimming pool, and access to good stream fishing. The park makes a good base for hikers to explore the Presidential Range to the south and the Appalachian Trail in the Mahoosuc Range to the northeast.

Past the park turnoff, the highway climbs steeply up Gorham Hill, flattens out, and reaches a scenic roadside view of the lofty Presidential Range to the south. Peaks seen from here include Mount Madison, Mount Quincy Adams, Mount Adams, and Mount Washington, the 6,288-foot high point of the White Mountains. Mount Washington, the highest peak in the Northeast, was a sacred place called *Agiocochook* or "place of the Storm Spirit" by American Indians. Darby Field made the first recorded ascent in 1642 and brought back a handful of "diamonds," which turned out to be quartz crystals. The summit is renowned for some of the world's worst weather, including a world record 231-mile-per-hour wind gust in 1934.

Past the viewpoint, the highway drops west into the wide glaciated Moose River Valley, passing numerous trailheads that lead south into the Presidential Range. The scenery beyond the asphalt is simply spectacular, with some of New Hampshire's best offerings. The Crescent and Pliny Ranges hem in the valley to the north with high, forested mountains. The rugged profile of the Presidential Range dominates the southern horizon. The road crests a low divide near Lowe's Cabins and begins following the upper waters of the Israel River, a west-flowing tributary of the Connecticut River. The highway slowly angles northwest along the northern fringe of the hilly valley, with vistas of Franconia Notch and the Franconia Range unfolding to the southwest.

After 12.5 miles the highway reaches its intersection with New Hampshire Highway 115. A few miles down this road is the excellent 5,304-acre **Pondicherry Wildlife Refuge,** part of the Silvio Conte National Fish and Wildlife Refuge, a nature preserve designated a National Natural Landmark. The refuge, including dense woods around ponds, bogs, and streams, offers superb animal habitat for moose, beaver, otter, mink, deer, muskrat, fox, and coyote. Numerous bird species also live here, including green-winged teal and ring-necked ducks, both rarely seen in New Hampshire.

The drive route descends through a secluded residential area and skirts the southern edge of the Pliny Range, topped by 4,020-foot Mount Waumbek, then passes the Starr King Cemetery. In summers past, the Waumbek theater was considered *de rigeur* for those seeking fine summer entertainment. Farther along is the Jefferson Historical Society Museum, housed in an 1869 church, and a scenic viewpoint with two picnic tables. The town of Jefferson is just past this point.

Jefferson is an unadorned village perched on open slopes above the Israel River Valley. Superb views from this town often lure travelers from below the notches in autumn. Jefferson is named for the author of the Declaration of Independence and second U.S. president. It was settled in 1772, incorporated in 1796, and since then has been a popular summer community. Look for local maple syrup for sale here in early spring. Splendid stands of sugar maple drape the hills, yielding syrup in spring and colorful foliage in autumn.

Jefferson to Groveton

The next segment of the drive travels 16 miles north along a series of lovely, winding back roads to Groveton. These can be avoided by driving on to Lancaster and heading north on U.S. Highway 3 to Groveton, but doing so means missing out on great adventures. To start this segment, continue 0.2 mile past the junction of US 2 and NH 116 and turn north (right) onto North Road. This rough, two-lane road runs northwest along the western edge of the Pliny Range. Rural farms with tree-lined pastures abut the tar road.

Prospect Mountain, the conical centerpiece of John Wingate Weeks Historic Site, rises to the west. The park, dignified by a stone tower on its summit, is named for John W. Weeks, a U.S. senator and Cabinet member who authored and pushed through passage of the Weeks Law, which authorized the federal government to acquire and preserve forest land in the East. The law led directly to the establishment of White Mountain National Forest. A nearby 420-acre state park offers historical displays, a bird collection, information on John Weeks, and evening lectures. The mountain's summit is accessed via a fine hike, with views of the Whites and the Connecticut River Valley. The park is accessed from US 2 on the way to Lancaster.

After almost 4 miles North Road makes a sharp left turn, drops across Garland Brook, swings around Elm Ridge, and enters a residential area. After 5 miles turn right on Grange Road. The village of Grange, and all homes, are reached in another 0.5 mile.

On the north side of town, the road becomes Lost Nation Road. The drive's next 10 miles follow this narrow asphalt strip along the west flank of the Pilot Range, dipping across shallow valleys, crossing gurgling brooks, and passing thick woods filled with sugar maple, beech, white birch, spruce, and fir trees or, alternately, hayfields and pastures. Cape Horn, a rounded hump, separates the highway from the unseen Connecticut River. The road finally reaches Ames Brook, bends sharply west, and descends residential streets into the mill town of Groveton. This section of the scenic drive ends at its junction with New Hampshire Highway 110 on the southern side of town. Turn right here to continue the drive or left to dally "downstreet" in Groveton.

Groveton lies on the north bank of the placid Upper Ammonoosuc River. Like so many northern New England communities, the town saw more prosperous days during its logging boom. Today it's a slightly depressed town of brick buildings and houses built close to its streets. The town has an industrial feel, dominated as it is by an immense paper mill and large stacks of wood chips and sawdust. On the south side of town is a 136-foot covered bridge that was built in 1852 across the river and is now restricted to foot traffic.

Groveton to the Androscoggin River

The drive's third leg runs 17 miles from Groveton to NH 16. It begins on the south bank of the river at the junction of Lost Nation Road and NH 110. Head east on NH 110. The initial highway section is the Stark Scenic and Cultural Byway, a designated state scenic route. The road follows the Upper Ammonoosuc River for a couple of miles before turning away from it and crossing a low saddle. Beach Hill, to the north, separates the highway from the river's wide bend. High forested peaks in White Mountain National Forest loom to the south, including Hutchins Mountain, North Peak, and Square Mountain.

North of the river lies a trio of state forests—Devils Slide, Percy, and the 39,619-acre Nash Stream Forest. From 1900 until 1988 this area was the domain of loggers and timber companies. In the latter year it was sold to a developer. Preservationists, alarmed at the prospects, were able to acquire most of the land in the Nash Stream watershed for recreation and wildlife habitat. The area is reached via Emerson Road, 2 miles east of Groveton. Drive a logging road a dozen miles into the remote valley. Good adventures here include hiking up Percy Peaks via a 2-mile trail, trout fishing in Nash Stream, and a walk up to beautiful Pond Brook Falls. Here the creek tumbles in a long series of cascades and falls over polished granite benches. The falls are reached by parking at a culvert where Pond Creek crosses the road and hiking east along a trail a short distance to the lower cascades.

Back on NH 110, the drive rejoins the river valley and enters the picturesque village of Stark. Stark, with a white church and a 134-foot covered bridge, lies below Devil's Slide, a towering 800-foot-high cliff. The hamlet was incorporated in 1795 as Percy but later renamed for General John Stark, the Revolutionary War hero of the Battles of Bennington and Bunker Hill. Stark is also renowned for saying the famed words seen on every New Hampshire license plate—"Live Free or Die."

A pioneer cemetery ages peacefully near Stark along the Upper White Mountains Scenic Drive.

The village plodded along until the railroad came through in 1852 and opened up the area's vast timber reserves. The town later achieved notoriety as a World War II prisoner of war camp from 1944 to 1946. The camp's 250 inmates, captured in North Africa and Normandy, cut pulpwood for the paper industry before going home at war's end. The site of the camp, designated by a historic marker, sits just east of town along the highway. Stark hosts a lively fiddlers' contest the last Sunday of every June, concurrent with the annual "Blessing of the Bikes" farther north in Colebrook. Motorcyclists and fiddlers make this town hop that weekend.

The drive continues east up a bucolic valley that holds the meandering river, grassy pastures, and woods. An interesting pioneer cemetery sits alongside the road almost 3 miles past Stark. The highway gently ascends the valley to West Milan and its junction with NH 110A. Turn east (left) on NH 110A. The next 4 miles roll through thick spruce and fir forest, past Cedar Pond, and drop down to NH 16 and the Androscoggin River. Turn north (left) on NH 16.

The next 18-mile section of drive goes north through the Thirteen Mile Woods on a road with gorgeous backwoods scenery to Errol. The tone for the drive is set almost immediately by a road sign reading MOOSE CROSSING NEXT 17 MILES. The highway follows the west bank of the meandering Androscoggin River, which begins just northeast of here in Umbagog Lake on the Maine border. *Androscoggin* is an Indian word that means "fish curing place." Low rounded hillocks, densely wooded with spruce, fir, yellow birch, alder, and red maple, and low marshy areas flank the river and highway. The river, its flow interrupted only by Pontook Reservoir and a hydroelectric station, twists slowly between its wooded banks above the lake and plunges foamily over bedrock in short rapids below the dam.

The river offers great trout fishing, as well as canoeing and rafting on Class II and III whitewater. There are plenty of pullouts, including the **Androscoggin Wayside Park,** places to stop and picnic or watch the wildlife. Loons are often spotted on the glassy water. Listen for their unmistakable call at dusk. Moose, those ungainly symbols of the north woods, hang out in "moose stomps," obviously trampled earth, alongside the highway. Evening and early morning are the best times to spot them. Watch for them on the highway; a moose-car crash is not a pretty sight and there are no winners.

Through Dixville Notch

Errol, one of New Hampshire's northernmost villages, sits at a crossroads; two of the town's three highways head east into Maine. Errol is one of those old lumber towns that thrived during the spring timber drives when logs were driven downstream during high-water runoff. Now it relies on pulpwood cutting and serves as a supply center for outdoor recreationists exploring the backcountry. In Errol, turn west (left) onto New Hampshire Highway 26 for the last 21 miles of the scenic drive.

The highway quickly leaves Errol and runs northwest alongside Clear Stream up a glacier-carved valley. Akers Pond is a good-sized lake adjoining the highway a mile out of town. On the south side of the road is the single strip of what is called (tongue-in-cheek) Errol International Airport—its only international flights going to nearby Canada. The valley, lorded over by darkly forested mountains, gradually constricts. The flat valley floor filled with dense thickets is prime moose territory.

At 9.7 miles from Errol, the highway enters **Dixville Notch State Park.** This 127-acre state park, traversed in only 1.5 highway miles, protects Dixville Notch, an abrupt defile sliced through ancient shales metamorphosed into schist and phyllite. Just after entering the park, look for a picnic area on the west side of the highway. After picnicking here, walk up a short trail to Huntington Cascades, a pretty series of cascades in a damp, mossy ravine. A pioneer cemetery sits by the parking lot.

Farther up the highway is another picnic area at The Flume. A short trail leads from the parking area to **The Flume,** a sharp granite chasm 250 feet long and 40 feet deep excavated by the rushing waters of Flume Brook. The trail winds along the gorge rim. Below the edge the brook rumbles over a series of cascades before making a 15-foot plunge off a rock ledge. Look for a 7-foot-deep pothole carved into the bedrock by swirling water.

In the state park the highway steeply climbs up a 10 percent grade through the narrowing vale into an upper canyon lined with broken cliffs and pinnacles. Finally, 11 miles from Errol, the road reaches the crest of 1,990-foot **Dixville Notch,** New Hampshire's northernmost notch and certainly its most rugged. The precipitous walls of the notch, named for early land-grant holder Timothy Dix, form an abrupt V with only enough room on its floor for the highway and a brook. The state's other notches exhibit glacial characteristics with their U-shaped contours, but Dixville Notch was sculpted by running water. One of New Hampshire's last places to be free from glacial ice, the notch is only 15,000 years old. It offers a cold, windy climate for the few hardy plants and trees clinging to its steep slopes. The trees, including white birch, red spruce, and balsam fir, are stunted by both weather and poor soil.

Park on the far west side of the notch at a southside parking area for the trailhead to Table Rock, a jutting rocky prow towering above the western end of the notch. The 0.3-mile trail climbs very steeply up a ravine to the crag's narrow summit platform. Table Rock yields a marvelous but hard-earned view of Dixville Notch, the surrounding mountains, and the famed resort hotel called The Balsams.

From the notch the highway drops 0.1 mile to Lake Gloriette and The Balsams. The latter, a grand 204-room hotel built against the stunning mountain

Table Rock offers a spectacular view of Dixville Notch.

backdrop, offers golf courses, tennis courts, a full slate of family activities, boating, swimming, and award-winning cuisine, including a heaped 100-foot buffet table in summer. *Golf Magazine* calls it "one of America's best golf resorts," while the National Trust for Historic Preservation designates it a "Historic Hotel of America." Nearby is the tiny hamlet of Dixville Notch, traditionally the first town to report its results in New Hampshire's presidential primary elections.

From here to Colebrook and the drive's end, NH 26 follows the gentle valley of the Mohawk River. The Balsams Wilderness Ski Area lies just past the hotel on the mountains south of the road. The area offers a 1,000-foot vertical drop and numerous intermediate runs along with 95 kilometers of groomed cross-country ski trails. Only 4 miles from the hotel at Kidderville is Diamond Pond Road. The road leads north 6 miles to 1,530-acre Coleman State Park with a twenty-four-site campground on the spruce-forested shores of Little Diamond Pond. The lake allows fine fishing for trout.

As the highway descends west, the land opens up to low, undulating hills creased by shallow valleys. Hill farms with hayfields and dark woods scatter alongside the highway. The road enters **Colebrook,** an old lumber town lying on the Connecticut River not far from its headwaters at the Connecticut Lakes.

Colebrook was first settled by Eleazer Rosebrook in 1774 on a land grant given to Sir George Colebrooke of the British East India Company. The town later grew and prospered with dairying and potato farming. The first road through Dixville Notch in 1804 further opened the area to settlement. The Colebrook area also was the center of the logging industry during the late nineteenth century. Huge log drives on the Connecticut River every spring floated millions of board feet of lumber down the snowmelt-swollen river to sawmills, with as much as 100 miles of the river solidly packed with logs going to market. The log drives are now a thing of the past, and the upper Connecticut River basin has reverted back to quiet farming days with its rustic, weathered barns, dairy farms dotted with black and white cows, and the ever-present mountains brushed green with thick forests.

The drive quietly ends at the intersection of NH 26 and US 3 in town. Quebec lies a scant 10 miles north of here. A good scenic return drive back to Groveton and Lancaster follows US 3 south along the Connecticut River through hilly countryside.

22

Mid-Coast Scenic Drive

General description: A 123-mile scenic drive exploring several of the long finger peninsulas jutting into the Atlantic Ocean on Maine's Mid-Coast.

Special attractions: Bowdoin College, Bowdoin Pines, Basin Cove Falls, Bath, Maine Maritime Museum, Morse Mountain, Popham Beach State Park, Fort Popham, Salt Bay, Damariscotta Reversing Falls, Wiscasset, Fort Edgecomb, Boothbay, Boothbay Harbor, Pemaquid Point, Fort William Henry, Pemaquid Beach Park, Rachel Carson Salt Pond Preserve, fishing, hiking, nature study, lighthouses.

Location: Central Maine.

Drive route numbers: U.S. Highway 1, Maine Highways 123, 24, 209, 27, 238, 130, and 32.

Travel season: Year-round.

Camping: Many private campgrounds are found along the drive. One of the best is Hermit Island Campground off Maine Highway 216 near Popham Beach. It has 275 sites along the beach. Ocean View Park Campground is a popular camp spot at Popham Beach. Other private campgrounds are at Pemaquid Point, Orrs Island, and Boothbay. Public campgrounds are at Bradbury Mountain State Park west of Freeport and Interstate 95, and Camden Hills State Park just north of Camden.

Services: All services in Brunswick, Topsham, Bath, Wiscasset, Boothbay Harbor, Newcastle, Damariscotta, New Harbor, and Waldoboro.

Nearby attractions: Freeport, Wolfe's Neck Woods State Park, Desert of Maine, Bradbury Mountain State Park, Portland attractions, Reid State Park, Josephine Newman Wildlife Sanctuary, Augusta, Head Tide, Damariscotta Lake State Park, Rockland, Camden, Camden Hills State Park, Monhegan Island.

The Drive

Beginning off Interstate 95 at Brunswick, this scenic drive follows several long, fingerlike peninsulas that jut southward into the Atlantic Ocean on Maine's Mid-Coast. This serene seaside landscape is dotted with fishing villages and summer cottages, isolated beaches and surf-swept headlands, quiet coves and picturesque lighthouses, and hundreds of offshore islands. The Mid-Coast is characterized by narrow, rocky peninsulas separated by bays and river channels that reach far inland. The area is a classic "drowned coast," shaped by huge glaciers that overrode the land and excavated valleys that later filled with seawater. Several major Maine rivers empty into the Gulf of Maine via these channels, including the Kennebec, Sheepscot, and Damariscotta Rivers. The ragged coastline has long provided numerous excellent harbors for both fishing boats and pleasure craft.

The scenic drive, stitched together by busy U.S. Highway 1 on the north, follows a series of state highways that explore the thin peninsulas to their blunt tips. Most of the roads require travelers to retrace their steps back to US 1 before

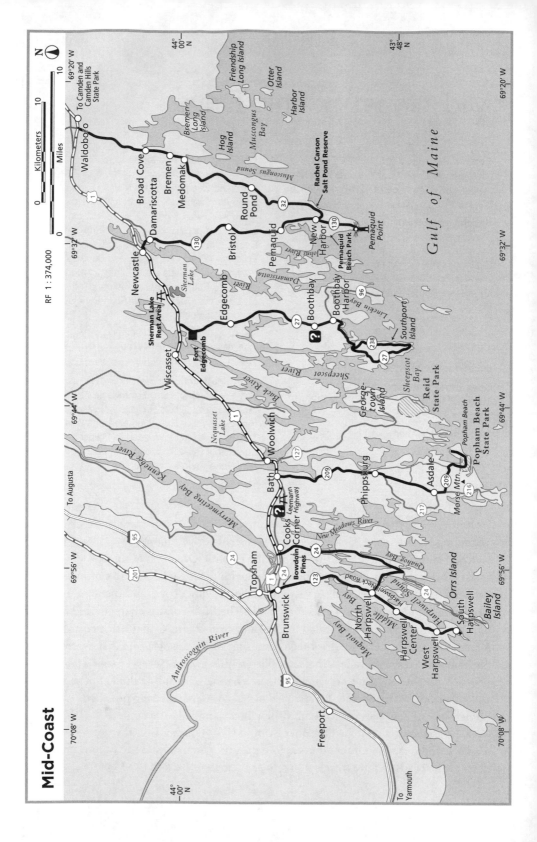

Mid-Coast

RF 1 : 374,000

embarking down the next finger projection. Each peninsula offers its own particular charms and attractions, giving explorers a sense of a Maine that is far removed from the hustle and bustle of commercial US 1. Allow a full day to drive these roads and sample their beauty. As always, lots of back roads beckon intrepid drivers to take the road less traveled. By all means, follow that urge and discover other secret places not included in this description.

Brunswick

The drive officially begins at I–95's exit 22 at Brunswick, just north of Freeport and its sprawling L. L. Bean store and outlet shops. Since 1912, Freeport has been the headquarters for L. L. Bean's mail-order business and retail store. The huge store is open year-round, twenty-four hours a day, seven days a week. Bradbury Mountain State Park, west of Freeport, makes a good base camp from which to explore the Mid-Coast. The park offers a wooded forty-one-site campground and some great hiking trails on its granite bluff.

Exit the interstate and immediately get on US 1 in west **Brunswick.** Seat of the excellent Bowdoin College, the town spreads along the south bank of the Androscoggin River, which soon thereafter empties into Merrymeeting Bay and mingles with the Kennebec River. Indians, calling this place *Ahmelahcogneturcook* or "place of much fish, birds, and animals," protected it as a favorite hunting ground. Thomas Purchase began a trading post here in the 1620s and a thriving business that cured salmon caught in the river before Indian raids forced the post and settlers out. Later Fort Andros was built here and by 1715 the town of Brunswick was laid out. Named for Brunswick, Germany, the town boasts a Maine Street, its principal north-south thoroughfare, which was made 12 rods wide and still remains the widest street in Maine. Brunswick flourished as a lumber, textile, paper, and industrial center through the 1800s, using cheap power generated by a dam on the Androscoggin River.

Bowdoin College, the town's cultural center, was established in 1794, opened in 1802, and named for Massachusetts governor James Bowdoin. Many famed Americans matriculated from the college, including Admiral Robert Peary, discoverer of the North Pole; Thomas Reed, a Speaker of the House; Hannibal Hamlin, fifteenth vice president; and the big three from the class of 1825—novelist Nathaniel Hawthorne, poet Henry Wadsworth Longfellow, and Franklin Pierce, fourteenth president of the United States. Writer Harriet Beecher Stowe, whose husband was a Bowdoin professor, lived nearby when she wrote the famous anti-slavery novel *Uncle Tom's Cabin* in the early 1850s. The book, which sold 305,000 copies in its first year alone, heightened awareness of the inhumanity of slavery and helped lead the nation toward irreconcilable differences and the Civil War.

Brunswick's past is well preserved in the **Federal Street Historic District,** which includes the 110-acre Bowdoin College campus and the Lincoln Street Historic District. The Pejepscot Historical Society owns the Joshua L. Chamberlain Museum and the Skolfield-Whittier House, which houses the society's museum. The college's two museums make an interesting visit. The Peary-Macmillan Arctic Museum displays the northern adventures of these two grads. Peary's memorabilia details his 1908 North Pole expedition, while Donald Macmillan's collection includes an excellent display of Inuit culture amassed during twenty-seven Arctic expeditions. Nearby is the Bowdoin College Museum of Art with an eclectic display that includes a Winslow Homer Gallery, a collection of paintings and sculptures by Gilbert Stuart, John Sloan, Daniel Chester French, and Augustus Saint-Gaudens, and some Mediterranean and Oriental artworks.

Down Harpswell Neck

US 1 bends through Brunswick and after a mile bears right onto Maine Street. Follow signs for Maine Highway 123/24. The road cuts through the busy downtown business district, passing old homes and churches. After skirting the Bowdoin campus and its magnificent stand of 90-foot-tall, old-growth white pines, watch for ME 123, where you'll turn south on Harpswell Neck Road. The first drive segment travels almost 15 miles on ME 123 down Harpswell Neck to the hamlet of South Harpswell on its southern tip. Harpswell Neck is a narrow peninsula flanked by Middle Bay on the west and Harpswell Sound on the east along with tattered chains of islands, some separated from the mainland by narrow channels. Orrs and Bailey Islands, the two largest, are immediately east of the neck. The long peninsula and the surrounding islands are collectively called The Harpswells.

The drive runs through fields and dense woods dotted with occasional houses. After 9 miles the road passes Mountain Road in North Harpswell; put a marker here, because after exploring the neck you'll return and follow this road northeast.

Harpswell Center lies a couple of miles farther south. This lovely old village boasts a white, Gothic-style Congregational Church built in 1843 for early pastor Elijah Kellogg. The burying ground outside has many graves dating from the 1700s, including that of Elisa Eaton, the first Harpswell reverend, who died in 1764. Nearby is the simple white-clapboard 1757 Harpswell Meeting House, the oldest surviving meetinghouse in Maine.

The road continues south through low forested hills and after 16 miles reaches the edge of the house- and cottage-lined harbor. About 0.5 mile later the highway dead-ends on the thin spit of land. Picnic tables by the turnaround here allow for a pleasant seaside lunch and a great view south across Merriconeag Sound to Bailey Island. The middle and west points of land on the trident-shaped tip of Harpswell Neck are separated by quiet Basin Cove. The narrow channel leading into the cove from Potts Harbor is the site of Basin Cove Falls, a reversing falls caused by the tide rising and falling through a gap.

To continue the scenic drive, turn north and retrace your path on ME 123 for 7 miles to Mountain Road in North Harpswell. Turn east (right) onto Mountain Road. A bridge leads across Ewin Narrows to the western lobe of Sebascodegan Island, an irregularly shaped island fringed by rocky inlets, bays, and coves. After 2.6 miles the road intersects ME 24. Turn north (left) on ME 24.

A right turn takes you on a good side-trip to Orrs and Bailey Islands. Cribstone Bridge, an unusual honeycombed granite bridge, connects the two. It's supposedly the only remaining example in the world of a bridge fashioned in an open checkerboard pattern that allows the tides to ebb and flow through its 1,200-foot span. The granite blocks were laid without mortar in the joints. The tip of Bailey Island was a military lookout in World War II, meant for spotting German U-boats. A rags-to-riches story here says fisherman John Wilson came upon an iron kettle filled with Spanish gold while duck hunting and set himself up with the finest farm on Bailey Island.

The main scenic drive route heads north on ME 24, edging along Quahog Bay, crossing Gurnet Strait, and reaching US 1 almost 9 miles later on the east side of Brunswick, a scant couple of miles from downtown. Turn right on US 1 and follow it for 5 miles. The highway crosses the wide New Meadows River, passes an information station and picnic tables, and enters the town of Bath—the City of Ships. Turn right in Bath on Maine Highway 209.

Bath to Popham Beach

On the west bank of the Kennebec River's tidal channel, Bath is one of America's greatest shipbuilding ports with more than 4,000 ships built and launched here. The town, settled in 1660 and named for the old Roman town of Bath, England, flourished after 1762 when the *Earl of Brute,* the first full-rigged ship built here, was launched. Earlier English colonists had constructed the thirty-ton pinnace *Virginia,* the first ship built in the New World, at Popham Point near here in 1607.

A combination of factors made Bath an ideal shipbuilding center. The sloped shore allowed for the laying of the keel. The river's deep channel permitted easy launching and protected anchored ships from ocean storms. Lastly, the Kennebec River ran straight north to the heart of Maine's timber, giving shipbuilders an almost inexhaustible supply of wood. During those halcyon days Bath was a lively, cosmopolitan town. Speedy half-clipper ships were built here to haul miners to California gold fields; the *Wyoming,* the largest wooden sailing ship built, and the only seven-masted schooner were fashioned here; early gunboats, destroyers, and navy ships left the yards to protect American interests.

After iron-hulled steamships replaced wooden sailing ships, Bath went into a slow decline until General Thomas Hyde founded the Bath Iron Works in 1890 and brought new prosperity to the Mid-Coast. The massive works, with its red-and-

Popham Beach is one of Maine's best and longest sand strands.

white crane (fourth largest in the country) looming over US 1, is now a modern shipbuilding complex and the single largest industry and employer in Maine. The Bath Iron Works builds frigates for the U.S. Navy and merchant container vessels.

Despite its industrial feel, Bath still retains historical charm. The town's old residential district offers numerous houses, once the homes of prosperous sea captains, as bed-and-breakfasts. The Winter Street Church, built in 1843 on the town green, merges Greek Revival and Gothic styles with its towering steeple and temple facade. The most interesting place in Bath is the Maine Maritime Museum, just east of the drive route and ME 209, at the site of the old ten-acre Percy & Small Shipyard. This excellent museum depicts the history of Maine shipping, shipbuilding, and seafaring with interpretative exhibits, tools, dioramas, and models. Of particular interest is the lobstering history and technology exhibit.

North of Bath is Merrymeeting Bay, a large inland bay that is the meeting place of six rivers—the Androscoggin, Kennebec, Abagadasset, Cathance, Muddy, and East. The 164-mile Kennebec River, called *Quinnebequi* or "River God" by the Indians, originates in Moosehead Lake far to the north, while the 174-mile Androscoggin begins in Umbagog Lake on the Maine–New Hampshire border. These two great rivers drain more than half of Maine's total area. Merrymeeting Bay is supposedly named because all these rivers so merrily met here. In her book

The Coast of Maine, Louise Dickinson Rich offers a more plausible explanation: "The name originally was spelled Maremiten, which I think could be translated roughly to mean 'inland sea'; and I believe Merrymeeting to be only a rather charming corruption." The Kennebec flows 17 miles south from the bay before emptying into the Gulf of Maine.

The next 17-mile segment of the drive heads south from Bath on High Street. After a couple of miles, it exits town, becomes ME 209, and jogs across Winnegance Creek. The wide highway, often busy in summer with visitors flocking down to Popham Beach, quickly dashes south through swamp and forest. At 5 miles it skirts Drummore Bay, passing historic Phippsburg and skirting another quiet cove, then continues south through rolling, wooded hills. The highway's junction with Maine Highway 217, a spur road to Sebasco, is at 11 miles.

Bend left on ME 209 at its intersection with Maine Highway 216. The road drops east through low hillocks to a broad marsh flat blanketed with salt grass. A short, private trail begins along here and winds through the marsh to the 600-acre Bates-Morse Mountain Preserve and a low hill between the Sprague and Morse Rivers. The hilltop offers views of the surrounding estuary, offshore islands, and, on a clear day, Mount Washington in New Hampshire.

The road next twists and turns around Spirit Pond and a mile later reaches **Popham Beach State Park.** Popham Beach is a lovely piece of oceanfront property with a long, sweeping sand strand that is one of Maine's best as well as its longest. Needless to say, this park is a very popular destination on warm summer week-ends. Better to wait until a quieter off-season day to walk the beach and listen to the Atlantic rollers breaking on the shore. A good hike during low tide is crossing the tombolo, or sandbar, that connects Fox Island to the mainland. The wide beach is open daily, with lifeguards in summer, and is a fee area. There are more than 7 miles of beach in the area, including Hunnewell Beach, crescent-shaped Head Beach, and The Nature Conservancy–owned Seawall Beach. Seawall is one of the finest undeveloped barrier spits left in Maine. It also boasts the state's largest parabolic dunefield.

Past the beach, the highway turns north onto a jutting cape and 2 miles later reaches **Fort Popham State Historic Site** and a parking area at the end of the road. The Fort Popham seen here today is the stone remains of a Civil War fortification. The two-story, 30-foot-high citadel, composed of massive granite blocks, sits at a strategic point overlooking the mouth of the Kennebec River. Its intents (and its thirty-six cannons) were to protect Bath's valuable shipbuilding industry from possible Confederate attacks. The fort was never finished, but garrisoned troops during the Civil and Spanish-American wars. Nearby are some bunkers that were manned in both world wars.

Just west of the fort on the opposite side of the cove lies the site of the 1607–1608 Popham Colony, the first English settlement in New England—predating the

The ruins of strategic Fort Popham protect the mouth of the Kennebec River.

Pilgrims' landing by fourteen years. The colony shares with Jamestown, Virginia, the honor of being the first English settlement in the New World. George Popham and Raleigh Gilbert led a hardy band of nearly a hundred pioneers from England. They landed here in August 1607 and established what they called the "Northern Virginia Colony." Constructing a storehouse and crude fort, they set about preparing for winter.

Things went from bad to worse through that cold season. Food stores were inadequate. Relations with local Indians fell apart after, as one settler noted, "They beat them, abused them, and they set their dogs on them with little restraint." The Indians retaliated by killing eleven English settlers. But it was finally the weather that did the brief colony in. The variable winter weather and frigid temperatures discouraged the colonists. Popham died that winter, and Gilbert left for England in the spring. The disenchanted settlers stuck it out until summer but, fearing another New England winter, packed up and departed for England or Virginia.

From the Fort Popham parking lot, turn the car around and drive back north 17 miles to the junction of ME 209 and US 1 in downtown Bath. The road wanders a bit in Bath, but keep an eye open for US 1 signs and you'll stay on course. Turn east (right) on US 1 in Bath. An old girder bridge swings over the mighty Kennebec here, offering views of the immense shipyard. On the far side of the span is Maine Highway 127. This charming road, not part of this drive, makes a great side-trip down Arrowsic and Georgetown Island/Peninsulas. At the end of the highway, 14 miles from here, is Reid State Park, Mile and Half Mile Beaches, and the Audubon Society's 119-acre Josephine Newman Sanctuary.

Wiscasset

The scenic drive continues northeast on US 1 from the highway bridge. US 1 runs through low hills covered with leafy woods and, 10 miles from Bath, enters **Wiscasset** on the west bank of the broad tidal channel of the Sheepscot River. *Wiscasset,* an Indian word meaning "meeting of three tides," is a charming town with a name that rolls off the tongue. It was occupied in the early 1700s, abandoned during King Philip's War, then permanently settled in 1730. After the Revolution Wiscasset prospered, like so many Maine coastal towns, as a shipping and lumber center. Numerous immense homes and mansions testify to the wealth that once flowed through town.

Wiscasset's historic district, encompassing the waterfront and older part of town, preserves some of New England's finest old houses. The Nickels-Sortwell House, built in 1807 by Captain William Nickels for the princely sum of $14,000, is a handsome, three-story Federal house with an elliptical stairway lit by a skylight. After Nickels's death in 1815, the house went through a long period as a succession of inns before Alvin Sortwell, mayor of Cambridge, Massachusetts, purchased it as a summer home in 1900. It is now a museum operated by the Society for the Preservation of New England Antiquities. Other buildings of note include the 1807 Red Brick Schoolhouse and the Lincoln County Museum and Old Jail. The cold, clammy jail, built in 1809, housed prisoners until 1953.

Lying in the Sheepscot River, just off US 1, are the rotting, barnacle-festered hulls of the 1918 *Hesper* and the 1917 *Luther Little.* The two schooners, local landmarks, were the last four-masted schooners built in New England and are the only two remaining of the 562 made in the United States.

Today, Wiscasset dubs itself "the prettiest village in Maine." That's not far removed from the truth. The classic buildings and houses from centuries past meld with the town's antiques and hardware shops, restaurants, and bed-and-breakfasts, giving it the perfect New England coastal town look. But watch out in summer when congested traffic makes the village a driver's nightmare.

US 1 bends east in Wiscasset and crosses the wide Sheepscot River on a long bridge. The southern tip of Davis Island, on the east side of the river, is the site of old Fort Edgecomb. The fort was built in 1808 to protect the Wiscasset port from English attack after Congress passed the Embargo Act of 1807. This act closed American ports to English ships during an escalation in hostilities between England and France. During the War of 1812, the fort guarded the harbor but saw no action. It was later manned during the Civil War when the Confederate ship *Talla-hassee* sailed into Maine waters. Little remains today except some disappearing earthworks, a massive octagonal blockhouse, and a reconstructed stockade. Watch for seals, which are often sighted in the water off the fort.

The Boothbay Peninsula

After reaching the east bank of the Sheepscot River, turn south almost immediately on Maine Highway 27 for the next drive section, a 22-mile exploration of the Boothbay Peninsula. This long, ragged peninsula between the Sheepscot and Damariscotta River estuaries extends south to Boothbay Harbor and Linekin Bay. ME 27 is not a back road by any stretch of imagination, but rather a fast highway that carries throngs of summer tourists. Plan your visit for the right time of year. Boothbay Harbor's year-round population is only 2,400. Summer brings more than 30,000 people on busy days, but the mid-July sailing regatta swells the weekend count to more than 100,000.

The road runs quickly south over rolling hills and past summer homes. Boothbay is reached after 8 miles. Just 2 miles later is Boothbay Harbor and the highway's junction with Maine Highway 96. Boothbay was purchased from local Indians for twenty beaver skins and settled in 1630 as Newagen. It was abandoned during the Indian wars, but resettled in the 1750s by Scotch-Irish emigrants. The village grew as a seaport and shipbuilding center.

Boothbay Harbor, lying on the north end of the placid anchorage, is a favorite port for pleasure sailors and a busy coastal resort. The town separated from Boothbay and incorporated in 1889. The narrow streets are lined with well-kept cottages and houses, craft and trinket shops, dockside motels and inns, art galleries, and restaurants. Hungry visitors should head to the locally owned Lobstermen's Cooperative for a look at a working lobster pound and some no-frills, very fresh seafood. Boothbay's summer theater is rightly famous, with a couple theaters and the Lincoln Arts Festival. Parking can be problematic. Calling itself "The Yachting Capital of New England," Boothbay Harbor offers several famous summer sailing festivals. The popular Windjammer Days in June bring myriad yachts to the festivities. Travelers might also want to sample a harbor cruise, deep-sea fishing excursion, whale-watching trip, or day-long tour to beautiful Monhegan Island.

Maine boasts somewhere between two and three thousand islands, depending on what is one's definition of an island. Monhegan Island, lying 20 miles east of Boothbay Harbor, is perhaps Maine's finest offshore island not accessed by a bridge. Described in 1569 as "a great island that was backed like a whale," it measures 1 mile wide and just over 2 miles long. John Cabot, the intrepid English explorer, visited it in 1498, a scant six years after Columbus's New World landing.

With lobstering, fishing, and an artists' colony, Monhegan offers startling scenery. It faces the unbroken Atlantic with a front of grand cliffs that plunge more than 160 feet into the frothy surf. The quiet Cathedral Woods, on the northern part of the isle, is a forest of pine and spruce. Watch out for abundant poison ivy.

To continue the scenic drive, head south on ME 27 through Boothbay Harbor, bending to the right in downtown. The narrow street winds west above the bay, passing a marina and houses. After a couple of miles, the road crosses a narrow strait on a swing bridge to Southport Island. The drive follows ME 27 and Maine Highway 238 on a 13-mile loop around the island's perimeter. The tree-shaded road, lined with cottages, offers views of Sheepscot Bay on the west and a fine craggy coast. Midway through the loop ME 27 melds with ME 238, which runs up the east shore.

Upon completing the loop at Boothbay Harbor, follow ME 27 back north to US 1. A good side-trip goes east from here on ME 96 to East Boothbay, a working fishing village, and continues down Linekin Neck to sea views at Ocean Point.

The main route takes US 1 northeast for 5 miles to Newcastle. Sherman Lake Rest Area, with picnic tables and restrooms, sits on the lake's north shore 2 miles from the highway junction. Upon reaching Newcastle, trend right onto US 1A and Maine Highway 130 across the Damariscotta River to Damariscotta. Turn south (right) on ME 130 toward Bristol.

Damariscotta to Pemaquid Point

Newcastle and **Damariscotta** are twin villages on opposite banks of the wide river. Newcastle is the site of the first Catholic parish in Maine, established in 1796 by Irish settlers. The church, St. Patrick's, was erected in 1803 and dedicated by Father Jean de Cheverus, the first Roman Catholic bishop in New England. The 300-year-old altarpiece is from France, while many of the paintings were taken from a convent during the Mexican War.

Damariscotta is an Indian word for "meeting place of the alewives." The townsite was a longtime Indian fishing spot. For centuries the native people congregated here in the spring, netting bushels of alewives or herrings swimming upstream to spawn in fresh water. The town, at the upper end of the Bristol Peninsula, was settled in 1625, abandoned during the Indian wars, and then resettled to prosper in the nineteenth century as a shipping and shipbuilding center. The clipper ship *Flying Scud* was built here and later made a record 448 miles in twenty-four hours. An 1845 fire consumed much of the town, but the Main Street Historic District preserves the rebuilt village. Points of interest upriver include the Damariscotta Reversing Falls, caused by tidal flow; Salt Bay, a shallow bay that offers excellent birding with many migrating shorebirds; and prehistoric shell heaps or middens deposited over thousands of years by American Indian hunter-gatherers.

Pemaquid Point stretches south from the Mid-Coast Scenic Drive into the Gulf of Maine.

The scenic drive turns south in Damariscotta on ME 130 for its last 35 miles on the last finger peninsula. The first 15 miles head down narrowing Bristol Peninsula to Pemaquid Point. The road then turns northeast along the peninsula's eastern shore for 20 miles to the drive's end in Waldoboro. ME 130 heads south above the Damariscotta River's east bank. Keep right on ME 130 at the Y intersection reached after 3 miles. The right branch, Maine Highway 129, continues down to South Bristol and Christmas Cove.

A couple of miles later, the road runs through the small hamlet of Bristol, graced with an 1800 Town Hall. Old houses and worn farms line the asphalt south of the village. The highway passes **Pemaquid** and the Harrington Burial Ground with graves as old as 1716 before wheeling left across the Pemaquid River and entering New Harbor, a fishing and resort area. The townsite was the ancestral home of Samoset, an Indian chief who greeted the Plymouth Pilgrims in 1621 with the words "Much welcome, Englishmen." He had learned a smattering of English from passing sailors. Later, when the Pilgrims were starving, he led them to a store of precious corn on Pemaquid Neck. European explorers were well aware of the Pemaquid Beach and Harbor area. David Ingram visited in 1569, Bartholomew Gosnold in 1602, Raleigh Gilbert and Francis Popham in 1607, and Captain John Smith, who spent Christmas Day in Christmas Cove to the west, in 1614. Merchants from Bristol, England, had a trading center here in 1600.

A reproduction of Fort William Henry, one of America's first stone fortresses, sits west of the drive near Pemaquid Beach. The first fort here, built in 1630, was sacked by Indians. A second, Fort Charles, was erected in 1677 and subsequently burned by pirates. The third, supposedly impregnable Fort William Henry, was built in 1692, but wrecked four years later by the French and Indians. Fort Frederic, a fourth citadel, was built at the same place in 1729. This, writes Louise Dickinson Rich, "establishes a record, not only for the number of forts on the same foundation, but for optimism in continuing to build on a jinxed spot as well." This fourth fort was dismantled by American patriots in 1775 so that it wouldn't fall into British hands. The existing stone tower was put up in 1906 and houses a collection of weapons and military equipment along with details of the complicated history of the site.

Past New Harbor, the highway narrows and winds through forest and past gift shops for 3 miles before emerging onto **Pemaquid Point.** This southernmost tip of Pemaquid Neck is a bare, rocky point jutting into the Atlantic surf. **Pemaquid Lighthouse,** one of Maine's prettiest lighthouses, perches on ledges above the water. The now unmanned, automatic light has guided mariners since 1827. Its 11,000-candlepower beam can be seen from 14 miles away. The adjoining lightkeeper's cottage is now an interesting fishing museum that displays fishing tools, maps, photographs, models, and a mounted twenty-eight-pound lobster.

The real beauty of Pemaquid Point is the ceaseless surf clashing against the bedrock coast. This spectacular place, one of the most photographed scenes on the Maine coast, is alive with constant movement. Heavy waves break constantly against the ledges and crags of tilted metamorphic rock and granite, an austere shoreline. Gulls dive and wheel above the surf. The point is one of the best spots to visit during a violent storm. Towering waves are driven ashore, pounding against the rocky walls with a constant roar. When the tide is low, stand on the west side of the point and listen to round boulders tumble back and forth in grooved channels. The point is a popular attraction, except on stormy days, with hundreds of visitors milling about on the clifftops. Come early or late to avoid the crowds. Also, take extreme care when walking on the rock ledges. Better yet, stay beyond the reach of the sea on the benches by the lighthouse. Every year visitors are swept off the rocks into the turbulent water by rogue, or sleeper, waves and drowned.

Continue the drive by heading back north on ME 130 to its junction with Maine Highway 32 in New Harbor. Turn east (right) onto ME 32 for the last 20 miles of the drive. This lovely highway stretch bordering Muscongus Bay and Medomak River is much more scenic and pleasant than ME 130. The road reaches the coast in a mile and passes the **Rachel Carson Salt Pond Preserve.** This seventy-eight-acre preserve owned by The Nature Conservancy is best visited at low tide when the tidal salt pond is exposed. Famed naturalist Rachel Carson spent countless hours researching in this area for data later used in her best-selling book *Edge of the Sea*. A brochure at the registration box details the many marine animals seen here, including starfish, sea urchins, crabs, blue mussels, and periwinkles.

The road leaves the bay at Long Cove and twists inland through pastoral hills. Round Pond is a quaint village poised above a round cove off Muscongus Sound. A white clapboard Methodist Church rises above the village center. Nearby is the oldest schoolhouse in Maine, a rough granite building with plank benches inside. The highway runs north past a cemetery and the little village of Bremen, then at 17 miles climbs onto a high ridge that offers far views across bays and coves to the east. East of here off the Keene Neck Road is land held as Hockomock Point Trail and Todd Wildlife Sanctuary. Both are Audubon Society properties. The mile-long trail exploring the flora and fauna of the neck offers good views down Muscongus Sound. The road is lined with homes as it nears Waldoboro. At 20 miles is a picnic area on the right. Only 0.1 mile later the drive ends where the highway intersects US 1 in Waldoboro.

Waldoboro, named for General Samuel Waldo who obtained a large land grant here, was settled by German emigrants. One grave marker in the cemetery at the 1772 Old German Church states, "This town was settled in 1748 by Germans . . . with the promise and expectation of finding a prosperous city, instead of which they found nothing but wilderness." The town, on the Medomak River, relied on shipping and shipbuilding like other coastal Maine towns. The Waldoboro Historical Society Museum maintains the town history with a restored schoolhouse, local memorabilia, and the Town Pound, a large stone corral to contain stray livestock.

Some excellent points of interest lie up US 1 and the coast from Waldoboro, including the picturesque town of Camden and the excellent Camden Hills State Park. The park offers marvelous views of West Penobscot Bay from its high mountains, spacious campground, and many hiking trails.

23

Acadia National Park Scenic Drive

General description: A 27-mile loop that explores the glacier-scoured mountains and rock-bound coast of Acadia National Park.

Special attractions: Acadia National Park, Hulls Cove Visitor Center, Sieur de Monts, Wild Gardens of Acadia, Robert Abbe Museum of Stone Age Antiquities, Acadia National Park Nature Center, Champlain Mountain and Precipice Trail, Sand Beach, Thunder Hole, Otter Cliffs, Otter Point, Jordan Pond, Jordan Pond House, Cadillac Mountain summit, scenic overlooks, nature study, photography, hiking, rock climbing, camping.

Location: The coastline of south-central Maine.

Drive route name: Park Loop Road.

Travel season: April through November. The drive is not maintained in winter. Be prepared for varied weather. Summer temperatures climb as high as 85 degrees Fahrenheit but can drop to the 40s. Spring and autumn highs range from 30 degrees to 70 degrees. Since it can rain or be foggy on any given day, hikers should carry rain gear.

Camping: Two park campgrounds with 541 sites are available. Blackwoods, on Maine Highway 3 about 5 miles south of Bar Harbor, is open year-round. Reservations can be made through the Acadia National Park Web site, www.nps.gov/acad. Seawall Campground, off Maine Highway 102A, is open from mid-May through early October. It operates on a first-come, first-served basis. Summer is very busy, so campgrounds fill quickly. Get there early to reserve a site. No overnight backpacking is allowed in the park. Many private campgrounds are found nearby. Check with the local chamber of commerce offices for information on these.

Services: All services, including gas, food, restaurants, lodging, and camping, are found in Ellsworth, Bar Harbor, and many of the surrounding small towns.

Nearby attractions: Schoodic Peninsula and Point, Lamoine State Park, Camden Hills State Park, Deer Isle, Isle au Haut, Bangor attractions.

The Drive

This spectacular 27-mile scenic drive explores Acadia National Park, New England's jewel in the nation's National Park system. Acadia, a place of matchless beauty and startling contrasts, is the most famous part of Maine's ragged, 2,500-mile coastline. The superlative park, covering 46,856 acres on Mount Desert Island, Isle au Haut, and Schoodic Peninsula, is a natural crossroads where the forested mountains march down to the relentless sea. Cadillac Mountain, its high point, is also the highest point on the entire eastern seaboard and the place where the rising sun first gilds the United States. The park is biologically diverse, with its northern coniferous forests interlaced with temperate deciduous forest. Arctic tundra, found in Canada's treeless north, crowns the park's high peaks. It's the dra-

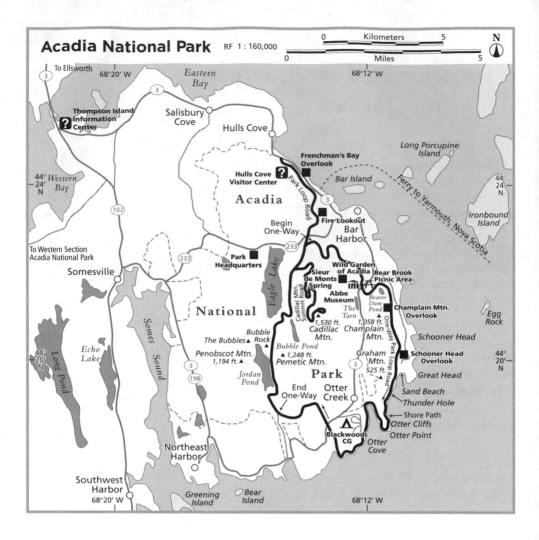

Acadia National Park   RF 1 : 160,000

matic interface between the land and sea, however, that defines the essence of Acadia National Park. Here the great Atlantic rollers pound against the rock-bound shoreline in a thundering show of sound and fury. This place is the distilled essence of maritime Maine.

The one-way, paved drive following Park Loop Road tours the eastern lobe of Mount Desert Island, the largest of the many islands that dot the Gulf of Maine. The curvy road is the major sightseeing route through Acadia National Park, and easily explores the park's highlights—numerous spectacular overlooks, trails, and points of interest. The road, unmaintained in winter, is often very busy, particularly on weekends, in July, August, and in late September during foliage season. It's best to avoid driving this route then. At the very least, plan on taking your time. The drive begins at Hills Cove Visitor Center just off Maine Highway 3, passes Bar Harbor, and makes a one-way loop through the park's southeast sector.

Mount Desert Island (pronounced "dessert" by locals) is connected to the mainland by a bridge over the Mount Desert Narrows on its northwest corner. The heart-shaped island, about 16 miles long and 13 miles wide, is divided into two lobes by Somes Sound, the only true fjord or glacier-carved inlet on America's Atlantic coast. Acadia National Park encompasses about 60 percent of the island's land area, including most of the eastern half. The western part of the isle, accessed via Maine Highway 102, includes Long Pond, Echo Lake and its beach, and Seawall Campground, near its southernmost point.

To reach Acadia National Park, drive south from Ellsworth and U.S. Highway 1 on ME 3. Past Trenton, keep on ME 3 and cross a bridge onto Mount Desert Island. The park's Thompson Island Information Center, with picnic tables and restrooms, lies on the south side of the bridge. Continue east (right) on ME 3 through Salisbury Cove and a few more miles to Hulls Cove. Just past Hulls Cove, take a right at the marked park sign and the start of the scenic drive's Park Loop Road. The town of Bar Harbor is 4 miles from this junction on ME 3.

Frenchman Bay and Bar Harbor

The Hulls Cove Visitor Center, just past the turnoff, is the starting point for the drive. The small visitor center offers an introductory video program in an auditorium, an overview diorama map, a small bookstore that sells interpretative literature and guides, and rangers who can answer questions and dispense park maps and brochures. A self-guided taped tour is also available. To begin the drive, leave the visitor center parking lot and make a right turn.

The road heads southeast from the visitor center through a mixed forest that includes red oak, mountain ash, black cherry, paper birch, striped maple, and poplar. **Frenchman Bay Overlook** is reached after a scant 0.6 mile. The pulloff yields a great view of the broad bay, one of the largest and most scenic on Maine's coast. Its coves are fringed with dark forest. Wooded isles, including Bar, Sheep Porcupine, Burnt Porcupine, Long Porcupine, Bald Porcupine, Stave, Jordan, and Ironbound Islands, dot its wide expanse. A sign identifies the islands spread below the viewpoint. The bay reaches depths of 290 feet, offering good shrimping and lobstering for local fishermen.

The bay is named for early French explorer Samuel de Champlain. In 1604, almost twenty years before the Pilgrims landed in Massachusetts, Champlain investigated the entire coast of Maine, making the first reliable maps of the coast, and claimed it all for France. The ship, flying the fleur-de-lis over its dozen crew members and Indian guides, sailed into the bay on September 5, passing an island "about four or five leagues long." Champlain dubbed the island, crowned by treeless, craggy peaks, *L'Isle des Monts Deserts*—"The Island of Bare Mountains." Later the name was Anglicized to Mount Desert Island. A smaller island to the west, now part of the national park, he called *L'Isle au Haut* or "The High Island." Champlain's ship ran ashore on a shoal off Otter Point, and landed on Mount Desert Island while repairs were made to the hull. The wild, lonely coast was part of a land the French called *Acadie*. The word probably derives from *Arcadia*, the name of an ancient Greek region that was given to Maine by Florentine mariner Giovanni da Verrazano in 1524. Champlain, greatest of the French explorers, later explored the entire New England coast to Cape Cod and founded the city of Quebec, earning him the nickname "The Father of New France."

The road continues southeast on a hillside above **Bar Harbor.** This affluent town has long been one of the most popular and famous resorts on the New England coast. The town began as Eden, a fishing and farming village, that was later discovered by artists and tourists after the Civil War. Huge hotels proliferated around Bar Harbor and Mount Desert Island. One, serviced by a cog railroad, perched atop nearby Cadillac Mountain. Steamships and trains brought thousands of summer sightseers and dropped them at Bar Harbor.

The era of the hotels ended in the 1880s when wealthy city folks began buying up land and building elaborate "summer cottages," which turned out to be small mansions and palaces. During the Gay Nineties more than 200 of these cottages dotted the area, and merchants from the big cities to the south opened exclusive shops for people with names like Rockefeller, Ford, Pulitzer, Morgan, Vanderbilt, Astor, and Carnegie. A local newspaper noted: "The discontented hand of progress has transformed the struggling fishing hamlet of a few years ago into a fashionable summer resort, at whose shrine the beauty, wealthy and fashion of the country pay homage."

Bar Harbor still retains some of that sophisticated charm and doesn't at all resemble the quaint Maine fishing village some visitors expect to find here. Instead, the town offers the greatest selection of hostelries, eateries, and stores on the island. A walk around reveals almost every other house has been converted into a bed-and-breakfast. Ferry service to Yarmouth, Nova Scotia, a six-hour trip each way, is available from the town's ferry terminal.

The road crosses a stone bridge, passes a turn to Bar Harbor, and climbs to the Fire Lookout at 2.4 miles. This viewpoint overlooks an area swept by forest fire in October 1947. The inferno, beginning at the Bar Harbor dump, burned for twenty-six days and consumed more than 17,000 acres along the island's east coast. The fire burned a third of the park's forest, some 8,700 acres, after one of the island's driest summers on record. Ferocious winds, one eyewitness recalled, "flung a wide sheet of flame past all opposition. Houses in its path exploded on contact. The wall of fire leveled forests and seared mountains." Today the forest is slowly

Breathtaking Bar Harbor can be seen from along Park Loop Road.

creeping back, with pioneer species such as quaking aspen providing cover for the pine, fir, and spruce of the slower-growing mature forest.

Past the lookout, the drive bends inland away from the bay and comes to an intersection with Maine Highway 233. A left turn on ME 233 leads to Bar Harbor and a right turn heads to Somesville and Northeast Harbor. Another 0.5 mile down the Park Loop Road is a left turn and the beginning of a 14.5-mile, one-way road section. This part of the drive, running southeast, skirts the apron of 407-foot Kebo Mountain and passes four trailheads. Acadia National Park offers more than 120 miles of trails for hikers. North Ridge Trail, reached at 3.5 miles, is a popular 4.4-mile round-trip up the open north ridge of Cadillac Mountain. Gorge Path begins 4.1 miles from the start of the one-way section, just past a small stone bridge. Dorr Mountain North Ridge Trail is another 0.4 mile down the road. The drive bends into a broad, open valley floored with dense mats of vegetation and a placid beaver pond. Dorr Mountain walls in the valley's west side with a wide, wooded escarpment. The turnoff for **Sieur de Monts Nature Center,** the next point of interest, is at 5.9 miles. ME 3, intersecting the park road here, goes south to the park's Blackwoods Campground.

The side-road leads to the Wild Gardens of Acadia, the Robert Abbe Museum of Stone Age Antiquities, and the Acadia National Park Nature Center. The Sieur de Monts Spring here, purchased along with other Mount Desert Island lands by a group of preservationists known as the Hancock County Trustees of Public Reservations in 1909, was the birthplace of Acadia National Park. Afraid that timber companies were going to level the island's forests, the trustees offered the land to the federal government. In 1916 President Woodrow Wilson established Sieur de Monts National Monument. After World War I the acreage was expanded and designated by Congress as Lafayette National Park in honor of the French Revolutionary War hero. It was the first national park in the East and the only one composed of private land donations. Later the owners of Schoodic Peninsula across the bay wanted to donate their holdings to the park, but objected to the name. A compromise was reached and the growing park was renamed Acadia National Park in 1929. George B. Dorr, a trustee and conservationist, became the park's first superintendent after tirelessly working to preserve this spectacular clash of land and sea.

The nature center introduces visitors to Acadia's cultural and natural history. The nearby privately owned Abbe Museum exhibits stone artifacts, antiquities, and dioramas of Maine's prehistoric Indians. An admission fee is charged. The Wild Gardens of Acadia are a worthy stop for anyone interested in the park's fascinating botany. The gardens, maintained by the Bar Harbor Garden Club, acquaint visitors with the island's many habitats, plant communities, and plants. This is an easy place to spend a lot of time, kneeling and stooping to read identification tags and exploring the area's rich biological diversity on a short path through the one-acre site.

Champlain Mountain, Sand Beach, and Otter Cliffs

Back on the drive, the road passes Bear Brook Picnic Area after 0.5 mile and swings around Beaver Dam Pond 0.1 mile later. The pond is a good place, on quiet evenings, to spot a nocturnal beaver swimming across his calm domain. The industrious beavers, North America's largest rodents, are natural engineers. They gnaw down trees and shrubs to create their lodges and dams, which stair-step up valleys. The chains of lakes constructed by flat-tailed beavers combat erosion, provide flood control, and create superb habitat for birds and fish. Their ponds silt up over time, creating rich soil for meadows.

At 7 miles the drive reaches **Champlain Mountain Overlook,** the first of the road's many spectacular viewpoints. Frenchman Bay dominates the view, its waters spreading east to rocky Schoodic Peninsula. A light station, sitting on tiny Egg Rock, marks the bay's wide entrance. Nearby is The Thrumcap, a rocky outcrop that provides a rookery for gulls and cormorants. Humped Champlain Mountain rears its rounded granite shoulders above the overlook. The road heads south, dropping past smooth, glacier-polished cliffs on the mountain flank. At the bottom of a hill sits The Precipice trailhead. A 0.8-mile trail scales The Precipice, the abrupt east face of 1,058-foot Champlain Mountain, climbing almost 1,000 feet from road to summit. The airy path, a must-do hike for the intrepid walker, winds steeply through slabs and cliffs broken by jumbled boulder fields and tree-clad ledges and benches. Iron rungs and ladders aid wary hikers on the more exposed trail sections. The trail is often closed to use because of rockfall or nesting raptors, including endangered peregrine falcons.

The road continues along a forested terrace. The turn to Schooner Head Overlook is 1.1 miles from The Precipice. This low point views Schooner Head, a private holding in the park. The road passes through a park fee collection station manned by rangers. Just past the station is the Sand Beach parking area on the left. This large lot is often filled to capacity, especially in July and August. Parking, unless otherwise indicated, is available in the right lane of the park road.

Sand Beach is exactly that—the park's largest sand beach and one of the biggest on the Maine coast north of Portland. Much of the white sand here is the crushed shells of marine creatures tossed onto the shore of this arcing cove. Occasional swimmers brave the turbulent waves and numbing water—the bracing water temperature rarely climbs above fifty-five degrees. A storm often reveals the hull of the *Tays*, a lumber schooner that beached here in 1911. Great Head Trail, a good 1.5-mile round-trip loop, begins at the parking lot, crosses Sand Beach, and follows a path up and right to the top of 145-foot Great Head and some great views of the rugged coastline. The Beehive Trail begins on the opposite side of the road from the parking area. This strenuous, 0.8-mile trail works up cliffs and ledges to the rounded, rocky summit of The Beehive, a 520-foot knob.

The next 5 miles are the most spectacular stretch of road in the park. The curved asphalt twists along the rock-bound coast within sight and sound of the crashing waves. The road ambles south from Sand Beach and reaches Thunder Hole in 0.5 mile. Incoming surf funnels up a narrow channel hemmed in by cliffs. When the surf is high, particularly after a storm, the water fills the chasm, trapping air and then suddenly releasing it with a sharp thunderclap. The stretch of granite coast along here is a great place to walk or simply sit and watch the surf roll in. The Ocean Trail parallels the road for 1.5 miles along this coastal segment.

The road runs along the cliff-top and climbs to the Otter Cliffs parking area. The **Otter Cliffs,** reaching heights of 100 feet, lie below the lofty overlook. These chiseled granite cliffs, rising vertically from the frothy sea, are a favorite setting for rock climbers at low tide. The cliffs are also the highest headland on the Atlantic coast north of Rio de Janeiro in Brazil. Seven miles of open water lie between here and Schoodic Point to the east. Just offshore below the cliffs is The Spindle, an underwater rock marked with a buoy. It was this rock that Champlain's ship struck, forcing him to land at Otter Cove to the west to repair the damage. A scenic path goes 0.3 mile south to Otter Point.

Climbers ascend Otter Cliffs at Acadia National Park.

Otter Point, Jordan Pond, and Eagle Lake

Back on the drive, the road reaches **Otter Point** parking lot after 0.3 mile. Park and cross the road and drop down to the Shore Path. This is a good place to examine the many tidepools in the zone between high and low tides. The road bends west around Otter Cove and passes Fabbri Memorial, the abandoned site of a naval radio station, and Fabbri Picnic Area at the head of the cove. The drive continues along the coast through a spruce forest. Several pullouts offer excellent and usually deserted views of the shore and the Atlantic Ocean. Hunters Head, a rocky headland jutting into the water, provides the last ocean view before the drive turns north and inland.

The road twists through a dense woodland of spruce and fir with occasional maples, and passes Wildwood Stables, which offer horse and carriage tours along the park's network of carriage roads that date from the early part of the century, and reaches the junction of the park road and ME 3. Two-way traffic resumes here. Keep straight on the two-lane road. **The Jordan Pond House,** sitting amid the grassy lawns on the southern end of Jordan Pond, has been a purveyor of afternoon tea and Acadia tradition since 1871. Although the restaurant, rebuilt after a 1979 fire, serves lunch and dinner, it's the pot of tea, warm popovers, and jam served with Victorian elegance on the manicured lawn that lure visitors. The view from the tables is simply marvelous. Jordan Pond, a long lake lying in a glacier-scoured basin, is surrounded by mountains—Penobscot Mountain encloses the western flank, and Pemetic Mountain the eastern. *Pemetic* is an Indian word that means "sloping land." The Bubbles, a handsome pair of rounded knobs, dominate the pond's northern end. The mile-long Jordan Pond Nature Trail details the area's natural history, while the 3.3-mile Jordan Pond Shore Trail follows the lake's shoreline. The pond offers trout and salmon fishing.

The drive heads north on the east side of Jordan Pond and quickly climbs away and edges across Pemetic Mountain to a low saddle. The Bubbles rise sharply to the left. The cliff perched on the East Bubble is a popular climbing crag. Bubble Rock, an immense boulder weighing between eleven and fourteen tons, perches precariously on the edge of the Bubble. The boulder, called a glacial erratic, was deposited by a glacier after being carried some 20 miles from the north. The Bubble Pond pullout, almost 3 miles from Jordan Pond House, is a narrow lake tucked into a valley between Pemetic and Cadillac Mountains. The 2.4-mile, round-trip hike up Pemetic Mountain begins here. The drive continues north on the sloping, forested slope of Cadillac Mountain above 425-acre **Eagle Lake,** the largest lake in the park.

The many elongated lakes, such as Eagle Lake, and rounded mountains, such as Cadillac Mountain, at Acadia National Park are part of an immense granite batholith that was excavated, incised, smoothed, polished, and sculpted by huge glaciers that blanketed most of New England. Swiss geologist Louis Agassiz, while teaching at Harvard in 1864, postulated that Mount Desert Island was once covered by a great ice sheet. He wrote, "Mount Desert . . . must have been a miniature Spitzbergen, and colossal icebergs floated off from Somes Sound into the Atlantic Ocean." Geologists today say the sheet reached thicknesses of 9,000 feet here, or six times as thick as Cadillac Mountain is tall. The last glacier only retreated about 15,000 years ago from Acadia and the Maine coast.

Cadillac Mountain

After a couple of miles, the road reaches the turnoff to 3.5-mile **Cadillac Mountain Summit Road.** Turn right here. The well-engineered road, with no grade greater than 7 percent, quickly climbs via switchbacks up the mountain's broad north flank. Several pullouts along the way offer great views. The spur road ends atop Cadillac's spacious 1,530-foot summit. This rounded granite mountaintop, the highest point along the Atlantic seaboard, yields one of New England's farthest and most breathtaking views on a clear day. A carpet of forest spreads across mountains, hills, and valleys below. Emerald lakes, glimmering in the sunlight, nestle among the mountain folds. Frenchman Bay is a rich blue, studded with wooded islands. And to the south stretches the endless Atlantic Ocean beyond the rocky coastline. A good time to be atop the peak is at sunrise. For much of the year, Cadillac Mountain is the first place in the United States that the rising sun illuminates. The paved Summit Trail makes a 0.3-mile loop around the summit, offering panoramic views and a look at the glaciated bedrock. Glacial erratic boulders, transported from other regions and left stranded atop the summit when the ice melted, dot the mountain. In other places the glacial movements etched and polished the granite. Stay on the trail to avoid damaging the fragile summit grasses and the stunted wind-blasted balsam fir trees called *krummholz*. A gift shop and restrooms are beside the summit parking lot.

Acadia National Park, a natural wonderland spread out around Cadillac Mountain, is a very small protected area of Maine's coast, It's an idyllic place that is surrounded by burgeoning development that threatens the park's character and existence. This park, one of the most popular national parklands in America, is also in real danger of being loved to death. Remember to walk softly and leave no trace of your passage.

From Cadillac's summit the drive twists back down the Summit Road to its intersection with Park Loop Road. Take a right turn. The road drops northward and reaches the turnoff to the drive's one-way portion. Continue straight on the loop road, past the turn to Bar Harbor, for 3 miles and the end of the drive at the park's Hulls Cove Visitor Center.

24

Sunrise Coast Scenic Drive

General description: A 134-mile drive along the rocky northern coastline of Maine from Ellsworth to West Quoddy Head, the easternmost point in the United States.

Special attractions: Acadia National Park, Schoodic Point, the Great Heath, Burnham Tavern Museum, Great Wass Island, Bold Coast, Quoddy Head State Park, Quoddy Head Lighthouse, Cobscook Bay State Park, Reversing Falls State Park, Roosevelt Campobello International Park, camping, hiking, nature study, birding, scenic viewpoints, blueberry picking, clamming.

Location: Northeastern Maine.

Drive route numbers and name: U.S. Highway 1, Maine Highways 186, 187, and 191, South Lubec Road.

Travel season: Year-round. Winters can be cold, snowy, and icy. Fog is common on the

drive. While this isn't as busy as the lower coastal routes, try to avoid driving here during the hectic July and August vacation season.

Camping: Acadia National Park, south of the drive's start at Ellsworth, has two campgrounds—Blackwoods and Seawall. Lamoine State Park, south of Ellsworth on Maine Highway 184, has a sixty-one-site campground. Many private campgrounds are in the Ellsworth/Mount Desert Island vicinity. Cobscook Bay State Park, northwest of the drive off US 1, offers 125 wooded campsites.

Services: All services in Ellsworth, Steuben, Milbridge, Harrington, Columbia Falls, Jonesboro, Machias, East Machias, and Lubec.

Nearby attractions: Acadia National Park, Cadillac Mountain, Bar Harbor, Camden State Park, Deer Isle, Castine, Moosehorn National Wildlife Refuge.

The Drive

The 134-mile Sunrise Coast Scenic Drive follows Maine's panoramic northeast coast from Ellsworth to West Quoddy Head, the easternmost point in the United States. This coastal rim, one of the first places the morning sun strikes the country, is a landscape of stunning beauty defined by rocks. The granite bedrock here— scraped, gouged, and polished by great ice sheets—meets the restless ocean at a spectacular boundary between rock and water.

Maine's irregular coastline is only 225 miles long as the crow flies, but its convoluted length, not including the shores of its many islands, is 2,379 miles—a distance almost twice that of the California shoreline and longer than the rest of the Atlantic seaboard. The bedrock foundation, pounded by breaking waves, is carved into innumerable inlets, coves, and bays. Bold headlands, points, and promontories reach out like fingers into the Gulf of Maine. Forested islands and chains of tiny islets, the submerged summits of hills, stick their noses above the turbulent sea. Early explorers were impressed by this rocky shoreline. Explorer John Smith wrote, "This coast is mountainous and Iles of huge Rockes, but overgrowne for most part with most sorts of excellent good woods." This drive curves around wide bays,

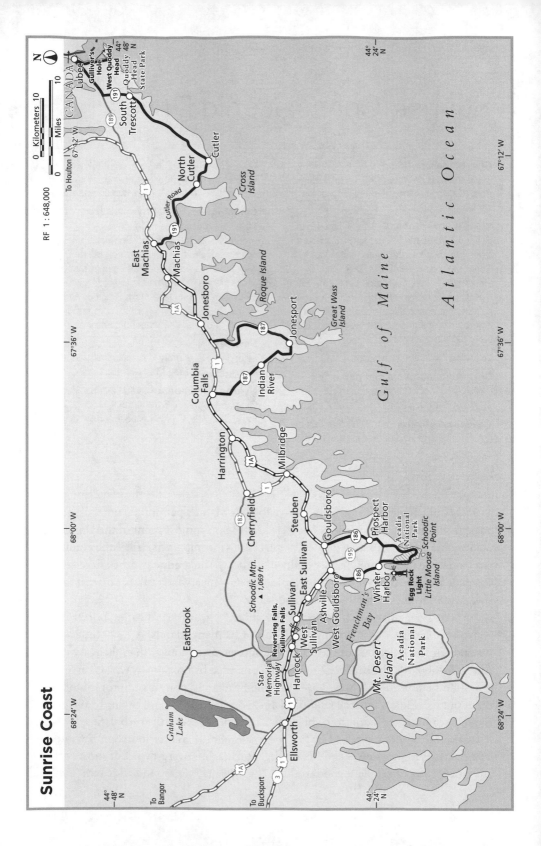

Sunrise Coast

RF 1 : 648,000

N

0 Kilometers 10

0 Miles 10

CANADA

Lubec
Gulliver's Hole
West Quoddy Head
Quoddy Head State Park
44°48' N

44°24' N

To Houlton

South Trescott
189
191

Cutler
North Cutler
Cross Island
Cutler Road
191

East Machias
Machias
Jonesboro
1A
1
Roque Island

11
187
Indian River
Jonesport
Great Wass Island
187
Columbia Falls

Harrington
Milbridge
1A

Cherryfield
182
1
Steuben
Gouldsboro
Prospect Harbor
186
195
Acadia National Park
Schoodic Point
186
Winter Harbor
Egg Rock Light
Little Moose Island
West Sullivan
Sullivan
East Sullivan
Ashville
West Gouldsboro
Frenchman's Bay

Schoodic Mtn. ▲ 1,069 ft.

Eastbrook

Star Memorial Highway
Reversing Falls, Sullivan Falls
Hancock

Graham Lake

Ellsworth
1
3
1A
To Bucksport
To Bangor

Mt. Desert Island
Acadia National Park

Gulf of Maine

Atlantic Ocean

67°42' W
67°36' W
68°00' W
68°24' W
67°12' W

edges onto points, meanders through dark woodlands, passes quaint fishing villages and historic towns, and ends atop a rocky headland at the very end of the country.

Ellsworth

This area of Maine is called Down East, a sailing term that confuses landlubbers. Ships heading east to Europe from Boston and Portland had the advantage of sailing Down East or down wind with the prevailing westerly winds along the Maine coast. The drive begins along a commercial strip on U.S. Highway 1 on the southeastern outskirts of **Ellsworth,** a crossroads town on the east bank of the Union River. The gateway to Acadia National Park and Mount Desert Island, Ellsworth dates back to 1763. The town, using waterpower generated by 60-foot Union River Falls, was an industrial center with lumber mills and ship-building yards. Although much of the older part of town was destroyed in a 1933 fire, many grand buildings remain. The white Ellsworth Congregational Church, built in 1846, dominates the town from its perch above the river.

The most famous building here is the Colonel Black Mansion, on West Main just west of the town center. Colonel Black emigrated from England at the age of thirteen and clerked for Maine land baron William Bingham. By 1810 he was an agent and, shortly afterwards, a general agent. He constructed this marvelous Georgian brick home in the years 1824 to 1827, sparing no expense on material or craftsmanship. The bricks were shipped from Philadelphia. The tall front windows on the porch make an architectural oddity and focal point—there is no front door on the porch, so the colonel's visitors came and went via the triple-hung windows. In 1930 the house and the surrounding 150-acre wooded estate were donated to Hancock County by Black's grandson. The mansion's rooms are filled with original period furniture, porcelain, and glassware and open daily for tours between May and October. Other historic Ellsworth sites include the brick and stone 1886 Old Jail and the Public Library, housed in the 1817 Seth Tisdale House, named for its Revolutionary War hero builder.

Ellsworth is the largest town on the drive, offering all visitor services including gas, groceries, restaurants, and lodging. The community's 79 square miles make it Maine's largest town, too, one that has unfortunately succumbed to the strip-mall mentality so often found beside great natural attractions these days. Factory outlets, fast-food joints, nondescript malls, and tourist trinket shops line many of the area roads. Shining spots, however, are the many roadside lobster (pronounced "lobstah" up here) pounds that line the highways between here and Mount Desert Island to the south. These shacks are great places to pick a fresh lobster and let the cooks drop it in a kettle of boiling seawater. When it's bright red, they'll put it in a basket on the table with a side of slaw, french fries, and a pile of napkins—all for about ten bucks.

Your sojourn starts on the southeast side of Ellsworth at the junction of US 1 and Maine Highway 3. Go east (left) on US 1, the main coastal thoroughfare. Nicknamed "The East's Main Street," this highway is the most celebrated in New England. After all, it is "number one." For much of its long East Coast run, this slender asphalt ribbon is a noisy, congested, cluttered, overbuilt highway mess. Up here, however, on the rockbound coast beyond Ellsworth, US 1 becomes a scenic route.

The highway goes east for several miles past businesses and development before breaking free into the open countryside. The road climbs into rolling hills broken by woods, fields, and roadside businesses. Great views of Acadia National Park, crowned by the rounded bulk of Cadillac Mountain, spread south from the highway. After 7 miles the road enters Hancock. This small village settled in 1764 sits on a broad peninsula between the Skillings and Taunton Rivers just north of Frenchman Bay. Hancock was briefly in national news back in World War II when two bold German spies, quickly apprehended by FBI agents, landed by submarine here.

Past Hancock, the highway crosses over the channel connecting Taunton Bay upriver and Sullivan Harbor to the south, running along the far bank. A narrow neck of land, constricting the channel between two bays, juts into the river to the right about a mile past the bridge. Sullivan Falls is a reversing falls caused by the tidal flow between the bays, the spectacular result of this constriction. The falls occur when tidewater pours out of the upper bay during low tide. The scenic area is a popular training ground for canoeists and kayakers. A pullout yields a good view south across Sullivan Harbor to Frenchman Bay and Mount Desert Island's humps.

The highway runs through Sullivan, a small hamlet strung along the pavement. A few miles north, off Maine Highway 200, is the Schoodic Mountain trailhead. Its 3-mile trail gains 1,000 feet over rock ledges to the bare summit of 1,069-foot Schoodic Mountain, the high peak northeast of Sullivan. Past town is Long Cove Rest Area, alongside a placid cove. The road continues southeast and after 17 miles reaches its junction with Maine Highway 186 in West Gouldsboro. Turn south (right) on ME 186 for the second leg of the trip, which makes a 25-mile loop down the west side of Schoodic Peninsula to a one-way park road then, after ME 186, drives up the peninsula's east side to rejoin US 1.

The Schoodic Peninsula

The Schoodic Peninsula is a wide stub jutting into the Gulf of Maine. A host of islands and Frenchman Bay flank it on the west, while Gouldsboro and West Bays mark its eastern boundary. A thin veneer of woods blankets the peninsula's rolling, granite hills. Numerous streams and swamps and occasional ponds nestle in hollows here. The southern tip of the peninsula is a detached segment of Acadia National Park and, unlike the Mount Desert Island section, is relatively peaceful.

ME 186 leaves West Gouldsboro, a picturesque village of old homes, and crosses a neck between Jones Cove and Jones Pond. The road crests a hill after a couple miles, as a good view of Frenchman Bay and nearby Stave Island unfolds from the windshield. South Gouldsboro is at 3.3 miles. From here the road turns inland and runs over undulating hills for another 3 miles to **Winter Harbor.** This is a lovely coastal village perched at the head of a wide cove separated from Frenchman Bay by Grindstone Neck. Tidy Cape Cod–style houses overlook the cove. The view south to the open sea is spectacular. Frenchman Bay has been known to freeze solid during frigid winters, but this sheltered anchorage, with an average depth of 42 feet, has never frozen during recorded history—hence the name Winter Harbor.

The highway bends left in Winter Harbor and 0.5 mile later reaches the marked turnoff to Acadia National Park's Schoodic Point. The drive turns south (right) on this narrow road. Prepare for stunning scenery ahead. The road runs south through woods at first, then at 8.6 miles enters the national park and crosses a narrow inlet. A park information kiosk is located here. At 8.8 miles is the Frazier Point turn, where the park road becomes one-way. The drive edges onto the rock-rimmed shoreline of Frenchman Bay and runs south. Numerous pullouts allow shoreline access. Many ideal reverie spots are found atop wave-polished boulders. Watch the blue water lap against the shore and the sunlight glimmering off the choppy bay. Angular blocks of granite plunge into the sea along this coastal stretch. A dark conifer forest, dominated by arbor vitae and jack pine, lines the park road. The road continues south and bends around a small, rocky cove at 11 miles. Pond Island rears above the cove's entrance. Past a swamp area is the right turn to Schoodic Point.

Reached by a 0.3-mile spur road, **Schoodic Point** is a dramatic meeting place of land and water. Here, at the end of this broad finger, the great breakers of the Atlantic Ocean roll ashore, exploding in foam against granite bedrock. The pink granite shelves and ledges are creased with basaltic dikes that formed long ago when molten material was intruded into fissures in the older granite. These dark dikes, less resistant to the ceaseless waves than the granite, erode more quickly leaving long, empty channels. Schoodic Point was shaped by glaciation, which chiseled, pecked, and smoothed its stone foundation. Be careful when walking about on the bedrock along the water; it's slippery, and the dropoffs to the water are abrupt. Large, sneak waves often crash on shore and can sweep unsuspecting visitors off their feet.

Back on the main park road, the drive continues along the blunt tip of Schoodic Peninsula. Little Moose Island sits just off the coast, separated from the mainland by a land bridge exposed at low tide. About 0.5 mile up the drive is the parking area for Blueberry Hill scenic viewpoint. This overlook sits on the southeast corner of the point, providing views of the choppy sea, floating lobster pots, and hills covered with shrubs including lowbush blueberry.

Waves break on rocks at Schoodic Point in Acadia National Park.

The next 11 miles of the scenic drive run north along the east coast of the peninsula to US 1. The road edges along broad Schoodic Harbor then bends east to Bunkers Harbor, a narrow cove. Here the one-way stretch of road ends. Farther north are Birch Harbor and the fishing village of Prospect Harbor. Continue straight on ME 186 through Prospect Harbor. A good side-trip goes right on Maine Highway 195 to Corea, an old fishing village set among windswept dunes covered with sea grass. The main drive route heads north, however, through rolling, wooded hills with occasional glimpses of West Bay on the right.

Gouldsboro to Columbia Falls

At US 1 in Gouldsboro, turn right. Steuben, the next town, straddles Tunk Stream at the head of Joy Bay. It was named for Baron Friedrich von Steuben, a Prussian army officer who fought in the Revolutionary War as inspector general of the Continental Army. The highway continues northeast through pleasant, forested hills and reaches Milbridge almost 5 miles later. The highway bends through the town as its Main Street, bordering the Narraguagus River's outlet in Narraguagus Bay. The town, incorporated in 1848, has long been a commercial fishing and lobstering center. One of Maine's first canneries opened here just after the Civil War.

On the north side of town, go right on US 1A. The highway swings across a bridge over the river and goes through rural countryside for 8 miles before rejoining US 1 on the east side of Harrington. On the meandering banks of the Harrington River, the town was settled in 1765 as a fishing center. A good side-drive begins just east of Harrington and heads down to the tip of Ripley Neck, a narrow peninsula that separates the Harrington and Pleasant Rivers.

The scenic drive continues east on US 1 through lovely hills wooded with conifers, a scattering of hardwoods, and quaking aspen. Columbia Falls, incorporated in 1863, is a couple of miles up the road. North of Harrington and Columbia Falls is the Great Heath, the largest raised bog or peatland in Maine with 5,681 acres. Just west of the bog is Pineo Ridge, an excellent example of a washboard moraine. This glacial moraine is the remnant of a 25-square-mile delta where the ocean once lapped against a retreating glacier leaving parallel ridges, a prominent wave-cut cliff on the ridge's south face, and now-dry streambeds.

This entire region of Maine is now a renowned blueberry-growing area. The Milbridge-Cherryfield area is nicknamed "Blueberry Capital of the World." More than 200,000 acres of blueberry barrens in Washington County produce 90 percent of the nation's crop.

Columbia Falls began, like many Maine coastal towns, as a lumber and shipbuilding center. The quiet village is now a blueberry center, but recalls its prosperous past with some old homes including the Thomas Ruggles House. This beautiful home, open for tours, was built in 1818 by Thomas Ruggles, a town judge, lumberman, store owner, and local postmaster. The house exhibits fine craftsmanship with its flying staircase and detailed woodwork.

Jonesport to Machias

After leaving Columbia Falls, turn south (right) onto Maine Highway 187 for the next leg of your journey. The next 23 miles follow ME 187 as it makes a rough, V-shaped back road jaunt over hills and along the coastline of a broad peninsula. The road heads southeast through woods and past occasional swamps until it crosses the Indian River. The next few miles pass shallow coves and tidal flats. After 10 miles the road reaches Jonesport. This is the most active Down East fishing village, not a place discovered by tourists and their accompanying trendy shops and high-priced real estate. Jonesport, with neighboring Beals, boasts the largest lobster fleet north of Penobscot Bay. Beals is also home to the Regional Shellfish Hatchery, which raises and plants millions of clams annually in surrounding mudflats.

A bridge in Jonesport leads south across Mooseabec Reach to Beals Island and onto **Great Wass Island,** with its 1,540-acre Nature Conservancy preserve. Great Wass Island reaches farther into the Gulf of Maine than any other bit of Maine land. The island's cool, foggy climate hosts many rare plants, including marsh felwort, bird's-eye primrose, and beach-head iris as well as a large, magnificent stand of stunted jack pines shaped like Japanese bonsai trees.

The drive works through Jonesport, passing homes, businesses, and boatyards piled with lobster traps before bending northeast past Sawyer Cove. The quiet highway runs along the edge of Englishman Bay, past many homes, cottages, and Sandy River Beach. Roque Island looms above the bay to the east. The road bends west and works around Mason Bay to Peasley Corner, and reaches US 1 about 10 miles from Rockport. Turn east (right) on US 1. A mile later the road passes through Jonesboro, a small farming and blueberry community on the Chandler River. Roque Bluffs Road, beginning just past the river bridge, goes 8 miles southeast to Roque Bluffs State Park.

The drive then runs northeast to **Machias, Machiasport,** and **East Machias.** These three towns sit on the wide Machias River as it empties into Machias Bay. *Machias* is a Passamaquoddy Indian word that means "Bad Little Falls." The falls, in Bad Little Falls Park on the edge of town, are a tumultuous torrent of whitewater split by a rocky outcrop. The towns figure prominently in Maine's early history. Although the area was first explored in the 1600s, territorial disputes between England and France kept it from being permanently settled until 1763. Machias, established as a township in 1770, was the first village east of the Penobscot River. Settlers here built a sawmill and within a year were producing more than a million board feet of lumber.

Shortly afterward, during the Revolutionary War, Machias was the site of the first naval engagement of the revolution. Local Loyalists, supported by the armed British schooner *Margaretta*, brought goods from Boston to support the British war effort. In 1775 irate patriots met in the still-standing Burnham Tavern, now operated as a museum by the Daughters of the American Revolution, and plotted to capture the ship. They attempted to capture the local British commander at church, but failed after he retreated to the protection of the schooner. The next day, June 12, forty men armed with guns, swords, axes, and pitchforks and led by Jeremiah O'Brien sailed downriver to the *Margaretta*, and attacked and boarded the vessel. The Brits surrendered. The Yankee rebels had won the first naval battle of the war.

At Machiasport stand the remains of strategically located Fort O'Brien, formerly Fort Machias. The fort was constructed after the *Margaretta* affair to protect the townspeople from British retaliation. The fort was sacked and destroyed during the War of 1812, but was rebuilt during the Civil War. Little remains of this important site today except low, grassy mounds scattered with cannons. The Burnham Tavern, listed on the National Register of Historic Places, displays mementos from the *Margaretta* and other period artifacts. It was also chosen as one of twenty-one buildings in the United States that were significant in the American Revolution.

The lovely First Congregational Church overlooks Machias on the Sunrise Coast Scenic Drive.

The tri-towns flourished in the nineteenth century with lumber mills and as a shipping center for the vast quantities of Maine lumber produced here. Machiasport was the end of the narrow-gauge Machias-Whitneyville Railroad. It was built in 1841 and used for fifty years to haul export lumber to market. Today the Machias area still relies on the lumber industry, as well as fishing, lobstering, and, of course, blueberries. Every August the town celebrates its Blueberry Festival.

The drive runs through Machias's town center, crosses the broad Machias River, and runs east a couple of miles to East Machias. This village is split by the narrow channel of the East Machias River. On the east side of town, the drive turns south (right) on Maine Highway 191 at an old bridge over the river. The road passes a beautiful First Congregational Church, perched on a commanding hilltop above the river and town.

Along the Bold Coast

The next drive segment travels 28 miles on ME 191 along upper Maine's wild, rugged, unpopulated coast. The highway winds south and bends east among worn granite hills above Holmes Bay. Many houses and cottages line the shore. At 7 miles rise the landmark 900-foot towers and wires of the Naval Communications Unit, scattered across a wide plain. The road reaches Little Machias Bay, a wide bay fringed by large mudflats at low tide. Dense conifer forest abuts the asphalt on its landward side.

Past the bay, the drive turns east to Little River, and, at its ocean mouth, the picturesque fishing village of **Cutler.** The town's secluded, horseshoe-shaped harbor, protected from the ocean by Little River Island, offers one of the most sheltered anchorages during storms on the upper coast. Cutler is the sailing point for excursions to Machias Seal Island, the outermost isle of the Grand Manan group. The island is the southernmost breeding site of the Atlantic puffin and other sea birds, including the razorbill auk. Landing is not permitted on the ecologically sensitive island.

Past Cutler, the drive enters what is called the **Bold Coast,** a lonely, virtually uninhabited coastline of rocky headlands and serene coves. The area, a region of ecological diversity, is the last undeveloped coastal area in Maine and one of the last on America's Atlantic Seaboard. The highway turns north in Cutler and runs for 14 miles over rolling hills dark with forest and interrupted by boglands. The ocean is occasionally glimpsed through the trees. South Trescott is a small hamlet perched on the edge of a small bay dubbed Bailey's Mistake. Supposedly a sea captain ran aground here because of a major navigational mistake, so his crew unloaded the lumber and settled here. Past the bay, the highway takes its leave of the coast and heads north to West Lubec.

Down to West Quoddy Head

Your basic stop-on-the-road, West Lubec is also the junction of ME 191 and Maine Highway 189. Go right on ME 189 towards Lubec. The road goes past homes and business and, after 4 miles, reaches South Lubec Road. Take a right on this narrow, winding road following the low coastline of a wide bay. After 3 miles a sharp left turn leads northeast onto a narrow neck and then West Quoddy Head. About 1.5 miles later the road divides, its right spur going to Quoddy Head State Park and its left one ending abruptly at Quoddy Head Lighthouse.

West Quoddy Head has the distinction of being the easternmost point in the United States at 67°, 57' longitude. East Quoddy Head lies in Nova Scotia on the opposite side of the channel. This dramatic, windswept seascape, a place rarely seen by casual travelers, is a wild and spectacular setting. It's a world of rocky headlands, plummeting ravines, wheeling seabirds, and vast views—on the rare clear day—of distant shores across the Bay of Fundy. Spruce forests cover the tops of ragged cliffs that plunge into the ocean. The candy-cane, red-and-white-striped lighthouse, one of Maine's historic landmarks, perches atop an 80-foot seacliff and is visible from 20 miles out at sea. The light, operated by the U.S. Coast Guard, was built in 1808 and rebuilt in 1852. Nearby is **Quoddy Head State Park,** a 532-acre parkland that offers picnicking and hiking trails atop the oceanside cliffs. Another popular point of interest is Gulliver's Hole, a foaming sea pocket etched into the cliff wall. The lighthouse is open daily year-round, and the state park is open from late May to mid-October.

Quoddy Head makes a fitting finale to this spectacular sea-drive. After following the long coastline, the drive's best scenery lies at the very end. Here one can stand with all of America behind and 3,000 empty miles of the Atlantic Ocean ahead. Here one can feel the first light of a new day spread its flush across the cliffs and woods of this remote headland at the edge of the continent.

There are lots of other points of interest near West Quoddy Head, including the town of Lubec, Cobscook Bay State Park, and the immense tides that characterize the Bay of Fundy and its side-channels. **Lubec,** the easternmost town in the United States, fills Lubec Neck where a bridge across a narrow channel leads to Campobello Island and Canada. Settled in 1780, Lubec was once the thriving center of the sardine industry. It wasn't until the Civil War that canned products became popular and Maine, with its sardine fishery, became an important player in the canning industry. At its height, Lubec produced more than 120 million tins of sardines a year. The town's Old Sardine Village Museum preserves and interprets the industry's past.

Across the narrow strait from Lubec is the island of Campobello in the Canadian province of New Brunswick. Here is the 2,800-acre Roosevelt Campobello International Park and Natural Area. Former President Franklin D. Roosevelt sum-

The lighthouse at West Quoddy Head sits on the farthest east point in the United States.

mered here beginning in 1883 when he was one year old until 1921 when he contracted polio. The park interprets the Roosevelt family's long relationship with the island and also offers 8 miles of trails.

North of Lubec off US 1 is **Cobscook Bay State Park,** a lovely natural area with campsites in the forest along the edge of Whiting Bay. Whiting and Dennys Bays, and the larger Cobscook Bay to the east, are famous for their extremely high tides. Although the head of the nearby Bay of Fundy in Canada boasts the world's highest tides, including one at a record 53 feet, this region is not far behind. The average tide at Cobscook Bay (*Cobscook* itself is an Indian word meaning "boiling tides") is 24 feet and the interval can run as high as 28 feet. Compare this with Baltimore's 13-inch tide; New York City's 4-foot, 5-inch tide; and Portland's 8-foot, 11-inch tide.

The great tides here create one of Maine's strangest natural wonders at **Reversing Falls Park** in the narrows between Mahar Point and Falls Island between Cobscook Bay and Dennys and Whiting Bays to the west. The rising tide squeezes through the gap into the twin bays, filling the tidal flats with seawater. The huge tidal difference backs water up in the bays as the tide alternately comes in and goes out, creating a frothy reversing falls/rapid. The park is south of Pembroke at the tip of Leighton Neck.

25

Grafton Notch Scenic Drive

General description: A 37-mile scenic drive that traverses rugged Grafton Notch in the Mahoosuc Range near the Maine and New Hampshire border.

Special attractions: Grafton Notch State Park, Step Falls Preserve, Screw Auger Falls Gorge, Mother Walker Falls Gorge, Moose Cave Gorge, Table Rock, Old Speck Mountain and trail, Appalachian Trail, Umbagog National Wildlife Refuge, Umbagog Lake (NH), Umbagog State Park (NH), camping, hiking, fishing, rock climbing, backpacking, picnicking.

Location: Western Maine.

Drive route numbers: Maine Highway 26, New Hampshire Highway 26.

Travel season: Year-round. Expect snow and icy conditions in winter.

Camping: No public campgrounds along the drive. Mount Blue State Park north of Dixfield off Maine Highway 142 has an excellent campground. Dixville State Park, in New Hampshire west of the drive's end at Errol, also offers camping. Private campgrounds are found in the drive vicinity, including one at Lake Umbagog.

Services: All services in Bethel and Errol.

Nearby attractions: White Mountain National Forest, Rangeley Lakes, Mount Blue State Park, Tumbledown Mountain, Dixville Notch (NH), Nash Stream Forest (NH), Pinkham Notch (NH), Mount Washington (NH), Great Gulf Wilderness Area (NH), Moose Brook State Park (NH).

The Drive

Beginning in Bethel, Maine, and ending in Errol, New Hampshire, this 37-mile scenic drive explores the deep, glaciated valley of Grafton Notch as it slices across the northern edge of the rugged Mahoosuc Range. The range, an eastern extension of the White Mountains, stretches northeast from Gorham at the northern end of New Hampshire's Presidential Range to the notch. It offers striking, remote backcountry topped with numerous high peaks, including 4,180-foot Old Speck Mountain, Maine's third highest. The range crest is a well-defined ridgeline that is closely followed by the Appalachian Trail. Backpackers call the trail segment through the Mahoosuc Range the single roughest section on the entire trail, especially the jumbled boulder maze in Mahoosuc Notch.

Bethel, Newry, and North Newry

The drive begins in Bethel at the junction of U.S. Highway 2 and Maine Highway 26. Straddling a bend on the Androscoggin River amid the Oxford Hills on the eastern edge of the White Mountains, **Bethel** is a lovely, classic New England village on the southern edge of Maine's vast northern wilderness. The town, founded

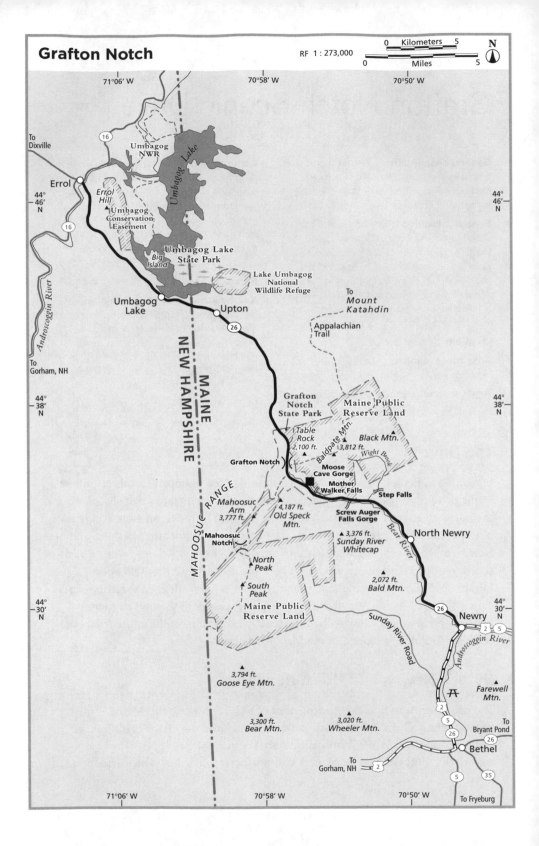

Grafton Notch

RF 1 : 273,000

Kilometers
0   5

Miles
0   5

N

71°06' W   70°58' W   70°50' W

To
Dixville

16

Umbagog
NWR

Umbagog
Lake

Errol

44°
46'
N

Errol
Hill

Umbagog
Conservation
Easement

Big
Island

Umbagog Lake
State Park

Lake Umbagog
National
Wildlife Refuge

Umbagog
Lake

Upton

26

To
Mount
Katahdin

Appalachian
Trail

To
Gorham, NH

44°
38'
N

Androscoggin River

MAINE
NEW HAMPSHIRE

Grafton
Notch
State Park

Maine Public
Reserve Land

Table
Rock
2,100 ft.

Baldpate Mtn.
3,812 ft.

Black Mtn.

Wight Brook

Grafton Notch

Moose
Cave Gorge

Mother
Walker Falls

Step Falls

Screw Auger
Falls Gorge

Bear River

North Newry

MAHOOSUC

Mahoosuc
Arm
3,777 ft.

4,187 ft.
Old Speck
Mtn.

Mahoosuc
Notch

RANGE

North
Peak

3,376 ft.
Sunday River
Whitecap

44°
30'
N

South
Peak

Maine Public
Reserve Land

2,072 ft.
Bald Mtn.

Sunday River Road

Newry

26

2   5

Androscoggin River

3,794 ft.
Goose Eye Mtn.

Farewell
Mtn.

2

3,300 ft.
Bear Mtn.

3,020 ft.
Wheeler Mtn.

5

To Bryant Pond

26

26

Bethel

To
Gorham, NH

2

5

35

To Fryeburg

71°06' W   70°58' W   70°50' W

44°
46'
N

44°
38'
N

44°
30'
N

in 1774 as Sudbury, Canada, was the site of the last hostile Indian raid in Maine in 1781. Raiders sacked the town and carried off three captives. One escaped, but the other two were kept prisoners in Canada until the end of the Revolutionary War.

The town center is Bethel Common, a lovely green fronted by numerous elegant old houses, including the historic Moses Mason House. This 1813 Federal house owned by the Bethel Historical Society was built for civic leader Moses Mason. The house was one of the area's first clapboards to be painted white and was the first erected on a stone foundation, although locals warned Mason that the wind would surely blow it off. The entryway walls are covered with magnificent landscape murals created by primitives painter Rufus Porter about 150 years ago. The house has nine period rooms and is open year-round by appointment, Tuesday through Sunday afternoons in July and August. Other notable buildings in Bethel include the Major Gideon Hastings House with a columned Greek Revival front portico, the spare 1847 West Parish Congregational Church, and the campus of the Gould Academy, a renowned preparatory school chartered in 1835.

Nearby on the Green is the Bethel Inn, originally built in 1913 as a spa for wealthy patients at the Gehring Clinic for nervous disorders. The inn, one of Maine's best known hostelries, also entertains guests with golf, tennis, cross-country skiing, boating, and swimming. With mountain vistas above every street, Bethel is a fine base camp for hikers setting off for the nearby mountains. In winter the town serves skiers who flock to cross-country ski areas in the surrounding woods or busy Sunday River Ski Resort north of town. The growing alpine ski resort boasts 128 trails and is famed for its snowmaking capabilities. A few years ago, it made enough snow that a run, albeit meager, stayed open until June.

The scenic drive heads out of downtown Bethel from the intersection of US 2 and ME 26. Head north on the combined highways. The first 6 miles run along the fertile west floodplain of the Androscoggin River after it makes an abrupt elbow turn at Bethel. The Androscoggin, arising in Lake Umbagog on the Maine–New Hampshire border, meanders 175 miles through both states before emptying into the Kennebec River at Merrymeeting Bay, a scant 10 miles from the Gulf of Maine. A rest area with picnic tables sits alongside the road and river at 3.8 miles.

A good side-trip goes up Sunday River Road, almost opposite the rest area, to the ski resort. Only 3 miles up this road is the 1870 **Artist's Bridge,** the most photographed and painted of Maine's eight covered bridges.

Back on the main drive route, continue another 2.5 miles before turning left on ME 26 in Newry as it branches northwest up the Bear River and taking leave of the Androscoggin, which won't be seen again until its headwaters at the drive's northern end. The highway heads northwest up the broad intermontane valley. Slabby cliffs break the dense forested walls, while the twisting river sweeps by pastures on the flat valley floor. The massive ramparts of 3,812-foot East Peak and its subsidiary summits, including West Peak and Mount Hittie (with a white landslide scar), tower to the northwest above the highway and the tiny town of North Newry.

Screw Auger Falls is a tumbling series of waterfalls tucked in a compact granite gorge on the Grafton Notch Scenic Drive.

Slowly the valley narrows and the road gently climbs. Glimpses of the small tumbling river are seen through the foliage below. **Step Falls Preserve** is reached after about 8 miles. Park at a small lot just before the highway crosses Wight Brook. A marked trail beginning here winds north through thick hardwood and balsam fir forest to this gorgeous twenty-four-acre preserve managed by The Nature Conservancy. Here the brook tumbles more than 200 feet in 0.2 mile, creating a series of stepped falls over granite ledges and polished boulders. The base of the cascades, a good picnic spot, is a short 0.5-mile walk up the path.

Through Grafton Notch

About 0.5 mile past Wight Brook, the highway enters 3,112-acre **Grafton Notch State Park,** one of Maine's most scenic natural areas. The park encompasses the valley floor and the highway, with dark, looming mountains hemming in the U-shaped glaciated valley. Several gorges, relatively rare in New England, are deeply incised into the granite bedrock along the drive through the park. **Screw Auger Falls Gorge,** on the south side of the highway a mile into the park, is a spectacular 40-foot-deep, 150-foot-long gorge that is less than 10 feet wide at its narrowest point. The river, here a mere brook, riffles over polished bedrock before dropping in a series of waterfalls into the abrupt chasm. Smooth granite walls, sculptured and rounded by glacial meltwater laden with cobbles and boulders, drop away below a guardrail and an overlook. Leafy ferns fill cracks and crevices on the vertical walls of the moist ravine. The gorge is so named because it looks like a screw auger, a logging tool, crazily turned like a corkscrew through the rock. The lower part of the narrow, twisted slot is choked with large boulders and log jams.

Below the gorge the river emerges into a wider canyon and continues to other downstream appointments. **Mother Walker Falls** lies on the right another 1.1 miles up the narrowing and steepening road. A short trail heads right from a parking area and drops to a viewpoint above this gorge. Some 50 feet below the overlook, the Bear River races through the 1,000-foot-long, steep-walled chasm with its 98-foot drop. This gorge, punctuated by occasional waterfalls and cascades, has been excavated in the weak contact zone between erosion-resistant granite and softer metamorphic rocks. Dense woods surround the gorge while ferns and moss cling to its moist walls. At the head of the gorge is a small natural bridge. This bridge and one at Screw Auger Falls are the only known natural bridges in Maine. The gorge is named for Mother Walker, one of the last homesteaders to reside in Grafton. Remains of the old carriage road that originally came through the notch can be seen just left of the parking lot.

Another 0.7 mile up the drive and 2.8 miles from the park's eastern entrance is the **Moose Cave Gorge** pullout, on the right. A 0.4-mile nature trail loops near this rugged gorge and its moss gardens. The path winds down to the rimrock

Autumn leaves and cobbles at Grafton Notch State Park.

above the river as it plunges through the narrow, rock-strewn gorge. The 200-foot-long slot formed, like Mother Walker Falls, in a fault or contact zone between granite and metamorphic rocks. The semi-subterranean stream channel is partially enclosed by immense boulders, also home to Moose Cave. This 3-foot-wide "cave" overhanging the gorge was created when a large granite slab broke away from the mountainside above. When an unfortunate moose slipped into the slot, a passing hunter heard its cries and mercifully shot the injured animal, hauling it home for his dinner table.

Farther up the loop nature trail is the **Moss Garden** along the walls of the moist gorge. Dense mats of moss cling to the misty rocks here, and delicate ferns, including upland lady fern and long beech fern, fill rocky crevices. Lichens, a symbiotic association of fungi and algae, cover exposed rock surfaces, including large colonies of misleadingly named reindeer moss. Much of this delicate vegetation has been damaged and trampled by passing hikers, however. Stay on the path to avoid further damage and to allow this fragile ecosystem to re-establish itself.

Past Moose Cave Gorge, the valley widens into Grafton Notch's dramatic gateway. Wild scenery and tall wooded mountains surround the drive route as it continues. High granite cliffs and slabs dotted with lone trees and ledges tower to the north. On the south are mossy slabs, such as The Eyebrow cliff, which rear up the north flank of Old Speck Mountain. This 4,180-foot peak, rising some 2,700 feet above the Bear River Valley floor, is Maine's third-highest point and the northern-most peak in the rugged 30-mile-long Mahoosuc Range.

A parking area a short distance up the highway from Moose Cave forms the trailhead for Old Speck and the Appalachian Trail. The trail climbs steeply over rugged terrain for 4 miles up windswept spruce- and fir-clad ridges to the peak's summit and marvelous views of the surrounding mountains. From here it marches southwest as the Appalachian Trail along the ragged, lofty crest of the Mahoosuc Range. This section of the 2,100-mile AT, a long-distance footpath that runs from Georgia's Springer Mountain to Mount Katahdin in Maine, is considered the roughest, toughest trail segment by thru-hikers. The mile-long trail section through Mahoosuc Notch itself just south of Old Speck is an obstacle course that threads and squeezes through an immense, jumbled boulder field. Snow lingers among the boulders here until July in most years. Hikers must scramble over the slippery rocks, often taking off their backpacks while they crawl under boulders or slip through narrow passageways.

On the opposite side of the highway from the Old Speck trail is the trailhead for **Table Rock.** This path climbs 900 feet in a mile up the southwest flank of Bald-pate Mountain, reaching a stunning ledge viewpoint called Table Rock. For a good loop hike, experienced hikers can continue west on a spur trail to the Appalachian Trail and descend back into the notch. Consider all the hikes in Grafton Notch to be fairly difficult and best attempted by hikers who are prepared for rough trails and inclement weather.

Back on the scenic drive, the notch valley widens and, 1 mile past the trail-heads, reaches the Spruce Meadow Picnic Area on the left. The wetland surround-ing the picnic area is a boggy peatland formed, at least partially, from silted-in beaver ponds. A taiga forest of red spruce and balsam fir, both trees of the far north, lines the valley. Balsam yields an aromatic fragrance that is contained in sap blisters on its trunk. Bushes such as blueberry and flowers such as gentian, golden saxifrage, wild iris, and wood sorrel grow on the spongy bog surface.

Lake Umbagog

Past the picnic area, the valley broadens even more. A mile later the drive leaves the state park and begins a gradual descent northwest along the Swift Cambridge River toward New Hampshire. A forest of spruce, fir, and tamarack abuts the pave-ment. The highway passes an old cemetery, a reminder, as are the occasional apple orchards and low stone fences, that this region was once settled and cleared for farmland. After a couple of miles, the road bends away from the river and traverses a low hillside into Upton, a remote outpost perched above Lake Umbagog. **Lake Umbagog National Wildlife Refuge** lies directly north on the marshy southeastern corner of the lake. After Upton the highway continues a gradual descent and in less than 2 miles passes into New Hampshire. The last 9 miles of the drive run from here to Errol.

Lake Umbagog, a huge 7,850-acre lake straddling the state border, is dotted with islands. Headwaters of the Androscoggin River, the lake is roughly 10 miles long with a 60-mile shoreline. The relatively shallow lake, at a maximum depth of 48 feet, offers excellent fishing for salmon, brook and brown trout, pickerel, yellow perch, and smelt. The diverse habitats along the shore include bogs, swamp forests, marshes, and hardwood forests, allowing for abundant wildlife. Moose, bear, loons, various duck species, and raptors live here. Several bald eagle nesting sites, monitored by wildlife biologists, are scattered across the area. Umbagog Lake State Park, with 1,350 acres, borders the southern end of the lake, and the 156-acre Big Island, owned by the Society for the Protection of New Hampshire Forests, yields hiking and primitive camping.

The highway runs along the edge of Sargent Cove and past a boat ramp and private campground before re-entering forest. Occasional secluded homes dot the woods as the level road skirts the southern edge of Mill Mountain and Errol Hill. Good views south toward Mount Washington and the White Mountains unfold across the low Androscoggin River Valley. The road makes a final steep (9 percent grade) descent, crosses the river on a steel girder bridge, and enters the old logging town of Errol. This scenic drive officially ends at the highway's junction with New Hampshire Highway 16 in downtown Errol. A left turn here leads down the Androscoggin River to Pinkham Notch and Mount Washington. Drivers keeping straight on NH 26 will travel up to scenic Dixville Notch.

Rangeley Lakes Scenic Drive

General description: An 84-mile open loop through the scenic mountains and Rangeley Lakes region of western Maine.

Special attractions: Webb Lake, Mount Blue State Park, Rangeley, Rangeley Lake, Rangeley Lake State Park, Height of Land, Coos Canyon, Smalls Falls, Tumbledown Mountain, Swift River Falls, camping, hiking, fishing, boating, canoeing, fall foliage, scenic views.

Location: Western Maine.

Drive route numbers and name: Maine Highways 142, 4, and 17, Byron Road.

Travel season: Year-round. Expect snow and icy conditions in winter.

Camping: Mount Blue State Park, on the southwest side of Webb Lake, has an excellent 136-site campground. Rangeley Lake State Park offers fifty sites on the south shore of Rangeley Lake.

Services: All services in Dixfield, Mexico, Rumford, Phillips, Rangeley, and Oquossoc.

Nearby attractions: Grafton Notch State Park, White Mountain National Forest, Bethel, Artist's Bridge, Sunday River Ski Resort, Sebago Lake, Mahoosuc Range, Carrabassett Valley, Sugarloaf/USA Ski Resort, Bigelow Range.

The Drive

This 84-mile scenic route forms a loop drive that explores the rugged mountains and river canyons between Rangeley Lake and the towns of Rumford and Mexico on the Androscoggin River. This lake-and-peak district, straddling the state's developed southern region and the wild north country, is a spectacular and beautiful landscape filled with looming mountain massifs, creased by swift rivers and abrupt gorges, dotted with wild ponds and wind-ruffled lakes, and populated by few people. The scenic drive follows paved highways except for a 10-mile gravel segment that threads across the southern slopes of Tumbledown Mountain.

The drive begins in **Mexico,** one of Maine's many towns named for foreign countries and places. The towns were not named by settlers from those places, but rather by Mainers who admired the struggles for freedom in faraway countries. A glance at a Maine highway map reveals an assortment of towns so-named—Peru, Norway, Paris, Denmark, Sweden, Naples, Poland, Italy, and China. Mexico was incorporated in 1818 and flourished as an industrial center. Today the town sprawls over hills as a bedroom community for Rumford, its busy paper mill neighbor and "twin city" to the west.

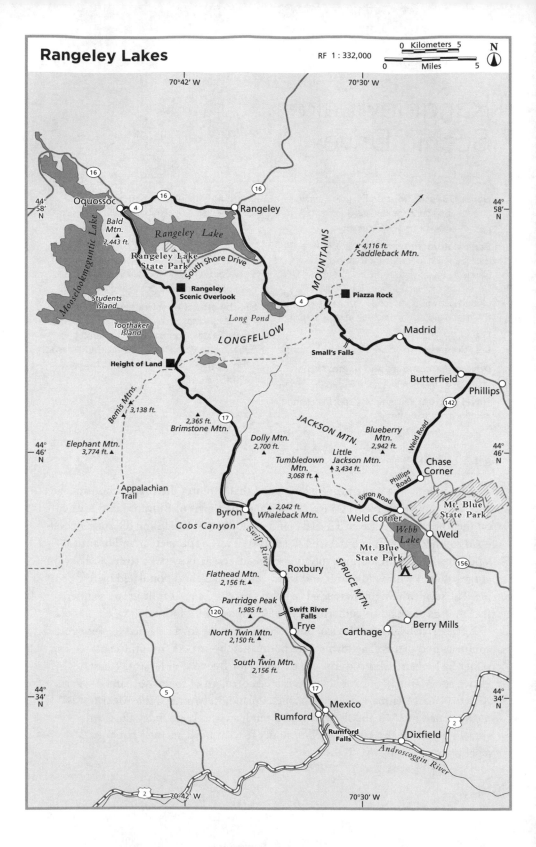

Rangeley Lakes

RF 1 : 332,000

Kilometers 0 5
Miles 0 5

N

70°42' W
70°30' W

44° 58' N

16
Oquossoc
4
16
16
Rangeley

Bald Mtn. 2,443 ft.
Rangeley Lake

Mooselookmeguntic Lake

Rangeley Lake State Park
South Shore Drive

LONGFELLOW   MOUNTAINS

4,116 ft. Saddleback Mtn.

Rangeley Scenic Overlook

Students Island

Long Pond

4
Piazza Rock

Toothaker Island

LONGFELLOW

Small's Falls

Madrid

Height of Land

Butterfield
Phillips

Bemis Mtns.
3,138 ft.

2,365 ft. Brimstone Mtn.

17

JACKSON MTN.

Blueberry Mtn. 2,942 ft.

142

Dolly Mtn. 2,700 ft.

Weld Road

44° 46' N

Elephant Mtn. 3,774 ft.

Little Jackson Mtn. 3,434 ft.

Chase Corner

Tumbledown Mtn. 3,068 ft.

Phillips Road

Appalachian Trail

Byron
2,042 ft. Whaleback Mtn.

Byron Road

Weld Corner

Mt. Blue State Park

Coos Canyon

Webb Lake
Weld

Swift River

Mt. Blue State Park

156

Flathead Mtn. 2,156 ft.
Roxbury

SPRUCE MTN.

Partridge Peak 1,985 ft.

Swift River Falls

North Twin Mtn. 2,150 ft.

120

Frye

Carthage

Berry Mills

South Twin Mtn. 2,156 ft.

44° 34' N

5

17

Mexico

2

Rumford

Dixfield

Rumford Falls

Androscoggin River

70°42' W
70°30' W

Rumford, besides being home to the Boise Cascade mill, also has the Strathglass Park District. This area, with its fifty-one brick buildings in a park setting with pines and maples, was a planned community built in 1901 for hard-working mill laborers by Hugh Chisholm, an owner of the Oxford Paper Company. Both towns lie on the Androscoggin River, Maine's third-longest river, amid the rolling Oxford Hills. The river roars over a granite bench in town, forming spectacular Rumford Falls and providing hydroelectric power for the town's pulp and paper mills. Rumford was home to native son Edmund Muskie, a former Maine governor, senator, and vice presidential candidate in 1968.

Up the Swift River Valley

The drive begins at the junction of U.S. Highway 2 and Maine Highway 17 in Mexico. Turn north on ME 17. The drive's first 36 miles go from here to Oquossoc. The road runs through quiet residential neighborhoods and after almost 2 miles takes leave of town. Most of ME 17 north of here is a designated Maine Scenic Highway. The highway twists upriver alongside the shallow, stony Swift River, as it tumbles over boulders and pools in deep reflective hollows between tree-lined banks. **Swift River Falls** lie off the road at 7 miles. Look for a large, unmarked pullout on the left. Here the river drops over a series of frothy cascades and a few short drops interrupted by deep pools in the rounded metamorphic bedrock. The exposed rock here is polished and smoothed by erosion into an outdoor sculpture filled with hollows, potholes, and short cliffs.

The highway continues north under tall mountains flanking the Swift River Valley. A long row of peaks marches along the western skyline—North and South Twin Mountains, 1,985-foot Partridge Peak, 2,156-foot Flathead Mountain, and Record Hill. The river is intermittently calm or rough. The tar road swings through Roxbury, a quiet village with a few homes, a cemetery, and an antiques shop. The Roxbury area (as well as most of Oxford County) is a notable mineral collecting district for rockhounds. Finds here include deposits of feldspar, quartz, aquamarine, amethyst, and prized tourmaline, the Maine state gemstone. The 4-mile river stretch from here to Byron has yielded small amounts of flaked gold and an occasional nugget to panners. Rumor says the nation's first gold strike was made here. Periodic gold rushes came later, too, after the 1849 California gold discoveries brought the fever to poor New Englanders looking to get rich mining. Fraudulent paper mines and mining companies also enticed get-rich-quick investors to quickly part with and lose their money.

Past the falls, the valley widens to Byron, with the river meandering past flat, grassy pastures studded with grazing cattle. The 13-mile Swift River run from Byron to Mexico is a great canoe trip for experts, crossing both flat water and Class II and III rapids. A few spots require portages or lining along the bank.

Byron is a small residential village that was once a busy mill town. It was named Byron for the romantic English poet Lord Byron after its 1833 incorporation. **Coos Canyon,** sitting alongside the highway at Byron, is a natural wonder. Here the Swift River carved a 1,500-foot-long gorge into the tilted metamorphic bedrock. This scenic gorge is filled with potholes, water-polished cliffs, foamy cascades, and small waterfalls. Park at a rest area near the bridge where Byron Road comes in from the north and walk along the fenced overlooks to view the canyon.

Byron to Oquossoc

The next highway segment runs 23 miles from Byron to Oquossoc. The asphalt continues north along the Swift River for 5 miles before crossing the river and bending up Mott Stream's broad valley. The road climbs steeply, swinging around 2,365-foot Brimstone Mountain. After 3 miles it crests a saddle on the mountain's northern shoulder and angles around Beaver Pond, a thin lake tucked among the woods, before edging steeply across a bare mountain slope. Almost 3 miles from the pond, the highway reaches its high point at a spectacular and unexpected scenic overlook called **Height of Land** on the left shoulder of the road. To the west is a high ridge topped by 3,774-foot Elephant Mountain and the long, bumpy ridge of Bemis Mountain, traversed by the Appalachian Trail. Farther west and southwest stretch the humped White Mountains in northern New Hampshire.

Below the lookout lies the dark expanse of Bemis Valley. The choppy waters of huge Mooselookmeguntic Lake to the north are broken by Toothaker and Students Islands and its forested shoreline. The islands comprise a private wilderness area called the Stephen Phillips Memorial Preserve. The area, open to the public, was set aside by the late Stephen Phillips to keep the islands unspoiled by the rampant commercial development that had occurred on the main lakeshore. The preserve offers hiking and camping, with most of the sites accessible only by boat.

Just past the vista, the road begins a gradual descent northward, alternately dropping down slopes and leveling out atop flattened ridges. Another good pulloff is the **Rangeley Scenic Overlook,** on the east side of a rounded knob. Rangeley Lake spreads out below the viewpoint. The highway steeply drops past the turnoff to South Shore Drive, which leads to 869-acre **Rangeley Lake State Park** and its campground, then onto a neck between Rangeley and Mooselookmeguntic Lakes. Here it levels and bends around 2,443-foot Bald Mountain to the western edge of Rangeley Lake. Cabins and homes sit along the shore.

Oquossoc to Rangeley

After a couple of miles, the highway reaches Oquossoc and its junction with Maine Highways 4/16. Turn east (right) on ME 4/16 toward Rangeley. The drive runs east

The Swift River races over metamorphic bedrock in Coos Canyon on the Rangeley Lakes Scenic Drive.

for 7 miles to the resort town of Rangeley, passing through woods and swamps north of the lake. As the road nears town, houses and businesses line the road. **Rangeley,** sitting at the relatively high elevation of 1,545 feet, has long been a destination for hunters, anglers, and outdoor recreationists who come to sample northwestern Maine's remote backcountry. The town makes a great fishing base camp, with more than forty lakes and ponds offering trout and salmon fishing within 10 miles of town. It has a wide assortment of hotels, lodges, restaurants, stores, and sports facilities, including the Mingo Springs Golf Course and tennis courts. The town also attracts visitors with numerous concerts, arts and crafts festivals, and seaplane rides during the summer months.

Rangeley boasts that it lies halfway between the Equator and the North Pole. The town was named for an English squire named Rangeley who built an immense estate here in 1825 and gave tracts of land to incoming settlers. He also erected a sawmill for building lumber and financed a 10-mile road through the woods to the outside world. By the mid-1800s Rangeley was a popular sailing spot for summer vacationers. The Rangeley Lakes Region Historical Society documents the area's history with a collection of photographs, an Abenaki Indian culture display, and an account of the first white explorers and their hardships in 1860. Rangeley was also the home of the controversial psychiatrist Wilhelm Reich, a disciple of Freud, who applied Freud's sexual behavior theories in a clinical setting. Smitten by the region, Reich settled here in 1942 and built a stone house called Orgonon overlooking the lake. The house, a few miles west of town off ME 4, is open in summer for tours.

Rangeley to Butterfield

To begin the next 21-mile segment of the drive, keep right in the Rangeley center on ME 4. The road climbs steeply out of town on a long hill and passes the turn to Saddleback Ski Area after a mile. It continues through pastures and cleared fields and past an old cemetery before dropping along Greenvale Cove at Rangeley Lake's southeastern tip. At 3.6 miles from the town center is South Shore Drive. A right turn here leads to Rangeley Lake State Park.

The highway begins to ascend Long Pond Stream's broad, wooded valley. A couple of miles later, it swings around Long Pond. This large lake nestles against 3,160-foot Beaver Mountain. The road tops a low divide then drops down the Sandy River Valley. Past a string of ponds is the turnoff to the parking area for Saddleback Mountain Trail and Piazza Rock. The trail climbs 5 miles, gaining 2,400 feet and passing numerous small tarns en route to the mountain's barren, 4,116-foot summit. Far-reaching views of the surrounding lakes and mountains are gained from the top. Piazza Rock, just up the trail, is a huge boulder with overhanging sides and a flat top capped with mature trees.

The highway turns southeast and crosses the Appalachian Trail at 10 miles.

Jackson Mountain lifts its wooded summit above a back road.

The valley narrows as it descends, with the river tumbling over a rough, cobbled bed. At 12.7 miles is a rest area with picnic tables and restrooms near a lovely waterfall called **Small's Falls.** Here the river, following a narrow gorge incised in the underlying bedrock, drops 80 feet in four waterfalls. Deep basins filled with crystal water sit between each dropoff, while ragged metamorphic rock cliffs tower above.

The drive continues down the birch-lined highway. As the road and river descend, the valley slowly broadens. At 16 miles is Madrid, a small village of homes. Below the town the Sandy River funnels through a tight, rocky gorge. A couple of miles later, the highway crosses the river and climbs out of the valley to the junction of ME 4 and Maine Highway 142. The drive turns southwest (right) here onto ME 142.

Mount Blue and Tumbledown Mountain

The last drive segment goes southwest on ME 142 for just over 9 miles to Weld Corner before turning west on Byron Road. From here it goes 10.5 miles to Byron and ME 17. The road works upward into rolling hills broken by fields and good views of the surrounding mountains. Pope Mountain lifts its 2,185-foot crown to the left, while Blueberry Mountain rises steeply to the right.

After 6 miles the highway begins a long descent down East Brook, the valley slowly broadening and flattening. The road makes a sharp turn to the right at Chase Corner and runs along the west edge of the marshy vale to Weld Corner. Here, after 9.7 miles, the drive route makes a right turn to the west onto narrow Byron Road.

Before turning here to complete your loop, make a side-trip to **Mount Blue State Park.** The park is reached by driving down ME 142 along Webb Lake for a couple of miles to the town of Weld. This pretty little town, founded in 1816, was named for settler Benjamin Weld. Turn left at the village center onto Center Hill Road, which climbs steeply onto the western slopes of Mount Blue, offering great views of sprawling Webb Lake and Jackson Mountain along the way. Atop a high hill, the road passes a long row of sugar maples before becoming a narrow dirt road and entering the 5,021-acre state park. At a fork in the road, go right to Center Hill and a short nature trail and picnic area, or left down a one-lane dirt track to the trailhead for the Mount Blue summit trail. The 0.75-mile trail climbs through a dense forest of white pine, red oak, sugar maple, hemlock, red spruce, basswood, and white ash to a balsam fir woodland just below the 3,187-foot summit. Total elevation gain from trailhead to apex is 1,800 feet.

Back on the main drive route, turn west onto Byron Road from ME 142 at Weld Corner. This last drive section follows a superb narrow road as it dips and winds through hills and shallow valleys for 10.5 miles. After 0.5 mile the road reaches West Road. A left turn here leads south a few miles to a detached unit of Mount Blue State Park on the west shore of Webb Lake. This park offers an excellent campground, as well as a sand beach, boat launching area, and occasional ranger-led hikes. Webb Lake is a 4-mile-long lake that is a popular boating and fishing spot.

Past West Road, Byron Road becomes gravel and runs through dense forest on the south slopes of **Tumbledown Mountain.** After 5 miles the track reaches the trailhead for Tumbledown Mountain. This three-summited mountain looms high over the road. A good 5.5-mile loop follows the Brook and Parker Ridge Trails as it scales the mountain, passing jewel-like Tumbledown Pond en route. More experienced hikers with climbing skills can ascend the steep and rugged Chimney Trail directly to the rocky summit of the 3,068-foot mountain. The chimney is a sharp cleft in a rock outcrop with a large boulder balanced above. It requires rock climbing ability and expertise with a rope. The slabby 600-foot-high granite face of Tumbledown Mountain also offers vertical adventure for rock climbers.

The road slowly climbs into a wide saddle past the trailhead before beginning a long, gradual descent to the East Branch of the Swift River. Watch for oncoming traffic on the sharp, blind curves. The narrow road drops along the gurgling river. A couple of miles later, the road becomes paved and swings southwest around Whaleback Mountain, then falls steeply to Byron, Coos Canyon, and the drive's end at ME 17. Turn left on ME 17 and retrace the first 13 miles of the drive to Mexico and Rumford.

27

Moosehead Lake–Kennebec River Scenic Drive

General description: A 125-mile scenic route through the Moosehead Lake region, the Moose River Valley, and the Kennebec Valley in west-central Maine.

Special attractions: Moosehead Lake, Mount Kineo, Moose River Valley, Kennebec River, Lily Bay State Park, Big Moose Mountain, scenic cruises, mountain biking, river rafting, camping, hiking, fishing, boating, canoeing, fall foliage, scenic views, ice fishing.

Location: West-central Maine.

Drive route numbers: Maine Highways 6 and 15 and U.S. Highway 201.

Travel season: Year-round. Expect snow and icy conditions in winter.

Camping: Lily Bay State Park, with ninety-one campsites, lies 8 miles northeast of Greenville on the east shore of Moosehead Lake. The Maine Forest Service's Squaw Brook Campground is 5 miles north of Greenville off ME 15/6. There are many private campgrounds in the Jackman area.

Services: All services in Dover-Foxcroft, Guilford, Moscow, Bingham, Greenville, Rockwood, and Jackman.

Nearby attractions: Gulf Hagas, Hermitage Preserve, Katahdin Iron Works, Baxter State Park, Mount Katahdin.

The Drive

Northwestern Maine is a rough, muscular land filled with lakes that pool in glacial depressions, swift rivers that tumble and foam over boulders and bedrock, rolling hills and lofty mountains, and dark, brooding forests. With more than seventeen million acres of woodland, Maine is the most heavily wooded state in the nation. Forest covers almost 90 percent of the land here. It's also very watery, with 6,000 lakes and ponds and more than 5,000 streams and rivers covering a full tenth of Maine's 33,000-square-mile area. Few major roads penetrate this remote, wooded shoulder of New England. Those that do offer quiet highway stretches with less traffic in a year than Boston's Storrow Drive sees in a day. The 125-mile Moosehead Lake–Kennebec River Scenic Drive explores the lower North Woods of Maine, passing Moosehead Lake, Maine's largest lake, and traversing scenic river valleys and mountains. This excellent drive tours the empty Maine backcountry without requiring travel on rough dirt logging tracks or total abandonment of civilization. The drive forms an open loop that begins in Guilford, just west of Dover-Foxcroft, and ends at Moscow-Bingham.

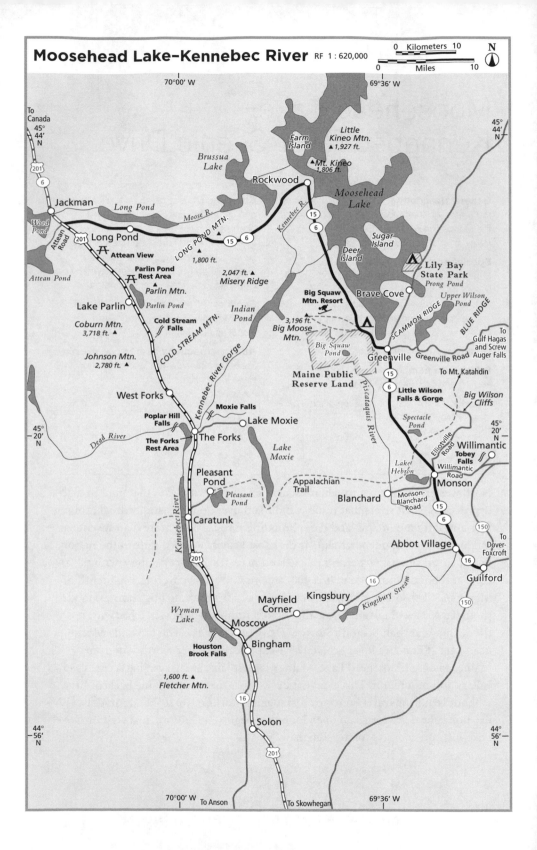

Guilford to Greenville

The drive begins in farm country at Guilford, 8 miles west of Dover-Foxcroft and 27 miles north of Newport and Interstate 95. At an elevation of 430 feet, Guilford is an old industrial town straddling the Piscataquis River. The town was established in 1803 by seven men who would admit no person as a settler who was not "industrious, orderly, moral, and well-disposed." A few years later the seven were called, tongue-in-cheek, "the seven wise men of Guilford." The drive takes off from a crossroads in downtown Guilford where Maine Highways 150, 23, 15, 16, and 6 intersect on the south side of a river bridge. Go west on ME 15/6, following signs to Greenville, 26 miles north.

The highway heads west on the south bank of the Piscataquis River among low hills broken by swampy vales. The river, originating on Bald Mountain to the northwest, offers a good 10-mile canoe trip from above Blanchard to Abbot Village. The road crosses a small, rocky gorge carved by Kingsbury Stream then bends north into Abbot Village. Past the village, the highway swings over the river and heads straight north. Thick forest abuts the asphalt, hiding the surrounding countryside. After 11 miles the highway drops down a hill into Monson, a small village atop a rounded ridge. The hills around town are gouged by slate quarries. Lake Hebron, a good trout lake, spreads west from town. Tobey Falls, three drops into scoured potholes, lie on Big Wilson Stream off Willimantic Road about 5 miles east of Monson.

After another 0.5 mile the highway leaves Monson and gently rises into wooded hills. After a few more miles, the Appalachian Trail crosses the tar. Occasional ponds break the forest, including Spectacle Pond at 16.5 miles. As the road heads farther into North Woods country, houses become few and far between and the vistas widen to views of dark hills and sodden clouds. Higher mountains, dotting the horizon to the northeast, lord over low, broad valleys filled with meandering rivers, glimmering ponds, and bogs. After 22 miles the highway enters the southern outskirts of Greenville. At 24 miles is the Greenville Rest Area with picnic tables and excellent views of Blair Hill and Blue Ridge to the east. The local chamber of commerce information station sits on the right just after the highway slows, drops downhill, and enters town.

Along Moosehead Lake

At the very southern tip of Moosehead Lake, **Greenville** is a jumping-off point for hunters, fishermen, hikers, and boaters. The town offers all visitor services, including lodging, private campgrounds, outfitters and wilderness guides, and seaplane service. It also hosts some unusual events. MooseMainea, during May and June, celebrates the ubiquitous moose with moose forums, moose-sighting safaris and

Ferns line the Kennebec River in autumn.

cruises, a moose theme craft fair, and The Taste of Moose Reception where gourmet moose recipes such as moose stew and barbecued moose are served—no chocolate mousse, however. The International Seaplane Fly-In, attracting pilots from across the continent, is held on the weekend after Labor Day every year. A popular summer excursion is a lake cruise on the 110-foot SS *Katahdin,* a classic steamboat operated by the Moosehead Marine Museum. The ship, sailing twice daily for two-hour cruises, dates from 1914 when it towed acres of logs across Moosehead Lake to the Kennebec River outlet.

Numerous natural wonders and scenic attractions lie around Greenville and are worth the extra time. Most of them lie in the deep forest east of Greenville. Little Wilson Falls and Gorge, with a 40-foot waterfall, lie southeast of town along the Appalachian Trail. Rugged 1,947-foot Borestone Mountain, east of Little Wilson Falls, lies within 1,639-acre Borestone Mountain Audubon Sanctuary. The mature forest here hasn't been harvested since the 1890s. **Gulf Hagas,** the "Grand Canyon of Maine," lies about 20 miles east of town off Greenville Road. This spectacular 3-mile-long gorge, flanked by vertical slate walls up to 300 feet high, contains five major waterfalls (including Screw Auger Falls) as well as numerous chutes and deep pools along the West Branch of the Pleasant River. The river drops more than 400 feet through the canyon, a registered National Natural Landmark. The 8-mile loop Gulf Hagas Rim Trail, a blue-blazed spur of the Appalachian Trail, winds along the canyon rim. Adjacent to the gorge is the Hermitage Preserve, an area run by The Nature Conservancy to protect a large grove of old-growth white pine on a bluff above the river. Northeast of Greenville along the eastern shore of Moosehead Lake is **Lily Bay State Park,** with a ninety-one-site campground, swimming beach, and boat ramps.

Moosehead Lake, however, is the real attraction for this part of Maine. It's not only the largest lake in both Maine and New England, but also the largest lake in the nation wholly within a single state. More than 1,000 feet above sea level, the lake covers 74,890 acres, stretches more than 40 miles from end to end, measures 12 miles at its widest point, and boasts 420 miles of shoreline. The lake's maximum depth is 246 feet. Numerous large islands, including Moose, Deer, and Sugar Islands, poke out of the windy lake.

Famed nineteenth-century naturalist Henry David Thoreau paddled a birch bark canoe up the west shore of Moosehead Lake from Greenville in 1857. His observations are still apt today for visitors driving up the lakeshore. Thoreau noted in *The Maine Woods* that "After leaving Greenville, you see but three or four houses for the whole length of the lake, and the shore is an unbroken wilderness." He spent a night along the shore with his companion and an Indian guide and remarked that the forest was so dense that it was almost impossible to find a space to comfortably lay down.

In Greenville the highway jogs left, passing the Moosehead Historical Society before it leaves town and bends north along the western lakeshore. The next section of the scenic drive runs 19 miles northwest to Rockwood. From Greenville ME 15/6 arcs around a knoll and passes the Maine Forest Service's Squaw Brook Campground. Big Moose Mountain dominates the view. A 3-mile trail climbs 2,000 feet from here to the summit of 3,196-foot Big Moose Mountain, offering far-ranging panoramic vistas on clear days from an abandoned fire lookout. The fire tower, the first built in the United States, was erected in 1905. Gems found on the peak's upper reaches include tourmaline and garnet. The trail begins from a dirt road that heads west from the highway at 5.3 miles. Drive a mile to the trailhead.

The highway continues past Big Squaw Mountain Resort, a good family ski area cut onto the peak's north slopes. The area offers thirty-three downhill trails with a 1,750-foot vertical drop, as well as several cross-country trails. Back on the drive, the level road runs north with a thick forest screen blocking any views of the lake—and hiding the growing vacation-home subdivisions springing up on Moosehead's western shore. After 11 miles the highway crosses the East Outlet of the Kennebec River. The lake forms the headwaters of the mighty Kennebec, Maine's largest and most storied river. The road runs north past more bogs and woods for 5 miles before dashing over the river's smaller West Outlet. The village of Rockwood sits on a rounded point a couple of miles farther north.

Rockwood to Jackman

Rockwood is a lovely small tourist town that spills across slopes above the lake. There's not a lot here—cabins, a bed-and-breakfast, some hotels, a couple of restaurants, boat and canoe rentals, and ferry service to looming Mount Kineo, a famous landmark to the north. **Mount Kineo,** thrusting its 1,806-foot summit encircled by glacier-sculpted rhyolite cliffs, dominates Moosehead Lake's midsection. Kineo's sheer east face, dropping almost 800 vertical feet to the water, towers above the Kineo Deep Hole, the deepest spot in Moosehead Lake. The peak's 800-acre peninsula is connected to the east shore by a thin neck but is usually accessed by boat from Rockwood. A series of rough logging roads do end up at the neck, however. Hikers who take the motorboat ferry from Rockwood's dock can hike two trails, the Indian Trail and the Bridle Trail, to the rocky summit plateau. One trail passes under a flint cliff that was mined by many New England Indian tribes for use as spear and arrow points.

The next drive section continues along ME 15/6, running 30 miles from Rockwood to Jackman through a wilderness of lakes and hills. At Rockwood the highway turns west and drops down to the lake edge. In a mile it reaches the Moose River and a small collection of cabins and stores at the river's inlet. The road continues west on a terraced floodplain between the river and Blue Ridge. In 3 miles it leaves all vestiges of civilization behind and departs from the river briefly before dropping back down to a southern arm of Brassua Lake. An overlook yields a good view across the wide lake. At the west end of the arm just north of the asphalt is a primitive camping area among the trees.

The highway runs up a valley along Misery Stream for a few miles before crossing the brook and rolling over Long Pond Mountain, a long uphill followed by a long downhill. Almost 20 miles from Rockwood, the road drops along the Moose River's Long Pond, a narrow, 8-mile-long lake with a wide, rocky shore. Good views of low hills to the north unfold across open clearings. Past the lake, the road bends away from the Moose River and its swampy lowland, reaching U.S. Highway 201 a mile south of Jackman.

A scant 16 miles south of Quebec, Jackman is another hunting and fishing outpost, as well as a canoeing center. The scenic drive's last leg goes south from here on US 201 for 50 miles to Bingham. At the intersection of U.S. Highway 202 and ME 15/6, gravel Attean Road heads west a couple of miles to Attean Pond and the put-in for the Moose River Bow Trip, one of New England's premier canoe trips. Here too is the trailhead for the Sally Mountain Trail. The 34-mile, two-day Bow Trip paddles across Attean Pond, portages a mile to Holeb Pond, crosses 3 miles of Holeb Pond to a stream connection to the Moose River, then returns to the lake and put-in via the Moose River, with a portage around Holeb Falls.

Driftwood along the rocky shore of Brassua Lake.

Down the Kennebec River

Turn south on US 201. The highway begins hill-climbing immediately. Good views of the Moose River Valley stretch east from the driver's window. **Attean View** is reached after 4.3 miles. This lofty lookout and rest area gives a marvelous view of the western lakes and mountains. A dense forest undulates down to shining Attean Pond, a huge lake dotted with wooded isles. Beyond rise high, hump-backed mountains, their rounded shoulders laden with dark forest half-hidden beneath veils of clouds. Farther west, a long row of peaks parades along the Maine-Quebec boundary.

Past the overlook, the highway rises another 0.5 mile to a broad, high ridge. Great views of conical Parlin, Coburn, and Cold Stream Mountains reach to the south. The road gently descends along Bean Brook, skirts Parlin Pond and Parlin Pond Rest Area with its picnic tables on the lakeshore, and climbs again to a low saddle. As it edges above Cold Stream's broad valley, look for a left turnoff that drops to the stream and a short trail to Cold Stream Falls, in a small gorge. The asphalt drops steeply off Johnson Mountain's south shoulder, rolls across a boggy plain to the Dead River and The Forks. The Forks, with a general store, sits at the confluence of the Dead and Kennebec Rivers. The Forks Rest Area is near the river junction.

The Forks is the headquarters for whitewater rafting on the Kennebec and Dead Rivers. The 9-mile Kennebec section from here to Caratunk offers a great whitewater experience for beginners. Above The Forks is the Kennebec River Gorge, a deep, 10-mile-long canyon filled with turbulent whitewater below Indian Pond and the hydroelectric plant at Harris Station. When Maine Central Power releases sufficient water from the dam there, the river thunders with whitewater and Class IV rapids.

A good side-trip from The Forks is to **Moxie Falls,** New England's tallest waterfall. To reach it, turn east (left) on the gravel road on the south side of the bridge over the Kennebec River and drive 2.2 miles to the parking area and trail-head. A short 1.2-mile, round-trip trail leads to the 90-foot-high waterfall on Moxie Stream.

The last 24 miles of the drive continue south on US 201 along the east bank of the Kennebec River. The Kennebec, with its source at Moosehead Lake, flows 150 miles south through a glacier-scoured rift to the Maine coast. The historic river has long been a pathway to the north country and Canada. Parts of it were explored as early as 1600. Later the river was used for immense log drives. Trees were cut and floated downriver to mills at Skowhegan and Waterville. The last log drive was in 1976.

The highway stretch along the river offers spectacular views of the inner canyon and of rounded mountains above. The small stopover of *Caratunk,* an Indian word meaning "rough and broken," is reached after 10 miles. As the river drops south, the canyon slowly broadens and the water, backed up by a dam at Moscow, widens and calms. Hardwood and birch forests now line the hills above the highway, replacing the taiga conifer forest of the north. Wyman Lake Rest Area sits on the right above the lake at 40 miles. About 8 miles later the highway passes Wyman Dam, a 155-foot-high, 2,250-foot-long earthen dam, and enters Moscow and Bingham. **Bingham,** the older of the two, was founded in 1785 and was named for Philadelphia banker Bill Bingham, who held title to the township. A town sign notes that Bingham lies halfway between the Equator and the North Pole. The scenic drive ends here. Continue south on US 201 to Skowhegan or follow scenic ME 16 east through rolling rural countryside for 29 miles to Abbot Village just above Guilford and the drive's starting point.

28

Baxter State Park Scenic Drive

General description: A 94-mile, back-roads route around Mount Katahdin and Baxter State Park in northern Maine.

Special attractions: Baxter State Park, Mount Katahdin, Katahdin Stream Falls, Doubletop Mountain, Travelers Pond, South Branch Pond, Sandy Stream Pond, Roaring Brook Nature Trail, Appalachian Trail, Little Niagara and Big Niagara Falls, Daicey Pond Nature Trail Visitor Center, camping, backpacking, hiking, fishing, wildlife observation, ski touring, canoeing, mountaineering, rock climbing, fall foliage.

Location: North-central Maine.

Drive route number and names: Park Tote Road, Grand Lake Road, Maine Highway 159. The park gates are open from 6:00 A.M. to 10:00 P.M. The park roads are closed to motorhomes, trailers, motorcycles, and off-road vehicles. Vehicles may not be over 9 feet high, 7 feet wide, or 22 feet long for a single vehicle or longer than 44 feet for a combined vehicle.

Travel season: Mid-May through mid-October.

Camping: Eight campgrounds in Baxter State Park—Roaring Brook (nine lean-tos/ten tent sites/one eight-person bunkhouse); Abol Campground (twelve lean-tos/nine tent sites);

Katahdin Stream Campground (twelve lean-tos/nine tent sites); Daicey Pond Campground (ten cabins); Kidney Pond Campground (twelve cabins); Nesowadnehunk Field Campground (eleven lean-tos/twelve tent sites); South Branch Pond Campground (twelve lean-tos/twenty-one tent sites/one eight-person bunkhouse); and Trout Brook Farm (one lean-to/fourteen tent sites). Backcountry/backpacking campsites are also available at Chimney Pond and Russell Pond. Camping is by reservation only in authorized campgrounds and campsites. Most are open from mid-May through mid-October. Reservations are by mail or in person and can be made beginning in mid-January. Write to Baxter State Park, 64 Balsam Drive, Millinocket, ME 04462. All camping reservation information is available on the Baxter State Park Web site, www.baxterstateparkauthority.com. There are numerous private campgrounds in the Millinocket area.

Services: All services in Millinocket. Limited services in Patten and Island Falls at the north end of the drive.

Nearby attractions: Gulf Hagas, Hermitage Preserve, Katahdin Iron Works, Moosehead Lake, Mount Kineo, Moose River Valley, Kennebec River, Lily Bay State Park.

The Drive

Mount Katahdin lifts its glacier-sculpted crown high above Maine's North Woods, a dense boreal forest that blankets the state's unpopulated upper half. The lofty 5,270-foot mountain and its surrounding satellite peaks tower above the horizon, their old, glaciated ridges etched against the pale sky on a clear day and visible from most of Maine. While the procession of seasons changes the mountain's

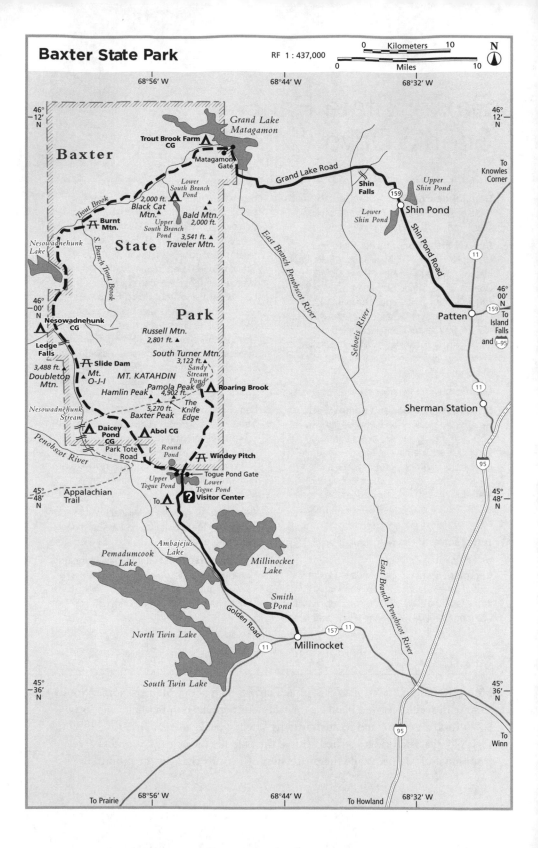

Baxter State Park

RF 1 : 437,000

Kilometers 10

Miles 10

N

68°56' W 68°44' W 68°32' W

46°12' N

Grand Lake Matagamon

Trout Brook Farm CG

Matagamon Gate

Baxter

Grand Lake Road

To Knowles Corner

Shin Falls

159

Upper Shin Pond

Shin Pond

Lower South Branch Pond

2,000 ft. Black Cat Mtn.

Bald Mtn. 2,000 ft.

Upper South Branch Pond

3,541 ft. Traveler Mtn.

Burnt Mtn.

Trout Brook

Nesowadnehunk Lake

State

S. Branch Trout Brook

Lower Shin Pond

Shin Pond Road

11

46°00' N

159

Patten

To Island Falls and I-95

East Branch Penobscot River

Seboeis River

Park

Russell Mtn. 2,801 ft.

46°00' N

Nesowadnehunk CG

Ledge Falls

3,488 ft. Doubletop Mtn.

Slide Dam

Mt. O-J-I

MT. KATAHDIN

South Turner Mtn. 3,122 ft.

Sandy Stream Pond

Pamola Peak 4,902 ft.

Roaring Brook

11

Sherman Station

Hamlin Peak

5,270 ft. Baxter Peak

The Knife Edge

Nesowadnehunk Stream

Daicey Pond CG

Abol CG

Park Tote Road

Round Pond

Windey Pitch

95

Penobscot River

Upper Togue Pond

Togue Pond Gate

Lower Togue Pond

45°48' N

Appalachian Trail

To

? Visitor Center

45°48' N

Ambajejus Lake

Pemadumcook Lake

Millinocket Lake

Smith Pond

Golden Road

157 11

East Branch Penobscot River

North Twin Lake

11

Millinocket

45°36' N

South Twin Lake

45°36' N

To Winn

To Prairie

68°56' W 68°44' W To Howland 68°32' W

outward appearance—leafy green forests spreading across the lower slopes in springtime, the blaze of summer wildflowers in a forest clearing, autumn trees papering the peak with gaudy colors, and a dazzling carpet of snow enveloping them in winter—the colossal mountain seems unchanging, eternal, and aloof as seasons pass across its face.

Mount Katahdin, Maine's highest peak, is the centerpiece of Baxter State Park, the fourth-largest state-owned preserve in the United States and the largest public parkland in New England. Baxter is an immense swath of magnificent wilderness that stretches across Maine's North Woods region. The pristine park, covering 204,733 acres, is rightly called Maine's Yellowstone. This park, a Katahdin-guarded realm, is a forest primeval that has recovered from the ravages of logging, a wildlife sanctuary filled with moose, deer, and bear, and a place, said its creator Percival Baxter, "where nature rules and where the creatures of the forest hold undisputed dominion."

The Baxter State Park Scenic Drive threads 94 miles through the western and northern edge of the park on the Park Tote Road, a dusty narrow track that leads to quiet campsites, ponds, waterfalls, tumbling brooks, and spectacular scenic views. Travelers need to remember that recreation is a mere secondary use of the park. Travelers should also be advised that Baxter does not cater to motorists. Expect a bumpy ride on a narrow dirt road. As one man said, "Baxter is heaven, but its roads are hell." Speed limits range up to only 20 miles per hour on the axle-breaking dirt roads. No motorhomes, trailers, motorcycles, trail bikes, pets, radios, TVs, or other fancy recreational paraphernalia are allowed in the park. Mountain bikes are allowed in the park, but may be ridden only on the Park Tote Road. Motorboats cannot be used on any lake or pond within the park. Neither are there any fast-food joints, hotels, or tacky souvenir shops anywhere in the park. Camping is closely regulated and restricted, and no more than 1,000 people can spend the night in the park. This is a place, Baxter said, for people to return to nature simply, or go somewhere else.

The drive, easily approached from Interstate 95, is open from mid-May to mid-October. Late summer and early fall are ideal times to drive the route, although expect unsettled and unpredictable weather at times with cool temperatures and prolonged periods of rain and clouds. Hikers and climbers need to be especially cautious and prepared for inclement weather. Wear proper waterproof boots or shoes; carry a rain parka and an extra coat or sweater; carry a flashlight; bring at least two quarts of water for a day hike and treat all park water before drinking; and stay on trails. The majority of park fatalities and accidents are caused by hikers leaving the trails and becoming lost.

Baxter State Park is one of the great success stories of American conservation and owes its existence to the efforts and vision of one man—Percival Baxter. Baxter, as mayor of Portland and later as a two-term governor of Maine, lobbied the

Maine state legislature to take action and preserve the Katahdin area from further devastation at the hands of the powerful logging industry. None of his bills or lobbying efforts panned out, although the legislature did create a game preserve on 90,000 acres of the mountain. Baxter, with a stubborn Yankee streak, refused to let his noble idea go. He later remembered, "I was attacked as a dreamer and branded as a socialist" for his efforts. So as a capitalist, Baxter began acquiring the land, piece by piece, from the lumber companies and turning over each precious parcel to the state with deed restrictions to preserve its wild nature. Over the next few decades, he gift-wrapped more than 200,000 acres along with some operating funds and turned them over to the State of Maine as a nature preserve to be kept in its "natural wild state." Today the park is operated by the Baxter Park Authority, a state entity distinct from the state parks department.

Millinocket to Sandy Stream Pond

The drive begins in Millinocket and runs northwest to the park. Millinocket lies 10 miles west of I–95's exit 56. Go west on Maine Highways 11/157 to the town. Millinocket, lying at the low elevation of 359 feet, was not settled early like so many other Maine towns. It was populated almost overnight in 1899 when the Great Northern Paper Newsprint Plant, one of the largest pulp paper mills in the country, decided to locate on the Penobscot River and use its water for hydroelectric power. The cost of shipping raw materials to the plant was cut by being closer to the source. Millinocket is still a paper town as well as headquarters for hikers, backpackers, anglers, and hunters who venture into the vast north woods. Northern Maine is traversed by only a handful of major highways, but laced with a network of logging tracks that spread out through all the commercial timber reserves. While pockets of undisturbed wilderness like Baxter State Park are found, most of the north woods belong to timber companies that manage them by a cycle of harvesting and replanting the trees.

The drive begins on the west side of Millinocket. Follow signs out of town to Baxter State Park. The paved road runs northwest through undulating, wooded hills. Smith Pond is passed at 3 miles. As the road swings by Hammond Ridge, an overgrown clearcut lines the road. At 6.8 miles the road crosses a narrow neck that separates Ambajejus Lake (on the left) from Millinocket Lake. The mostly level asphalt, paralleled by a forest access road on the left, runs through dense hardwood forest. After 11 miles mighty Mount Katahdin towers above the surrounding hills. At 13.8 miles is a turnoff to the New England Outdoor Center and Penobscot Outdoor Center, both wilderness outfitters. A massive boulder alongside the highway says "Keep Maine Beautiful" and has a mural of mountains, forest, a bear, a leaping trout, and flying geese painted on its flank.

Mount Katahdin fills the horizon above Sandy Stream Pond.

The road enters **Baxter State Park** at its south entrance 14.5 miles from Millinocket. Deciduous forest encloses the road and large glacier-deposited boulders scatter beneath the trees. At 15.9 miles is a small visitor center on the right. This is a mandatory stop for maps, camping, and park information. Only 0.1 mile past the center, the pavement ends and the gravel road begins. Togue Pond Picnic Area sits on the left alongside Togue Pond. The road gate is just up the road and the Togue Pond Gatehouse is a little farther along. Nonresident visitors must stop here to pay a $12 entrance fee; Maine residents are free. During summer the road is open from 6:00 A.M. to 10:00 P.M.

The road forks at the gatehouse. The left fork is the Park Tote Road, and the right fork is a rough, dead-end road that climbs 8.1 miles to Roaring Brook Campground and allows access to several of Mount Katahdin's trails. Take the right fork for a great side-trip to the north flank of Katahdin. This narrow dirt road drops and rolls up the forested slopes, crossing a succession of brooks. At 1.4 miles is Rum Brook Picnic Area with picturesque streamside picnic sites. The road slowly climbs through the shady hardwood forest, passing glacial deposits of rough, unsorted boulders. Past Windey Pitch is Avalanche Field Group Campsite and 2 miles farther is Roaring Brook Campground and day-use area. A large parking area marks the road's terminus.

This area is the main jumping-off point for hikers and climbers venturing on Katahdin and the surrounding peaks. A good, short day-hike begins at the Roaring Brook ranger station at the far west end of the parking area and follows the Sandy Stream Pond Trail about a half-mile to **Sandy Stream Pond** through a mixed deciduous and coniferous forest. This lovely glacial lake nestles in the woods and offers great views of Katahdin and South Turner Mountain. It's also an excellent wildlife habitat and superb wild-watching area. Moose are often spotted browsing in the waters, especially at dawn and dusk. Other animals in this area include beaver and deer as well as herons, woodpeckers, and songbirds. Those with more energy can continue around the lake or hike up 3,122-foot South Turner Mountain via a 4-mile round-trip trail from the pond.

The parking lot is also the trailhead for several trails that climb south to the almost-mile-high summit of **Mount Katahdin.** Katahdin is actually composed of several summits on a lofty ridge with the highest point named Baxter Peak. The imposing granite monolith, its upper treelined slopes often mantled in clouds and swept by wind, is prominent in Penobscot Indian mythology. They believed three great spirits inhabited the stormy mountain. The powerful Stormbird *Pamola,* with the fierce beak and talons of an eagle, the arms and torso of a man, and the head and antlers of a moose, was easily angered and vented his rage by brewing up storms. *Wuchowsem* was the spirit of the benign night winds. And last was the *Spirit of Katahdin,* a giant human with stony features who inhabited the mountain with his wife and children. The 3.2-mile Helen Taylor Trail works up Keep Ridge to the top of Pamola Peak, a 4,902-foot spur summit, before edging across the razorlike Knife Edge to the twin high points of South and Baxter Peaks. The famed Knife Edge, in places less than 3 feet wide with almost 2,000 feet of open space gaping below your boots, is a jagged, rocky arête that separates two cirques excavated by glaciers. It's not treacherous on calm days for experienced hikers, but watch out when it's windy or visibility is poor. The arête will then seem as narrow as its name suggests. Many a hiker has crawled across the mile-long ridge in foggy conditions. Many who cross the edge call it the most exhilarating stretch of trail in all New England. The 360-degree view from the mountain's rock-strewn summit, the northern end of the 2,100-mile Appalachian Trail, is simply marvelous. The green mat of forest, studded with gleaming jeweled lakes, spreads out below, while mountain upon mountain recede to the horizon. The Great Basin, an immense alpine cirque below Katahdin, offers some excellent moderate rock climbs along with snow and ice routes for mountaineers. Climbers and mountaineers should be competent and able to self-rescue. Helmets are required, along with proper climbing equipment and ropes, foul weather gear, and a headlamp for night descents. Bivouacs are not permitted.

Along Park Tote Road

To continue the drive, retrace your route 8 miles back to the fork at the Togue Pond Gatehouse and go left on the Park Tote Road. The road travels 41 miles from here around the western and northern edge of the park to the Matagamon Gatehouse, the park's northern entrance. All the mileages to the drive's end in Patten begin here. The road heads northwest on low, marshy land below the mountain flank, passing many small ponds. Look for moose here in morning or evening. The haunting cry of loons echo across these lonely ponds in summer and fall.

The first couple miles of roadway traverse the Katahdin Esker. An esker, a glacial feature, is a deposit of sediment and boulders left by streams that ran over the glacier's surface or in tunnels below. As the stream ran downhill, boulders and cobbles were deposited along the hemmed-in streamcourse. After the glaciers melted the gravel deposits were stranded as long, winding ridges. Esker comes from the old Gaelic word *eiscir*, meaning "ridge."

At 2 miles the road passes **Round Pond** on the right. Abol Pond Picnic Area, at the west end of Abol Pond, is a mile farther. The Abol Campground turnoff sits at 5.8 miles. The Abol Trail to Katahdin's summit begins here. The path winds up the mountain's southwest flank. At 8 miles is Katahdin Stream Campground and the final Appalachian Trail section up Katahdin Stream. Just over a mile up the trail hides **Katahdin Stream Falls,** a spectacular, four-tiered, 75-foot waterfall tucked into a mossy ravine.

The road continues past Tracy Pond to the Daicey Pond Campground turn at 10 miles. The campground sits 1.5 miles south of the Park Tote Road on the edge of Daicey Pond. The pond offers great views of the Katahdin massif towering above the forest-fringed water. A short nature trail explores the area. Another trail heads south for just over a mile through a white birch, spruce, fir, and cedar forest along the Nesowadnehunk Stream to Little and Big Niagara Falls. Both falls are short but pretty as they tumble over polished granite bedrock. They were named in jest, since both are less than 20 feet high. The stream was once the scene of numerous log runs when cut timber was floated down to the West Branch of the Penobscot River. The remains of the old Toll Dam can be seen above the falls. The dam controlled the water so logs could be sent downstream without jamming the channel. Other good hikes here include Sentinal Mountain, some outlying pond walks, and great canoeing. Just up the park road is Kidney Pond Campground with twelve wilderness cabins on a spur road to the left.

The next road section is spectacular. The narrow track, now following Nesowadnehunk Stream, turns north and enters a steep-walled valley flanked by tall mountains. To the right is Mount O-J-I, named for landslide-formed letters on its side. To the left is 3,488-foot Doubletop Mountain with long granite slabs exposed on its abrupt slope. At 13.8 miles is Slide Dam Picnic Area and a couple

Mount Katahdin dominates the skyline along Park Tote Road.

miles later is **Ledge Falls.** Park below the falls in a small parking area and walk up to this scenic spot. Here the creek riffles over granite ledges before pooling in a wide bedrock hollow. The road edges past the cascade and enters a broader valley north of the gap.

Nesowadnehunk Campground lies to the left at 17 miles. The road runs through thick underbrush and a conifer forest to Nesowadnehunk Lake, the origin of the creek. The 5-mile stream run from here to the campground is an excellent, easy canoe trip with deep pools and negligible rapids. The large lake is also a popular canoeing locale, although care needs to be taken as the winds quickly build up.

Nesowadnehunk Lake to Patten

The last leg of the drive in the state park goes 23 miles from Nesowadnehunk Lake to Matagamon Gate. This section, paralleling Trout Brook for most of the distance, crosses low, brushy flatlands before dipping and rolling over hills above the creek. Burnt Mountain Picnic Area is at 28.8 miles and the Webster Lake Trail is a couple miles farther. After mile 33 the brook is encased in a deep, rocky gorge below the road. The South Branch turnoff is at 35 miles. This spur track leads south to a campground on the edge of Lower South Branch Pond. This scenic pond sits amid high peaks, including Black Cat Mountain on the west and Traveler Mountain, a dark gray peak composed of lava cooled from an ancient volcano, on the east. A short nature trail explores the pond area near the site of a massive 1903 forest fire that denuded the mountains. Another good hike works up to Upper South Branch Pond. Back on the drive, the road leaves the creek and skirts knobby Trout Brook Mountain, passing Trout Brook Farm Campground at 39 miles and Littlefield Pond Trail 0.5 mile later along the way. At 41 miles the road drops alongside **Grand Lake Matagamon,** a large, serene lake surrounded by a rock- and forest-bound shoreline. Several canoe-access sites are located on the lake's pristine shore. The Matagamon Gate, the park's northern entrance, is reached at 42 miles.

The drive leaves the park and passes under huge, dark cliffs on the north slope of Horse Mountain. At 44 miles the drive, now on Grand Lake Road, becomes smooth and paved—much to the relief of your dusty car. The road crosses the East Branch of the Penobscot River and dashes eastward through rolling hill country studded with lakes and ponds. Deep woods line the asphalt. The Seboeis River crossing is at 51 miles. Look for a river-side picnic area on the left. A short distance later is an unmarked pulloff on the right. A rough trail leads to scenic **Shin Falls,** a 50-foot, three-tiered waterfall over slate bedrock in a rocky gorge. The road bends southeast and drops down to Shin Pond. Past here, the road, once a lumber supply route, becomes Maine Highway 159 and enters more open country dotted with homes and farms. Just over 67 miles from the park's Togue Pond entrance, the highway makes a sharp left turn through grassy pastures and fields and enters Patten a mile later. **Patten,** like so many northern Maine towns, has a lumber-based economy with area wood going to paper mills or sawmills for lumber. The Patten Lumberman's Museum in town is an interesting stop. The three-building museum exhibits the role and development of logging in Maine as well as displaying various lumbering tools that include a steam log hauler. The drive ends in Patten at the intersection of ME 159 and ME 11. Continue east on ME 159 a few miles across swamps to I–95's exit 59 at Island Falls.

Sources of More Information

For more information on lands and events, please contact the following agencies and organizations.

Connecticut

Bluff Point State Park
90 Walbach Street
New London, CT 06320
(860) 444–7591
http://dep.state.ct.us/stateparks/parks/
    bluffpoint.htm

Campbell Falls State Park Reserve
385 Burr Mountain Road
Torrington, CT 06790
(860) 482–1817
http://dep.state.ct.us/stateparks/
    reserves/campbell.htm

Connecticut Commission on Culture
    and Tourism
Tourism Division
505 Hudson Street
Hartford, CT 06106
(860) 270–8080, (888) CTVISIT
www.CTVISIT.com

Connecticut State Parks Division
Bureau of Outdoor Recreation
79 Elm Street
Hartford, CT 06106-5127
(860) 424–3200, (866) 287–2757
http://dep.state.ct.us/stateparks/

Dennis Hill State Park
385 Burr Mountain Road
Torrington, CT 06790
(860) 482–1817
http://dep.state.ct.us/stateparks/parks/
    dennishill.htm

Fort Griswold Battlefield State Park
90 Walbach Street
New London, CT 06320
(860) 444–7591
http://dep.state.ct.us/stateparks/parks/
    fort_griswold.htm

Greater New Milford
    Chamber of Commerce
11 Railroad Street
New Milford, CT 06776
(860) 354–6080
www.newmilford-chamber.com

Hammonasset Beach State Park
P.O. Box 271
1288 Boston Post Road
Madison, CT 06443
(203) 245–2785
http://dep.state.ct.us/stateparks/parks/
    hammonasset.htm

Harkness Memorial State Park
275 Great Neck Road
Waterford, CT 06385
(860) 443–5725
http://dep.state.ct.us/stateparks/parks/
    harkness.htm

Haystack Mountain State Park
385 Burr Mountain Road
Torrington, CT 06790
(860) 482–1817
http://dep.state.ct.us/stateparks/parks/
    haystack.htm

Housatonic Meadows State Park
Route 7
Sharon, CT
(860) 927–3238
http://dep.state.ct.us/stateparks/parks/
    housatonic.htm

Kent Falls State Park
Route 7
Kent, CT
(860) 927–3238
http://dep.state.ct.us/stateparks/parks/
    kentfalls.htm

Lake Waramaug State Park
30 Lake Waramaug Road
New Preston, CT 06777
(860) 868–2592
http://dep.state.ct.us/stateparks/parks/
    lakewaramaug.htm

Macedonia Brook State Park
159 Macedonia Brook Road
Kent, CT 06757
(860) 927–3238
http://dep.state.ct.us/stateparks/parks/
    macedonia.htm

Mohawk State Forest
20 Mohawk Mountain Road
Goshen, CT 06756
(860) 491–3620
http://dep.state.ct.us/stateparks/forests/
    mohawk.htm

Mount Tom State Park
30 Lake Waramaug Road
New Preston, CT 06777
(860) 868–2592
http://dep.state.ct.us/stateparks/parks/
    mounttom.htm

Mystic Seaport
P.O. Box 6000
75 Greenmanville Avenue
Mystic, CT 06355-0990
(860) 572–0711
www.mysticseaport.org

Northwest CT Convention &
    Visitors Bureau
P.O. Box 968
Litchfield, CT 06759-0968
(860) 567–4506
www.litchfieldhills.com

Old Saybrook Chamber of Commerce
P.O. Box 625
146 Main Street
Old Saybrook, CT 06475
(860) 388–3266
http://oldsaybrookchamber.com/cms/

Rocky Neck State Park
P.O. Box 676
Niantic, CT 06357
(860) 739–5471
http://dep.state.ct.us/stateparks/parks/
    rockyneck.htm

Sharon Audubon Center
325 Cornwall Bridge Road (Route 4)
Sharon, CT 06069
(860) 364–0520
www.audubon.org/local/sanctuary/
    sharon

Sloane-Stanley Museum
P. O. Box 917
Route 7
Kent, CT 06757
(860) 927–3849
www.chc.state.ct.us/sloanestanley
    museum.htm

White Memorial Conservation Center
80 Whitehall Road
Litchfield, CT 06759
(860) 567–0857
www.whitememorialcc.org

Maine

Acadia National Park
P.O. Box 177
Eagle Lake Road
Bar Harbor, ME 04609-0177
(207) 288–3338
www.nps.gov/acad

Bar Harbor Chamber of Commerce
93 Cottage Street
Bar Harbor, ME 04609
(207) 288–5103, (800) 288–5103
www.barharborinfo.com

Baxter State Park
64 Balsam Drive
Millinocket, ME 04462
(207) 723–5140
www.baxterstateparkauthority.com

Bethel Area Chamber of Commerce
P.O. Box 1247
8 Station Place
Bethel, ME 04217
(207) 824–2282, (800) 442–5826
www.bethelmaine.com

Boothbay Harbor Region Chamber
    of Commerce
P.O. Box 356
Boothbay Harbor, ME 04538
(207) 633–2353
www.boothbayharbor.com

Eastport Chamber of Commerce
P.O. Box 254
Eastport, ME 04631
(207) 853–4644
www.eastport.net

Ellsworth Area Chamber of Commerce
P.O. Box 167
163 High Street
Ellsworth, ME 04605
(207) 667–5584
www.ellsworthchamber.org

Grafton Notch State Park
1941 Bear River Road
Newry, ME 04261
(207) 824–2912
www.state.me.us/cgi-bin/doc/parks/
    find_one_name.pl?park_id=1

Katahdin Area Chamber of Commerce
1029 Central Street
Millinocket, ME 04462
(207) 723–4443
www.katahdinmaine.com

Machias Bay Area Chamber of
  Commerce
P.O. Box 606
Machias, ME 04654
(207) 255–4402
www.machiaschamber.org

Maine Bureau of Parks and Lands
22 State House Station
18 Elkins Lane (AMHI Campus)
Augusta, ME 04333-0022
(207) 287–3821
www.state.me.us/doc/parks/

Maine Office of Tourism
#59 State House Station
Augusta, ME 04333-0059
(888) 624–6345
www.visitmaine.com/home.php

Moosehead Lake Region Chamber
  of Commerce
P.O. Box 581
Main Street
Greenville, ME 04441
(207) 695–2702
www.mooseheadlake.org

Mount Blue State Park
299 Center Hill Road
Weld, ME 04285
(207) 585–2347
www.state.me.us/cgi-bin/doc/parks/
  find_one_name.pl?park_id=18

Popham Beach State Park
10 Perkins Farm Lane
Phippsburg, ME 04562
(207) 389–1335
www.state.me.us/cgi-bin/doc/parks/
  find_one_name.pl?park_id=22

Quoddy Head State Park
Box 1490
Lubec, ME 04652
(207) 733–0911, (207) 941–4014
  (off-season)
www.state.me.us/cgi-bin/doc/parks/
  find_one_name.pl?park_id=10

Rangeley Lake State Park
HC 32 Box 5000
Rangeley, ME 04970
(207) 864–3858
www.state.me.us/cgi-bin/doc/parks/
  find_one_name.pl?park_id=25

Rangeley Lakes Chamber of Commerce
P.O. Box 317
Rangeley, ME 04970
(207) 864–5364, (800) MT–LAKES
www.rangeleymaine.com

Roosevelt Campobello International
  Park
P.O. Box 97
Lubec, ME 04652
(506) 752–2922
www.nps.gov/roca/

Southern Midcoast Maine
  Chamber of Commerce
59 Pleasant Street
Brunswick, ME 04011
(207) 725–8797, (877) 725–8797
www.midcoastmaine.com

Southwest Harbor/Tremont Chamber
  of Commerce
P.O. Box 1143
Southwest Harbor, ME 04679
(207) 244–9264, (800) 423–9264
www.acadiachamber.com

Massachusetts

Beartown State Forest
69 Blue Hill Road
Monterey, MA 01245
(413) 528–0904
www.mass.gov/dcr/parks/western/bear
.htm

Berkshire Hills Visitors Bureau
Berkshire Common Plaza
Pittsfield, MA 01201
(413) 443–9186, (800) 237–5747
www.berkshires.org

Cape Cod Chamber of Commerce
P.O. Box 790
307 Main Street
Hyannis, MA 02601
(508) 862–0700, (888) 33–CapeCod
www.capecodchamber.org

Cape Cod Museum of Natural History
869 Route 6A
Brewster, MA 02631
(508) 896–3867
www.ccmnh.org

Cape Cod National Seashore
99 Marconi Station Site Road
Wellfleet, MA 02667
(508) 349–3785
www.nps.gov/caco/
Salt Pond: Visitor Information
(508) 255–3421
Province Lands: Visitor Information
(508) 487–1256

Central Massachusetts Tourist Council
30 Worcester Boulevard
Worcester, MA 01608
(508) 755–7400
www.worcester.org

Chesterfield Gorge Reservation
River Road
Chesterfield, MA 01012
(413) 684–0148
www.thetrustees.org/pages/291_chester
field_gorge.cfm?searchterm=chester
field-gorge

Clarksburg State Park
1199 Middle Road
Clarksburg, MA 01247
(413) 664–8345, (413) 663–8469 (off-
season)
www.mass.gov/dcr/parks/western/clsp
.htm

D.A.R. State Forest
Route 112
Goshen, MA
(413) 268–7098
www.mass.gov/dcr/parks/western/darf
.htm

Greater Boston Convention and
Visitors Bureau
2 Copley Place, Suite 205
Boston, MA 02116-6501
(617) 536–4100, (888) See–Boston
www.bostonusa.com

Hancock Shaker Village
P.O. Box 927
Pittsfield, MA 01202
(413) 443–0188, (800) 817–1137
www.hancockshakervillage.org

Historic Deerfield
Old Main Street
Deerfield, MA 01342
(413) 774–5581
www.historic-deerfield.org

Kenneth Dubuque Memorial
    State Forest
740 South Street
Pittsfield, MA 01202
(413) 442–8928
www.mass.gov/dcr/parks/western/
    dubq.htm

Massachusetts Office of
    Travel & Tourism
10 Park Plaza, Suite 4510
Boston, MA 02116
(617) 973–8500, (800) 227–MASS
www.massvacation.com

Mohawk Trail Association
P.O. Box 1044
North Adams, MA 01247
(413) 743–8127
www.mohawktrail.com

Mohawk Trail State Forest
175 Mohawk Trail
Charlemont, MA 01339
(413) 339–5504
www.mass.gov/dcr/parks/western/
    mhwk.htm

Mount Greylock State Reservation
Rockwell Road
Lanesboro, MA 01237
(413) 499–4262, (413) 499–4263
www.mass.gov/dcr/parks/western/
    mgry.htm

Nickerson State Park
Route 6A
Brewster, MA 02631
(508) 896–3491
www.mass.gov/dcr/parks/southeast/
    nick.htm

North Adams–Northern Berkshire
    Chamber of Commerce
57 Main Street
North Adams, MA 01247
(413) 663–3735
www.berkshirechamber.com

Provincetown Chamber of Commerce
P.O. Box 1017
307 Commercial Street
Provincetown, MA 02657-1017
(508) 487–3424
www.ptownchamber.com

Savoy Mountain State Forest
Central Shaft Road
Savoy, MA 01247
(413) 663–8469
www.mass.gov/dcr/parks/western/
    svym.htm

Shawme-Crowell State Forest
42 Main Street
Sandwich, MA 02563
(508) 888–0351
www.mass.gov/dcr/parks/southeast/
    schr.htm

Tolland State Forest
P.O. Box 342
410 Tolland Road
East Otis, MA 01029
(413) 269–6002
www.mass.gov/dcr/parks/western/toll
    .htm

Windsor State Forest
River Road
Windsor, MA 01270
(413) 684–0948, (413) 268–7098
    (off-season)
www.mass.gov/dcr/parks/western/
    wnds.htm

New Hampshire

Castle in the Clouds
P.O. Box 687
Route 171
Moultonborough, NH 03258
(603) 476–2352, (800) 729–2468
www.castleintheclouds.org/

Claremont Chamber of Commerce
The Moody Building-Tremont Square
Claremont, NH 03743
(603) 543–1296
www.claremontnh.com/visitors

Crawford Notch State Park
U.S. Route 302
Harts Location, NH 03812
(603) 374–2272
www.nhstateparks.org/ParksPages/
    CrawfordNotch/CrawfordNotch
    .html

Dixville Notch State Park
NH Route 26
Dixville, NH 03576
(603) 538–6707
www.nhstateparks.org/ParksPages/
    DixvilleNotch/Dixville.html

Franconia Notch State Park and Flume
    Gorge
Franconia, NH 03580
(603) 823–8800
www.franconianotch.org

Greater Lebanon Chamber of
    Commerce
P.O. Box 97
1 School Street, Village House
Lebanon, NH 03766
(603) 448–1203
www.lebanonchamber.com

Greater Ossipee Area Chamber of
    Commerce
127 Route 28
Ossipee, NH 03864
(603) 539–6201
http://ossipeevalley.org/index.html

Hanover Chamber of Commerce
P.O. Box 5105
47–53 Main Street, 216 Nugget Building
Hanover, NH 03755
(603) 643–3115
www.hanoverchamber.org

Lincoln-Woodstock Chamber of
    Commerce
NH Route 12
Kancamagus Highway
Lincoln, NH 03251
(603) 745–6621
www.lincolnwoodstock.com

Littleton Area Chamber of Commerce
P.O. Box 105
Littleton, NH 03561
(603) 444–6561
www.littletonareachamber.com

Moose Brook State Park
Route 2, Jimtown Road
Gorham, NH 03581
(603) 466–3860
www.nhstateparks.org/ParksPages/
    MooseBrook/MooseBrook.html

Mount Washington Valley Chamber of
    Commerce & Visitor's Bureau
P.O. Box 2300
North Conway, NH 03860-2300
(800) 367–3364
www.mtwashingtonvalley.org

New Hampshire Division of Travel and
Tourism Development
P.O. Box 1856
172 Pembroke Road
Concord, NH 03302-1856
(603) 271–2665, (800) FUN–IN–NH
www.visitnh.gov

Squam Lakes Area Chamber of
Commerce
(603) 968–4494
www.squamlakeschamber.com

Umbagog Lake State Park
Route 26
Cambridge, NH 03579
(603) 482–7795
www.nhstateparks.org/ParksPages/
Umbagog/Umbagog.html

Wellington State Park
Route 3A
Bristol, NH 03222
(603) 744–2197
www.nhstateparks.org/ParksPages/
Wellington/Wellington.html

White Mountain Attractions
Box 10MG
North Woodstock, NH 03262
(603) 745–8720, (800) 346–3687
www.visitwhitemountains.com

White Mountain Gateway Visitor &
Interpretive Center
200 Kancamagus Highway
North Woodstock, NH 03262
(603) 745–3816, (800) 346–3687

White Mountain National Forest
719 Main Street
Laconia, NH 03246
(603) 528–8721
www.fs.fed.us/r9/forests/white
_mountain

Wolfeboro Chamber of Commerce
P.O. Box 547
32 Central Avenue
Wolfeboro, NH 03894
(603) 569–2200, (800) 516–5324
www.wolfeboro.com/chamber/index
.html

Rhode Island

Beavertail State Park and Lighthouse
Beavertail Road
Jamestown, RI 02835
(401) 884–2010
www.riparks.com/beaverta1.htm

Blackstone Valley Tourism Council
175 Main Street
Pawtucket, RI 02860
(401) 724–2200, (800) 454–BVTC
www.tourblackstone.com

Burlingame State Park
Sanctuary Road
Charlestown, RI 02813
(401) 322–8910
www.riparks.com/burlingastatepark
.htm

Charlestown Breachway State Park
1 Burlingame State Park
Charlestown, RI 02813
(401) 364–7000
www.riparks.com/charlesbreach.htm

Charlestown Chamber of Commerce
4945 Old Post Road
Charlestown, RI 02813
(401) 364–3878
www.charlestownrichamber.com

East Matunuck State Beach
950 Succotash Road
South Kingston, RI 02881
(401) 789–8585
www.riparks.com/eastmatunuck.htm

Fisherman's Memorial State Park
1011 Point Judith Road
Narragansett, RI 02882
(401) 789–8374
www.riparks.com/fisherma.htm

Fort Wetherill State Park
Fort Wetherill Road
Jamestown, RI 02835
(401) 423–1771
www.riparks.com/fortweth.htm

Gilbert Stuart Birthplace
815 Gilbert Stuart Road
Saunderstown, RI 02874
(401) 294–3001
www.gilbertstuartmuseum.com

George B. Parker Woodland
1670 Maple Valley Road
Coventry, RI 02827
(401) 295–8283
www.asri.org/parker.htm

George Washington Management Area
2185 Putnam Pike
Chepachet, RI 02813
(401) 568–2013

Misquamicut State Beach
257 Atlantic Avenue
Westerly, RI 02891
(401) 596–9097 (seasonal)
www.riparks.com/misquamicut.htm

Narragansett Chamber of Commerce
P.O. Box 742
Ocean Road
Narragansett, RI 02882
(401) 783–7121
www.cshell.com/ncc/

Narragansett Indian Tribe
P.O. Box 268
Charlestown, RI 02813
(401) 364–1100
www.narragansett-tribe.org/

Ninigret National Wildlife Refuge
Box 307
3679D Old Post Road
Charleston, RI 02813
(401) 364–9124
www.fws.gov/refuges/profiles/index
     .cfm?id=53542

Rhode Island Tourism Division
One West Exchange Street
Providence, RI 02903
(800) 556–2484
www.visitrhodeisland.com

Scarborough State Beach
870 Ocean Road
Narragansett, RI 02882
(401) 789–2324, (401) 782–1319
www.riparks.com/scarborough.htm

South County Tourism Council
4808 Tower Hill Road
Wakefield, RI 02879
(401) 789–4422, (800) 548–4662
www.southcountyri.com/index.cfm

Tomaquag Indian Memorial Museum
Arcadia Village
390A Summit Road
Exeter, RI 02822
(401) 539–7213, (401) 491–9063
www.tomaquagmuseum.com/

Trustom Pond National Wildlife
    Refuge
Box 307
3679D Old Post Road
Charlestown, RI 02813
(401) 364–9121
www.fws.gov/refuges/profiles/index
    .cfm?id=53545

Vermont

Addison County Chamber of
    Commerce
2 Court Street
Middlebury VT 05753
(802) 388–7951, (800) SEE–VERMONT
www.midvermont.com

Branbury State Park
3570 Lake Dunmore Road, Route 53
Salisbury, VT 05733
(802) 247–5925
www.vtstateparks.com/htm/branbury
    .cfm

Central Vermont Chamber of
    Commerce
P.O. Box 336
Barre, VT 05641
(877) 887–3678
www.central-vt.com/chamber/

Coolidge State Park
855 Coolidge SP Road
Plymouth, VT 05056
(802) 672–3612
www.vtstateparks.com/htm/coolidge
    .cfm

Elmore State Park
856 VT Route 12
Lake Elmore, VT 05657
(802) 888–2982
www.vtstateparks.com/htm/elmore
    .cfm

Emerald Lake State Park
65 Emerald Lake Lane
East Dorset, VT 05253
(802) 362–1655
www.vtstateparks.com/htm/emerald
    .cfm

Gifford Woods State Park
34 Gifford Woods
Killington, VT 05751
(802) 775–5354
www.vtstateparks.com/htm/gifford
    .cfm

Green Mountain National Forest
231 North Main Street
Rutland, VT 05701
(802) 747–6700
www.fs.fed.us/r9/gmfl/

Groton State Forest
303 Boulder Beach Road
Groton, VT 05046
(802) 584–3822

Lamoille Valley Chamber of
    Commerce
P.O. Box 445
43 Portland Street
Morrisville, VT 05661
(802) 888–7607
www.stowesmugglers.org/

Manchester and the Mountains
    Chamber of Commerce
5046 Main Street, Suite 1
Manchester Center, VT 05255
(802) 362–2100, (800) 362–4144
www.manchestervermont.net

Merck Forest and Farmland Center
Route 315, Rupert Mountain Road
Rupert, VT 05768
(802) 394–7836
www.merckforest.com

Mount Mansfield State Forest
324 North Main Street
Barre, VT 05641
(802) 479–3241

Northeast Kingdom Chamber
51 Depot Square, Suite 3
St. Johnsbury, VT 05819
(802) 748–3678, (800) 639–6379
www.nekchamber.com

Quechee State Park
764 Dewey Mills Road
White River Junction, VT 05001
(802) 295–2990
www.vtstateparks.com/htm/quechee
    .cfm

Silver Lake State Park
214 North Road
Bethel, VT 05032
(802) 234–9451
www.vtstateparks.com/htm/silver.cfm

Smugglers' Notch Area Chamber
    of Commerce
P.O. Box 364
Jeffersonville, VT 05464
(802) 644–2239
www.smugnotch.com/index.htm

Smugglers Notch State Park
6443 Mountain Road
Stowe, VT 05672
(802) 253–4014
www.vtstateparks.com/htm/smugglers
    .cfm

Stowe Area Association
P.O. Box 1320
Main Street
Stowe, VT 05672
(802) 253–7321, (877) GOSTOWE
www.gostowe.com

Vermont Department of Tourism and
    Marketing
6 Baldwin Street, Drawer 33
Montpelier, VT 05633-1301
(802) 828–3676, (800) VERMONT
www.travel-vermont.com

INDEX

ABOUT THE AUTHOR

Stewart M. Green is a freelance writer and photographer based in Colorado Springs, Colorado. He has written many other books for Globe Pequot Press, including *Scenic Driving Colorado, Scenic Driving California, Rock Climbing Utah, Rock Climbing Colorado, Rock Climbing New England,* and *Rock Climbing Europe.* Stewart's photographs are widely published in many magazines, books, catalogs, and advertisements. He is currently writing a collection of essays about rock climbing and climbers. Check out www.stewartgreen.com for more information about Stewart Green and his photography.